THE COMMON CORE OF EUROPEAN ADMINISTRATIVE LAWS

General Editors

GIACINTO DELLA CANANEA
MAURO BUSSANI

Procedural Requirements for Administrative Limits to Property Rights

THE COMMON CORE OF EUROPEAN ADMINISTRATIVE LAWS

General Editors:
Giacinto della Cananea, Professor of Administrative Law at Bocconi University; and Mauro Bussani, Professor of Comparative Law at the University of Trieste and Adjunct Professor of Comparative Law at the University of Macau

Other titles in the series:

Tort Liability of Public Authorities in European Laws
Edited by Giacinto della Cananea and Roberto Caranta

Administrative Justice Fin de siècle
Early Judicial Standards of Administrative Conduct in Europe (1890–1910)
Edited by Giacinto della Cananea and Stefano Mannoni

Judicial Review of Administration in Europe
Procedural Fairness and Propriety
Edited by Giacinto della Cananea and Mads Andenas

European Research Council
Established by the European Commission

The Common Core of European Administrative Law (CoCEAL) project has received funding from the European Research Council (ERC) under the Horizon 2020 Research and Innovation Programme 'Advanced Grant' Excellent Science (Grant Agreement No 694697).

Procedural Requirements for Administrative Limits to Property Rights

Edited by
MARTINA CONTICELLI AND THOMAS PERROUD

OXFORD
UNIVERSITY PRESS

OXFORD
UNIVERSITY PRESS

Great Clarendon Street, Oxford, OX2 6DP,
United Kingdom

Oxford University Press is a department of the University of Oxford.
It furthers the University's objective of excellence in research, scholarship,
and education by publishing worldwide. Oxford is a registered trade mark of
Oxford University Press in the UK and in certain other countries

First Edition published in 2022

Impression: 1

Published in the United States of America by Oxford University Press
198 Madison Avenue, New York, NY 10016, United States of America

British Library Cataloguing in Publication Data
Data available

Library of Congress Control Number: 2022935961

ISBN 978–0–19–886758–6

DOI: 10.1093/oso/9780198867586.001.0001

Printed and bound by
CPI Group (UK) Ltd, Croydon, CR0 4YY

General Editors' Preface

This is the fourth book of the series, *The Common Core of European Administrative Laws* (*CoCEAL*), based on a comparative research for which the European Research Council has awarded us an Advanced Grant. From the outset it was decided that this research would have two major themes. The first concerns the methodology of comparative analysis. Our intent is to compare a plurality of legal systems, going beyond the mainstream scrutiny of the most influential ones, and seeking to understand the role of various legal formants therein. Secondly, and more importantly, this comparison has a particular end in view. Our intent is to launch a large-scale debate not only on commonalities and diversities within the European legal space but also, and more importantly, on how commonality and diversity have stretched out and interact with one another, within and across legal systems, both diachronically and synchronically, in the past and today.

From the first point of view, the methodology adopted in our research owes a great deal to the pioneering seminars held at Cornell Law School during the 1960s and to the 'Common Core of European Private Law' project launched in 1993. This methodology is based on a 'factual analysis' in the sense that it is based on hypothetical cases that are first subject to scrutiny during workshops with the experts of the legal systems selected for comparison, in order to ascertain whether those cases are plausible and meaningful. Only at a later stage are these cases sent to the experts, who elaborate their answers on the basis of all relevant legal formants. A further step consists in comparing these answers, with a view to understanding the relevance and significance of both the commonality and diversity.

From the second point of view, this new research is strongly focused on administrative procedure and thus considers various types of administrative action, including adjudication and rule-making, without overlooking the importance of traditional sets of issues, such as those relating to judicial review and government liability in tort. These are precisely the ones with which we have chosen to open this new series, because they are, at the same time, both 'classic' and important. They allow us to take into due consideration the works of those who have gone before, using legal comparison for various purposes. They permit us to call for heightened attention to what is new and original in the European legal space, where national legal systems interact one with one another and with the two regional organizations, the European Union and the Council of Europe.

The project website, www.coceal.it, provides useful information on past initiatives and next steps.

Giacinto della Cananea and Mauro Bussani
Rome and Trieste, 19 July 2021

General Editors' Preface

Editors' Preface

This book develops a subtopic within the Common Core of European Administrative Law Project (CoCEAL), which examines specific groups of administrative procedures.

Our study aims to discuss procedures that interfere with the right to private property. Unlike—and in addition to—previous studies on expropriation, we consider at the same time traditional 'takings' and so-called 'regulatory expropriation'. Also unlike other comparative studies in both private and public law, we concentrate on the exercise of public power, focusing our analysis on procedural constraints.

Our research began many years ago, with Giacinto della Cananea and Mario Bussani including this subtopic in the CoCEAL studies from the very beginning. They recognised how these themes provide a meaningful framework for representing the various issues concerning administrative procedures and highlighting the controversial choices they bring to light.

While the other volumes in this series thus far have dealt with topics likely to provide a comprehensive viewpoint on administrative law, our contribution concentrates on a somewhat limited category of administrative procedures.

Through a comparative survey spanning twelve legal systems and a transnational regime, our research aims to shed light on the core of administrative activity that exemplifies the 'negative State'. Within the vast field of adjudication, this volume deals with one of the most traditional sets of procedures, namely the exercise of public powers affecting property and trade. This is a fascinating area of investigation in the field of administrative law, as the topic stands at the crossroad between public authority and private rights *par excellence*. Many other reasons, such as its proximity to private law, are examined later in this volume, which suggests approaching this topic from a common core research perspective.

As in the CoCEAL project as a whole, the structure of our questionnaire takes the fundamentals of expropriations in a given legal order as its starting point and examines a number of cases: the main requirements for property rights restrictions are presented briefly through national reports and discussed through hypotheticals, while our search for comparative evidence focuses on procedural propriety and fairness, leaving aside other aspects, such as the right to compensation.

Our main conjectures are as follows: first, that a new property paradigm is emerging; second that this paradigm regards both what property is and how it might be protected, and third that a common core is emerging, whose relevance counts especially at the level of procedural propriety. Our findings support the idea that much of this shift is grounded in the very essence of a shared understanding of procedural requirements protecting private property against any kind of public restrictions.

We express our gratitude to Giacinto della Cananea and Mauro Bussani for involving us in such a challenging enterprise and for their countless input. We also wish to thank Angela Ferrari Zumbini, Marta Infantino, and Laura Muzi from the

CoCEAL research team for their daily contribution to the research and their work to fine-tune the questionnaire.

The original idea behind this book and a rough version of the questionnaire were first presented during a workshop in Rome in October 2018, attended by Jean-Bernard Auby, Paul Craig, Spyridon Flogaitis, Takis Tridimas, and Ferdinand Wollenschläger.

The final version of the questionnaire, including various hypothetical cases, was drawn up in the subsequent months and sent to the national experts, who were invited to discuss it in the course of an international workshop in Rome in May 2019.

Roberto Caranta, Otto Pfersmann, Ulrich Stelkens, Gaia Taffoni, and Rocio del Pilar Trujillo Sosa joined the group, generously adding their contribution to the general debate.

Our deepest gratitude also goes to all the participants involved in any way in this project. We learned so much from all the exchanges we had during this time.

The answers provided by the national experts served as a basis for the comparative exercise that followed, aiming to shed light on the commonalities and diversities among the selected legal systems. We extend our thanks to the national experts who agreed to engage in this legal research and participate in this collective work, filling many roles at different steps along the way.

We owe a profound debt of gratitude to Adrian Bedford and Martin Maguire, who carefully reviewed the text from the linguistic point of view, faithfully respecting the authors' intentions.

Heartfelt and special thanks go to Paola Monaco, who patiently but rigorously assisted us throughout, collecting the reports, editing the texts according to the OUP guidelines, and helping us with the overall drafting of the book.

Special thanks are due to Sabino Cassese, not only for his teaching input but also for introducing one of the editors to the world of property and expropriation studies.

Last but not least, we gratefully acknowledge the support of Ctif, the Interdepartmental Center for Teleinfrastructures, and especially Paola Paniccia and Paolo Paolini. We also thank 'Tor Vergata' University of Rome: Claudio Franchini, for his continuous support, and Francesca Dominici, Danilo Aceto Zumbo, Elisa Baldazzi, Sabrina Bozzoli, Maria Antonietta Compostella, and Gabriella Lisi, as well as Bocconi University (Paola Calogero in particular), and the University of Trieste.

Martina Conticelli and Thomas Perroud
Tor Vergata University of Rome, Panthéon-Assas University
Rome, Paris, 30 June 2021

Contents

PART IV COMPARATIVE ANALYSIS

Detailed Table of Contents

PART III CASES

The authors of the respective country reports in Cases 2-11 are the same as in Case 1 unless otherwise noted

PART IV COMPARATIVE ANALYSIS

List of Abbreviations

A1P1	Article 1 of Protocol No 1 of the European Convention on Human Rights
AC	Law Reports, Appeal Cases (Third Series)
AJCL	American Journal of Comparative Law
AJIL	American Journal of International Law
AJDA	*Actualité Juridique, Droit Administratif*
BauGB	*Baugesetzbuch* (Federal Building Code—Germany)
BayPAG	*Polizeiaufgabengesetz Bayern* (Police Task Law Bavaria—Germany)
BGB	*Bürgerliches Gesetzbuch* (German Civil Code—Germany)
BIC	Asset of Cultural Interest (Bien de interés cultural) (Spain)
BJIL	Berkeley Journal of International Law
BPCHPV	Basis for the Policy of Cultural Heritage and its Protection and Valorisation (Portugal)
BPN	*Banco Português de Negócios*
Br Yearb Int	British Yearbook of International Law
Buff L Rev	Buffalo Law Review
BVerfGE	*Entscheidungen des Bundesverfassungsgerichts*
CAP	Code of Administrative Procedure (Poland)
C Cass	*Cour de cassation* (France)
CC	*Conseil constitutionnel* (France)
CE	*Conseil d'État* (France)
CE	Portuguese Code of Expropriations (Portugal)
CE	Spanish Constitution (*Constitución Española de 1978*) (Spain)
Chic J Int Law	Chicago journal of international Law
Colum J Eur L	Columbia Journal of European Law
CPO	compulsory purchase order
CPTA	Code of Process in the Administrative Courts of Law (Portugal)
Dir amm	*Diritto Amministrativo*
DPR	Decree of the President of the Republic of Italy
DS	*Droit social*
ECHR	European Convention on Human Rights
ECtHR	European Court of Human Rights
ed(s)	editor(s)
edn	edition
EEG NW	*Landesenteignungs—und—entschädigungsgesetz Nordrhein-Westfalen* (Expropriation and Compensation Act of North Rhine-Westphalia—Germany)
eg	*exampli gratia*
EIA	Environmental Impact Assessment (Sweden)
EPLJ	European Property Law Journal

Eur J Int Law	European Journal of International Law
Eur Law J	European Law Journal
EWCA Civ	England and Wales Court of Appeal (Civil Division)
ExK	Expropriation Act (Sweden)
ExL	Expropriation Regulation (Sweden)
FET	fair and equitable treatment
ff	following
FJ	Legal basis (*Fundamento Jurídico*) (Spain)
Foro It	Il Foro italiano
GG	*Grundgesetz* (Basic Law for the Federal Republic of Germany—Germany)
Harv Int Law J	Harvard International Law Journal
Harv L Rev	Harvard Law Review
HRA 1998	Human Rights Act 1998
ICLQ	International and Comparative Law Quarterly
ICSID	International Centre for Settlement of Investment Disputes
ie	that is
IJPL	Italian Journal of Public Law
Int J Bus Manag	International Journal of Commerce and Management
IPMA	Immovable Property Management Act of 21 August 1997
ISDS	investor–state dispute settlement
JPL	Journal of Public Law
KB	Law Reports, King's Bench Division
KGSG	*Kulturgutschutzgesetz* (Cultural Property Protection Act—Germany)
King's L J	King's Law Journal
Law Am	Lawyer of the Americas
LC	Coastal Act (*Ley 22/1988 de Costas*) (Spain)
LEA	Act on Environmental Impact Assessment (*Ley 21/2013 de Evaluación del Impacto Ambiental*) (Spain)
LEF	Act on Expropriation (*Ley de Expropiación Forzosa de 1954*) (Spain)
LJCA	Judicial (Contentious) Administrative Act (*Ley 29/1988 de la Jurisdicción Contencioso-Administrativa*) (Spain)
LOEAES	Organic Law on the States of Alarm, Emergency, and Siege (*Ley 4/1981 Orgánica de los Estados de Alarma, Excepción y Sitio*) (Spain)
LPAC	Administrative Procedure Act (*Ley 39/2015 de Procedimiento Administrativo Común*) (Spain)
LPAP	Act on Public Property (*Ley 33/2003 de Patrimonio de las Administraciones Públicas*) (Spain)
LPH	Historical Heritage Act (*Ley 16/1985 de Patrimonio Histórico*) (Spain)
LPIL	Land Planning Instruments Law (Portugal)
LPN	Act on National Parks (*Ley 30/2014 de Parques Nacionales*) (Spain)
LPNB	Nature and Biodiversity Protection Act (*Ley 42/2007 de Protección de la Naturaleza y la Biodiversidad*) (Spain)

LPPSPU	Law of Public Policy for Land, Planning and Urban Planning (Portugal)
LR	Noise Pollution Act (*Ley 37/2003 del Ruido*) (Spain)
LRJSP	Act on the Legal Regime of Public Authorities *(Ley 40/2015 de Régimen Jurídico del Sector Público*) (Spain)
LUA	limited use area
LuftVG	*Luftverkehrsgesetz* (Air Traffic Act—Germany)
Maastricht J Eur & Comp L	Maastricht Journal of European and Comparative Law
Minn L Rev	Minnesota Law Review
no(s)	number(s)
NVwZ-RR	*Neue Zeitschrift für Verwaltungsrecht Rechtsprechungs-Report*
NYU L Rev	New York University Law Review
PolG NW	*Polizeigesetz Nordrhein-Westfalen* (Police Law North Rhine-Westphalia—Germany)
Prop	Proposition (Government Bill) (Sweden)
QPC	Priority Question of Constitutionality (France)
RD	*Regio decreto* (Italy)
RDP	*Revue du droit public* (France)
Rec	*Recueil des décisions du Conseil d'État* (France)
Rec	*Recurso* (Spain)
REF	Regulation on Expropriation (*Reglamento de Expropiación Forzosa de 1957*) (Spain)
RJ	*Repertorio de Jurisprudencia* (Spain)
SOU	*Statens offentliga utredningar* (Swedish Government Official Reports) (Sweden)
SPDA	Spatial Planning and Development Act of 27 March 2003
SSSIs	sites of special scientific interest
STC	Constitutional Court Judgment (*Sentencia del Tribunal Constitucional*) (Spain)
STS	Supreme Court Judgment (*Sentencia del Tribunal Supremo*) (Spain)
SvJT	*Svensk Juristtidning* (Sweden)
TEU	Treaty on European Union
TCPA	Town and Country Planning Act 1990
TRLS76	Land Act of 1976 (recast) (*Texto Refundido de la Ley del Suelo de 1976*) (Spain)
TRLSRU	Land and Urban Renovation Act (recast) (*Texto Refundido de la Ley del Suelo y Rehabilitación Urbana de 2015*) (Spain)
Univ Ill Law Rev	University of Illinois Law Review
U Pa J Const L	University of Pennsylvania Journal of Constitutional Law
U Pa L Rev	University of Pennsylvania Law Review
VwGO	*Verwaltungsgerichtsordnung* (Code of Administrative Court Procedure—Germany)
VwVfG	*Verwaltungsverfahrensgesetz* (Administrative Procedure Act—Germany)
WL	Water Law (Portugal)
WLR	Weekly Law Reports
Yale LJ	Yale Law Journal

Table of Cases

(Chronological order except where otherwise specified)

BELGIUM

THE NETHERLANDS

FRANCE

GERMANY

POLAND

PORTUGAL

SPAIN

SWEDEN

Supreme Administrative Court (*Regeringsrätten*)

UKRAINE

Constitutional Court (*Конституційний Суд України*)

THE UNITED KINGDOM (ALPHABETICAL ORDER)

THE UNITED STATES (ALPHABETICAL ORDER)

THE EUROPEAN COURT OF JUSTICE

THE EUROPEAN COURT OF HUMAN RIGHTS (ECtHR)

AD HOC ARBITRATION TRIBUNALS

LONDON COURT OF ARBITRATION (LCIA)

PERMANENT COURT OF ARBITRATION (PCA)

UNCITRAL

Table of Legislation

ITALY

THE NETHERLANDS

POLAND

PORTUGAL

SPAIN

SWEDEN

UKRAINE

THE UNITED KINGDOM

THE UNITED STATES

Essential Provisions

Belgian Constitution (1831)

Article 16
No one can be deprived of his property except in the case of expropriation for a public purpose, in the cases and manner established by the law and in return for fair compensation paid beforehand.

Article 17
Assets may not be confiscated as a means of punishment.

Basic Law for the Federal Republic of Germany (1949)

Article 14
[Property—Inheritance—Expropriation]
(1) Property and the right of inheritance shall be guaranteed. Their content and limits shall be defined by the laws.
(2) Property entails obligations. Its use shall also serve the public good.
(3) Expropriation shall only be permissible for the public good. It may only be ordered by or pursuant to a law that determines the nature and extent of compensation. Such compensation shall be determined by establishing an equitable balance between the public interest and the interests of those affected. In case of dispute concerning the amount of compensation, recourse may be had to the ordinary courts.

Constitution of the Italian Republic (1948)

Article 42
Property is public or private. Economic assets may belong to the State, to public bodies or to private persons. Private property is recognised and guaranteed by the law, which prescribes the ways it is acquired, enjoyed and its limitations so as to ensure its social function and make it accessible to all.
In the cases provided for by the law and with provisions for compensation, private property may be expropriated for reasons of general interest.
The law establishes the regulations and limits of legitimate and testamentary inheritance and the rights of the State in matters of inheritance.

Constitution of the Kingdom of the Netherlands (2008)

Article 14
1. Expropriation may take place only in the public interest and on prior assurance of full compensation, in accordance with regulations laid down by or pursuant to Act of Parliament.
2. Prior assurance of full compensation shall not be required if in an emergency immediate expropriation is called for.
3. In the cases laid down by or pursuant to Act of Parliament there shall be a right to full or partial compensation if in the public interest the competent authority destroys property or renders it unusable or restricts the exercise of the owner's rights to it.

Constitution of the Republic of Poland (1997)

Article 21
1. The Republic of Poland shall protect ownership and the right of succession.
2. Expropriation may be allowed solely for public purposes and for just compensation.

Constitution of the Portuguese Republic (1976)

Article 62
(Right to private property)
1. Everyone is guaranteed the right to private property and to the transmission thereof in life or upon death, in accordance with the Constitution.
2. Requisitions and expropriations in the public interest may only be undertaken on a legal basis and upon payment of just compensation.

Spanish Constitution (1978)

Article 33
1. The right to private property and inheritance is recognised.
2. The content of these rights shall be determined by the social function which they fulfil, in accordance with the law.
3. No one may be deprived of his or her property and rights, except on justified grounds of public utility or social interest and with a proper compensation in accordance with the provisions of the law.

Constitution of Sweden: The Instrument of Government (1974)

Chapter 2, Article 15. Protection of property and the right of public access
The property of every individual shall be so guaranteed that no one may be compelled by expropriation or other such disposition to surrender property to the

public institutions or to a private subject, or tolerate restriction by the public institutions of the use of land or buildings, other than where necessary to satisfy pressing public interests.

A person who is compelled to surrender property by expropriation or other such disposition shall be guaranteed full compensation for his or her loss. Compensation shall also be guaranteed to a person whose use of land or buildings is restricted by the public institutions in such a manner that ongoing land use in the affected part of the property is substantially impaired, or injury results which is significant in relation to the value of that part of the property. Compensation shall be determined according to principles laid down in law.

In the case of limitations on the use of land or buildings on grounds of protection of human health or the environment, or on grounds of safety, however, the rules laid down in law apply in the matter of entitlement to compensation.

Everyone shall have access to the natural environment in accordance with the right of public access, notwithstanding the above provisions.

Constitution of Ukraine (1996)

Article 41

Everyone has the right to own, use and dispose of his or her property, and the results of his or her intellectual and creative activity.

The right of private property is acquired by the procedure determined by law.

In order to satisfy their needs, citizens may use the objects of the right of state and communal property in accordance with the law.

No one shall be unlawfully deprived of the right of property. The right of private property is inviolable.

Forced alienation (expropriation) of objects of the right of private property may be applied only as an exception for reasons of social necessity, on the grounds of and by the procedure established by law, and on the condition of advance and complete compensation of their value. . Forced alienation (expropriation) of such objects with subsequent complete compensation of their value is permitted only under conditions of martial law or a state of emergency.

Confiscation of property may be applied only pursuant to a court decision, in the cases, in the extent and by the procedure established by law.

The use of property shall not cause harm to the rights, freedoms and dignity of citizens, the interests of society, aggravate the ecological situation and the natural qualities of land.

Constitution of the United States (1789)

Amendment V (1791)

No person shall be held to answer for a capital, or otherwise infamous crime, unless on a presentment or indictment of a grand jury, except in cases arising in the land or naval forces, or in the militia, when in actual service in time of war or public danger; nor shall any person be subject for the same offense to be twice put in jeopardy of life or limb; nor shall be compelled in any criminal case to be a witness against himself, nor be deprived of life, liberty, or property, without due process of law; nor shall private property be taken for public use, without just compensation.

Amendment XIV (Section 1) (1868)

All persons born or naturalized in the United States, and subject to the jurisdiction thereof, are citizens of the United States and of the state wherein they reside. No state shall make or enforce any law which shall abridge the privileges or immunities of citizens of the United States; nor shall any state deprive any person of life, liberty, or property, without due process of law; nor deny to any person within its jurisdiction the equal protection of the laws.

Charter of Fundamental Rights of the European Union (2000)

Article 17

Right to property

1. Everyone has the right to own, use, dispose of and bequeath his or her lawfully acquired possessions. No one may be deprived of his or her possessions, except in the public interest and in the cases and under the conditions provided for by law, subject to fair compensation being paid in good time for their loss. The use of property may be regulated by law in so far as is necessary for the general interest.
2. Intellectual property shall be protected.

Protocol No 1 to the European Convention on Human Rights (1952)

Article 1

Protection of property

Every natural or legal person is entitled to the peaceful enjoyment of his possessions. No one shall be deprived of his possessions except in the public interest and subject to the conditions provided for by law and the general principles of international law.

The preceding provisions shall not, however, in any way impair the right of the state to enforce such laws as it deems necessary to control the use of property in accordance with the general interest or to secure the payment of taxes or other contributions or penalties.

List of Contributors

Luis Arroyo Jiménez Jean Monnet Chair in European Administrative Law, University of Castilla-La Mancha (Spain)

Balázs Szabolcs Gerencsér PhD, Habil, Director of Ereky Public Law Research Center, Associate Professor, Pázmány Péter Catholic University, Faculty of Law, Budapest (Hungary)

Luca Ceci Assistant at Louvain University; Lawyer at the bar of the Walloon Brabant (Belgium)

Martina Conticelli Professor of Administrative Law, Tor Vergata University of Rome (Italy)

Caroline Delforge Scientific Collaborator at Louvain University; Lawyer at the bar of Charleroi (Belgium)

Halyna Dovhan PhD, Associate Professor, Ivan Franko National University of Lviv (Ukraine)

Filippo Fontanelli Senior Lecturer in International Economic Law, University of Edinburgh; Adjunct Professor, LUISS (Italy)

Emma Guernaoui PhD student in Public Law, University of Montpellier/Panthéon-Assas (France)

Rui Guerra da Fonseca Professor of the University of Lisbon Faculty of Law; Researcher, Lisbon Centre for Research in Public Law (CIDP) (Portugal)

Patricia Jonason Associate Professor of Public Law, Södertörns University (Sweden)

Inga Kawka Dr hab, Chair of European Law, Faculty of Law and Administration, Jagiellonian University in Krakow (Poland)

Łukasz Kozera Dr doc, Institute of Law and Economics, Pedagogical University of Krakow (Poland)

Nuria Magaldi Associate Professor (*Profesora Titular*) of Administrative Law, University of Córdoba (Spain)

Yseult Marique Senior Lecturer, University of Essex (United Kingdom); Research Fellow, FÖV Speyer (Germany)

Vincent Martenet Professor of Law and Dean of the Faculty of Law, Criminal Justice and Public Administration, University of Lausanne; Deputy Justice, Federal Supreme Court (Switzerland)

Silvia Mirate Associate Professor of Administrative Law, University of Torino (Italy)

Thomas Perroud Professor of public law at Université Panthéon-Assas (CERSA); Fellow of the Humboldt Foundation at Humboldt University (Berlin)

Kevin Polet Assistant at Louvain University; Lawyer at the bar of the Walloon Brabant (Belgium)

David Renders Professor at Louvain University; Lawyer at the bar of Brussels (Belgium)

Foroud Shirvani Professor of Public Law, University of Bonn (Germany)

Ilya Somin Professor of Law, George Mason University (USA)

Dolores Utrilla Fernández-Bermejo Professor of Administrative Law at University of Castilla-La Mancha; Law Clerk at the Spanish Constitutional Court (Spain)

Nikky van Triet PhD candidate, Radboud University (Nijmegen, the Netherlands); associate at BarentsKrans (The Hague, the Netherlands)

Jacques Sluysmans Professor of Expropriation Law, Radboud University (Nijmegen, the Netherlands); partner at Van der Feltz advocaten (The Hague, the Netherlands)

Emma Waring Senior Lecturer, York Law School, The University of York (United Kingdom)

PART I
INTRODUCTION
A Common Core Research on Property

1

Property Rights and Administrative Limits

A Procedural Perspective

Martina Conticelli

I. The object of this research in context

This book develops a sub-topic of the research on the 'Common Core of European Administrative Laws' (COCEAL) focusing on public restrictions to property rights.

The importance of the topic for comparative studies, the bases of our hypothesis, and the limits and boundaries of this investigation will become clear in the pages that follow. Before that, however, a few words must be dedicated to the general setting that provides the reference framework for this book.

As already pointed out by Giacinto della Cananea and Mauro Bussani, the 'Common Core of European Administrative Laws' project seeks to offer an advanced methodology for legal comparison in the field of administrative law in the light of the main achievements obtained by comparative studies in private law.[1]

This comparative approach sets out to investigate whether a common ground or a 'common core' of administrative laws is to be found among European countries and, if so, to what extent that dimension may be considered valid and which tools may be used to evaluate it, despite a certain degree of divergence and lack of uniformity.

Diversity is expressed in various terms across distinct traditions. As in the previous volumes in this series, our comparative inquiry addresses administrative law, mostly viewed through the lens of procedure.[2]

The main hypothesis of the Common Core of Administrative Laws in Europe project is that behind, beyond, and despite divergences, administrative experiences have much in common. We aim therefore to assess the nature and importance of the main commonalities, both in terms of their function as elements of connection, reshaped in legal terms in the guise of general principles of law, and from the viewpoint of the mechanisms for applying them in diverse contexts—the idea being that minor differences do not undermine the validity and robustness of our basic assumptions.

Rather than merely juxtaposing legal systems, our goal is to compare jurisdictions with a view to establishing the conditions for the advancement of knowledge

[1] The main assumptions, methodology, and structure of the new comparative research project are discussed in G della Cananea and M Bussani, 'The Common Core of European Administrative Laws: A Framework for Analysis' (2019) 26 Maastricht J Eur & Comp L 217. See also the research website www.coceal.it (accessed July 2021).

[2] G della Cananea and S Mannoni (eds), *Administrative Justice Fin de Siècle: Early Judicial Standards of Administrative Conduct in Europe (1890-1910)* (OUP 2021); G della Cananea and R Caranta (eds), *Tort Liability of Public Authorities in European Laws* (OUP 2020).

Martina Conticelli, *Property Rights and Administrative Limits* In: *Procedural Requirements for Administrative Limits to Property Rights.* Edited by: Martina Conticelli And Thomas Perroud, Oxford University Press. © Martina Conticelli 2022.
DOI: 10.1093/oso/9780198867586.003.0001

by examining the differences—but also the common elements—running through the European legal systems.

This chapter is structured as follows. Section II explains why the field of property is an interesting terrain for our comparative study. In section III, we define the contextual framework, the conceptual map for our cartography, and the boundaries of our research. Section IV focuses on the importance of procedural fairness in proceedings for the restriction of property rights for reasons of public interest. Section V addresses some methodological issues, including the nature of our 'factual analysis', as well as the choice of the specific legal systems to include in our comparison. We shall also outline the structure of this book.

II. Property matters

As mentioned above, our study concerns property rights and how they are limited by public powers.

Why property?

The relevance of our choice, its place within the general project concerning administrative laws in Europe, and its potential impact, are rooted in a number of different factors affecting the assumptions of our research and the expected findings.

First of all, this is not only a traditional topic; it opens up a field of investigation on a broad variety of authoritative and discretionary powers: those may include expropriation, confiscation, and the so-called regulatory expropriation.

Secondly, property has long been studied from the private lawyer's perspective but much less from the viewpoint of the public lawyer. More specifically, few comparative studies have been dedicated to property issues, albeit with a number of exceptions—mainly in private law scholarship.[3] Nevertheless, most of the private law research focuses on substantive issues, while our study seeks to provide an opportunity to investigate procedural questions.[4] Even among comparative studies in public law,[5] the procedural side of the topic is rarely explored, if not totally neglected—again, with some exceptions.[6]

Besides focusing on procedures, the added value of our perspective lies in the target of the comparison: most comparative analysis, specifically in the field of private law, focuses on elaborating a common frame of reference within a broader perspective of preparing the terrain for developing uniform rules. As we mentioned in the opening remarks of this introductory section however, we do not approach the issue with a

[3] M Graziadei and L Smith, *Comparative Property Law, Global Perspectives* (Edward Elgar 2017); U Mattei, *Basic Principles of Property Law: A Comparative Legal and Economic Introduction* (Greenwood Press 2000); I Kim, H Lee, and I Somin, *Eminent Domain. A comparative perspective* (CUP 2017).

[4] U Mattei, 'The History, Present Day Applications, and Future of Property Law: Basic Principles of Property Law: A Comparative Legal and Economic Introduction' [2002] Int J Bus Manag 126 ff.

[5] A Van der Walt, *Constitutional Property Clauses. A comparative Analysis* (Kluwer Law International 1999) 5.

[6] On both property and public restrictions see JAMA Sluysmans, S Verbist, and E Waring, *Expropriation Law in Europe* (Wolters Kluwer 2015); JAMA Sluysmans and EJL Waring, 'Core Principles of European Expropriation Law' (2016) EPLJ 142 ff; T Allen, *The Right to Property in Commonwealth Constitutions* (CUP 2009).

view to such a normative objective or purpose-oriented goal. Essentially, our aim is to also bring a new perspective to comparative studies in property law.

Third, none may doubt that the protection of property rights stands at the crossroads between private and public law. Against this backdrop, a study centred on property provides a chance to test the view in terms of the common core proposed in CoCEAL.

One of the key arguments in the approach adopted by the general project is that the common core methodology already adopted for private law may be successfully applied also in the field of Public and Administrative Law, albeit with some adjustments. Our choice is likely to challenge the methodological approach with regard to its distinctive features and will eventually confirm its validity.

More recently, although strongly linked to the experience of 'state', the field of property issues has provided an opportunity to open up our perspective on supranational influences as well as transnational ones, leading us to evaluate whether exercising public powers affecting property is still to be considered the prerogative of the state, and to what extent jurisdictions beyond state level may form useful means of connection among legal systems.

We shall return to these questions shortly; suffice it to say at this stage, as a mere introduction, that the inclusion of property rights in the catalogue of human rights paved the way for a system of multilevel protection and led the way to the emergence of a cross-system regime. This was not only due to the role played by the European Convention on Human rights, whose implications are important from the substantive and procedural perspectives alike (if we consider Article 1 Protocol No 1 to the Convention and Article 6 ECHR, respectively). Besides defining property as a human right, the rationale behind the interest shown in the status of property rights by legal regimes beyond municipal level was also triggered by increasing market integration. Confirmation comes from the concern shown by supranational legal systems such as the European Union, where, despite references in the catalogue of fundamental rights (the Charter of Nice, Article 47, and Article 17 on property), private property has a bearing on the European 'economic constitution', notwithstanding the wording of Article 345 TFEU. Further evidence is provided by the prominence given to property rights in the legal regimes protecting foreign investments in the various bilateral and multilateral investment agreements (BITs).[7]

Although property is strictly connected to sovereignty, municipal regimes are now increasingly supplemented by supranational and international rules. Thanks to global interconnection, the ultra-national dimension of a discourse on property can no longer be denied, nor can its consequences for its regime, due to the transnational reach of legal systems beyond the state. Thus, one may wonder whether a regime of property law with general principles and rules applying to all forms of property—movable, immovable, and claims—is emerging.

[7] S van Erp, *European and National Property Law: Osmosis or Growing Antagonism?* Sixth Walter van Gerven Lecture, Leuven Centre for a Common Law of Europe, Ius Commune Research School (Europa Law Publishing 2006).

III. Setting boundaries

Some other preliminary remarks are due as we state our standpoint on the category of restrictions on property rights. These regard property itself and our decision to mention property rights themselves rather than referring more concisely to the right to property. We suggest that some clarifications are needed on this issue and conclude with a synthesis concerning the extent of our work.

Clearly, not only may property be studied from widely divergent perspectives, but also the way property is conceptualised may vary profoundly, depending on the meaning and the importance assigned to the stable rights and forms of appropriations in each jurisdiction and, more generally, in any societal community.

The issue of property, like the regime governing its limitations, is deeply rooted in a specific social environment and political context, and it depends largely on the constitutional framework of any given jurisdiction, whose evolution—from a diachronic point of view—has historically led to profound changes in ownership status.

The same differences between legal systems as far as the label and the concept is concerned, need not be overemphasised here as a cultural impediment to discussing property.

Whatever is formalised in a written charter or simply considered conventional, thanks to the legacy of the shared environment of philosophical and political thought across the centuries, the roots of property in Europe may seem to have more in common than national constitutional traditions themselves when taken as a whole.[8]

Yet legal structures vary worldwide and even throughout Europe.

If we look at the common law tradition for instance—just to cite one example—most jurisdictions associate the notions of trust and property,[9] but the experience of trust may be less relevant for civil law countries and therefore allows for few comparisons.[10] Furthermore, in the UK, a fundamental distinction is drawn between personal property and real property, especially in the jurisdiction of England and Wales.

Generally speaking, property rights in other jurisdictions may be classified differently depending on whether a distinction is drawn between public or private property, or between forms of collective property and individual ones, while in other cases those distinctions may count for less.

Property clauses rarely state definitions of property.[11] Yet the two should be interconnected: even so, property clauses tend to avoid too many definitions. In reality, the major differences are to be found in the object of property rights: according to different viewpoints, 'property' may refer, as far as its object is concerned, to movables, immovables, intangibles (intellectual properties, rights),[12] entitlements,[13] or claims

[8] See della Cananea and Bussani (n 1) 217.

[9] For the opposite view see J Langbein, 'The Contractarian Basis of Trust Law' (1995) 105(3) Yale LJ 625.

[10] H Hansmann and U Mattei, 'The Functions of Trust Law: A Comparative Legal and Economic Analysis' (1998) 73(2) NYU L Rev 434 ff.

[11] See eg Italian Civil Code, art 832; French Civil Code, art 544; German Civil Code, arts 854 ff, 903 ff.

[12] See KJ Vandevelde, 'The New Property of the Nineteenth Century: The Development of the Modern Concept of Property' (1980) 29 Buff L Rev 325 ff.

[13] See on this point the seminal work by C Reich, 'The New Property' (1964) 73 Yale LJ 733 ff.

for access to essential facilities[14] and, more recently, even to body parts and virtual forms of property.[15]

Moreover, and against this backdrop, the concept of property has been understood as an amphibological one, potentially referring to its object as well as to rights and prerogatives over the object itself.[16] This stems mainly from the common law experience, and it specifically rests on theories claiming that property must refer to a bundle of rights: just to mention some, the privileges afforded to the owner may include, for instance, the right to exclude, the right to enjoy, the right to peaceful enjoyment, and the right to dispose.[17] Rooted particularly in the US legal tradition, besides the recognition of the existence of different prerogatives, this notion also encompasses the idea that each component may circulate autonomously even if pertaining to the whole.

Along with its conceptualisation, a second aspect is the importance of property in contemporary democracies.

From a diachronic perspective, the Constitutional charters of the last century play their part by allowing the sacrifice of what was considered the subjective right par excellence,[18] provided that deprivation takes place in the forms—and according to—the limits that find expression in the 'expropriation measure for reasons of public interest', and with due compensation. Therefore, the change consolidates a reading of the protection of the right of property in terms of guarantees regarding the actions of public authorities, whose intervention supposedly meets specific requirements.

Hence, our interest in the topic refers almost entirely to the period circumscribed by the approval of democratic constitutions and focuses on the system of guarantees, and in particular the forms of protection accorded to private individuals from the exercise of public power in the cases provided for by the law. These—we argue—are likely to support comparable standards of perception of private property and to express core social values relating to ownership and control.

The decision to investigate public interference and the countervailing procedural requirements also stems from the fact that this topic has not been so frequently studied in an organic and systematic way, and still less from a synchronic and comparative perspective, for the reasons mentioned in the second section of this introduction.

In the light of the above, the content and characteristics of this regime are addressed across an array of different jurisdictions, and the legal status of the owner vis-à-vis public authority is one of the topics examined here.

Our main interest is land, and we have adopted the following definition of land expropriation: 'the forced transfer of ownership ordered for reasons of general interest'.

[14] A Bell and G Parchomovsky, 'Givings' (2001) 111 Yale LJ 547 ff.

[15] JM Moringiello, 'Towards a System of Estates in Virtual Property' (2008) 1 IJPL 3.

[16] In these terms see A Gambaro, *Property, Propriété, Eigentum* (Cedam 1992) 16. The issue is discussed particularly with regards to the US environment: see FS Philbrick, 'Changing conceptions of Property in Law' (1938) 86(7) U Pa L Rev 691 ff; JE Cribbett, 'Concepts in Transition: The Search for a New Definition of Property' (1986) 95 Univ Ill Law Rev 1 ff.

[17] See M Honoré, 'Ownership' in AG Guest (ed), *Oxford Essays in Jurisprudence* (Clarendon Press 1961) 107 ff.

[18] Since the approval by the National Assembly of France, of the Declaration of the Rights of Man and of the Citizen, of 26 August 1789, whose art XVII provided that: 'Since property is an inviolable and sacred right, no one shall be deprived thereof except where public necessity, legally determined, shall clearly demand it, and then only on condition that the owner shall have been previously and equitably indemnified.'

But we also argue that the concept of property in the broader sense requires some investigation, which is why we have included references to a wider definition both in the introductory questions and occasionally in our questionnaire, where we focus on statutory restrictions regarding cultural heritage, licences, and regulatory taking.

We are confident that our comparative exercise in the field of direct expropriation can contribute by checking the validity and resistance of the traditional categories, as well as assessing the robustness of protection mechanisms against emerging forms of limitations. Thus, we include specific measures among the forms of public interference in question. These include the taking of property (expropriation) and the regulation of private property that is likely to produce an effect tantamount to expropriation.

This choice reflects the growing importance of legal regimes beyond the state, where economic assets are seen as proprietary and protected as such. The jurisprudence of the ECHR takes a broad view, thanks to the meaning assigned to the term 'possessions' in the jurisprudence of the Court of Strasbourg when interpreting the wording of Article 1, protocol 1, to the Convention. Whether possessions may refer to an autonomous and distinct concept with respect to property depends on various factors, such as the efficacy of the ECHR in domestic systems, including in terms of Article 6 TEU, and the protection afforded. Despite growing global interest in the topic, some have argued—on the basis of these premises—that the sheer importance of the issue shifts the very boundaries between private and public law.

The proposed approach has a two-fold goal: on the one hand, we aim to investigate the traditional forms of restrictions, while—on the other—we aim to discuss whether new forms of property may be emerging, taking as our starting point the circumstances deserving protection.

We therefore aim to study and compare all the procedures allowing interference with property rights and the procedural requirements for doing so. Besides adjudication, we are also interested in rule-making. Generally speaking, therefore, we may also consider general statutory provisions on acquisitions and the enjoyment of an individual's possessions, although the various forms of administrative restrictions are of greater interest to our study, both from a quantitative standpoint and a qualitative perspective.[19] We include measures such as compulsory acquisitions, deprivations, the extinguishing or modification of rights, requisitions, transfers of either ownership or possession, takings, and regulatory takings. These include regulation in the broad sense, and enabling powers, not so much in the constitutive phase but mostly in the revocation of licences, in changes to administrative terms and conditions that may be considered important limitations, assuming that the underlying status may be considered to be of a proprietary nature.

Ascertaining whether a special regime for properties and their limitations protects property from compulsory acquisitions and from police-power regulatory deprivations, or from both, is another issue to be addressed. The study also examines issues of judicial review in order to evaluate procedural fairness and the consequences of breaches of procedural fairness.

[19] Current reference is made in constitutional studies to the work by B Ackerman, *Private property and the Constitution* (Yale University Press 1977).

IV. The concept of procedural fairness in protecting property rights

To a greater extent than other public decisions, restrictions on property rights may differ depending not only on the interests at stake—those a particular society may believe more deserving of special protection—but also on the basis of a scale of values following a given, and established, hierarchical order.

Protection of individuals from state interference commonly relies on a set of minimum requirements, ie a public interest, compensation for loss, and a procedure defined according to standards provided for by law.

Constitutional questions concern the scope of administrative power over property rights in relation to the parliamentary role of statutes—and the characteristics of the restrictive measures are crucial. Differences may emerge at different stages; these may regard the nature of the expropriation procedure (whether administrative or judicial), its structural development, its codification (whether they are covered by a general administrative procedure act or they depend on sector-specific regulation), the nature of the expropriating body, the object of the expropriation, the amount of compensation, and the respective sub-procedures. The countries selected for our study may adopt different solutions to this regard.

This is why discussing 'how' property may be seized within a given framework may look more interesting than exploring when, and under what circumstances, it may occur, even if these aspects cannot be simply set aside. The answers to these questions form the basis for a substantial comparative analysis of the subject matter.

Our conjecture is that there really is a common core of procedural guarantees in the jurisdictions surveyed here, so our aim is to investigate to what extent this statement can be considered valid, and under what circumstances.

In order to do so, procedural due process of law is at least as relevant as substantive due process. The former includes the main rights expressed within the development of a certain procedure, such as the right to be heard, the right to be informed, the right to a reasoned decision, the protection of legitimate expectations, and the right to good administration and impartial treatment. To these we may add compliance with procedure, the way different values come into the procedure, the rights of third parties, and the position of the directly aggrieved party, as well as the effects on the treatment of procedural irregularities, absence of review, and the relative rectification procedures. In addition, procedural factors may include specifications of the criteria for using discretionary powers with a view to preventing arbitrary procedures. The context, which may affect procedures and lead to changes is also fundamental and deserves attention in terms of a general assessment. For example, a procedure that is ordinarily unreasonable may be considered reasonable in times of emergency.

A more frequently studied aspect is substantive fairness, whose standard covers compensation and public interest, for instance. It envisages principles of reasonableness and proportionality, conceived as a form of control over substantive immoderation among the criteria for valid restrictions.

V. In search of the 'common core'

After explaining the importance of protecting property from administrative action 'for reasons of public interest', thus situating the function played by the limitation of property rights within the system of administrative law, it is necessary to clarify the aim of this research and its place within the scope of the broader CoCEAL research project as a whole.

A. A 'common core' research

The main purpose of this study is to explore commonalities, and not only divergences. To this end, a questionnaire was circulated among the compilers of the national reports.

Due to the variety of procedures for limiting property rights, the first part of the questionnaire refers to a set of general introductory questions aiming to outline some broad features of their domestic jurisdictions from the outset.

First, we start from an examination of constitutional provisions (or conventions) concerning both land expropriation in the traditional sense, and limitations to property rights in the broad sense.[20]

Secondly, the distribution of legislative competences (in addition to administrative ones) needs to be taken into adequate consideration. In this domain, competences regarding expropriation may be distributed among different levels of government (namely in regional, federal or confederal states). In composite states, the situations presented in the questionnaire should be addressed by looking at the legislation in force in the entire country while mentioning some examples of rules applicable only in specific parts of the territory, thus emphasising the relationship between a minimum floor of common principles and the diversity of rules.

Thirdly, a brief analysis of procedure is required, listing the formal acts necessary for expropriation. Whatever the substantive provisions concerning expropriation, the choice between a pre-established general procedure or a set of sector-specific procedures may not look neutral for our purposes. In both cases, specific attention should be given, in our view, to potential and important differences with regard to the procedural requirements set out for other administrative procedures. Due to the specific connection between the different procedures, all of which affect property rights, the relationship between urban planning procedures and expropriation, and the relationship between environmental impact assessment and expropriation, must also be considered, not only to understand which procedural requirements are essential, but also at which stage they must be granted. For this reason, an overview of the structure of procedures limiting property rights through expropriation may not be sufficient, as expropriations and deprivations, like other procedures seeking to limiting property rights, might be connected with previous procedural steps or deliberations, such as planning. One issue

[20] See the 'Essential Provisions' table in this volume, xxxv.

we have had to face is to understand the relationship between the urban planning stage and the concrete limitations of property rights. This is such an important topic that a further line of research in this regard is expected within the broader project.[21]

Finally, the consequences of a court ruling that the expropriating measure is unlawful on grounds of substance and/or of process must be highlighted, and it must be ascertained whether it will be merely quashed or there will be other consequences, such as the award of damages.[22]

Part II of the questionnaire exemplifies the heart of the 'common core' method, as described in the research project on the common core of European administrative laws.

Comparison is never easy. This is why cases have been imagined which may give an understanding of how each one would be handled, and why, within a given legal context. The cases cover a variety of circumstances that help contextualise the underlying problem in the light of the main assumptions of each legal system. 'living law', encompassing legislative and regulatory provisions, judicial decisions, scholarly works and governmental practice, but also background theories, is likely to play an important role.

B. A 'factual' analysis

Although much has been written on the common core method by the editors of this collection, and discussions may be found in previous works published there, it is worth recalling the main assumptions underlying our choice of methodology.

As has already been pointed out, our 'factual' analysis originates with the comparative enquiry carried out by Rudolf Schlesinger in the 1960s as implemented by Bussani and Mattei in the framework of the Trento project on European private law.[23] According to the methodology developed by the German American legal scholar, an effort to move beyond the descriptive stage was needed when comparing legal institutions. This implied focusing on how problems would actually be addressed from jurisdiction to jurisdiction. Importantly, hypothetical cases need to be formulated in factual terms so they can be understood by scholars coming from different realities.

Against this backdrop, our questionnaire features eleven hypothetical cases formulated according to the methodology set out by della Cananea and Bussani for administrative law issues. These were then the object of discussion about how they would be solved in each of the selected jurisdictions.

Two cases (nos 1 and 2) discuss procedural deviations from classic expropriation. Furthermore, while the relationship between procedural requirements in urban planning and expropriations are addressed in Cases 3 and 10, Case no 4 looks at a further

[21] The research on Administrative rulemaking and planning carried out under the 'Common Core of European Administrative Laws' (CoCEAL) project will be published in 2023 by Oxford University Press in the sixth volume of the series.

[22] On this topic see G della Cananea, 'Commonality and Diversity in Administrative Justice: Fin de siècle' in della Cananea and Mannoni (eds) (n 2) 3 ff.

[23] See M Bussani and U Mattei, 'The Common Core Approach to European Private Law' (1997–1998) 3 Colum J Eur L 339; JM Smits, 'Convergence of Private Law in Europe: Towards a New Ius Commune?' in E Örücü and D Nelken (eds), *Comparative Law: A Handbook* (Hart Publishing 2007) 219.

factor of complexity, namely when expropriations take place under exceptional circumstances requiring urgent decisions.

Other cases consider the place and relevance of procedural requirements in the event of different forms of public interference arising from partial, indirect, or regulatory expropriations likely to affect the enjoyment of property rights, or representing a deprivation of property (Case nos 5, 6, 7, 8, 9, and 11).

A condition for this analysis is that the cases must be formulated in terms likely to make sense in all the legal systems taken into consideration. The questionnaire was therefore discussed during a seminar held in Rome in May 2019. The cases were duly amended in accordance with the findings of the debate. The discussion sought to set common ground for comparison and to provide a first glance at the basic foundations and assumptions from which to depart to frame the protection of property rights within the various administrative systems. In addition, the debate aimed to ascertain, first, whether the questions were pertinent to all the legal systems selected for comparative analysis.

The participants were leading scholars selected for their expertise in the field of property law and expropriation in each legal order. They sought to discover how the same hypothetical cases would probably be solved in their system. Participants were expected to provide answers to the questions raised for each case on the basis of the laws of their countries.

C. The legal systems selected for our comparison

It is also worth explaining how the jurisdictions for comparison were selected.

The structure of the comparative framework must be explained, both in terms of the choice of jurisdictions to be considered for submitting the questionnaire to the national rapporteurs and regarding the reasons for our choices when grouping the countries and their responses.

As for the first issue, faced with the choice of limiting our horizons to the major traditional European jurisdictions, we favoured the alternative, opting to cover a greater number of legal systems.

As a methodological choice shared with previous lines of research within the broader project on the Common Core of European Administrative Laws, we decided to embrace a series of jurisdictions perhaps best likely to represent a suitable and representative mix of legal systems across Europe. The sample therefore includes countries belonging to different kinds of systems, coming from both common law and civil law traditions, with different forms of government, and with recently adopted constitutions and less recent ones. In addition to EU Member States, we included two countries from outside the European Union, namely Ukraine and the US. Also—and exceptionally—we considered the legal regimes for the protection of foreign investments for a separate report. This is due to the growing importance of the 'jurisprudence' of arbitration tribunals in the field of property law in its wider sense.

To this end, EU rules, recommendations from the Council of Europe, and the OECD need only be quoted, while references from the ECHR must be taken into due consideration where relevant to the resolution of the cases. Further, the respondents were asked to shed light on the background theories or sets of beliefs and ideas about the law that the courts or other public agencies would refer to when dealing with the cases.[24]

As far as the horizontal reports are concerned, they discuss solutions common to all the jurisdictions or more widely shared among only some of them, possibly giving reasons explaining similarity and diversity.

The rationale behind grouping countries for comparison is also worth mentioning. We placed the main traditional jurisdictions in one group, treating them as dominant systems, with the purpose of outlining the main features of property protection rights in those legal contexts.[25] Accordingly, in our view, 'big systems' such as those of France, Germany, the UK, and the United States deserve to be considered together.

Conversely, we placed Italy, Portugal, and Spain in a second group in order to verify the assumption that they might be influenced by other jurisdictions. A third group embraces countries such as Ukraine and Poland, which shared the experience of a socialist regime and have young Constitutions, all features of undoubted importance when assessing the place assigned to private property—both countries share a lack of specific constitutional protection of property, for instance.

D. The structure of this book

Notwithstanding the traits of our analysis that distinguish it from previous ones, the structure of this work follows the general model of the volumes already hosted in this series.

The work is divided into four parts. The first aims to place our sector-oriented research within the general framework of the CoCEAL project.

The second and the third parts, however, gather the reports on the jurisdictions selected for our comparative analysis. This includes, on the one hand, answers to general 'constitutional' questions regarding property clauses, competences, and procedures—with their possible codification. On the other, it collects answers to the hypothetical cases at the heart of our factual analysis that provide the basis for actual comparison. To facilitate this, answers are listed and presented for each case.

The fourth part brings together comparative essays where the answers given to the hypothetical cases are discussed. The aim is to compare the findings of the questionnaire, with specific regard to suggesting which underlying problems are shared, to what extent, and with reference to which jurisdictions among those taken into consideration in addition to stating reasons for the outcome. The concluding chapter discusses the relationship between the common and distinctive traits of modern administrative systems.

[24] R Sacco, 'Legal Formants: A Dynamic Approach to Comparative Law I' (1991) 39 AJCL 1.

[25] In this regard see M Fromont, *Droit administratif des Etats membres de l'Union européenne* (PUF 2006) 15.

PART II
THE LEGAL SYSTEMS SELECTED FOR COMPARISON
Law, Administration, and Procedures

2

Procedural Requirements for Administrative Limits to Property Rights in Belgium

David Renders, Luca Ceci, Caroline Delforge, and Kevin Polet

I. Is there any constitutional provision or convention concerning land expropriation in the traditional sense (ie the forced transfer of ownership ordered for reasons of general interest) in the cases provided for by the law, and with provisions for compensation? If not, please elaborate.

Various provisions applicable in Belgium can be mentioned relating to expropriation in the traditional sense of the term. These are: Article 16 of the Belgian Constitution, which provides that: 'No one can be deprived of his property except in the case of expropriation for a public purpose, in the cases and manner established by the law and in return for fair compensation paid beforehand.' In addition, Article 1, paragraph 1, of Protocol No 1 to the European Convention on Human Rights to which Belgium is a party—provides that: 'No one shall be deprived of his possessions except in the public interest and subject to the conditions provided for by law and by the general principles of international law.' Lastly, Article 17, subparagraph 1, second sentence, of the Charter of Fundamental Rights of the European Union—of which Belgium is a Member State—provides that: 'No one may be deprived of his or her possessions, except in the public interest and in the cases and under the conditions provided for by law, subject to fair compensation being paid in good time for their loss.'

II. Is there any constitutional provision or convention concerning limitations to property rights in the broad sense? If not, please elaborate.

Various other provisions applicable in Belgium may be mentioned in relation to limits on the right to property in the broadest sense of the term.

Article 17 of the Belgian Constitution contains a provision on confiscation as a criminal sanction. It provides that: '[a]ssets may not be confiscated as a means of punishment'.

For its part, Article 1, subparagraph 2, of Protocol No 1 to the European Convention on Human Rights provides that: 'The preceding provisions shall not, however, in any way impair the right of a State to enforce such laws as it deems necessary to control the use of property in accordance with the general interest or to secure the payment

David Renders, Luca Ceci, Caroline Delforge, and Kevin Polet, *Procedural Requirements for Administrative Limits to Property Rights in Belgium* In: *Procedural Requirements for Administrative Limits to Property Rights.* Edited by: Martina Conticelli And Thomas Perroud, Oxford University Press.
DOI: 10.1093/oso/9780198867586.003.0002

of taxes or other contributions or penalties.' Article 17, subparagraph 1, third sentence, of the Charter of Fundamental Rights of the European Union further provides that: '[t]he use of property may be regulated by law in so far as is necessary for the general interest'.

In addition to the constitutional and conventional instruments mentioned, the case law has sometimes recognised that very severe limitations to the right to property amount to expropriation and therefore justify compliance with the conditions required for expropriation in the strict sense of the term.

III. How are competences regarding expropriation distributed among different levels of government (ie in regional, federal, or confederal states)?

The Belgian State is a federal state consisting of a federal authority and federated entities. The latter are called either regions or communities.

On the question of how expropriation law is organised within the Belgian Federation, three elements should be considered.

Article 16 of the Constitution enshrines the requirement of a 'public purpose' and a 'fair compensation paid beforehand', without delegating anything to the law on these questions.

As a result, these two requirements are imposed as such on the federal authority, the regions, and the communities.

Article 16 of the Constitution further provides that expropriation may only be carried out 'in the cases ... established by the law'.

The 'law' that may determine the cases in which expropriation may be carried out is:

- either a legislative act of the federal authority, called a 'law';
- a legislative act of a region, called a 'decree' in the Walloon and Flemish Regions and an 'ordinance' in the Brussels Region;
- a legislative act of a community, called a 'decree' in the French, Flemish, and German-speaking communities.[1]

Article 16 of the Constitution also provides that expropriation can only be carried out 'in the manner' established 'by the law'.

The 'law' that establishes the 'manner' in which expropriation may be carried out is, as of 2014 and in principle, the 'law' of the regions, called a 'decree' in the Walloon and Flemish Regions and an 'ordinance' in the Brussels Region.

This 'law' remains, however, the federal 'law' for any expropriation carried out by the federal authority or by a legal person empowered by or by virtue of the federal 'law'.[2]

[1] See art 79 of Special Act 'on institutional reforms' (8 August 1980; publication in the Belgian Official Gazette on 15 August 1980).

[2] ibid art 6*quater*.

IV. Please include a brief description of the procedure, listing the formal acts necessary for an expropriation. What is the relationship between urban planning procedures and expropriation? When is an environmental impact assessment needed?

Expropriation for a public purpose involves a three-step procedure.

In the *first step*, the legislative power—federal, regional, or community—must establish, in a general and abstract manner, the 'cases' in which public authorities will be able to resort to expropriation: for example, in order to acquire land for the establishment of industrial or commercial firms; in order to acquire buildings to fulfil the requirements of planning schemes, or to protect the immovable cultural heritage. *Contra legem*, however, case law recognises that it is not prohibited to proceed without the intervention of the legislative power if the expropriated property is assigned 'a public purpose'.

In the *second step*, the executive power, which will be federal, regional, or community, depending on the entity competent in the area in which the expropriation is intended—or, in some cases, the municipal council—must give a public authority specific and concrete authorisation to expropriate a given piece of land for a given purpose, following a given procedure. This authorisation is theoretically preceded by a so-called 'administrative' phase, which consists of drawing up the expropriation project and leads to the adoption of the reasoned decision authorising the expropriation.[3]

In the *third step*, the public authority to which the specific and concrete authorisation has been granted by the executive power can at last implement the authorisation it has received from the executive power. If it does so, an amicable agreement must first be sought. In practice, such an agreement is reached in 95 per cent of cases. If an amicable agreement is not reached, the public authority is then obliged to submit a request for expropriation to a court. It is then up to the court to assess the legality of the expropriation authorisation and, consequently, to grant—or not—the forced transfer of property, by ordering the deposit of fair compensation beforehand, knowing that the exact amount to be paid will be set by a subsequent court decision.

With regard to the connection between expropriation and land use planning, expropriation can serve as a land policy instrument for planning by implementing the requirements of a planning scheme, as pointed out above. However, expropriation can also be used in many other circumstances, so it is not only of interest in terms of its interaction with land use planning.

As to whether the expropriation should be subject to an environmental impact assessment, this is necessary only if it forms part of a 'plan' or 'programme' which is in itself likely to have a significant impact on the environment and is therefore subject to assessment.

[3] P Bouvier, R Born, B Cuvelier, and F Piret, *Éléments de droit administratif* (2nd edn, Larcier 2013) 252.

V. What are the consequences of a court finding that an expropriation is unlawful on the grounds of substance and/or of process? Is it merely annulled, or are there other consequences, for example the award of damages?

As pointed out in section IV above, expropriation does not take place on the basis of a unilateral administrative act but after a decision by a court in response to a request from a public authority that has itself received authorisation from the executive power, be it federal, regional, or community, or else from the municipal council.

This question is not relevant to Belgian law because if an expropriation request is found to be irregular—whether on a matter of form or substance—a court will not allow it to go ahead.

However, it may happen that the public authority resorting to expropriation has not used the expropriated property for the public purpose that was stated as the reason for the expropriation, or it has not started the works necessary to achieve the public purpose. Another possibility is that it has not transferred the property to a third party that was meant to achieve the public purpose. The Walloon Region legislation, for example, provides that, under these circumstances, the expropriated person may request retrocession of the property in question after five years have elapsed.

VI. Is there any difference between expropriation and nationalisation?

There is no general text in Belgian law establishing a nationalisation procedure.

If a public authority were to seek to become the owner of a property belonging to a private person, it would logically be necessary to pass a legislative act in this sense and to grant financial compensation for the loss suffered by the private person concerned.

3

Procedural Requirements for Administrative Limits to Property Rights in France

Emma Guernaoui

I. Is there any constitutional provision or convention concerning land expropriation in the traditional sense (ie the forced transfer of ownership ordered for reasons of general interest) in the cases provided for by the law, and with provisions for compensation? If not, please elaborate.

If the first considerations of the liberals of the French Revolution tended to consecrate a right of private property, a bulwark against royal abuses and synonymous with freedom, the right of expropriation was not exempt from reflection. It is worth noting the Declaration of the Rights of Man and of the Citizen of 1789, which symbolically consecrates the right of ownership while allowing its exceptional infringement to serve the general interest. In its Article 17, the Declaration mentions: 'Since the right to Property is inviolable and sacred, no one may be deprived thereof, unless public necessity, legally ascertained, obviously requires it, and just and prior indemnity has been paid.' Rousseau, the Age of Enlightenment thinker, was himself quick to allude in the establishment of his Social Contract to the necessary and useful existence of a property whose enjoyment would be 'common' for the benefit of all; a property that must nevertheless be regulated so as not to infringe upon the precious right of private property.

Consequently, the law of 8 March 1810 consecrated this right of expropriation in order to make possible the great public works undertaken by the Emperor Napoleon without offending the owners, who represented a class essential to the support of the regime in place. This law was thus established to frame the regime of Article 545 of the Napoleonic Civil Code. Legislatively regulated, the expropriation procedure has never ceased to evolve and has now constituted a Code since 1977, the latest version being issued in 2014. The French Constitution contains no mention of the right of expropriation, while the right of property does have a constitutional value.[1] Therefore,

[1] A value gained since the Declaration of 1789 entered the '*bloc constitutionnel*'. This 'constitutionality bloc' is an expression coined by French Law Professor Louis Favoreu to describe the set of norms outside the Constitution—which are therefore not mentioned in the strict sense—that have gradually acquired constitutional value. This makes it possible to strengthen the constitutionality review of laws, since the Constitutional Council can rely on more principles. See L Favoreu, 'Le principe de constitutionnalité: essai de définition d'après la jurisprudence du Conseil constitutionnel' in L Favoreu, *Mélanges Eisenmann* (Cujas 1975) 33. This makes it possible to strengthen the constitutionality review of laws since the Constitutional Council can rely on more principles (Conseil Const, Decision of July 16, 1971, No 71/44 DC 'Law completing the provisions of Articles 5 and 7 of the Law of 1 July 1901 on association agreements').

Emma Guernaoui, *Procedural Requirements for Administrative Limits to Property Rights in France* In: *Procedural Requirements for Administrative Limits to Property Rights*. Edited by: Martina Conticelli And Thomas Perroud, Oxford University Press.
 DOI: 10.1093/oso/9780198867586.003.0003

following a decision of the Constitutional Council in 1982,[2] which was expected to scrutinise the legality of the nationalisation policy initiated by the socialist government, the Constitutional Council reiterated the importance of respecting the right to property when nationalisations are carried out.[3] Thus, the Council revoked these nationalisations, which violated Article 17 of the Declaration of the Rights of Man and of the Citizen because fair and prior compensation had not been respected. Since then, the Constitutional Council has strictly regulated the exercise of expropriation so that those who are expropriated are not disadvantaged.[4]

French law separates two cases in which property rights are infringed upon. These two dissociated situations lead to radically different regimes. The first occurrence is the one that has been previously reviewed: a total deprivation of the right to property, in particular when expropriation occurs. Then, actual dispossession occurs. Given these specific circumstances, the 'fair and prior compensation' resulting from Article 17 of the Declaration of 1789 is required.

In contrast, where it is 'only' a matter of infringement or limitation of the right to property, the regime of Article 17 of the Declaration does not apply. To illustrate this difference, Professor Favoreu referred to the image of an 'artichoke'.[5] The protective regime of Article 17 will only come into force if the heart of the artichoke is affected. In the case of infringement, it will not apply. The Constitutional Council has imposed this conception in these terms and only on those occasions when: 'Such limitations are so serious that the resulting infringement of the right to property distorts the meaning and scope of this right guaranteed by Article 17 of the Declaration of the Rights of Man and of the Citizen.'[6] The Constitutional Council will tolerate infringements of property rights if the existence of an aim of general interest is ascertained. On the contrary, if 'neither the terms of the provision under review nor the parliamentary debates specify the reasons of general interest justifying'[7] the infringement, the legislative provision will be censured.

[2] Conseil Const, Decision of 16 July 1982, No 81/132 DC, 'Law of nationalization'.

[3] It recalls that, despite the limitations that may be placed on the right of ownership, it remains that the very principles set out in the Declaration of Human Rights have full constitutional value both with regard to the fundamental character of the right of ownership, the preservation of which constitutes one of the goals of political society and which is placed on an equal footing with freedom, security, and resistance to oppression, and with regard to the guarantees given to the holders of this right.

[4] It recently recalled the conditions that must be met for an expropriation to take place because of a priority question of constitutionality. These 'questions' of constitutionality refer to a procedure established in French constitutional law that allows the supreme administrative court (*Conseil d'Etat*) and the supreme judicial court (*Cour de cassation*) to address questions to the Constitutional Council. In its Decision No 2012/226 (QPC of 6 April 2012), the Constitutional Council recalled, by a statement of principle, that:

> the law can only authorize the expropriation of buildings or real estate rights for the realization of an operation whose public utility is legally established; that the taking of possession by the expropriator must be subject to the prior payment of compensation; that, in order to be fair, the compensation must cover the entire direct, material and certain prejudice caused by the expropriation; that in the event of disagreement on the amount of compensation, the expropriated party must have an appropriate remedy.

[5] L Favoreu, 'La jurisprudence du Conseil constitutionnel et le droit de propriété proclamé par la Déclaration de 1789' in Conseil constitutionnel (ed), *La Déclaration des droits de l'homme et du citoyen et la jurisprudence. Colloque des 25 et 26 mai 1989 au Conseil constitutionnel* (PUF 1989) 138.

[6] Conseil Const, Decision of 9 April 1996, No 96-373.

[7] Conseil Const, Decision of 20 July 2000, No 2000/434.

Finally, the right to property can be understood as a 'second-class' right despite its constitutional value. Infringements may be allowed if necessary to serve the public interest, unlike other public freedoms that are subject to much stricter control (for example, freedom of movement, freedom of assembly, freedom of opinion, and freedom of enterprise). It is possible to infringe the right to property, but it is not one of the strictly protected 'fundamental freedoms'. Indeed, three guarantees must be strictly respected to ensure such a level of protection. First, it is not possible to impose prior authorisations for the exercise of these supreme freedoms. Secondly, the legislator may limit the exercise of these rights only on rare occasions (for example, in the event of a health emergency or a natural disaster). Finally, these freedoms must be exercised freely and uniformly throughout the territory.

II. Is there any constitutional provision or convention concerning limitations to property rights in the broad sense? If not, please elaborate.

Historically, the recourse to expropriation was limited to major public works under state responsibility. As such, it was the 'public necessity' that had to be established, and this was limited to the construction of roads, canals, or railways, for example. Afterwards, the '*Etat gendarme*'—a model of minimal state following the principles of liberalism—became a welfare state, from which more was expected than the exercise of exclusively regalian competences. In this way, the social vocation of the state, which was supposed to ensure a minimum of well-being, imposed itself. As multiform interventionism developed, it was no longer limited to 'necessary' work, so much so that the notion of 'public necessity' was replaced by the broader notion of 'public interest'.[8] However, the development of expropriation has not distorted the nature of this right: it remains an exclusive right granted by the state, which evades the process of decentralisation. Thus, only state authorities are entitled to expropriate. If local governments are willing to benefit from expropriation, they may only do so with the central state's agreement.

Expropriation is not, however, the only limitation of the right of ownership. Although this right is protected both constitutionally and conventionally, limitations to its exercise may be imposed.

Thus, legislative and regulatory limitations have been allowed as long as they are proportionate. For example, the owner's use of the property may be limited by town planning and historical heritage protection provisions. This is the case of buildings classified as 'historic monuments'; they cannot be worked on without prior authorisation. Moreover, 'natural monuments' are also protected so that works are lawful only if they do not modify the site.

[8] JF Couzinet, 'From Public Necessity to Public Utility: Changes in the Justifying Factor for Expropriation' ('*De la nécessité publique à l'utilité publique: les évolutions du fait justificatif de l'expropriation*') in G Koubi (ed), *Property Right and Revolution* (*Propriété et Révolution*) (CNRS and Toulouse University 1991) 197.

Also, the right of pre-emption allows a public person to have priority in the acquisition of a property put up for sale. The owner is limited in the choice of the purchaser. This right can also benefit private persons, such as tenants or co-owners, who also have priority. Finally, it should be noted that the exercise of the right of ownership may also be limited in areas where rents are capped, such as in Paris. A tax may be imposed on owners of vacant dwellings to encourage them to rent out the property in areas where demand exceeds supply.

The exercise of property rights is not absolute either. It is restricted because it must not be abused and cause a disturbance to others. Thus, jurisprudential limitations have been introduced. An owner can be subject to penalties if he causes abnormal neighbourhood disturbances. Moreover, if an owner intends to cause harm and develops his property only in this sense, without utility, he will be sanctioned for having abused his right in accordance with the theory of the abuse of right.

III. How are competences regarding expropriation distributed among different levels of government (ie in regional, federal, or confederal states)?

Even though expropriation may benefit a local authority, the state is the exclusive holder of the regalian power to expropriate, and the final decision remains with it. This procedure is therefore a derogation from the era of decentralisation. However, while the state has jurisdiction over the entire territory, local authorities have jurisdiction *ratione loci.*[9] It is not possible for them to request authorisation to expropriate on territories beyond their jurisdiction. Rare exceptions exist, but only when the public utility of the expropriation is qualified and cannot be carried out on communal land. The *Conseil d'État* has thus tolerated exceptions for the construction of water catchments[10] or the creation of access roads.[11]

Finally, the *Conseil d'État* has recently developed its jurisprudence concerning public institutions that did not have the power to expropriate. They now benefit from this faculty as a result of their public law personality. In rare cases, private individuals may benefit from this right, particularly when they carry out a mission of general interest.[12] This is notably the case of regional social security funds that directly manage a public service.[13] Lastly, competence remains the prerogative of the state, which supervises the right of expropriation. Nevertheless, the mutability of case law testifies to the adaptability of this right, which can benefit other public law entities if circumstances lend themselves to it.

[9] CE, Decision of 4 June 1954, Commune de Thérouanne, Rec 339.

[10] CE, Decision of 6 March 1981, Association de défense des habitants du quartier de la Chêvre-Morte, Rec 125.

[11] CE, Decision of 13 December 1967, Ville de Dreux, Rec 487.

[12] Expropriation Code, art L300-4.

[13] CE, Decision of 17 January, Sieur Ancelle et autres, *AJDA* 141 (1973), Rec 138.

IV. Please include a brief description of the procedure, listing the formal acts necessary for an expropriation. What is the relationship between urban planning procedures and expropriation? When is an environmental impact assessment needed?

The expropriation procedure is representative of French law because it consists of two distinct phases. The first is the administrative phase of expropriation, which involves several administrative acts. First, there is the preliminary inquiry procedure, which is used to ensure that the expropriation is useful and necessary. This stage also informs the public with the help of an inquiry file that is made available to them. Once completed, the prefect, the representative of the state in the local authorities, declares the utility of the project submitted to him and, if appropriate, issues a declaration of public utility. The third stage, the land survey, is used to determine precisely which parcels are to be expropriated before the final stage takes place. This is the cessation order adopted by the prefect in order to identify the expropriated parties and the parcels.

The judicial phase takes place consecutively. The judge receives the transferability order from the prefect. Then he issues an expropriation order equivalent to a property title for the expropriator before establishing the amount of the compensation. The procedure is finally concluded one month later and once all the compensation has been paid.

V. What are the consequences of a court finding that an expropriation is unlawful on the grounds of substance and/or of process? Is it merely annulled, or are there other consequences, for example the award of damages?

It may occur that the use of the expropriated property does not correspond to what was initially intended in the declaration of public interest. In this hypothesis, the former owner, having been dispossessed, benefits from the faculty of 'retrocession'.[14] This right allows the transfer of the expropriated property back to the former owner. This is not a 'resolution' consisting of returning the compensation that the expropriated party had previously received and finally returning the parties to the state they were in before the expropriation took place. In fact, retrocession refers to the payment of the value of the asset at the date of retrocession by the public authority to the expropriated party.

The public authority and the expropriated party may reach an amicable agreement to establish the retrocession of the property. However, in the event of a conflict, three cumulative conditions are necessary to grant the retrocession. On the one hand, the expropriation must have been completed, and therefore the order must have been

[14] In the event of expropriation, the right to retrocession is governed by art L 12-6 of the Expropriation Code.

issued. On the other hand, a period of five years must have elapsed between the expropriation order and the request. The expropriated owner benefits from a period of thirty years to submit a claim. Lastly, the property must not have been used or used in a non-conforming manner. In the first hypothesis, the expropriated person can formulate his or her request within five years after the expropriation order. In the end, a judicial court is responsible for determining whether the use of the affected building complies with the order. It is the *Tribunal des conflits*,[15] the court in charge of attributing jurisdiction between the administrative and judicial courts, which has established this distribution that has been previously accepted. Thus, the civil court interprets the object of the declaration of public interest and evaluates whether the beginning of the public works or the use of the building conform with the expected purpose. In the event of serious difficulty in interpreting the declaration of public interest, the court has the option of sending a question to the administrative court—this is called a 'prejudicial question'.

If retrocession is granted, two hypotheses are conceivable. First, if the property has remained unchanged and can be returned, in the event of disagreement between the two parties the court may rule on its value at the date of the decision. Secondly, it is plausible that the property cannot be returned. This is the case when it has been sold to a third party. Or, again, if the authority has already carried out public works: in respect of the 'intangibility principle' of public works, which means 'in its original purity'[16] that the judge may not harm the public work serving the general interest, even in the case of illegal expropriation. Consequently, retrocession will allow the expropriated party to benefit from damages. The value of these damages corresponds to the current value of the immoveable—its capital gain—from which the amount of the dispossession indemnity will be deducted.[17]

If the expropriation is unlawful,[18] the former owner may claim compensation for his or her loss. This is possible if the building has not been put to its intended use within five years or if it has ceased to be used after thirty years.

VI. Is there any difference between expropriation and nationalisation?

Lastly, it is necessary to distinguish the differences between two notions that are nevertheless very close: nationalisation and expropriation. At first glance, the similarities are the most obvious. These two notions share the same legal sources, namely Article

[15] See *Tribunal des Conflits* (23 February 2004) No 04/03.381 https://urlz.fr/ePoM (accessed 17 July 2021).

[16] See the definition given by Professor Jacques Petit: 'In its original purity, it prohibited any judge from prescribing any measure likely to harm a public work, even if illegally established, and, in particular, from ordering its demolition. It was based on two reasons. The main one was the use of the public work in the general interest. The public financial interest was also invoked: to order the destruction of a work that the administration could rebuild after correcting the illegality committed would be a waste of public money.' See J Petit, 'Intangibility and unfinished public work' (*Ouvrage public inachevé et intangibilité*) (2013) 1 RDP 79.

[17] Such is the application of art R.12-5-4 of the Expropriation Code given by the Supreme Civil Court, in its decision C Cass, Civ 3ème (17 November 2010) Cheilan, No 09616.797, https://urlz.fr/ePqb. https://www.marconnet-jodeau.com/__psa/PDF/retrocession.pdf (accessed 27 July 2021).

[18] Expropriation Code, art L 12-6.

34 of the Constitution relating to protecting ownership rights and nationalisations. In compliance with the principle of legality, they allow the public authorities to force the transfer of property for the purpose of general interest. Thus, on the one hand, in case of public necessity and in return for a 'fair and prior indemnity', the forced transfer will be justified. On the other hand, it is the object of such forced transfers that differs. On the one hand, nationalisations typically regard joint-stock companies. Therefore, they are shares, movable property, which will be allocated to the state's patrimony. In addition, nationalised companies pursue their industrial and commercial activities favouring the general interest and are no longer for profit. On the other hand, expropriations concern buildings or mobilised real rights directly assigned to the patrimony of the public authorities.

4

Procedural Requirements for Administrative Limits to Property Rights in Germany

Foroud Shirvani

I. Is there any constitutional provision or convention concerning land expropriation in the traditional sense (ie the forced transfer of ownership ordered for reasons of general interest) in the cases provided for by the law, and with provisions for compensation? If not, please elaborate.

Article 14 section 3 GG contains a provision on expropriation ('*Enteignung*') for reasons of the public good. Expropriation is the sovereign access to the property of the individual, which is aimed at the complete or partial deprivation of specific property rights and involves the acquisition of goods for the benefit of the public authorities ('*Güterbeschaffung*').[1]

First, expropriation requires a sovereign legal act. An expropriation can only be carried out by a public authority in the exercise of specific sovereignty. Secondly, the access to property must be intended and targeted by the public authority. The expropriation term of the German Basic Law excludes unforeseeable encroachments on property or 'coincidental expropriations'.[2] Thirdly, access to property must lead to a complete or partial deprivation of the property. Therefore, no expropriations are restrictions or prohibitions of use that, for example, exist in building and nature conservation legislation.[3] Fourthly, state access to property is only considered expropriation if the purpose is the fulfilment of public tasks.[4] If the legal act is aimed at balancing conflicting private interests, this does not constitute expropriation, but a determination of the content and limits of property ('*Inhalts—und Schrankenbestimmung*').[5] Fifthly, expropriation presupposes the acquisition of goods.[6] According to the case law of the Federal Constitutional Court, access to the right of property must simultaneously be an acquisition of goods for the benefit of the public authorities or another beneficiary of the expropriation.[7] The acquisition

[1] See BVerfGE 143, 246, paras 243 ff.

[2] cf J Wieland, 'Art 14' in H Dreier (ed), *Grundgesetz: Kommentar*, vol 1 (3rd edn, Mohr Siebeck 2013) para 97; R Wendt, 'Art 14' in M Sachs (ed), *Grundgesetz: Kommentar* (8th edn, CH Beck 2018) para 151.

[3] O Depenheuer and J Froese, 'Art 14' in H Mangoldt, F Klein, and C Starck, *Grundgesetz: Kommentar*, vol 1 (7th edn, CH Beck 2018) para 209.

[4] BVerfGE 100, 226 <239 and 240>; 104, 1 <9 and 10>.

[5] BVerfGE 101, 239 <259>; 104, 1 <10>.

[6] BVerfGE 104, 1 <10>; 143, 246 paras 246 ff.

[7] BVerfGE 143, 246 para 246.

Foroud Shirvani, *Procedural Requirements for Administrative Limits to Property Rights in Germany* In: *Procedural Requirements for Administrative Limits to Property Rights*. Edited by: Martina Conticelli And Thomas Perroud, Oxford University Press.
 DOI: 10.1093/oso/9780198867586.003.0004

of goods can, for example, consist in the transfer of land ownership. Altogether, these five requirements have led to a narrow understanding of the constitutional term of expropriation.

An expropriation in the described sense is only constitutional if it is carried out for the public good.[8] Expropriation may only be ordered by or pursuant to a law that determines the nature and extent of compensation. Such compensation shall be determined by establishing an equitable balance between the public interest and the interests of those affected.[9] Article 14 section 3 GG is, as mentioned above, also applicable to the expropriation of land.

II. Is there any constitutional provision or convention concerning limitations to property rights in the broad sense? If not, please elaborate.

Article 14 section 1 sentence 2 GG instructs the legislator to determine the content and limits of property rights in the broader sense. The legislator defines in a general and abstract manner the rights and obligations of those who have property in the sense of the constitution.[10] According to Article 14 section 2 sentence 2 GG, the use of property shall also serve the public good. The legislature must find a fair equilibrium and a balanced relationship between the owner's interests that are worthy of protection and the public good.[11]

The public good is not only the reason, but also the limit for restricting the powers of the owner. Therefore, when restricting property, the legislator must not undermine the core of the property guarantee. This core area includes both the nature of the property of being of private benefit and the owner's fundamental power of disposition over the property object.[12] The determination of content and limits must be clearly distinguished from expropriation as a specific individual deprivation of the right of property. An illegal determination of content and limits of property must be annulled by the courts.

III. How are competences regarding expropriation distributed among different levels of government (ie in regional, federal, or confederal states)?

The German *Bundesländer* have enacted expropriation laws that regulate general matters of expropriation.[13] The laws regulate the expropriation procedure, the competent expropriation authority, the compensation for expropriation, and the right to sue for compensation. In addition, there are expropriation provisions in the sectoral laws at

[8] Article 14 sec 3 sentence 1 GG.
[9] GG, art 14 sec 3 sentences 2 and 3.
[10] cf BVerfGE 52, 1 <27>; 110, 1 <24>.
[11] BVerfGE 100, 226 <240>; 143, 246 para 268.
[12] BVerfGE 100, 226 <241>.
[13] cf eg EEG NW.

federal level and the laws of the *Bundesländer*. The Federal Building Code regulates the conditions and consequences of expropriation measures that are used to implement urban planning.[14]

IV. Please include a brief description of the procedure, listing the formal acts necessary for an expropriation. What is the relationship between urban planning procedures and expropriation? When is an environmental impact assessment needed?

The expropriation laws of the *Bundesländer* contain an expropriation procedure. The procedure includes in particular the application for expropriation, an oral hearing involving the owners affected, and an expropriation decision by the expropriation authority.[15] According to the special provisions of the Federal Building Code, expropriation can be carried out in order to use a piece of land in accordance with the regulations of the land-use plan.[16] When a land-use plan is drafted, an environmental assessment must be carried out to determine the likely significant environmental impacts.[17]

V. What are the consequences of a court finding that an expropriation is unlawful on the grounds of substance and/or of process? Is it merely annulled, or are there other consequences, for example the award of damages?

If the expropriation measure is unlawful on grounds of substance or of procedure, the owners affected must take legal action against the measure. The court will annul the unlawful expropriation act. The owners have no right to choose whether to defend themselves against an unlawful expropriation act or to demand compensation for expropriation.[18] If the expropriation becomes incontestable, a later claim for compensation based on the expropriation will be dismissed.[19] The affected owners who take legal action against the expropriation may also have claims for damages under state liability law. In this case, a public liability claim based on § 839 BGB in conjunction with Article 34 GG is possible. The claim presupposes in particular that the civil servant who instructed the expropriation has violated his official duty, ie has misinterpreted or misapplied the applicable law.

[14] cf BauGB, §§ 85 ff.
[15] cf EEG NW, §§ 18 ff.
[16] BauGB, § 85 sec 1 No 1.
[17] BauGB, § 2 sec 4 sentence 1.
[18] cf BVerfGE 58, 300 <324>.
[19] ibid.

VI. Is there any difference between expropriation and nationalisation?

According to Article 15 GG, land, natural resources and means of production can be transferred to public ownership for the purpose of socialisation by a law that determines the compensation. Socialisation is not a special case of expropriation, but an additional authorisation addressed to the legislator to intervene in the right of property guaranteed by the constitution.[20] The characteristic feature of expropriation is that it specifically and individually removes property and transfers it to the state or a third party. In contrast, socialisation aims at changing the power to dispose of certain assets and is not necessarily associated with a change of ownership. The assets are no longer to serve individual profit-making, but rather social needs or objectives of the common good.[21] While the object of expropriation can be any right of property, Article 15 sentence 1 GG conclusively lists the goods that can be socialised (land, natural resources, and means of production). Both in case of expropriation and socialisation, the legal basis must determine the nature and extent of compensation.[22]

[20] W Durner, 'Art 15' in T Maunz and G Dürig, *Grundgesetz: Kommentar* (CH Beck 2020) paras 61 ff; B-O Bryde, 'Art 15' in I von Münch and P Kunig, *Grundgesetz: Kommentar*, vol 1 (7th edn, CH Beck 2021) para 9.

[21] cf HD Jarass, 'Art 15' in HD Jarass and B Pieroth, *Grundgesetz: Kommentar* (16th edn, CH Beck 2020) para 5; Bryde (n 20) para 14; Durner (n 20) para 51.

[22] GG, art 14 sec 3 sentence 2; GG, art 15 sentence 1.

5

Procedural Requirements for Administrative Limits to Property Rights in Italy

Silvia Mirate

I. Is there any constitutional provision or convention concerning land expropriation in the traditional sense (ie the forced transfer of ownership ordered for reasons of general interest) in the cases provided for by the law, and with provisions for compensation? If not, please elaborate.

In the Italian Constitution, Article 42 provides a general protection for private property at the constitutional level:

> Private property is recognised and guaranteed by the law, which prescribes the ways it is acquired, enjoyed and its limitations so as to ensure its social function and make it accessible to all. In the cases provided for by the law and with provisions for compensation, private property may be expropriated for reasons of general interest.

The location of the provision under Title III (Economic Rights and Duties) of the Constitution (and not under 'Fundamental Principles') shows how the nature of property rights is linked to economic needs and therefore subject to a balance with other values.

The provision expressly refers to the possibility of limiting ownership to ensure its social function and guarantee accessibility for the whole community. It contains an explicit reference to the forced transfer of ownership ordered for reasons of general interest (public utility) and there is an express provision for the granting of compensation. The constitutional rule, however, refers to the power of the legislature to define expropriation cases and to adopt the specific provision for compensation (the current discipline is provided by the DPR 8 June 2001, No 327, 'Consolidated Law on expropriation').

II. Is there any constitutional provision or convention concerning limitations to property rights in the broad sense? If not, please elaborate.

A constitutional provision used in a broad sense for limitations of property rights is the clause regarding the 'social function' of property, mentioned in Article 42.1

Silvia Mirate, *Procedural Requirements for Administrative Limits to Property Rights in Italy* In: *Procedural Requirements for Administrative Limits to Property Rights*. Edited by: Martina Conticelli And Thomas Perroud, Oxford University Press.
 DOI: 10.1093/oso/9780198867586.003.0005

of the Constitution. The reference to this clause has been used (by the legislator and case law) to limit property rights for various reasons of public interest (see, for example, in the agricultural sector the limitation imposed on landowners and farmers in order to improve particular crops or plantings of interest for national production).

Another constitutional provision is Article 9, according to which the Republic 'safeguards natural landscape and the historical and artistic heritage of the Nation'. This is a fundamental principle for the protection of the historical and artistic heritage. As historical and artistic assets are often private property, the provision might imply the adoption of laws aiming at limiting property rights not only through expropriation, but also in a broader sense (economic burdens of maintenance, limitations on private use).

For land property, we might also recall the provisions of the Civil Code concerning public limitations to property rights. Beside land expropriation (also dealt with in Article 834), Article 835 provides for requisition and the imposition of constraints arising from public needs.

Other limits are imposed by statute law on the basis of the nature of the private asset. See, for example, the system of laws for environmental protection; the provision of constraints imposed to ensure the respect of legal distances of buildings from 'zones of respect' (roads, railways, highways, etc); the easements and impositions on funds to ensure utilities for the public administration (telephone lines, road signs, electrical conduits); forestry, hydro-geological, and landscape constraints; the rules regarding mines, quarries, and peatland.

III. How are competences regarding expropriation distributed among different levels of government (ie in regional, federal, or confederal states)?

The legislative competences in the Italian system are attributed to the state and to the regions according to Title V of the Constitution, and in particular to Article 117, which distinguishes between exclusive, concurrent, and residual competences. In Article 117(2) there is a list of matters which are expressly devolved to the competence of the state; Article 117(3) defines the sectors where competence is concurrent because the state has to establish the general principles, while the regions have to provide detailed rules (for example 'land-use planning', which is usually interpreted as related to town planning, but not to land expropriation). Finally, Article 117(4) states that, for all the matters not expressly indicated in the previous paragraphs, the regions have legislative powers.

Expropriation is not explicitly indicated as a subject or sector in either Article 117(2) or (3). For this reason, expropriation is considered as a cross-function, not an autonomous 'matter', but rather a constituent part or portion of other matters.

In Italy, the interpretation has been transposed into Article 5 of the Consolidated Law on Expropriation. The article states that in the matter of expropriation 'instrumental' to matters of regional competence, the regions exercise concurrent legislative power in accordance with the fundamental principles of state legislation and the general principles established by DPR No 327/2001. The aim is to arrive at a single type of expropriation procedure, which is as far as possible uniform for all the different levels of government.

IV. Please include a brief description of the procedure, listing the formal acts necessary for an expropriation. What is the relationship between urban planning procedures and expropriation? When is an environmental impact assessment needed?

DPR No 327/2001 provides a general procedure for all the cases of execution of public works (implementation of town plans, housing plans, production, and tourist plans, etc). According to Article 2(2), the procedures for expropriation 'are inspired by the principles of economy, efficiency, efficacy, publicity and simplification of administrative action'.

The power of expropriation is exercised by the authority which has the competence for the execution of the public work or intervention of public utility.

For each expropriation, a person in charge of the procedure must be designated with the task of directing, coordinating, and implementing all the operations and documents related to the procedure, but only the head of the office has the authority to issue the final order.

The only exception is represented by the case in which the public work is carried out by a concessionaire, to whom the granting administration may delegate the expropriation powers in whole or in part.

The expropriation procedure comprises the following formal acts:

- Pre-established constraint for expropriation: this is the first formal deed of the procedure and it may derive from a general regulatory plan, from a variant, or from another deed which in any case entails a modification of the regulatory plan.
- Declaration of public utility: the deed may be also implicit (for example in the approval of the final project of the public work). This deed is a precondition of lawfulness for the continuation of the procedure, and it contains the deadline for the issuance of the final expropriation decree (otherwise Article 13 DPR No 327/2001 provides for a term of five years).
- Provisional determination of the allowance, which varies depending on the voluntary or non-voluntary transfer by the expropriated private owner.
- Expropriation decree: this closes the procedure and gives the private individual the right to demand compensation from the administration. Owners are compensated according to market prices. Expropriation orders are automatically reversed if construction on a project does not start within five years of the expropriation. In general, the public authorities acquire the ownership of expropriated land.

There are situations in which the public administration, for reasons connected with the expropriation procedure or force majeure, occupies the property without issuing the expropriation decree and carries out an activity that involves the transformation of the property, also irreversibly. These are the cases of emergency expropriation (special procedure provided for in Article 22-bis) and expropriation '*a posteriori*'—provided for by Article 42-bis, which finally replaces the constructive (or indirect) expropriation discipline declared unconventional by the European Court of Human Rights on numerous occasions (see *Scordino v Italy* in case law).

In providing for the need of a pre-established constraint for expropriation, linked to regulatory planning acts, as a prerequisite for the declaration of public utility and the issuance of the expropriation decree, the legislator intended to emphasise the functional interdependence between urban planning and expropriation matters.

The public work can consist in an intervention having an effect on the environment (eg the construction of a plant for the production of energy from renewable sources). In this case the declaration of public utility must be preceded by the environmental impact assessment procedure, which has to ascertain the feasibility of the work from the point of view of environmental protection.

V. What are the consequences of a court finding that an expropriation is unlawful on the grounds of substance and/or of process? Is it merely annulled, or are there other consequences, for example the award of damages?

The expropriation order can be quashed by an administrative court. If the expropriation is unlawful, even if there was a valid declaration of public utility at the beginning of the procedure, the ownership of the land is not transferred to the public administration. Therefore, an individual has the right to ask for restitution, or alternatively for compensation for damages (calculated on the basis of the whole period of expropriation, starting from the possible emergency occupation).

VI. Is there any difference between expropriation and nationalisation?

Nationalisation is regulated by Article 43 of the Italian Constitution:

> For the purposes of the common good, the law may establish that an enterprise or a category thereof be, through a pre-emptive decision or compulsory purchase authority with provision of compensation, reserved to the Government, a public agency, a workers' or users' association, provided that such enterprise operates in the

field of essential public services, energy sources or monopolies and are of general public interest.

Expropriation is the tool for the execution of a nationalisation procedure that has to be provided for by a statute law. There are no recent cases of nationalisation (we are reminded of the 1962 nationalisation of the companies that managed the electricity grid into ENEL, or of various rescue operations for banking groups), because starting from the early nineties there was a clear change of direction with the privatisation of numerous public enterprises in Italy.

6

Procedural Requirements for Administrative Limits to Property Rights in the Netherlands

Jacques Sluysmans and Nikky van Triet

Before answering the questions of both Part I and Part II, we would like to make an important introductory remark.

At the time of writing this country report for the Netherlands, Dutch expropriation law is governed by the Expropriation Act of 1851. However, new rules for expropriation have been adopted by Parliament as part of the so-called Environment and Planning Act (*Omgevingswet*). This Environment and Planning Act is scheduled to come into force sometime in the year 2022. With regard to expropriation law, we have based our answers on the forthcoming law rather than on the current law.

Environmental and planning law is currently regulated by a great deal of different legislation and regulations, of which the Spatial Planning Act is the most important. The future law, unfortunately, on certain aspects is still not clear. Therefore, in those matters, for clarity, we will refer to both the current and the future law.

I. Is there any constitutional provision or convention concerning land expropriation in the traditional sense (ie the forced transfer of ownership ordered for reasons of general interest) in the cases provided for by the law, and with provisions for compensation? If not, please elaborate.

Article 14 of the (Dutch) Constitution succinctly states that expropriation may only take place in the public interest and if compensation has been ensured in advance. Compensation need not be ensured in advance in cases of emergency. This article forms the basis for the expropriation regulations in the Environment and Planning Act, which brings together all the relevant codified rules concerning expropriation.

The fact that—in general—all regulations on Dutch expropriation law can be found in just one code suggests a simplicity, which Dutch expropriation law lacks. Although all the procedural rules can indeed be found in one code, the above-mentioned Environment and Planning Act, the material rules—and especially those rules pertaining to the determination of compensation—have primarily been developed by the Dutch Supreme Court and can only be found in case law. It is significant that the

Jacques Sluysmans and Nikky van Triet, *Procedural Requirements for Administrative Limits to Property Rights in the Netherlands* In: *Procedural Requirements for Administrative Limits to Property Rights.* Edited by: Martina Conticelli And Thomas Perroud, Oxford University Press. DOI: 10.1093/oso/9780198867586.003.0006

standard handbook concerning expropriation law mostly consists of a discussion and clarification of Supreme Court case law, rather than of an explanation of the codified rules.[1]

It should further be noted that in the Netherlands there is no constitutional court. It is—on the contrary—explicitly forbidden for Dutch courts—including the Supreme Court—to test legislation that has been passed by Parliament against the constitution. It is, however, permitted to test such legislation against directly applicable rules of international law. In the field of expropriation law, the most relevant of such rules is Article 1 of Protocol 1 of the European Convention on Human Rights. In the past, the Supreme Court of the Netherlands has, for example, declared Article 42 of the Expropriation Act to be in violation of Article 1 of Protocol 1, and therefore not applicable in the specific case at hand.[2]

II. Is there any constitutional provision or convention concerning limitations to property rights in the broad sense? If not, please elaborate.

The above-mentioned constitutional article is the only constitutional provision concerning limitations to property rights. There is no 'convention' in this respect, other than Article 1, Protocol 1 of the above-mentioned European Convention on Human Rights.

Property may only be taken through expropriation in accordance with the rules laid down in the Environment and Planning Act.

The use of property may be limited in various ways.

In cases where public works have to be carried out on, in, or above someone's property and expropriation is not necessary, the Environment and Planning Act allows the possibility for a public authority to decide—by way of an administrative decision—that a property owner has to tolerate those public works. Common examples of such works are pipelines and electricity cables. A property owner may appeal such a decision before the administrative courts. The decision to tolerate public works entitles the property owner to full compensation for damage. This claim may be brought before the civil courts.

Of course, there are many other decisions that limit property rights. A well-known example is a (new) environment plan that limits the existing possibilities to develop a plot of land. Should damage arise from such a decision, Dutch law allows the possibility of compensation for loss resulting from administrative acts.

[1] GCW van der Feltz and others, *Schadeloosstelling voor Onteigening: Telders, Nieuw voor Oud* (Kluwer 2006).

[2] Supreme Court 30 November 1994, NJ 1995/668 (*Witte Paard*).

III. How are competences regarding expropriation distributed among different levels of government (ie in regional, federal, or confederal states)?

The tool of expropriation may be used by different levels of government. The authorities that may make use of the instrument, and the grounds on which they may do so, are all listed in the Environment and Planning Act. Article 11.2 of the Environment and Planning Act states that an expropriation may take place in the name of a municipality, a water authority, a province, the state, or any corporation that has been entrusted with the development, use, or protection of the physical environment. The expropriation decision itself can only be taken by public authorities, as stipulated in Article 11.4 of the Environment and Planning Act: the municipal council, the general board of the water authority, the provincial council, or the responsible minister.

IV. Please include a brief description of the procedure, listing the formal acts necessary for an expropriation. What is the relationship between urban planning procedures and expropriation? When is an environmental impact assessment needed?

The Environment and Planning Act exhaustively lists all the criteria for expropriation, as the Expropriation Act did previously.

According to Article 11.5 of the Environment and Planning Act, an expropriation decision may only be taken: (a) in the interest of the development, use, or management of the physical environment; or (b) if expropriation is necessary; and/or (c) urgent.

There is only an interest (for expropriation) as mentioned in Article 11.5 if (see Article 11.6) the envisaged path of development, use, or management of the physical environment has been laid down in (in short) an environmental decision (such as the environment plan, a modern version of a zoning plan), that excludes the current development, use, or management of that physical environment.

The is only a necessity as mentioned in Article 11.5 if (see Article 11.7) the expropriating party has seriously—but unsuccessfully—tried to purchase the property in question before resorting to an expropriation procedure. Moreover, there is a lack of necessity if the property owner sufficiently proves that they are capable and willing to develop, use, or manage the (new) environment plan underlying the envisaged expropriation themselves in accordance with the wishes of the public authority (see also Article 11.7).

Article 11.11 stipulates that there is no urgency as mentioned in Article 11.5 if it is not likely that the development of the environment plan underlying the proposed expropriation will start within three years of the actual transfer of property.

It may be that in the course of deciding on the environment plan (the new version of the zoning plan introduced by the Environment and Planning Act) an environmental impact assessment is needed, but there is no direct relationship between such an environmental impact assessment and the possibility of expropriation.

Interested parties (such as owners of property within or adjacent to the new plan) may participate in the decision-making process regarding a new environment plan. Once the municipal council (or, in the case of a provincial environment plan, the provincial council or, in the case of a state environment plan, the minister responsible) has decided on a new environment plan the above-mentioned interested parties may appeal the plan before the judiciary branch of the Council of State.

The public interest of a subsequent expropriation aimed at the development of the environment plan is—in general—already enshrined in the decision on the environment plan.

There is no room in the expropriation procedure to raise questions about choices that are made in the environment plan.

A rare decision where a lack of sufficient public interest stood in the way of expropriation was the situation in which a municipality tried to expropriate a part of someone's garden in order to add this appropriated piece of garden to someone else's garden.[3]

The expropriation procedure starts—if legally prescribed prior negotiations to amicably obtain the property have failed—with a draft expropriation decision (by the public authority that wants to develop the environment plan, usually the municipal council). Interested parties may comment on the draft decision. Taking into account these comments, the public authority will take a final expropriation decision. This decision can only come into force after it has been acknowledged by the (administrative) court. A decision by the court in such an acknowledgement procedure may be appealed before the Council of State.

This 'acknowledgement procedure' is a unique procedure within the framework of Dutch administrative law.

Under the Expropriation Act of 1851, expropriation (ultimately) took place by force of a judgment of a civil court, in a civil procedure. Under the Environment and Planning Act it is—as mentioned above—a public authority that decided on expropriation via an expropriation decision. There were serious concerns within the Dutch parliament that in such a system—following the normal system of administrative law—the expropriation decision would become final in the event it was not appealed in time (that is, within six weeks) by an interested party, which would mean that a person could lose his or her property without the court being involved. Coming from a time-honoured system in which a (civil) court was (necessarily) involved in every expropriation, Parliament wished to maintain the existing standard of legal protection and asked the government to devise a system that could safeguard the continued involvement of the (administrative) court in each and every expropriation.

It is against this background that in the Environment and Planning Act a system was developed—only for expropriation procedures—that has no precedent in Dutch administrative law and differs significantly from the regular administrative procedure.

[3] Royal Decree of 12 October 1984, BR 1985/642 (Amsterdam).

In this system, the (expropriation) decision taken by a public authority has to be brought before the administrative court by that same public authority in order to have the expropriation decision acknowledged by the court. In this way, it is ensured that even in those cases in which no interested party makes a timely appeal against the expropriation decision the court will still investigate the merits of that decision.

Article 11.15 stipulates that transfer of property takes place once the expropriation decision has been entered into the public registry by a notary. Before doing so, the notary has to check whether the requirements for such a registration are met. Those requirements are to be found in Article 11.16 subsection 1 of the Environment and Planning Act. First, the expropriation decision has to be irrevocable. Secondly, the environment plan has to be irrevocable. Thirdly, an advance payment on the compensation for the expropriation has to be paid.

The expropriated party is entitled to full compensation for damage caused by the expropriation. The amount of compensation is assessed in separate proceedings before the civil court. In these proceedings the court is under a legal obligation to appoint experts who have to advise the court on the amount of compensation. Of course, the court is not bound by the outcome of the expert advice, but in practice this advice is very much relied on by the court. The decision of the court on the compensation for expropriation may only be appealed before the Supreme Court.

V. What are the consequences of a court finding that an expropriation is unlawful on the grounds of substance and/or of process? Is it merely annulled, or are there other consequences, for example the award of damages?

In the event an expropriation decision is not acknowledged by the district court or any acknowledgement decision is annulled by the Council of State, the consequences of such a judgment for the expropriation will very much depend on the reason for the decision of the court.

In the event procedural formalities have been neglected—such as a lack of serious negotiations preceding the start of the expropriation procedure—there will be ample opportunity to safeguard the expropriation. The court may open the possibility for the public authority to make reparations within the current procedure, or the public authority could simply start new proceedings.

In the event that the court sees substantial obstacles to expropriation—such as a lack of necessity—the expropriation is—unless factual conditions change—essentially off the table. An example would be the situation in which a property owner claims that he or she will develop the part of the environment plan that applies to his or her property themselves (the so-called self-realisation argument). If this is a feasible argument, there is no need for expropriation in order to come to a (timely) development of the environment plan. Should a court accept such an argument, there is no viable way for a public authority still to arrive at expropriation under the existing environment plan.

VI. Is there any difference between expropriation and nationalisation?

Expropriation is limited to real estate, and is only possible on the grounds listed in the Environment and Planning Act. Nationalisation is an effort usually not just aimed at real estate, and is moreover not listed in the above-mentioned code. Nationalisation is therefore not an effort that the Environment and Planning Act aims to facilitate.

A (sort of) nationalisation has been made possible in the Financial Supervision Act (*Wet op het financieel toezicht*), where the minister of finance has been given the authority to expropriate financial institutions that are on the brink of failure. The authority has so far only been used once, when the minister decided to expropriate (nationalise) all the assets of the SNS Bank.[4] The decision of the minister can be appealed before the Council of State within a period of two weeks. This special procedure has been tested by the European Court of Human Rights. Expropriated parties are entitled to (full) compensation, in the same way as in regular expropriation procedures. The compensation procedure in the SNS Bank case has not yet come to a final end.

For the sake of completeness, we should also mention the Requisition Act (*Vorderingswet*). This act makes it possible to expropriate (movable and immovable) property and proprietary rights in situations of (imminent) disaster and/or war.

[4] Decision of 1 February 2013. This (administrative) decision has led to both administrative (Council of State 25 February 2013, ECLI:NL:RVS:2013:BZ2265) and civil (Supreme Court 17 November 2017, ECLI:NL:HR:2017:2904) proceedings.

7

Procedural Requirements for Administrative Limits to Property Rights in Poland

Inga Kawka and Łukasz Kozera

I. Is there any constitutional provision or convention concerning land expropriation in the traditional sense (ie the forced transfer of ownership ordered for reasons of general interest) in the cases provided for by the law, and with provisions for compensation? If not, please elaborate.

Although there exist no provisions in the Polish Constitution referring to land expropriation, it does contain a general principle related to the protection of the right of ownership. As it is not an absolute rule, the Constitution also provides for some exceptions to it, one of them being the institution of expropriation, ie carrying out an administrative dispossession of ownership of movable and immovable property.[1] In turn, detailed material and procedural provisions on expropriation of the latter are contained in the Immovable Property Management Act of 21 August 1997[2] (IPMA).

Pursuant to Article 21(1) of the Constitution, 'the Republic of Poland shall protect ownership and the right of succession'. The norm expressed in this cited provision is one of the fundamental systemic principles of the Republic of Poland, which results from its placement in Chapter I of the Constitution titled 'The Republic'. The chapter in question contains the most important decisions of the constitutional legislator allowing for the definition of the form of statehood.[3] According to the case law of the Polish Constitutional Court:

> [i]n the light of that provision, to guarantee the protection of ownership is a constitutional duty of the state, which is materialised by both legislative activity (shaping fundamental legal institutions lending specificity to the essence of ownership as well as

[1] The Constitution takes up the notions of ownership protection and possible ownership dispossession and removal in several of its provisions. Of key importance are those of arts 21 and 64 discussed in this document, yet one should also point out: art 20, which mentions 'private ownership' as one of the foundations of a 'social market economy'; art 46, which specifies the conditions of cases when 'property may be forfeited', linking them to court protection; art 165(1), which guarantees to local government units 'rights of ownership and other property rights'; art 218, which foresees the existence of the state treasury and leaves it to highest-rank 'Acts' of law (*ustawas*) to specify its organisation and the manner of its asset management; L Garlicki and M Zubik, 'Article 21' in L Garlicki and M Zubik (eds), *Konstytucja Rzeczypospolitej Polskiej: Komentarz*, vol 1 (2nd edn, Wydawnictwo Sejmowe 2016).

[2] Immovable Property Management Act of 1 August 1997 (Journal of Laws (JoL) of 2020, item 65, as amended).

[3] M Kallas, *Konstytucja Rzeczypospolitej Polskiej: Komentarz* (Wydawnictwo Prawnicze PWN 1997).

Inga Kawka and Łukasz Kozera, *Procedural Requirements for Administrative Limits to Property Rights in Poland* In: *Procedural Requirements for Administrative Limits to Property Rights.* Edited by: Martina Conticelli And Thomas Perroud, Oxford University Press. © Inga Kawka and Łukasz Kozera 2022. DOI: 10.1093/oso/9780198867586.003.0007

defining measures for the protection of the right of ownership) and the actual actions of state bodies related to goods belonging to a person.[4]

As a consequence, the discussed norm postulates the establishment of legal guarantees ensuring the right to use property by natural and legal persons, as well as the prohibition of excessive interference with property by all public authorities.[5] Further, Article 21(1) of the Constitution establishes a guarantee of inheritance of property left behind after deceased persons by their statutory and testamentary heirs. The norm in question—as indicated in the CC judgment of 25 February 1999—constitutes a 'call for state authorities to establish such legal provisions that would not be an obstacle but, to the contrary, ensure ... the succession of rights and obligations by means of inheritance. In its essence, the said right correlates with, as well as complements, the right of ownership and makes its continuation possible after the death of the owner'.[6]

The principle expressed in Article 21(1) of the Constitution does not differentiate between private and public ownership. It must be perceived in the context of one of the foundations of Poland's economic system, which is the fact of ownership remaining in private hands. This means that Article 21(1) of the Constitution not only formulates a guarantee of ownership (inheritance) protection but also expresses a more general guarantee: of a macro-social existence of private ownership and its fundamental role in shaping a social market economy, next to economic freedom and solidarity, dialogue, and cooperation of social partners.[7] Consequently, these provisions preclude an evolution of ownership relations in Poland towards the restitution of a dominant role of ownership by the state or other public entities.[8]

Article 21(2) establishes a detailed norm (an exception to the ownership protection rule), setting up conditions and methods of one form of ownership removal, that is expropriation.[9] The said article reads that it 'may be allowed solely for public purposes and for just compensation'. The Constitution does not define the term 'expropriation'. The notion, however, has been the subject of the case law of the Constitutional Court on numerous occasions.[10] According to the Constitutional Court's settled stance, Article 21(2) of the Constitution 'pertains to forced disposal (removal) of

[4] Constitutional Court judgment of 12 January 1999, P 2/98, OTK 1999/1/2.

[5] P Tuleja, 'Article 21' in P Tuleja (ed), *Konstytucja Rzeczypospolitej Polskiej: Komentarz* (Wolters Kluwer Polska 2019).

[6] Constitutional Court judgment of 21 May 2001, SK 15/00, Case law of the Constitutional Tribunal Official (OTK) collection 2001/4/85.

[7] J Paśnik, 'Wybrane aspekty ekonomicznych i normatywnych uwarunkowań zasad ustroju gospodarczego w Konstytucji RP z 1997 r' (2019) 9 Przegląd Prawa Publicznego 61.

[8] Z Ziembiński, *Wartości konstytucyjne* (Wydawnictwo Sejmowe 1993) 68; Kallas (n 3); Garlicki and Zubik (n 1); Constitutional Court judgment of 21 May 2001, SK 15/00, OTK 2001/4/85.

[9] K Świderski, 'Wywłaszczenie w świetle art 21 ust. 2 Konstytucji RP' (2006) 42 Casus 15.

[10] Constitutional Court judgments of: 12 December 2017, SK 39/15, OTK-A 2017/86; 14 March 2000, P 5/99, OTK 2000/2/60; 12 April 2000, K 8/98, OTK 2000/3/87; 24 October 2001, SK 22/01, OTK 2001/7/216; 3 April 2008, K 6/05, OTK-A 2008/3/41; 9 December 2008, K 61/07, OTK-A 2008/10/174; 9 December 2008, SK 43/07, OTK-A 2008/10/175; 13 December 2012, P 12/11, OTK-A 2012/11/135; 23 September 2014, SK 7/13, OTK-A 2014/8/93; 14 July 2015, SK 26/14, OTK-A 2015/7/101; 25 May 2016, Kp 2/15, OTK-A 2016/23.

the constitutional category of 'private ownership'. It is a legal institution allowing the state—by way of exception—to interfere in the constitutional ownership guarantees'.[11] The Constitutional Court has also pointed out the need for a possibly broad understanding of the constitutional term 'expropriation', stressing that it covers all forcible removal by a public authority of all kinds of private ownership entitlements.[12] This pertains not just to immovable property but also movable items and other owned goods (eg good protected by copyright).[13] That is why the meaning of the term 'expropriation' used in Article 21(2) of the Constitution cannot be automatically associated as identical with the narrower meaning assigned to 'expropriation' by the legislator for the purpose of applying the provisions of the IPMA, where expropriation means a removal or a restriction, introduced by means of a decision, of the right of ownership, the perpetual usufruct right, or other rights in rem related to immovable property (Article 112(2) of the IPMA). Expropriation may be effected if public purposes cannot be attained in any other way than by removing or restricting rights to immovable property and such rights cannot be acquired by means of an agreement (Article 112(3) of the IPMA). Immovable property may be expropriated solely for the benefit of the state treasury or a local government unit (Article 113(1) of the IPMA), which takes place in return for compensation (Article 128 of the IPMA).

Pursuant to Article 21(2) of the Constitution, expropriation shall be possible only when the following preconditions are met: expropriation is related to a public purpose; expropriation is performed under a highest-rank statute ('Act' of law or *ustawa*) and by means of a procedure specified therein; the expropriated party is awarded just compensation.

The definition of the term 'public purpose' is not precise. It is sufficient to link expropriation to any public purpose specified in an Act, also going beyond the purposes listed in the Constitution, particularly in Article 31(3).[14] The term 'public purpose' is general for a reason as this allows for embracing complex realities of social and economic life.[15] That does not mean, however, that there are no restrictions on the legislator when giving more precision to 'public purposes' in Acts of law. A purpose may be considered public only when it serves the general public, is commonly available, and constitutes a good of the public, ie the entire society or a regional community.[16]

Another condition for the admissibility of expropriation is the indispensability of its performance. Article 21(2) of the Constitution may not formulate that clearly enough, yet it uses the word 'solely'. That means that a removal of the right of ownership may

[11] Constitutional Court judgment of 13 December 2012 (n 10).

[12] Constitutional Court judgment of 3 April 2008 (n 10).

[13] K Zaradkiewicz, 'Artykuł 21' in M Safjanz and L Bosek (eds), *Konstytucja RP: Komentarz* (Wydawnictwo CH Beck 2016) 582; M Radajewski, 'Normatywna treść konstytucyjnych przesłanek dopuszczalności wywłaszczenia' (2018) 1(103) Przegląd Legislacyjny 27.

[14] Garlicki and Zubik (n 1); K Świderski, 'Konstytucyjne przesłanki dopuszczalności wywłaszczenia' (2007) 1 Casus 12.

[15] T Woś, *Wywłaszczanie nieruchomości i ich zwrot* (Wydawnictwo Prawnicze LexisNexis 2011) 41.

[16] T Woś, 'Wywłaszczanie nieruchomości i ich zwrot w orzecznictwie sądów administracyjnych' (2010) 5–6 Zeszyty Naukowe Sądownictwa Administracyjnego 455; Constitutional Court judgment of 9 December 2008 (n 10).

take place only when it is useful, necessary, and not excessive in order to attain a given public purpose, and hence is of a proportional nature.[17]

The Constitution does not limit expropriation to removing the ownership right by an individual act and it may be also effected by means of a general act. The notion of expropriation, however, does not include nationalisation, which means a large-scale property dispossession, for example in a given economic sector.[18]

The provision in question spells out just compensation, to be understood as that for an actual loss or lost benefits. However, the case law of the Constitutional Court does not exclude partial compensation, for example when necessitated by the principles of social justice.[19] Hence, 'just compensation' is a flexible notion and as such allows for the assumption that in certain cases, given that expropriation is effected for the common good, sometimes full compensation will not be just, while partial compensation may be considered to be such.[20]

Recognising that expropriation is an exception to the principle of protection of ownership and other property rights (Article 21(1) and Article 64(1) of the Constitution), the Constitutional Court has pointed out the need to establish equally strong guarantees serving to protect legitimate ownership interests of private entities. Such guarantees include, inter alia, the principle of return of expropriated immovable property, if it has become redundant for the public purpose for which it was expropriated. As argued in the Constitutional Court judgment of 24 October 2001,[21] that principle should be treated as an 'obvious consequence' of the application of the expropriation admissibility conditions specified in Article 21(2) of the Constitution. The right to demand that expropriated immovable property be returned constitutes a basic guarantee against the abuse of the expropriation instrument on the part of public authorities and—indirectly—is intended to guarantee real rather than merely theoretical protection of ownership and other property rights of private entities against the unconstitutional dispossession of these rights. Otherwise, the state would enjoy financial benefits at the expense of its citizens.[22]

II. Is there any constitutional provision or convention concerning limitations to property rights in the broad sense? If not, please elaborate.

Expropriation is an interference by public authorities in the very essence of the right of ownership. In the absence of such an interference, possible limitations of that right are regulated by Article 64(3) and Article 31(3) of the Constitution. Pursuant to the former, 'the right of ownership may only be limited by means of a statute and

[17] Garlicki and Zubik (n 1); Radajewski (n 13) 31; K Complak, 'Artykuł 21' in M Haczkowska (ed), *Konstytucja Rzeczypospolitej Polskiej: Komentarz* (Wydawnictwo Prawnicze LexisNexis 2014); W Skrzydło, 'Artykuł 21' in *Konstytucja Rzeczypospolitej Polskiej: Komentarz* (7th edn, LEX 2013).

[18] Tuleja (n 5); Radajewski (n 13) 28.

[19] Constitutional Court judgment of 29 May 2001, K 5/01, OTK 2001/4/87.

[20] R Hauser, 'Preambuła Konstytucji i postanowienia ustrojowe' in M Smolak (ed), *Wykładnia konstytucji: Aktualne problemy i tendencje* (Wolters Kluwer 2016).

[21] Constitutional Court judgment of 24 October 2001 (n 10).

[22] Constitutional Court decision of 6 November 2019, SK 21/18, OTK-A 2019/58; Tuleja (n 5).

only to the extent that it does not violate the substance of such right'. According to the Constitutional Court, that provision has a double function. First, it is an unambiguous and explicit constitutional basis for introducing ownership right limitations. Secondly, it provides a framework for admissible limitations of that right.[23] Article 64(3) of the Constitution, however, does not indicate any material conditions for ownership restrictions, and it should be assumed then that they stem from Article 31(3) of the Constitution, which has a fundamental significance as regards restrictions of all constitutional freedoms and rights. It also pertains to regulations that formulate detailed restrictive clauses, including Article 64(3) of the Constitution.[24] Pursuant to its Article 31(3):

> [a]ny limitation upon the exercise of constitutional freedoms and rights may be imposed only by an Act of law, and only when necessary in a democratic state for the protection of its security or public order, or to protect the natural environment, health or public morals, or the freedoms and rights of other persons. Such limitations shall not violate the essence of freedoms and rights.

In the case of ownership, the Constitution contains two indications, in Article 64(3) and Article 31(3), that ownership limitations need to be imposed in the form of the highest-rank statute, an 'Act' of law. According to the Constitutional Court, this means that the 'entire sphere of ownership right limitations belongs to the "statutory matter", and as a result the legislator may not delegate the law-making power in that regard to other bodies'.[25] It transpires from the Constitutional Court case law that if restrictions of the constitutional freedoms and rights may be established exclusively in an Act (of law), that includes the requirement to ensure that a limitation of a given right and freedom be complete, so that it is possible to delineate a full outline (contour) of such a restriction already on the basis of reading the statutory provisions.[26] Furthermore, normative acts of the local government cannot regulate matters of significant importance from the perspective of the constitutional freedoms and rights, although their objective scope may be broader than the scope of regulations (of a lower rank than Acts).[27]

The limit of ownership right restrictions is the prohibition of infringing on the essence of that right, expressed in the Constitution twice, in its Article 64(3) and Article 31(3). Such an infringement on the essence of a right in question occurs when the restrictions introduced pertain to fundamental entitlements making up the contents of that right and make it impossible for it to effect the function assigned to it in the legal order.[28] Defining the essence of the right of ownership, the Constitutional Court

[23] Constitutional Court judgment of 12 January 1999 (n 4); Constitutional Court judgment of 11 May 1999, K 13/98, OTK 1999/4/74; Constitutional Court judgment of 12 January 2000, P 11/98; OTK 2000/1/3.

[24] P Tuleja, 'Artykuł 31' in P Tuleja (ed), *Konstytucja Rzeczypospolitej Polskiej: Komentarz* (Wolters Kluwer Polska 2019); L Garlicki and K Wojtyczek, 'Artykuł 31' in L Garlicki and M Zubik (eds), *Konstytucja Rzeczypospolitej Polskiej: Komentarz*, vol 2 (2nd edn, Wydawnictwo Sejmowe 2016).

[25] Constitutional Court judgment of 5 March 2001, P 11/00, OTK 2001/2/33.

[26] Constitutional Court judgment of 12 January 2000 (n 23).

[27] Constitutional Court judgment of 8 July 2003, P 10/02, OTK-A 2003/6/62.

[28] Constitutional Court judgment of 9 July 2007, P 30/06, OTK-A 2007/7/74; Constitutional Court judgment of 8 October 2007, K 20/07, OTK-A 2007/9/102; Constitutional Court judgment of 10 October

invokes Article 140 of the Civil Code. It is made up of such entitlements as the possibility to use, derive benefits, or indirectly exploit the object of the ownership.[29]

Limitations of the constitutional freedoms or rights, including the right of ownership, may be justified by the principles listed in Article 31(3): public security or public order, environmental protection, public health and morality, or freedoms and rights of other persons. This list is exhaustive.[30]

Restrictions on ownership must comply with the proportionality principle, ie may be established 'only when necessary in a democratic state' (the first sentence of Article 31(3) of the Constitution). Although that principle is not listed in Article 64(3), it goes without saying that it is fully applicable to ownership. Breaching the proportionality requirement has been the most frequent charge leading to rulings where resolutions excessively interfering in the sphere of ownership have been found unconstitutional.[31]

III. How are competences regarding expropriation distributed among different levels of government (ie in regional, federal, or confederal states)?

Pursuant to Article 112(4) and Article 129(1) of the IPMA (prior to their change by the Act of 7 January 2000 amending the immovable property management act and other acts),[32] which entered into force on 15 February 2001, the competent authority for immovable property expropriation and compensation used to be the *voivode* (provincial governor, a local public administration authority in a voivodeship, ie province). That arrangement meant that the appellate body in cases related to such matters was the chairman of the Housing and Urban Development Authority[33] (a body of the central-government administration). Currently, after the amendments made to Article 112(4) and Article 129(1) of the IPMA by the Act of 7 January 2000, the competent authority for immovable property expropriation and compensation is the *starost*, or a county head, performing administrative tasks on behalf of the government. The *starost* is a county-level local government authority which at the same time has the function of

2000, P 8/99, OTK 2000/6/190; Constitutional Court judgment of 19 December 2002, K 33/02, OTK-A 2002/7/97.

[29] M Florczak-Wątor, 'Artykuł 64' in P Tuleja (ed), *Konstytucja Rzeczypospolitej Polskiej: Komentarz* (Wolters Kluwer Polska 2019); Constitutional Court judgment of 25 May 1999, SK 9/98, OTK 1999/4/78; Constitutional Court judgment of 1 July 2014, SK 6/12, OTK-A 2014/7/68.

[30] L Garlicki and S Jarosz-Żukowska, 'Artykuł 64' in L Garlicki and M Zubik (eds), *Konstytucja Rzeczypospolitej Polskiej: Komentarz*, vol 2 (2nd edn, Wydawnictwo Sejmowe 2016); Constitutional Court judgment of 23 May 2006, SK 51/05, OTK-A 2006/5/58.

[31] For instance: Constitutional Court judgment of 12 January 1999 (n 4); Constitutional Court judgment of 11 May 1999 (n 23); Constitutional Court judgment of 12 January 2000 (n 23); Garlicki and Jarosz-Żukowska (n 30).

[32] Act of 7 January 2000 amending the Immovable Property Management Act and other Acts of law, JoL 2000 no 6, item 70, as amended.

[33] On the basis of the Act of 8 October 2004, amending the Immovable Property Management Act and certain other Acts of law, JoL no 240, item 2408, the body was disbanded and its competences transferred to the minister competent for construction, local planning, spatial management, and housing.

the general government administration in the county.[34] The appellate body for decisions related to such matters now is the *voivode*.

IV. Please include a brief description of the procedure, listing the formal acts necessary for an expropriation. What is the relationship between urban planning procedures and expropriation? When is an environmental impact assessment needed?

Immovable property expropriation proceedings,[35] as those in individual administrative matters for which public administration bodies are competent (Article 112(4) and Article 129(1) of the IPMA) and which are resolved by means of administrative decisions (Article 112(2) and Article 129 of the IPMA), are jurisdictional administrative proceedings. Given the provisions of Chapters 4 and 5 of section III of the IPMA related to certain procedural issues, they should be seen as belonging to the category of 'separate' (special) administrative proceedings. In the course of such proceedings—in compliance with the general *lex specialis derogat legi generali* law interpretation principle—special procedural provisions of the IPMA (as a *lex specialis*) will be applied in the first place, followed by, in matters not regulated in the IPMA, the provisions of the Code of Administrative Procedure (CAP) as a *lex generalis*.[36]

An obligatory stage preceding the initiation of expropriation proceedings are 'negotiations concerning a contractual acquisition' of immovable property needed for the attainment of a public purpose (Article 114(1) of the IPMA). The negotiations are held between the *starost*, performing administrative tasks on behalf of the government, and the owner or perpetual user of the property in question, as well as a person holding a limited right in rem to it. As regards property expropriation sought by local government units, the negotiations are carried out by their executive bodies (Article 114(2) of the IPMA). In the course of the negotiations, replacement property may be offered.[37]

Expropriation proceedings are initiated after the two-month deadline for entering into an agreement by means of negotiations set by a public authority for the property owner, perpetual user as well as persons holding a limited right in

[34] Act of 23 January 2009 on the provincial governmental administration governor in the province (ie JoL of 2019, item 1464); P Niemczuk, 'Rządowe funkcje powiatu' (2009) 1(14) Administracja. Teoria—Dydaktyka—Praktyka 158 ff; P Niemczuk, 'Pozycja ustrojowo-prawna starosty' (2011) 1(22) Administracja. Teoria—Dydaktyka—Praktyka 75; J Dobkowski, 'Skutki wpływu przekształcenia modelu organu wykonawczego powiatu na funkcjonowanie administracji powiatowej' in K Małysa-Sulińska and M Stec (eds), *Pozycja ustrojowa organów wykonawczych jednostek samorządu terytorialnego* (LEX 2014).

[35] The legislator has regulated real property expropriation separately in 'special acts' aimed at accelerating the expropriation procedure. They serve the purpose of implementing infrastructural investment projects; M Kamiński, 'Uproszczone i przyspieszone postępowania w sprawach infrastrukturalnych' in I Niżnik-Dobosz (ed), *Przestrzeń i nieruchomości jako przedmiot prawa administracyjnego: Publiczne prawo rzeczowe* (LexisNexis 2012).

[36] The Code of Administrative Procedure Act of 14 June 1960 (JoL of 2020, item 256); T Woś, *Wywłaszczanie nieruchomości i ich zwrot* (LexisNexis 2011).

[37] Judgment of the Provincial Administrative Court in Rzeszów of 7 March 2006, II SA/Rz 943/05.

rem to that property (Article 115(2) of the IPMA)[38] has lapsed with no effect. Expropriation proceedings are initiated *ex officio* (when immovable property is to be expropriated for the benefit of the state treasury) or upon request (when immovable property is to be expropriated for the benefit of a local government unit). The legislator attaches special attention to a precise definition of the object of expropriation proceedings. Its manifestation is a detailed and exhaustive specification found in Article 116(1) and (2) of the IPMA of the aspects that should be included in the property expropriation application.

Pursuant to the provisions of Article 117(1) of the IPMA, the *starost*, performing on behalf of the government the administrative task of carrying out expropriation proceedings, is obliged to lodge, at the competent district court keeping land and mortgage registers for the area to be expropriated, a request for making an entry therein concerning the institution of expropriation proceedings or, if there no land and mortgage register related to the property in question exist, a notice of expropriation proceedings institution to be included in the existing case file.

The next obligatory aspect of expropriation proceedings is a hearing. It means an assembly bringing together all parties to the administrative proceedings aimed at collecting evidence (witness testimonies, expert opinion presentation, and hearing of the parties) as well as making them familiar with the evidence collected.[39] The hearing may also include a visual inspection of the property in question or its part covered by the application for expropriation.

The following stage is the issuance of the expropriation decision. Article 119(1) of the IPMA specifies which additional aspects, apart from those listed in Article 107(1) of the CAP should be included in that decision. The final resolution of an immovable property expropriation case is tantamount to reaching the consequence of expropriation proceedings, ie a transfer of the right of ownership to the state treasury or to a commune, county, or the local government of a province. The property acquisition is effective on the day when the expropriation decision has become final.[40] Pursuant to Article 16(1) of the CAP, the final administrative decision cannot be contested in the instant mode. That means that the administrative case has been finally resolved and it cannot be re-examined and resolved anew, under pain of ascertainment of its invalidity, as *res iudicata* pursuant to Article 156(1)(3) of the CAP.

The basic legal act that regulates the planning process in Poland is the Spatial Planning and Development Act of 27 March 2003 (SPDA).[41] Pursuant to its Article

[38] Constitutional Court judgment of 12 December 2017 (n 10).

[39] B Adamiak J Borkowski, *Postępowanie administracyjne i sądowoadministracyjne* (Wolters Kluwer 2009) 228; A Wróbel, 'Artykuł 89' in M Jaśkowska, M Wilbrandt-Gotowicz, and A Wróbel, *Komentarz aktualizowany do Kodeksu postępowania administracyjnego* (LEX 2019); J Wegner, 'Artykuł 89' in W Chróścielewski and Z Kmieciak (eds), *Kodeks postępowania administracyjnego: Komentarz* (Wolters Kluwer Polska 2019).

[40] IPMA, art 121; A Łukaszewska, 'Artykuł 121' in M Krassowska, A Łukaszewska, and J Szachułowicz, *Gospodarka nieruchomościami: Komentarz* (3rd edn, Wydawnictwo Prawnicze LexisNexis 2003).

[41] The Spatial Planning and Development Act of 27 March 2003 (JoL of 2020, item 293).

4, the specification of the land's intended use and location of public-purpose investment, as well as the specification of methods of land management and conditions for its development are effected by means of a local spatial development plan[42] and, in its absence, a planning permission decision, where: (1) the location of public-purpose investment projects is established by means of a decision on the location of public-purpose investment; (2) the method of land management and conditions for the development of other investments is established by means of a planning permit decision.

As regards expropriation, Article 112(1) of the IPMA sets a requirement—for areas covered by valid local plans—for a given piece of immovable property to be located in an area intended for public purposes. In the absence of a plan, property expropriation may take place also with relation to immovable property 'for which a decision has been issued regarding the specification of the location of public purpose investment projects'. The requirement to specify the location of public-purpose investment projects formalises expropriation when there exists no local plan, just like the requirement to specify in the local plan the intended use of a specific piece of property for some public purpose.[43]

Immovable property expropriation can also take place as regards pursuing public purposes related to environmental protection.[44] Environmental protection issues also have a bearing on the local spatial development plan, which requires prior performance of a strategic environmental impact assessment.[45] This is intended to guarantee that at an early stage of the investment process, which is defining the planning framework, environmental protection and sustainable development requirements are incorporated in compliance with the precautionary principle.[46] Furthermore, some public-purpose investments are projects that at the planning stage require proceedings related to the environmental impact assessment as well as the issuance of the environmental decision.[47]

[42] Z Czarnik, 'Istota i zakres władztwa planistycznego gminy' (2010) 3(20) Teoria—Dydaktyka—Praktyka 17 ff.

[43] M Szewczyk, 'Przedmiotowy zakres stosowania przepisów o formalnym expropriation nieruchomości' in Z Leoński, M Szewczyk, and M Kruś, *Prawo zagospodarowania przestrzeni* (LEX 2012); Decision of the Constitutional Court of 18 April 2000, SK 23/98, OTK 2000/3/93.

[44] Z Bukowski, 'Problematyka celów publicznych z zakresu ochrony środowiska określonych w ustawie o gospodarce nieruchomościami' in Z Bukowski (ed), *Zarządzanie nieruchomościami* (LEX 2013); M Czech, 'Działania starosty w procedurze wywłaszczenia nieruchomości na cele związane z ochroną środowiska' (2015) 18 Białostockie Studia Prawnicze 183 ff.

[45] Act of 3 October 2008 on making information (I) concerning the environment (E) and its protection available (A), the participation of society in environmental protection and environmental impact assessments (IEAA), JoL 2020.283, art 46(1).

[46] A Fogel, 'Strategiczna ocena oddziaływania na środowisko kluczowa dla sporządzania studium' https://www.prawo.pl/samorzad/strategiczna-ocena-oddzialywania-na-srodowisko-kluczowa-dla-sporzadzania-studium,96167.html (accessed 3 March 2020); R Bednarek (ed), *Strategiczna ocena oddziaływania na środowisko w planowaniu przestrzennym* (Polskie Zrzeszenie Inżynierów i Techników Sanitarnych 2012) http://mmm.rdos.gov.pl/doc/pozn/podrecznik_soos.pdf (accessed 27 March 2020).

[47] IEAA, arts 71 and 72; A Ociepa-Kubicka, 'Rola planowania przestrzennego w zarządzaniu ochroną środowiska' (2014) 17(1) Inżynieria i Ochrona Środowiska 135.

V. What are the consequences of a court finding that an expropriation is unlawful on the grounds of substance and/or of process? Is it merely annulled, or are there other consequences, for example the award of damages?

Expropriation decisions may be contested in proceedings before administrative courts. The adjudication competences of Polish administrative courts are largely of a cassation nature. Consequently, they cannot make resolutions as to the merits of the matter being the object of the contested act. They can only uphold the latter's validity or remove such an act from the system of legal transactions if a decision contradicts material law or the procedural rules. The consideration of a complaint against a decision or a resolution may consist in: (1) its repealing; (2) ascertaining its invalidity; or (3) ascertaining its issuance with a breach of law.[48]

The *ex delicto* liability for losses incurred by a public authority are regulated in the Civil Code Act (CCA).[49] Pursuant to its Article 417(1): '[t]he State Treasury or a local government unit or another person exercising public authority by force of law shall be liable for any damage caused by an unlawful action or omission while exercising public authority'.

Being guilty is not a condition for a public authority's *ex delicto* liability. As a consequence, that liability is based solely on the condition of illegality and is not linked to the behaviour of a specific public official but an illegal action of a given organisational structure exercising public authority.[50] In the case of the final expropriation decision, Article 417(2) of the CCA will apply. It reads as follows: 'If damage is caused by a final and non-revisable court decision or other final decision, remedy thereof maybe demanded once such decision has been declared incompliant with the law ... in the course of relevant proceedings.'[51]

VI. Is there any difference between expropriation and nationalisation?

In the Polish legal order, the institution of expropriation is distinguished from that of nationalisation. Currently, the latter is only of historical importance. It consisted in

[48] JP Tarno, 'Artykuł 145' in *Prawo o postępowaniu przed sądami administracyjnymi: Komentarz* (5th edn, Wydawnictwo Prawnicze LexisNexis 2011).

[49] The Civil Code Act of 23 April 1964 (JoL of 2019, item 1145, as amended).

[50] G Karaszewski, 'Artykuł 417' in J Ciszewski and P Nazaruk (eds), *Kodeks cywilny: Komentarz* (Wolters Kluwer Polska 2019).

[51] In the Supreme Court judgment of 16 January 2015 (III CSK 96/14, LEX no 1591900), it was pointed out that the required predicate ruling could be not just the ascertainment of a final administrative decision's invalidity under the provisions of the CAP (its art 156(1)), the ascertainment, under art 158(2) in conjunction with art 156(2) of the CAP, of the issuance of a contested decision in breach of law or the ascertainment of breaches of law that give grounds for the resumption of proceedings closed by a final decision under art 145(1) of the CAP. A predicate ruling can also take the form of an administrative court's judgment delivered under art 145(1) of the Act on proceedings before administrative courts. It is so as there are no reasons for including in the said category of relevant proceedings in the meaning of art 417(2) of the CCA solely extraordinary administrative proceedings (resumption of proceedings, ascertainment of a decision's invalidity), excluding administrative court proceedings (Supreme Court judgment of 21 October 2016, IV CSK 26/16, LEX No 2162818).

removing from private entities the right of ownership of an organised set of things, such as: agricultural holdings, industrial and trade enterprises, pharmacies or schools, but also running surface waters and land under such waters. Nationalisation was effected *ex lege*, but required administrative acts that individualised and specified its legal consequences. The Polish Constitution currently in force is silent on nationalisation. Consequently, one could conclude that the institution in question is foreign to the current Polish legal system.[52]

[52] M Szewczyk, 'Wywłaszczenie i instytucje zbliżone do wywłaszczenia' in Z Leoński, M Szewczyk, and M Kruś, *Prawo zagospodarowania przestrzeni* (LEX 2012); Z Leoński, *Materialne prawo administracyjne* (CH Beck 2009) 133; M Zimmermann, *Polskie prawo wywłaszczeniowe* (1939) 32; S Pawłowski, 'Wywłaszczenie z mocy prawa (ex lege) a nacjonalizacja: refleksje w przedmiocie publicznoprawnych ingerencji w prawo własności' (2019) 1 Ruch Prawniczy, Ekonomiczny i Socjologiczny 87.

8

Procedural Requirements for Administrative Limits to Property Rights in Portugal

Rui Guerra da Fonseca

I. Is there any constitutional provision or convention concerning land expropriation in the traditional sense (ie the forced transfer of ownership ordered for reasons of general interest) in the cases provided for by the law, and with provisions for compensation? If not, please elaborate.

There are actually several constitutional provisions regarding expropriation.

The main constitutional provision in this matter is Article 62(2) (protection of private property), according to which expropriation (as well as requisition) for reasons of general interest can only take place under the law and on the payment of fair compensation. This provision, with slight changes, has been present in Portuguese constitutionalism since our first modern constitution, of 1822.[1] It does not mention 'land' expropriation specifically, but that was always unequivocally the backdrop or typical situation for which the provision was designed. Of course, there were already other situations of deprivation of (non-land) property based on that constitutional provision.

There are other constitutional provisions in this pack. According to Article 65(4) (housing and urban planning), the state, the autonomous regions, and the municipalities define the rules regarding urban land occupation, use, and transformation, namely through urban planning (under the main laws) and can expropriate lands which are necessary for achieving ends of urban general interest.[2] Although this article does not mention it, because of Article 62(2) this cannot be done without the payment of fair compensation.

Both of these articles are in Part I of the Constitution—fundamental rights and duties, and more specifically in the title regarding economic, social, and cultural rights.[3]

[1] Portugal had various constitutions before the current one of 1976: 1822, 1826, 1838, 1911, and 1933. The first three corresponded to the period of the liberal constitutional monarchy. The fourth was the first republican constitution in Portugal, and the fifth was the constitution of an authoritarian regime.

[2] This provision was added in the first constitutional amendment (1982) of the Portuguese Constitution.

[3] This does not mean that private property is not seen as a fundamental civil liberty, namely for the purpose of 'restriction to restrictions'. Its presence within economic, social, and cultural rights has historical explanations (connected to the affirmation of a progressive transition to socialism, present in the original version of the constitution, but slowly purged throughout the constitutional amendments).

Rui Guerra da Fonseca, *Procedural Requirements for Administrative Limits to Property Rights in Portugal* In: *Procedural Requirements for Administrative Limits to Property Rights*. Edited by: Martina Conticelli And Thomas Perroud, Oxford University Press. © Rui Guerra da Fonseca 2022. DOI: 10.1093/oso/9780198867586.003.0008

The Portuguese Constitution has a Part II concerning the economic order or organisation which includes some relevant provisions, although some of them are sometimes considered 'dormant' nowadays (because of the influx of EU law and their original contextualisation: the above-mentioned one, and abandoned as a constitutional project, transition to socialism). Article 94 still contemplates the use of expropriation as an instrument to eliminate excessively large agricultural lands (considering as anachronic agricultural policy objectives: Article 93), which would then be given to or worked by small farmers or smaller forms of agricultural exploitation. Another provision in this part which mentions the possibility of the expropriation of abandoned means of production is Article 88. Technically, it is debatable if land can be considered a means of production (in a constitutional amendment, the expression 'land' was eliminated from Article 83, which contemplates the possibility of public appropriation of means of production). But historically our Constitution clearly considered it as such.

On another page, Article 165(1), al e) establishes a relative parliamentary legislative reserve regarding the general regime for requisitions and expropriations for reasons of general interest. This means that the power to pass general legislation on these matters lies with Parliament, which, however, can delegate it to the government.

II. Is there any constitutional provision or convention concerning limitations to property rights in the broad sense? If not, please elaborate.

Besides the provisions already mentioned in Section I, Article 86(2) allows for governmental intervention in the management of private corporations as an exceptional and transitional situation, again for reasons of general interest, in cases expressly considered by law, and normally subject to a previous judicial decision. This possibility is largely similar to what happened in the US with the *Still Seizure* cases.

In the broad—but still express—sense, the above-mentioned situations of requisition are limitations to property rights because they determine the temporary public use of private property (without transfer): when it is no longer needed, the proprietor recovers the full use of their property (and status as lone user).

Generally, in an implicit way, all the constitutional provisions regarding various rights and for general interests can be used as normative justifications for property limitations (eg environment and quality of life: Article 66; health: Article 64).

III. How are competences regarding expropriation distributed among different levels of government (ie in regional, federal, or confederal states)?

Expropriation is governed by an administrative procedure (at least up to a certain point). This procedure starts with a petition for expropriation coming from its beneficiary, which is normally a public body but not necessarily so (sometimes entities incorporated under private law but pursuing general interests may be beneficiaries).

This petition requires procedural standing. It is presented before the level of government with the power to issue the 'public utility declaration' which is the administrative act that constitutes the fundamental decision of expropriation (it does not transfer the property immediately to the public sphere, but from then on it is inevitable if everything is done according to the law).

The 'public utility declaration' (a free translation of the Portuguese '*declaração de utilidade pública*') is issued normally by the government (by the minister of the area of the justifying general interests: health, education, etc; if it is not possible to establish this with certainty, the power belongs to the Prime Minister). Municipalities may only issue a 'public utility declaration' if the purpose of the expropriation is to concretise a 'plan of urbanisation' or a 'plan of detail' (specific municipal urban plans). This power belongs to the municipal parliament under the proposal of the 'municipal executive'. In the autonomous regions of the Azores and Madeira, this power lies with the regional governments.

IV. Please include a brief description of the procedure, listing the formal acts necessary for an expropriation. What is the relationship between urban planning procedures and expropriation? When is an environmental impact assessment needed?

The Portuguese Code of Expropriations[4] contains three types of procedure: normal expropriation; urgent expropriation; and most urgent expropriation. Commonly, everything starts with the decision to expropriate, followed by the above-mentioned petition to the competent level of government, which will then issue the 'public utility declaration'. Before the latter, an attempt to buy the land from its owner according to civil law must take place; if this fails (normally because of disagreement about the price), then the 'public utility declaration' will be issued, and the beneficiary of the expropriation is granted possession of the land to start the execution of the project. If the expropriation is urgent, the attempt to buy is not mandatory and possession is immediate.

After this an arbitration takes place to settle the value of the land in terms of compensation. If the proprietor does not agree with the arbitral decision, it is possible to appeal to the ordinary courts. In brief, the transfer of property will take place by judicial decision at the end of the process, but the administration has already by then taken possession of the land to start the works.

Before administrative possession takes place, there is always a visit to the area in question in order rigorously to establish all the elements of value present that will be relevant at the time of fixing the compensation (inspection '*ad perpetuam rei memoriam*').

Expropriation is an instrument for the effectiveness of urban planning, but it assumes greater importance when specific plans are involved (i) for the 'face-lifting' of

[4] Law 168/99, 18 September (with several changes: the current text derives from Law 56/2008, 4 April).

certain parts of cities, (ii) the construction of roads, and (iii) other infrastructures for public use.

The object of the environmental impact assessment is not the expropriation itself, but eventually the project or infrastructure that justifies the expropriation.[5] In any case, this environmental impact assessment, when legally mandatory, must be sent along with the petition regarding the declaration of public utility (Article 12(1) al e) of the Code of Expropriations), in which case, if the environmental impact assessment is negative, this will impair the proposed infrastructure and consequently cancel the reasons of general interest that determined the expropriation and rendering it illegal.[6]

V. What are the consequences of a court finding that an expropriation is unlawful on the grounds of substance and/or of process? Is it merely annulled, or are there other consequences, for example the award of damages?

In that case, the expropriation (that is, the 'public utility declaration') is quashed (annulled or declared null),[7] and there might be also the award of damages. The administrative courts of law might decide so for substantive or procedural reasons, meaning that the 'public utility declaration' will no longer be effective. However, if it is proven that this illicit situation caused damages, they can be claimed, not as compensation for expropriation (and so, not following the criteria for establishing the value of the land), but as actual damages, according to another law (the regime on civil liability of the state and other public bodies).

VI. Is there any difference between expropriation and nationalisation?

This is a long-running debate in Portugal. In broad terms, a nationalisation is an expropriation in the sense that both concepts describe a deprivation of property rights for reasons of general interest. But right after this *minimum*, it is common to see various distinctions. First, expropriation would have specific goods as an object (namely land), while nationalisation would involve enterprises or similar (what we call universalities). Secondly, expropriation would have a specific justification or end, while nationalisation would have a broader purpose. Thirdly, expropriation has a specific code (which has seen many versions), while nationalisation follows a different and recent law (Law 62-A/2008) and a special procedure. Fourthly, nationalisation has been present in our constitutionalism since 1974 as a politically motivated act, while expropriation is a non-ideological administrative act.

[5] The legal regime of environmental impact assessment is contained in Decree-Law 151-B/2013, 31 October (with several changes: the current text derives from Decree-Law 152-B/2017, 12 December).

[6] See Decision of the Supreme Administrative Court (28 January 1998).

[7] Portuguese law has two different consequences for unlawful administrative acts: the law specifies which are null (or the causes for that) and these have no effect since their birth, thus they are *declared* null; and which must be cancelled, thus having normal effects until they are *annulled*.

But all these (debatable) differences have a focal point. Our Constitutional Court requires that in both situations there is compensation for the deprivation of property rights (otherwise it would be a confiscation), but accepts differences regarding the extension, value, and moment of payment (unlike what happens in Germany and France, for example). According to the Constitutional Court, the compensation for expropriation must be fair, while the compensation for nationalisation only needs to be reasonable or acceptable in order to meet constitutional provisions (and can be paid later, and eventually in public debt certificates).

In my opinion, as mentioned above,[8] all these differentiations are merely incidental, non-decisive as far as juridical reasoning is concerned, and utilised to justify a different kind of compensation which I find to be unconstitutional.

It is important to mention that we never had a general law on nationalisations before 2008; and when it saw the light of day it was because of the banks and the financial crisis. The same law had two different parts: the first one was this new legal framework on nationalisation; and the second part, the nationalisation of a bank ('*BPN—Banco Português de Negócios*') on the basis of the new general legal framework.

[8] See R Guerra da Fonseca, *Comentário à Constituição Portuguesa* II coord P Otero (Almedina 2008) 272 ff.

9

Procedural Requirements for Administrative Limits to Property Rights in Spain

Luis Arroyo Jiménez and Dolores Utrilla Fernández-Bermejo

I. Is there any constitutional provision or convention concerning land expropriation in the traditional sense (ie the forced transfer of ownership ordered for reasons of general interest) in the cases provided for by the law, and with provisions for compensation? If not, please elaborate.

Article 33(1) CE provides for the right 'to private property and inheritance'. As discussed in greater detail below, Article 33(2) allows for the right's content to be further regulated or defined by law in view of the 'social function of property'. Article 33(3) governs expropriation: 'No one may be deprived of his or her property and rights, except on justified grounds of public utility or social interest, with a proper compensation, and in accordance with the provisions of the law.' The Spanish Constitutional Court has broadly construed the notion of expropriation under Article 33(3). Such a wide interpretation has led the Court to define expropriation as follows: 'A single compulsory deprivation, carried out by public authorities, of privately owned property or property rights on grounds of public interest.'[1]

Such an extensive notion of expropriation stems from general statutory provisions on expropriation that were in force at the time of the enactment of the Constitution (Articles 1(1) LEF and 1(1) REF). These pieces of legislation were passed during the Franco regime; they have remained virtually unchanged and they are currently in force.

First, note that all private property, whether real estate or movable property, as well as property rights more broadly, can be subject to expropriation. In turn, neither (i) public property or assets owned by public bodies, nor (ii) mere expectations, non-effective, future, contingent entitlements, or non-vested rights can be expropriated.[2] Secondly, in order to qualify as an expropriation, the relevant measure should be a 'single or isolated deprivation' of the relevant rights or legal interests, ie it must entail:

> [a]n 'extraordinary loss' or a 'distinct sacrifice' to be borne by one or more parties, but not a general regulation or limitation of a given right. In other words, in order to qualify as such, expropriations must distinctly deprive of property rights, yet not define the right's content or amend a previous legal framework altogether.[3]

[1] STC 108/1986, FJ 20; 99/1987, FJ 6; 227/1988, FJ 11; 178/1989, FJ 9; and 41/1990, FJ 4.
[2] STC 227/1988, FJ 11; and 108/1986, FJ 20.
[3] STC 108/1986, FJ 20; and 99/1987, FJ 6.

Luis Arroyo Jiménez and Dolores Utrilla Fernández-Bermejo, *Procedural Requirements for Administrative Limits to Property Rights in Spain* In: *Procedural Requirements for Administrative Limits to Property Rights*. Edited by: Martina Conticelli And Thomas Perroud, Oxford University Press.
DOI: 10.1093/oso/9780198867586.003.0009

Furthermore, the deprivation must be decided by public authorities in order to serve a public purpose. These authorities will usually be administrative bodies, but Parliaments can also carry out so-called legislative expropriations. Finally, expropriations amount to a form of public power or prerogative intended to deprive a party of her property or rights. This clearly contrasts with public authority non-contractual liability potentially giving rise to loss or damage, which is subject to a different substantive and procedural public law regime (see Articles 106(2) CE, and 32 to 35 LRJSP).

II. Is there any constitutional provision or convention concerning limitations to property rights in the broad sense? If not, please elaborate.

Article 33(2) CE provides that 'the social function' to be fulfilled by private property shall 'determine' the content thereof 'in accordance with the law'. Therefore, having proclaimed the right to private property, the Constitution immediately instructs the legislature to define its substance. Accordingly, (i) the very legislature, who is actually bound by the fundamental right, must define its boundaries, but (ii) this legal scheme is constitutionally-driven. In fact, the Constitution provides that such definition of the content of the right to property must have regard to the underlying 'social function' of property. The Constitutional Court has noted that the social function to be fulfilled by private property depends on the type of asset. Therefore, the content of the right to private property may differ, based on the goods or assets involved.[4] As is the case with the 'public utility or social interest' clause regarding the grounds for expropriation (Article 33(3) CE), the 'social function' standard (Article 33(2) CE) further specifies the general principle laid down in Article 128(1) CE, which is worded as follows: 'The entire wealth of the country in its different forms, irrespective of its ownership, is subordinate to the general interest.'[5]

General statutory provisions define or delineate the content of property rights. Articles 11 to 17 TRLSRU are a paramount example of this: they define the rights and duties of landowners on a general basis in view of the type of land they own. However, these provisions may require public authorities to implement them by specific public action in the form of adjudication measures, thereby giving rise to single case 'administrative limitations'. In both cases, the measure's underlying rationale is the social function to be fulfilled by the relevant asset. Accordingly, in contrast with compulsory expropriation under Article 33(3) CE, these measures under Article 33(2) CE do not give rise to compensation.[6] A distinction between those statutory provisions defining the content of the rights of property and the so-called legislative expropriations—ie expropriations ordered by the Parliament—must be drawn: the first set out the various entitlements that make up the right's substance (hence do not give rise to

[4] STC 37/1987, FJ 8.

[5] L Ortega Álvarez and L Arroyo Jiménez, 'Artículo 128' in ME Casas and M Rodríguez-Piñero (eds), *Constitución Española* (Wolters Kluwer/BOE 2018) 833–34.

[6] STC 227/1988, FJ 11, 170/1989, FJ 8; STS of 20 March 1998, and of 20 June 2002.

compensation), whereas the latter provide for the single deprivation of specific rights or assets, thus giving rise to compensation payable to expropriated owners.[7]

In addition, those pieces of legislation that define the content of the right to property should preserve such fundamental right's essence (*contenido esencial*, *Wesensgehalt*) (Article 53(1) CE). There is an interesting Constitutional Court line of case law regarding those provisions that fail to abide by the right's essence—for example, when the legislative definition of the right's content deprives the asset of any economic value whatsoever. Reasonably, these provisions should be declared invalid, on top of the award of compensation payable for any loss or damage caused by the unconstitutional provision. Nonetheless, the Constitutional Court has stated that general measures violating the affected right's essence entail a deprivation of property and thus qualify as expropriation.[8] Thus, the Constitutional Court places these provisions outside the scope of Article 33(2), which covers those pieces of legislation regulating the content of the right to property, defining them as expropriatory measures in order for them to give rise to compensation under Article 33(3). In turn, it might have been more appropriate to strike down those provisions as unconstitutional for being contrary to Article 33(2) and 53(1) CE, since they violate the right's essence, and, if appropriate, award compensation for any loss or damage arising for public authority liability. The Constitutional Court's approach triggers two different legal notions of expropriation: the formal understanding of expropriation as a single deprivation, ie the deprivation of specific rights or assets determined by public authorities, including the legislature (Section I above), and the substantive understanding of the Constitutional Court, where the legislature generally regulates the right to property violating its essence.[9]

III. How are competences regarding expropriation distributed among different levels of government (ie in regional, federal, or confederal states)?

Spain has three government levels: national (that of the state); regional (that of autonomous regions); and local (that of provinces and municipalities). Under Article 149(1)(18) CE, the power to regulate expropriation is exclusively held by the state. This power includes parliamentary and administrative rule-making on expropriation. However, the Constitutional Court has provided a loose interpretation of this exclusive competence. Indeed, it has allowed regional governments to regulate certain expropriation-related aspects, due to the ties of expropriation with certain matters falling under the competence of autonomous regions (among others, urban planning, environment, transportation, and public works). Thus, the state is allocated the power to regulate the expropriation procedure and the assessment of fair compensation, whereas autonomous regions—duly abiding by these common rules and within their scope of power—are entitled to enact legislation on: (i) the public purposes that may

[7] STC 111/1983, FJ 9.

[8] STC 227/1988, FJ11; and 204/2004, FJ 5.

[9] JM Rodríguez de Santiago, 'Artículo 33' in ME Casas and M Rodríguez Piñero (eds), *Comentarios a la Constitución Española* (Wolters Kluwer/BOE 2018) 1165.

be pursued by expropriation and that render the use of expropriation powers lawful;[10] and (ii) certain specificities within the expropriation procedure laid down by the state, insofar as such specificities are reasonable—ie proportionate—with respect to the type of expropriation.[11]

The competence to carry out expropriations is incumbent upon authorities at all three government levels, as long as they do not overstep their territorial scope and sector-specific powers. Under Article 2(1) LEF, '[c]ompulsory expropriations shall only be determined by the state, the Province or the Municipality'. As from the entry into force of the 1978 Constitution, regional governments—ie autonomous regions—must be deemed included in this list. Therefore, the remaining public authorities (such as specialised instrumental bodies and independent public agencies), as well as publicly owned companies, foundations, or non-profit entities, and private entities exercising delegated public functions, have no power to carry out expropriations. The Supreme Court has traditionally upheld this exclusion.[12] This concentration of expropriation powers in the hands of territorial government bodies has usually been justified on the grounds that only their general, non-specialised position allows for a comprehensive balancing of the different public and private interests at stake.[13]

IV. Please include a brief description of the procedure, listing the formal acts necessary for an expropriation. What is the relationship between urban planning procedures and expropriation? When is an environmental impact assessment needed?

The standard expropriation procedure is governed by the LEF of 1954, which provides for a requisite or previous condition, and a complex procedure made up of three consecutive administrative procedural steps. The requisite is the so-called 'declaration of public utility or social interest', which is a previous formal declaration made by Parliaments or territorial administrative authorities of the public purpose of the expropriation (*causa expropiandi*), usually on a general basis in view of global categories of goods and assets (Articles 9–14 LEF).

Once this condition is met, the actual procedure with its three steps can start. The first one is a decision-making process to determine that a relevant right or asset must be expropriated, which ends up with an administrative decision called 'declaration of the need to expropriate' (Articles 15–23 LEF); the second one is conducted to set the

[10] STC 37/1987, FJ 6; 227/1988, FJ 32; and 186/1993, FJ 2. JM Baño León, 'Artículo 149.1.18º' in ME Casas and M Rodríguez Piñero (eds), *Comentarios a la Constitución Española* (Wolters Kluwer/BOE 2018) 1381–82.

[11] STC 37/1987, FJ 6; and 61/1997, FJ 21, 29, and 31. JR Fernández Torres, *Estudio integral de las expropiaciones urbanísticas* (Thomson-Aranzadi 2007) 31–49.

[12] STS of 27 October 1979 (RJ 3841/1979), of 25 October 1982 (RJ 6036/1982), of 4 June 1986 (RJ 3033/1986), of 27 October 1989 (RJ 3841/1989), and of 19 January 1998 (RJ 347/1998).

[13] E García de Enterría, 'Las expropiaciones legislativas desde la perspectiva constitucional. En particular, el caso de la Ley de Costas' (1996) 141 Revista de Administración Pública 46; L Tolivar Alas, 'Artículo 2: Administración expropiante y beneficiario' in F Sosa Wagner (ed), *Comentarios a la Ley de Expropiación Forzosa* (Thomson-Aranzadi 2003) 43.

amount of compensation and subsequently proceed to payment (Articles 24–47 LEF); the third procedural step is needed to take or actually seize the right or asset subject to expropriation (Articles 48–55 LEF). This procedural sequence, which is that of the standard expropriation procedure, will be modified for urgent or expedited expropriations. Although these are supposed to be exceptional, they are widespread in practice. Under these expedited procedures, the seizure of property or property rights occurs prior to setting and paying compensation (Article 52 LEF). Finally, the LEF also provides for special (non-standard) expropriations subject to their own procedural rules.

In contrast with German (*Enteignungsbeschluss*)[14] or French (*Ordonnance de expropriation*)[15] expropriation law, the LEF does not clearly attach the effects of expropriation to any of the formal acts adopted throughout the expropriation procedure. This has created uncertainty regarding various aspects, such as (i) when is fair compensation due and payable? (ii) at what time is the property right actually transferred? or (iii) when does it become mandatory—and what is the nature and contents of this obligation—to allocate the expropriated right or asset to the public purpose that justified the expropriation?[16]

Expropriations that are carried out on urban planning grounds are only subject to the LEF regarding those aspects not specifically governed by urban planning legislation. The most significant of these special rules is that the administrative procedure for urban planning expropriations is considerably streamlined, because the 'declaration of public utility or social interest' and the declaration of the need to expropriate are implied in the final approval of the territorial and urban plans (Article 42 TRLS).

As for environmental assessments, expropriation rules and regulations provide no further specificities. The general legal framework laid down in the LEA—which basically transposes EU secondary legislation—applies where an environmental assessment is required regarding plans or projects that ultimately need property to be expropriated.

V. What are the consequences of a court finding that an expropriation is unlawful on the grounds of substance and/or of process? Is it merely annulled, or are there other consequences, for example the award of damages?

The consequences arising from any flaws or defects in an expropriation are governed by the general legal framework applicable to administrative acts (Articles 47–52 LPAC) and to their judicial review (Articles 25, 31, 70, and 71 LJCA). Accordingly, in case of unlawful expropriations, the competent judicial authority shall (i) invalidate the challenged administrative action (Article 71(1)(a) LJCA); (ii) declare, if appropriate, the expropriated owner's right to property, subsequently ruling, if possible, to

[14] See eg art 31 of the Bayerisches Gesetz über die entschädigungspflichtige Enteignung (BayRS 2141-1-B).

[15] See art L 221-1 of the Code de l'expropriation pour cause d'utilité publique, enacted by Ordonnance no 2014-1345 of 6 November 2014, JORF no 0261 (11 November 2014).

[16] D Utrilla Fernández-Bermejo, *Expropiación forzosa y beneficiario privado* (Marcial Pons 2015) 220–65.

restore the statu quo prior to the unlawful act (Article 71(1)(b) and (c) LJCA); and (iii) declare that the expropriated owner is entitled to compensation for the loss or damage suffered (Article 71(1)(d) LJCA). The latter is conditioned to the general public law requirements of non-contractual liability set out in Articles 106(2) CE and 32 LRJSP: (i) that the claim be filed in a timely manner; (ii) that the injured party have sustained unlawful loss or damage; (iii) that there be a material causal link between the unlawful expropriation and the loss or damage suffered; and (iv) that the loss or damage can be legally attributed to the expropriating authority. In case of annulment, this last condition will require the expropriation to be manifestly illegal, since, according to the case law, public authorities will not be held liable for unlawful administrative acts if these were reasonably within their scope for discretion or interpretation (the so-called margin of tolerance).[17]

Regarding court invalidations of expropriation procedures, the case law had traditionally upheld the injured party's right to compensation for liability in an amount equal to 25 per cent of the 'fair compensation', on top of the amount for the loss actually sustained. This 'surcharge' was intended as some sort of punitive damages imposed on public authorities for their unlawful actions. However, the state (national) legislature amended the LEF in 2017 and ruled out such possibility:

> If the expropriation procedure is invalidated, regardless of the grounds, the expropriated owner's right to compensation will be justified as long as he/she appropriately evidences that he/she has sustained an actual loss due to the unlawful expropriation (Sole Additional Provision of the LEF).

VI. Is there any difference between expropriation and nationalisation?

Nationalisation has its own legal framework, provided by Article 128(2) CE. This provision reads as follows:

> Essential resources or services may be restricted by law [by the legislature] to the public sector [nationalisation], especially in the case of monopolies. Likewise, intervention in companies may be decided upon [by the legislature] when the public interest so demands.

As opposed to expropriation, intervention in companies entails temporary public management of specific private firms without transfer of capital. Nationalisation, in turn, has a wider scope, since it can apply to (i) broad categories of rights or assets (for instance, continental or superjacent waters, the coast, or radio frequency usage), as well as to (ii) broad economic activities (for example, waste collection, railway transport, or telecommunications).[18]

[17] STS of 17 February 2015 (Rec 2335/2012), and of 26 October 2011 (Rec 188/2009).

[18] JL Martínez López Muñiz, 'La publicatio de recursos y servicios' in L Cosculluela (ed), *Estudios de Derecho Público Económico: Libro Homenaje al Profesor Dr. S. Martín-Retortillo* (Civitas 2003) 687–718; Ortega Álvarez and Arroyo Jiménez (n 5) 837–40.

In the case of resources, the piece of legislation providing for nationalisation is an expropriatory measure, since it fails to regulate expropriation but does order the deprivation of specific rights or assets. Also, it qualifies as a general expropriation because it is addressed to an undefined, broad category of parties, namely, the former holders of the expropriated rights or assets. Thus, compensation must be established by law, striking a fair balance between the amount of compensation and the loss or deprivation. The legislative acts that nationalised continental waters and the coast, which were declared constitutional,[19] granted as compensation the right to use the expropriated assets for a long period of time.[20] Nationalising a category of assets under Article 128(2) CE does not only entail a transfer of ownership—being the state the new owner—but it also usually modifies the nationalised assets' legal framework, which fall under the category of public domain (*dominio público*) and thus become subject to a specific public law regime. The latter aspect is also tackled by the Constitution. In particular, Article 132 provides that such legal regime is based on the principle that they 'shall be inalienable, imprescriptible [ie not amenable to *usucapio*] and not subject to attachment or encumbrance'. This provision also states that the assets falling under this category are those 'established by law and shall, in any case, include coastal area, beaches, territorial waters and natural resources of the economic zone and the continental shelf'. In the case of services, nationalisation can also entail the compulsory expropriation of those assets held by the companies that had been providing the nationalised activity or service, according to Article 33(3) CE. However, in this case, public authorities may decide not to expropriate the relevant property. If so, the owners could claim compensation for loss of value under Article 106(2) CE. Finally, if the activity involved is new and no investment has been made so far to further develop it, nationalisations would not bring along the deprivation of rights or assets, thus not giving rise to any compensation. Such a nationalisation would not require payment of fair compensation, nor grant of damages.

[19] STC 227/1988 and 149/1991.
[20] García de Enterría (n 13) 131–52.

10

Procedural Requirements for Administrative Limits to Property Rights in Sweden

*Patricia Jonason**

I. Is there any constitutional provision or convention concerning land expropriation in the traditional sense (ie the forced transfer of ownership ordered for reasons of general interest) in the cases provided for by the law, and with provisions for compensation? If not, please elaborate.

The Instrument of Government (*Regeringsformen* 1974:152)[1] contains in the second chapter, which constitutes a catalogue of rights, a provision dedicated to expropriation and also to other limitations of property rights for reasons of public interest.[2]

According to section 15:

> The property of every person shall be so guaranteed that none may be compelled by expropriation or other such disposition to surrender property to the public institutions or to a private subject, or tolerate restriction by the public institutions of the use of land or buildings, other than where necessary to satisfy pressing public interests. A person who is compelled to surrender property by expropriation or other such disposition shall be guaranteed full compensation for his or her loss. Compensation shall also be guaranteed to a person whose use of land or buildings is restricted by the public institutions in such a manner that ongoing land use in the affected part of the property is substantially impaired, or injury results which is significant in relation to the value of that part of the property. Compensation shall be determined according to principles laid down in law.

The Constitution refers to 'full compensation for loss'[3] when the limitation of property is due to 'expropriation or other such disposition' but refers only to 'compensation' when it

* I would like to thank Jan Darpö, emeritus professor in environmental law for his valuable feedback.

[1] Which, together with three fundamentals laws, the Freedom of the Press Act, the Fundamental Law on Freedom of Expression, and the Act of Succession, form the Swedish Constitution.

[2] On the historic development of property rights in Sweden see Jonathan R Macey, 'Property Rights in Sweden: A Law and Economics Perspective' SNS occasional paper No 85 (January 2001) 44 ff. See also SOU 2007:29 *Hur tillämpas expropriationslagens bestämmelser*? at 17 ff (Preparatory work).

[3] The adjective 'full' was added during the constitutional reform of 2011.

Patricia Jonason, *Procedural Requirements for Administrative Limits to Property Rights in Sweden* In: *Procedural Requirements for Administrative Limits to Property Rights*. Edited by: Martina Conticelli And Thomas Perroud, Oxford University Press.
 DOI: 10.1093/oso/9780198867586.003.0010

concerns public restrictions on the use of land and buildings.[4] In practice, 'full compensation' means 125 per cent of the market value.

In order to prevent an interpretation of the constitutional protection which could encompass a protection and compensation for restrictions ordered for health, environmental, or safety purposes,[5] a passus has been introduced along with the last constitutional reform, which states:

> In the case of limitations on the use of land or buildings on grounds of protection of human health or the environment, or on grounds of safety, however, the rules laid down in law apply in the matter of entitlement to compensation.

This means that the above-mentioned rules do not apply in these cases and that it is for the legislator, in the acts endorsing the public powers with the right to restrict property rights for health, environmental, or safety purposes, to consider if a right to compensation should be introduced or not.[6]

II. Is there any constitutional provision or convention concerning limitations to property rights in the broad sense? If not, please elaborate.

There is no constitutional provision protecting limitations of property rights in a general manner. Nevertheless, in addition to the protection to limitations to property rights, as mentioned above, the Swedish Catalogue of rights laid down in Chapter 2 contains provisions for copyrights (section 16) and freedom of business (section 17).[7]

A specificity of the Swedish Constitution has to be mentioned. It is the so-called 'Everyman's right' (*allemansrätten*). According to this old principle, enshrined in the Constitution at the end of the 1990s, '[t]here shall be access for all to the natural environment in accordance with the right of public access, notwithstanding the above provisions',[8] the 'main import' of this principle being that '[e]veryone is entitled to walk on another person's property and remain there temporarily, provided their behaviour is not disruptive and they do not cause any damage'.[9]

[4] The enlargement of the protection to 'restrictions on the use of land or building' was made on the occasion of the incorporation of the European Convention on Human Rights into the Swedish legal order. See SOU 2008:125, *En reformerad grundlag* at 432–40 and Prop 2009/10:80, *En reformerad grundlag* at 167 (Preparatory works).

[5] For an example of the application of the former constitutional provisions see NJA 2014, s 332. See also J Darpö, 'Tradition och förnyelse på vattenrättens område: Om mötet mellan gamla tillståndsregimer och moderna miljökrav' (2014) 2 Nordisk Miljörättslig Tidskrift 101; see in particular 11 ff.

[6] J 80 (n 4) 167.

[7] Including a paragraph according to which: 'The right of the Sami population to practise reindeer husbandry is regulated in law.'

[8] By Act (1994:1468).

[9] See Anders Victorin, 'Real Property' in M Bogdan (ed), *Swedish Law in the New Millennium* (Norstedts Juridik 2008) 448.

III. How are competences regarding expropriation distributed among different levels of government (ie in regional, federal, or confederal states)?

Expropriative interventions may be possible according to many special laws such as the Real Property Formation Act (*Fastighetsbildningslagen* 1970:988), the Planning and Building Act (*Plan—och bygglagen* 2010:900), the Roads Act (*Väglagen* 1971:948), and the Railway Act (*Järnvägslagen* 2004:519).

The following will focus on the procedure of expropriation contained in the general legislation on expropriation, ie the Expropriation Act (*Expropriationslagen* 1972:719, ExL) and the related Expropriation Regulation (*Expropriationskungörelse* 1972:727, ExK).

As a general rule, the decision to expropriate is entrusted to the government (section 1, Chapter 3, ExL).[10]

However, the government may delegate to the county administrative board (*länsstyrelsen*) to take the decision, or when special reasons exist ('*särskilda skäl föreligger*') to another public authority, when the application has not been contested, or when the issue is of a minor importance from a general or individual perspective (section 1, Chapter 3, ExL).

The delegation from the government to the county administrative board is enforced through the Expropriation Regulation. According to this, a decision of expropriation is taken by the county administrative board[11] if the government had so decided or when the application concerning the permit to expropriate is not contested (section 4, ExK).

IV. Please include a brief description of the procedure, listing the formal acts necessary for an expropriation. What is the relationship between urban planning procedures and expropriation? When is an environmental impact assessment needed?

The following will focus on the procedure of expropriation contained in the Expropriation Act (*Expropriationslagen* 1972:719, ExL) and the related regulation Expropriation Regulation (*Expropriationskungörelse* 1972:727, ExK).

The procedure begins with the applicant sending to the government (section 1, ExK) the application stating the matter and the circumstances for the

[10] The reason for this rule of competence is twofold: first, it is to give guarantees for a uniform jurisprudence in the field but, secondly, it is also to take into consideration that 'many cases are of higher public importance (*större allmän betydelse*) or involve sensitive considerations of suitability (*lämpligh etsavvägningar*)'. See Prop 1972:109, *Kungl. Maj:ts proposition med förslag till expropriationslag* at 221 (Preparatory work).

[11] Or the Swedish Energy Markets Inspectorate (*Energimarknadsinspektion*) when it concerns electrical installations.

expropriation (eg the kind of right concerned (property rights, use rights, easements), the purpose for the expropriation, the grounds[12] on which the application is based, etc), information about the property involved in the application and the names and addresses of all the known property holders (section 2, Chapter 3, ExL). Other material that may be necessary for the current application also has to be furnished by the applicant (section 2, Chapter 3, ExL). In particular, the application 'shall be accompanied by such a complete description of the projected enterprise as is necessary in each particular case for the need for expropriation to be assessed' (section 2, ExK).

The application is then sent to the county administrative board,[13] which gives the property unit holders affected[14] and the municipality and public authorities who have an interest in the case[15] the opportunity to express their views (section 3, ExK).

The decision is taken by the county administrative board if the government has decided that the case is of minor importance from a public or individual point of you and therefore decides to transfer the decision-making power to it or when the application for the authorisation to expropriate and its approval is not contested (section 1 , Chapter 3, Exl, section 4, ExK).

When a county administrative board has taken a decision concerning expropriations, the government has to be informed (section 1 , Chapter 3, Exl, section 5, ExK).

The possibility to grant expropriation is limited by the requirement of an 'important public interest' (*angelägen allmänt intresse*) laid down by the Constitution,[16] but also by a provision contained in the ExL which provides for balance of interests. According to section 12, Chapter 2, ExL: 'Expropriation permits shall not be granted, if the purpose should be suitably satisfied otherwise or the inconvenience of expropriation from a general and individual point of view outweighs the benefits that might be gained by it.' This means, for example, that there should not be any decision of expropriation if the land can be used in a different, less drastic way—especially through voluntary settlement.[17]

The expropriation permit determines the extent of the expropriation, as well as with which right the expropriation is granted (section 4, Chapter 3, ExL). It will expire if a determination of compensation has not been submitted to a Land and Environment Court (*mark—och miljödomstolen*) within one year of the permit being granted (section 6, Chapter 3, ExL).[18] It is the Land and Environment Courts, which belong to the ordinary courts, who make the decision concerning the amount of compensation (section 1, Chapter 5, ExL).

[12] The (ten) grounds for the expropriation are specified in section 2, Chapter 2, ExL. They are, inter alia, urban development, public transport, protection and security, and cultural heritage.

[13] Prop 1972:109 (n 10) 280. The general rules from the Administrative Procedure Act (2017:900) are applicable, which include inter alia the application of the obligation to give the parties an opportunity to express their views. The rules also apply to the government. See A Dahlsjö, M Hermansson, and E Sjödin, *Expropriationslagen: En kommentar* (Norstedts Juridik 2010) 152.

[14] See Prop 1972:109 (n 10) 280.

[15] Section 3, ExK. Public authorities such as the National Board of Housing (*Boverket*) or the Environmental Protection Agency (*Naturvårdsverket*).

[16] B Bengtsson, *Speciell fastighetsrätt: Miljöbalken* (Iustus B 2018) 139.

[17] ibid 140.

[18] This rule was introduced after Sweden was criticised in the *Sporrong and Lönnroth* case, Application no 151/75 and 7152/75 (Judgment of 23 September 1982).

The special acts such as the Real Property Formation Act, the Planning and Building Act, the Roads Act, and the Railway Act have their own procedures. However, they refer to the Expropriation Act when it concerns the rules on compensation.

The Expropriation Act does not require an environmental impact assessment per se, but other acts such as the Roads Act (section 15) as well as the Railway Building Act (section 9, Chapter 2) do. The EIA concerns the permit for the project applied for.

V. What are the consequences of a court finding that an expropriation is unlawful on the grounds of substance and/or of process? Is it merely annulled, or are there other consequences, for example the award of damages?

The appeal against a decision of expropriation taken by a public authority (such as a county administrative board) is lodged with the government (section 9, Chapter 3, ExL).[19] Government decisions are not subject to appeals as such but to legal review before the Supreme Administrative Court, according to the Act on Legal Review of Certain Governmental Decisions (*Lagen om rättsprövning av vissa regeringsbeslut* 2006:304).[20]

The Supreme administrative courts, acting according to the Act on Legal Review of Certain Governmental Decisions, may quash the decision of expropriation when it is unlawful ('*strider mot en rättsregel*') and, if necessary, remand the case.[21]

In theory, both a violation of a substantial rule (regarding, for example, the balance of interests) and of a procedural rule (such as, for example, the obligation to provide a reasoned decision) may lead to the quashing of the decision. However, a decision is not quashed if it is obvious that the error is of no significance to the decision.

In theory, there are possibilities for the owners of an expropriated property to seek damages if the conditions provided in the Tort Liability Act (*Skadeståndslagen* 1972:207) are fulfilled, not least when 'the damage occurs as a result of the injured party's rights under the European Convention on the protection of human rights and fundamental freedoms have been violated by the state or municipality' (section 3, Chapter 2, Tort Liability Act).[22]

VI. Is there any difference between expropriation and nationalisation?

Nationalisation, as set out in the Constitution, equates with expropriation.[23]

[19] The petition has to be lodged within three weeks.

[20] The petition has to be lodged within three months.

[21] It is not very clear in which situations the court might only quash or quash and remand the decision. See eg RÅ 1996 ref 56 and RÅ 1996 ref 40.

[22] According to a provision that entered into force on 1 January 2018. See B Bengtsson, 'Skadestånd vid överträdelse av Europakonventionen: den nya lagstiftningen' (2018) 2 SvJT 93.

[23] SOU 2008:125 (n 4) 430.

11

Procedural Requirements for Administrative Limits to Property Rights in Ukraine

Halyna Dovhan

I. Is there any constitutional provision or convention concerning land expropriation in the traditional sense (ie the forced transfer of ownership ordered for reasons of general interest) in the cases provided for by the law, and with provisions for compensation? If not, please elaborate.

To start with, it is necessary to emphasise that the notion of 'land expropriation' is not used in Ukrainian legislation. Instead, the term 'forced alienation for the purpose of public necessity' is applied.[1]

There are no provisions in the Constitution of Ukraine dealing with land expropriation as such in the traditional sense.[2]

The Civil Code of Ukraine envisages the possibility of buying out land plots, other real property assets located on them, and private property for public needs or their forced alienation for the purpose of public necessity (Article 350).[3]

Provisions dealing with land expropriation are also included in the Land Code of Ukraine,[4] and a special law on land expropriation 'On the alienation of land plots

[1] The Ukrainian Law 'On the alienation of land plots, other Real Property Assets located on them which are private property for the public needs or on the grounds of public necessity' contains such a definition: forced alienation for the purpose of public necessity is a transfer of property rights on plots of land, and other real property located on them owned by natural persons or legal entities, to the state or territorial community for reasons of public necessity and on the base of a court decision. Comparing this definition with the notion of land expropriation given above, some identical features may be singled out, namely (1) the forced nature of the transfer, (2) special reasons justifying it (in case of land expropriation, general interest is mentioned; in Ukrainian legislation it would have to be public necessity), (3) obligatory compensation paid to the owner, (4) it may be applied only in exceptional cases provided for by law, (5) it should be done on the basis of an enforcement order. Thus, it seems that there is no difference between these two notions; it is merely a matter of terminology. This is a case of using Ukrainian terms to name legal procedures rather than borrowing from words of Latin origin.

[2] Assuming that the term used in the question refers to land expropriation in the traditional sense, this is not envisaged in the Constitution of Ukraine. There is a provision concerning the forced alienation of private property in general, not only of land plots.

[3] Civil Code of Ukraine (16 January 2003) https://zakon.rada.gov.ua/laws/show/435-15 accessed 5 May 2021.

[4] Land Code of Ukraine (25 October 2001) https://zakon.rada.gov.ua/laws/show/2768-14 accessed 5 May 2021.

Halyna Dovhan, *Procedural Requirements for Administrative Limits to Property Rights in Ukraine* In: *Procedural Requirements for Administrative Limits to Property Rights*. Edited by: Martina Conticelli And Thomas Perroud, Oxford University Press.
 DOI: 10.1093/oso/9780198867586.003.0011

and other Real Property Assets located on them which are private property for public needs or on the grounds of public necessity' was adopted in 2009.[5]

II. Is there any constitutional provision or convention concerning limitations to property rights in the broad sense? If not, please elaborate.

The Constitution of Ukraine contains general principles concerning limitations to property rights, namely, (1) the inviolability and inadmissibility of the unlawful deprivation of the right to property, (2) advance and full reimbursement of the value of private property assets, (3) application only as an exception for reasons of public necessity, (4) application on the grounds of, and according to, the procedure established by law, and (5) authorisation only under conditions of martial law or a state of emergency (Article 41). It is worth mentioning that a confiscation procedure is mentioned in the Constitution. It may, however, be applied only pursuant to a court decision.[6]

The Civil Code of Ukraine includes legal provisions concerning limitations to property rights in the broad sense.[7] It is stressed that the state must not intervene in the exercise of the right of ownership. Under Articles 319 and 321, the right of ownership is inviolable. Its restriction or deprivation are permissible only in some cases, and according to the procedure established by law.[8]

III. How are competences regarding expropriation distributed among different levels of government (ie in regional, federal, or confederal states)?

In Ukraine, the land expropriation procedure can be initiated by the executive authorities (Cabinet of Ministers of Ukraine, regional, or district state administrations) or local self-government bodies.

The executive authorities are entitled to take a decision if it is necessary to construct structures pertaining to (1) national security and defence; (2) communications, utility, transport, and energy facilities, and any facilities required for their use; (3) objects related to mining operations; (4) natural reserve fund objects of national importance (Article 8 of the Law of Ukraine 'On Alienation').[9]

[5] Law of Ukraine 'On the alienation of land plots, other Real Property Assets located on them which are private property for the public needs or on the grounds of public necessity' (17 November 2009) https://zakon.rada.gov.ua/laws/show/1559-17 accessed 5 May 2021.

[6] Constitution of Ukraine (28 June 1996) https://zakon.rada.gov.ua/laws/show/254%D0%BA/96-%D0%B2%D1%80 accessed 5 May 2021.

[7] Both the Constitution of Ukraine and the Civil Code of Ukraine contain principles concerning the limitation of property rights in general, thus not only as the result of forced alienation of land plots for purposes of public necessity.

[8] Civil Code of Ukraine (16 January 2003) https://zakon.rada.gov.ua/laws/show/435-15 accessed 5 May 2021.

[9] Law of Ukraine (n 5).

Self-governing bodies (rural, settlement, city councils) adopt decisions on forced alienation in case of necessity to construct structures pertaining to (1) communications, utility, transport, and energy facilities for the territorial community of a village, town, or city, and any facilities required for their use; (2) natural reserve fund objects of local importance; and (3) graveyards (Article 9 of the Law of Ukraine 'On Alienation').[10]

It is worth mentioning that forced alienation cannot be conducted on the basis of these decisions. Only a court order on forced alienation can constitute a legal basis for this procedure.

IV. Please include a brief description of the procedure, listing the formal acts necessary for an expropriation. What is the relationship between urban planning procedures and expropriation? When is an environmental impact assessment needed?

The documents necessary for expropriation are the following (the list reflects the procedural sequence):

1. a decision by executive authorities or local self-government bodies regarding the redemption of land plots for public needs and land management documentation prepared according to the Law of Ukraine 'On Land Management';
2. a report on expert pecuniary evaluation and state expertise regarding land management documentation;
3. written notification addressed to the owner including information about the object of redemption, its location, area, cadastral number, and land category; the purpose of the redemption; the conditions of redemption (estimated price of redemption, time limit, the source of financing for the procedure, information about land plots that could be proposed as an alternative); the rights and duties of the owner concerning the redemption; information about the house that could be proposed as an alternative. If the owner declines the offer, executive authorities or local self-government bodies are entitled to file a suit before an administrative court requesting forced alienation. But this is possible only in cases of public necessity;
4. a court decision on forced alienation of land plot;
5. documents confirming advance and full reimbursement of the value of the land plot or confirming the state registration of ownership of real property that is given rather than transferred.[11]

The Law of Ukraine 'On Alienation' provides that urban planning documentation should be taken into consideration during expropriation (Article 7(2)).

One of the principles of land expropriation provided by Law of Ukraine 'On Alienation' is the observance of requirements of ecological safety and guaranteeing of further rational use of land plots (Article 4(4)). Forced alienation is allowed if the

[10] ibid.
[11] Law of Ukraine (n 5).

planned construction of objects is to take into account ecological factors (among other things) (Article 15). Law of Ukraine 'On Environmental Impact Assessment' provides that a prior environmental impact assessment is not compulsory for the construction of all the structures covered by the notion of 'public necessity'. It should be carried out before the planning of construction of communications, utility, transport, and energy facilities, in addition to any facilities required for their exploitation, as well as objects related to mining operations (Article 3).[12]

V. What are the consequences of a court finding that an expropriation is unlawful on the grounds of substance and/or of process? Is it merely annulled, or are there other consequences, for example the award of damages?

The Code of Administrative Proceedings of Ukraine provides that damages must be awarded if an individual act is found to be unlawful and it is quashed by a court, or if any actions of an competent authority are judged to be unlawful (Article 245(2)).[13]

A similar provision is included in Ukraine's Land Code, which provides that unlawful acts will be invalidated, and ensuing damage must be fully indemnified by the authority that issued the act.[14]

VI. Is there any difference between expropriation and nationalisation?

Neither of these concepts is defined in Ukrainian law.[15] In spite of the lack of definition and the conditions of its usage, the term 'nationalisation' has actually been used

[12] Law of Ukraine 'On Environmental Impact Assessment' (23 May 2017) https://zakon.rada.gov.ua/laws/show/2059-19 accessed 5 May 2021.

[13] While examining appeals regarding the decisions of competent authorities, a court should ascertain whether any decisions have been adopted: (1) based on the scope of the authorities' power and in accordance with the Constitution and laws of Ukraine; (2) according to the purpose for which such powers have been conferred to the authority; (3) in terms of justifiably (sufficient lawfulness), taking into account all the circumstances relevant to decision making; (4) without bias; (5) in good faith; (6) reasonably; (7) observing the principle of equality, preventing all forms of discrimination; (8) proportionally, namely observing the proper balance between any adverse effects on the rights, liberties, or interests of persons and the purpose that the decision pursues; (9) taking into account the right of a person to participate in the decision-making; (10) in a timely manner (Article 2(2) of the Code of Administrative Proceedings of Ukraine). Code of Administrative Proceedings of Ukraine (6 July 2005) https://zakon.rada.gov.ua/laws/show/2747-15 accessed 5 May 2021.

[14] Land Code of Ukraine (n 4).

[15] Despite the lack of a legal framework for the process of nationalisation in Ukraine, this phenomenon has indeed occurred. The most high-profile case in this regard was the nationalisation of the PrivatBank. On 18 December 2016, the Cabinet of Ministers of Ukraine issued a decree 'On some issues of guaranteeing the stability of the financial system of Ukraine', according to which the Ministry of Finance of Ukraine took 100% of the shares in PrivatBank for the symbolic price of 1 hryvnia (https://zakon.rada.gov.ua/laws/show/961-2016-%D0%BF#Text). The notion of 'nationalisation' was not used in this document, but this case, which is still hotly debated, was seen in this light by society at large. In March 2021, the National Security and Defence Council of Ukraine made a decision to nationalise Motor Sich, one of the world's leading enterprises, manufacturing engines for airplanes and helicopters. Alongside expropriation and nationalisation, a notion and procedure of 'reprivatisation' are widely used in Ukraine but with no legislative definition.

in some legislation. For example, nationalisation is mentioned as one of the directions of economic policy of the state in the Commercial Code of Ukraine.[16] Besides this, the Law of Ukraine 'On investment activity' provides that investments cannot be nationalised or requisitioned without payment. Such measures may be implemented only on the basis of Ukrainian legislative acts with payment for all damages caused as a result of the termination of investment activity.[17] This procedure is not detailed at all, however.

In legal doctrine, nationalisation is considered as a termination of the right to property of natural and legal persons on the basis of law, and the reimbursement of its value is provided for. Prior to nationalisation, special law has to be adopted.[18]

As for expropriation, legal scholarship proposes three approaches to interpretation: (1) it has a broad meaning covering all cases of the forced alienation of property, namely requisition, nationalisation, buying out, etc; (2) expropriation is a synonym for requisition;[19] and (3) it covers cases of the paid alienation of immovable property.[20] VM Kossak defines expropriation as forced assignment of property (paid or without payment) by state authorities, usually without the consent of the owner. The matter of the expropriation can be both movable and immovable property. He notes that nationalisation, requisition, and confiscation are types of expropriation.[21]

This term describes the process of reverse privatisation, namely the return of previously privatised property to the state. Among the well-known examples of reprivatisation of key enterprises in Ukraine is the *Kryvorizhstal* case (one of the biggest steel producers in the world. See https://ips.ligazakon.net/document/view/SD042523?an=102&ed=2004_10_22 accessed 5 May 2021), the *Nikopol Ferroalloy Plant* case (https://zakon.rada.gov.ua/laws/show/v18_1600-05#Text accessed 5 May 2021), the Nikopol Yuzhnotrubny Plant, an attempt to reprivatise the biggest telecom operator, Ukrtelecom (https://reyestr.court.gov.ua/Review/91720858 accessed 5 May 2021 and https://www.epravda.com.ua/rus/publications/2018/04/16/636033/ accessed 4 July 2022).

[16] Commercial Code of Ukraine (16 January 2003) https://zakon.rada.gov.ua/laws/show/436-15 accessed 5 May 2021.

[17] Law of Ukraine 'On Investment Activity' (18 September 1991) https://zakon.rada.gov.ua/laws/show/1560-12#Text accessed 5 May 2021.

[18] V Bobrika, I Spasibo-Fateeva, and O Banasko (eds), *Civil Code of Ukraine: Scientific and Practical Commentary*, vol 5 (Strajd 2011) 242–44.

[19] D Meier, *Russian Civil Law* (Dvigatel 1914), in Russian.

[20] M Venetsianov, *Expropriation from the Point of View of the Civil Law* (Typography of Imperial University 1891), in Russian.

[21] VM Kossak, 'Expropriation' ('*Експропріація*') in VA Smoliy (ed), *Encyclopaedia of the History of Ukraine (Енциклопедія історії України)*, part 3 (Institute of History of Ukraine 2005) 24 http://history.org.ua/uk accessed 5 May 2021.

12

Procedural Requirements for Administrative Limits to Property Rights in the United Kingdom

Emma Waring

The law relating to land expropriation is known as 'compulsory purchase' in England and can 'appear daunting'[1] due to its 'complex and piecemeal nature'.[2] Compulsory purchase law in England has historically been derived from a combination of legislative powers, prerogative powers, and judicial decisions. A central tenet of the rule of law in English constitutional law has been that:

> It is clear that no minister or public authority can acquire land compulsorily except the power to do so be given by Parliament; and Parliament only grants it, or should only grant it, when it is necessary in the public interest ... I regard it as a principle of our constitutional law that no citizen is to be deprived of his land by any public authority against his will, unless it is expressly authorised by Parliament and the public interest decisively so demands. If there is any reasonable doubt on the matter, the balance must be resolved in favour of the citizen.[3]

The traditional understanding that land should only be taken compulsorily where the landowner's rights are outweighed by the public interest has been strengthened by the incorporation of the European Convention on Human Rights (ECHR)[4] into domestic law by the Human Rights Act 1998 (HRA 1998),[5] particularly Article 1 of Protocol 1 (A1P1). A1P1 famously guarantees that:

> Every natural or legal person is entitled to the peaceful enjoyment of his possessions. No one shall be deprived of his possessions except in the public interest and subject to the conditions provided for by law and the general principles of international law. The preceding provisions shall not, however, in any way impair the right of the state to enforce such laws as it deems necessary to control the use of property in accordance with the general interest.

[1] G Roots and others, *The Law of Compulsory Purchase* (3rd edn, Bloomsbury Professional 2018) 6 [4].
[2] EJL Waring, 'Expropriation Law in England' in JAMA Sluysmans, S Verbist, and EJL Waring (eds), *Expropriation Law in Europe* (Wolters Kluwer 2015) 129.
[3] *Prest v Secretary of State for Wales* (1982) 81 LGR 193, 198 (Lord Denning).
[4] Convention for the Protection of Human Rights and Fundamental Freedoms (European Convention on Human Rights, as amended) (ECHR) Rome (4 November 1950) Cmd 8969.
[5] The HRA 1998 came into force on 2 October 2000.

Emma Waring, *Procedural Requirements for Administrative Limits to Property Rights in the United Kingdom* In: *Procedural Requirements for Administrative Limits to Property Rights*. Edited by: Martina Conticelli And Thomas Perroud, Oxford University Press. © Emma Waring 2022. DOI: 10.1093/oso/9780198867586.003.0012

While A1P1 guarantees the right to the peaceful enjoyment of possessions, it does not prevent compulsory purchase of land where this is in the public interest and subject to legal principles set down by statute. States have a significant 'margin of appreciation' in deciding whether the public interest justifies compulsory purchase in a particular scenario. However, section 6 of the HRA 1998 requires that a public authority may not act in a way that is incompatible with the ECHR, so both the Secretary of State and local authorities will be subject to this obligation. It is possible for the confirmation of a compulsory purchase order (CPO) to be challenged on the basis that it breaches the HRA 1998 and undermines the ECHR rights of the claimant.

Today, the power to acquire land by compulsory purchase is governed almost exclusively[6] by a highly fragmented series of general statutes[7] that: (a) empower an authority to acquire land compulsorily; (b) authorise the acquisition; (c) implement the acquisition; and (d) provide compensation for the acquisition. There is no one all-encompassing statute or code governing compulsory purchase in England. Instead, there are a number of different statutes governing compulsory purchase including: the Land Compensation Act 1961; the Compulsory Purchase Act 1965; the Land Compensation Act 1973; the Highways Act 1980; the Acquisition of Land Act 1981 (as amended by the Planning and Compulsory Purchase Act 2004); the Compulsory Purchase (Vesting Declarations) Act 1981; the Town and Country Planning Act 1990; the Planning Act 2008; and the Neighbourhood Planning Act 2017. Further guidance for acquiring authorities is contained in the non-statutory government advice document *Guidance on Compulsory Purchase Process and the Crichel Down Rules*.[8] Generally, these powers enable the acquiring authority (a governmental body or sometimes a private entity) to expropriate land in specified situations or for various purposes, eg to expand a motorway or to encourage inner-city regeneration.

Typically, compulsory purchase entails a number of stages. First, any acquiring authority wanting to expropriate land must, in the abstract, possess the statutory power to do this. The acquiring authority must also then ensure that it can take the specified land for the particular desired purpose. This second stage of the process, which involves making and confirming a particular CPO is most often governed by the procedure set out in the Acquisition of Land Act 1981 (ALA 1981) and various common issues relating to compensation are set out in the Compulsory Purchase Act 1965.

[6] The Crown retains a residual power under the royal prerogative to take land in time of war (although compensation should be paid even in these circumstances, according to the House of Lords in *Burmah Oil Co (Burma Trading) Ltd v Lord Advocate* [1965] AC 75). However, this residual prerogative power should not be exercised where this overlaps with a statutory power of compulsory purchase (*AG v De Keyser's Royal Hotel Ltd* [1920] AC 508). The applicability of this residual prerogative power is almost completely academic today.

[7] There are so-called 'Private' Acts of Parliament which provide for compulsory purchase powers for specified land for a particular project, eg the Channel Tunnel under the Channel Tunnel Act 1987. Normally, compulsory purchase powers are general and contained in Public General Acts of Parliament that are of general applicability and do not refer to specific plots of land.

[8] *Guidance on Compulsory Purchase Process and the Crichel Down Rules* produced by the Department of Communities and Local Government (2015), updated in 2019 by the Department for Levelling Up, Housing & Communities https://assets.publishing.service.gov.uk/government/uploads/system/uploads/attachment_data/file/1071500/CPO_guidance_-_with_2019_update.pdf accessed 19 May 2022.

Challenges to planning decisions made by government ministers, local authorities, or other public bodies are normally made by way of judicial review. It is worth noting that this is not an automatically available remedy and that the court can refuse permission to bring a claim if the court cannot discern an arguable ground. Sections 23 and 24 of the ALA 1981 govern the process by which a CPO can be questioned before or after its confirmation. The validity of a CPO can be challenged on the grounds that the decision to authorise the CPO was ultra vires the authorising Act;[9] or that a 'relevant requirement' has not been complied with which means that the interests of the applicant have been 'substantially prejudiced'.[10] Any application under section 23 challenging a CPO has to be made within a six-week period beginning when the notice of the order's confirmation is first published. This short time period can have harsh consequences and commentators have noted that the time limit may 'deprive a person of a right to challenge if he is unaware of a matter that could give rise to a challenge until it is too late'.[11] If a successful challenge to a CPO is made, the court has two discretionary remedial powers: first, to grant interim relief suspending all or part of the CPO's operation until the court makes its final decision;[12] and, secondly, to quash all or part of the CPO.[13]

Planning decisions and challenges to the refusal to confirm a CPO may be brought by way of judicial review in the High Court. The grounds for judicial review continue to evolve, but predominantly focus around issues of illegality, irrationality, procedural unfairness, and legitimate expectations. Any legal challenge by way of judicial review must be undertaken promptly, with claims involving planning decisions to be filed within six weeks of the decision, rather than the usual three months for most judicial review claims.[14] The remedies available in a successful judicial review case involve quashing orders, mandatory orders compelling the public body to act in a particular way, or a prohibiting order preventing the public body from acting in a particular way. It is also possible for the court to make a declaration setting out the various legal rights and duties, an injunction, and in some limited cases damages may be awarded.

[9] ALA 1981, s 23(1).
[10] ibid ss 23(2) and 24(2)(b).
[11] B Denyer-Green, *Compulsory Purchase and Compensation* (11th edn, Routledge 2019) 48 [4.10].
[12] ALA 1981, s 24(1).
[13] ibid s 24(2).
[14] Civil Procedure Rules 1998, r 54.5.

13

Procedural Requirements for Administrative Limits to Property Rights in the United States of America

Ilya Somin

I. Is there any constitutional provision or convention concerning land expropriation in the traditional sense (ie the forced transfer of ownership ordered for reasons of general interest) in the cases provided for by the law, and with provisions for compensation? If not, please elaborate.

The Takings Clause of the Fifth Amendment of the federal constitution[1] forbids the taking of private property without 'just compensation'.[2] This restricts takings by all three levels of government: federal state, and local. Almost every state constitution has a similar provision, which constrains expropriation by its respective state and local governments. The Supreme Court has ruled that 'just compensation' generally requires the payment of 'fair market value' to the owner, estimated as of the date the property was appropriated.[3] Some state constitutions and federal statutes require additional compensation beyond that.

Compensation is automatically required when the government takes property by the use of eminent domain. The Supreme Court has also ruled that there is an automatic *per se* taking anytime the government imposes a 'permanent physical occupation' of property,[4] or regulates it in such a way as to wipe out 100% of its value.[5] In an important recent case, *Cedar Point* Nursery v Hassid, the Supreme Court ruled that 'temporary' physical occupations of property also usually qualify as *per se* takings.[6] Takings claims involving most other regulatory restrictions on property rights are subject to a complex and vague three part balancing test, under which the government usually prevails. The test requires courts to consider '[t]he economic impact of the

[1] For a much more detailed overview of condemnation law in the United States see I Somin, 'Eminent Domain in the United States' in I Kim, H Lee, and I Somin (eds), *Eminent Domain: A Comparative Perspective* (CUP 2017).

[2] US Const Amend V.

[3] See eg *Kirby Forest Industries Inc v United States* 467 US 1, 10 (1984).

[4] *Loretto v Teleprompter CATV Corp* 458 US 419 (1982).

[5] *Lucas v South Carolina Coastal Council* 505 US 1003 (1992).

[6] 141 SCt 2063 (2021). For my early assessment of this ruling, see I Somn, 'Supreme Court's *Cedar Point* Property Rights Decision Protects Both Sides' *The Hill* (23 June 2021) https://thehill.com/ opinion/ judiciary/559914-supreme-courts-cedar-point-property-rights-decision-protects-both-sides/ accessed 17 June 2022.

Ilya Somin, *Procedural Requirements for Administrative Limits to Property Rights in the United States of America* In: *Procedural Requirements for Administrative Limits to Property Rights*. Edited by: Martina Conticelli And Thomas Perroud, Oxford University Press. © Ilya Somin 2022. DOI: 10.1093/oso/9780198867586.003.0013

regulation on the claimant,' the 'extent to which the regulation has interfered with distinct investment-backed expectations,' and the 'character of the government action'.[7] It is often unclear how to apply these factors, or what happens when two of them come out in favour of one side, but the third supports the other. Some state courts have interpreted their state constitutions as providing greater protection for property owners than the federal Takings Clause (as currently interpreted by the federal Supreme Court) does.

The Fifth Amendment also requires that the use of eminent domain be limited to cases where the condemnation of property for a 'public use'.[8] For some 200 years, there has been a debate between advocates of the 'broad' and 'narrow' interpretations of this requirement.[9] The narrow view holds that a public use only exists when eminent domain is used to take property for a government-owned project, such as a road or a public building, or for a private entity that has a legal duty to serve the entire public (such as a public utility). By contrast, the broad view holds that a 'public use' simply requires that the condemned property be used for some purpose that might benefit the general public in some way—even if the government provides little or no evidence that the supposed public benefit will actually be realised.

The US Supreme Court has largely endorsed the broad view, most notably in cases such as *Berman v Parker* and *Kelo v City of New London*.[10] But some state supreme courts endorse the narrow view or some intermediate position between the two, in interpreting their state constitutional public use provisions.[11]

In the wake of the political backlash against the Supreme Court's decision in *Kelo*, which upheld the taking of homes for private 'economic development', some states have enacted amendments to their state constitutions or new statutory laws that explicitly endorse the narrow view, or at least ban many types of takings that transfer property to private parties.[12] The issue of 'public use' remains controversial, and it is possible that the Supreme Court will at some point either narrow or overrule the *Kelo* decision.[13]

II. Is there any constitutional provision or convention concerning limitations to property rights in the broad sense? If not, please elaborate.

As noted above, the Takings Clause of the Fifth Amendment provides substantial protection to property owners whose property has been taken by the government, requiring 'just compensation' and limiting the use of eminent domain to cases where there is a 'public use'. In addition to the Takings Clause, the Fifth and Fourteenth Amendments also forbid federal and state governments to deprive individuals of 'property' without 'due process of law'.[14] Most state constitutions have similar provisions,

[7] *Penn Central Transp Co v City of New York* 438 US 104, 123 (1978).

[8] US Const Amend V.

[9] For an overview see I Somin, *The Grasping Hand: Kelo v City of New London and the Limits of Eminent Domain* (rev edn, University of Chicago Press 2016) ch 2.

[10] *Berman v Parker* 348 US 26 (1954); *Kelo v City of New London* 545 US 469 (2005).

[11] For an overview see Somin (n 9) ch 7.

[12] For an overview of new state legislation and constitutional amendments enacted after *Kelo* see *Kelo v City of New London* (n 10) chs 5 and 6.

[13] See discussion of the prospects for such developments in *Kelo v City of New London* (n 10) 238–41.

[14] US Const Amend V; US Const Amend XIV, sec 1.

and some have additional protections for property rights that go beyond this. As currently interpreted by the Supreme Court, the Due Process Clauses provide primarily procedural protections for property rights, rather than substantive ones, although a few modest substantive constraints remain.[15]

In the late nineteenth and early twentieth centuries, the Due Process Clause of the Fourteenth Amendment was interpreted to provide considerable substantive protection against violations of property rights and economic liberties.[16]

III. How are competences regarding expropriation distributed among different levels of government (ie in regional, federal, or confederal States)?

The federal, state, and local governments can all condemn property for a wide range of purposes, such as infrastructure, development, building of public facilities, and so on. But most condemnations are in fact done at the local or state level.

At least as a general rule, the use of eminent domain must be expressly authorised by a specific federal or state statute.[17] It cannot simply be inferred from vague language in a statute, or from the general structure of government.

Most condemnations are undertaken by state or local governments, authorised by state statutes. Typical examples include condemnations for purposes of building public infrastructure, such as roads, public buildings, and public utilities. More controversially, most states also allow for condemnation of 'blighted' property for transfer to private developers, who, authorities hope, will alleviate the blight.[18]

Some states also permit condemnation of private property for transfer to private parties simply to promote 'economic development', a practice upheld by the Supreme Court in the controversial case of *Kelo v City of New London*, but rejected by numerous state courts applying the public use clauses of their state constitutions.[19]

The federal government uses eminent domain to build federal infrastructure and military facilities, among other purposes. In recent years, there has been great controversy over the use of eminent domain to take land for construction of President Donald Trump's now-aborted border wall project, on the southern border with Mexico.[20]

Some uses of eminent domain are undertaken by both state and federal governments. An important example is condemnation for pipelines, which—depending on the type of pipeline—can be done pursuant either to state or federal legislation.[21]

[15] See eg *Lingle v Chevron Inc* 544 US 285 (2005).

[16] For an overview of the history of public use property rights jurisprudence see Somin (n 9) ch 2. On economic rights under the due process clause more generally see DE Bernstein, *Rehabilitating Lochner: Defending Individual Rights Against Progressive Reform* (University of Chicago Press 2011).

[17] See eg *Delaware, L & W R Co v Town of Morristown* 276 US 182 (1928).

[18] See discussion of this in Somin (n 9) ch 3; see also WE Pritchett, 'The "Public Menace" of Blight: Urban Renewal and the Private Uses of Eminent Domain' (2003) 21(1) Yale Law & Policy Rev 1.

[19] See Somin (n 9) ch 7 (providing an overview of these cases).

[20] See eg I Somin, 'To Build the Wall, Trump Might Make Thousands of Americans Suffer' *Washington Post* (19 January 2019) https://www.washingtonpost.com/opinions/to-build-the-wall-trump-might-make-thousands-of-americans-suffer/2019/01/19/fd39abe6-150e-11e9-b6ad-9cfd62dbb0a8_story.html accessed 21 April 2021; G Dickerson, 'Property Musings at the US-Mexican Border' (2018) 33 Maryland J Int'l L 162.

[21] For an overview see JW Coleman and AB Klass, 'Energy and Eminent Domain' (2019) 104 Minn L Rev 659.

IV. Please include a brief description of the procedure, listing the formal acts necessary for an expropriation. What is the relationship between urban planning procedures and expropriation? When is an environmental impact assessment needed?

The answers to this vary somewhat by state, and also by issue area. But, as a general rule, authorities must have proper legislative authorisation, provide notice to owners of condemned property,[22] and also give them an opportunity to contest the legality of the takings in court.[23]

V. What are the consequences of a court finding that an expropriation is unlawful on the grounds of substance and/or of process? Is it merely annulled, or are there other consequences, for example the award of damages?

The answer to this depends on why the condemnation was found to be unlawful, and also varies between states. But, in nearly all cases, if the taking was found to be illegal because it was not for a 'public use' as required by the federal and/or state constitutions, then it is simply forbidden. The same applies if the taking is not properly authorised by legislation.

In general, such cases are adjudicated before the government actually takes over the property in question, so there is no need for compensation. However, there are some state and federal laws that allow for 'quick take' condemnations that enable swift seizure of property, with adjudication to follow only afterwards.[24] A notable federal example is that of takings for federally authorised pipelines.[25]

VI. Is there any difference between expropriation and nationalisation?

No. If a seizure or restriction on private property rights qualifies as a taking, the condemning authority cannot avoid legal liability by calling it 'nationalisation'. To my knowledge, there is no such category in American law.

[22] See eg Fed Rule of Civil Procedure 71.1 (requiring notice of the exercise of eminent domain for federal takings).

[23] For a detailed state-by-state overview of eminent domain procedures see JC Pipes, RJ Will, and W G Blake, *The Law of Eminent Domain: A Fifty State Survey* (American Bar Association 2012). A revised edition of this reference book is being planned, but it is not clear when it will be published.

[24] See eg *Mayor of Baltimore v Valsamaki* 916 A.2d 324, 356 (Md 2007) (describing and limiting such procedures); *Rhode Island Economic Development Corp v The Parking Co* 892 A.2d 87, 102 (RI 2006) (also describing and limiting such procedures).

[25] See eg *Mountain Valley Pipeline v 6.56 Acres of Land* 915 F.3d 197 (4th Cir 2019).

14

Procedural Requirements for Administrative Limits to Property Rights in the International Law on Promotion and Protection of Foreign Investments

Filippo Fontanelli

International law on the protection of foreign investments (international investment law, or IIL) consists of thousands of treaties and the customs on the protection of aliens and their property.[1] IIL treaties display a high degree of similarity,[2] which permits referring to a Platonic template of the recurring provisions. Other sources of protection, like contracts and statutes, are outside this study, since they escape generalisation. Published tribunal awards are a de facto source. They occasionally contradict each other—an unfortunate inconsistency. Given the similarity between the applicable norms and the importance of the practice, one would presume and prefer convergence in their interpretation.

All European countries have IIL obligations. By design, IIL supplements (without supplanting) domestic law, insuring foreign investors against rule of law failures. Rather than creating novel property rights, IIL provides rights recognised under domestic law with additional protection.[3] Therefore, IIL standards of protection mostly speak through principles—fairness, equity, equal treatment, full security, due process, and access to justice. These principles are ubiquitous in the domestic constitutional legal texture. Hence, state legislative acts rarely breach IIL. More commonly, state breaches happen through particular application of laws, often through administrative acts.

IIL-based protection for foreign investors is normally unavailable to their domestic counterparts. Foreign investors can enforce these privileged rights through a system of investor–state dispute settlement (ISDS) separate from the domestic judiciary. Typically, arbitration can be launched without resorting to local remedies—let alone

[1] For a primer on the international protection of foreign investments see C Schreuer, 'Investments, International Protection' *Max Planck Encyclopaedia of Public International Law* (2011).

[2] F Ortino, *The Origin and Evolution of Investment Treaty Standards: Stability, Value, and Reasonableness* (OUP 2019) 2: '[p]rovisions on transfer of funds (found in almost 100% of the treaties mapped by UNCTAD), MFN treatment (99%), investor–State dispute settlement (ISDS) (98%), expropriation (98%), subrogation (96%), fair and equitable treatment (FET) (95%), and national treatment (NT) (87%)'.

[3] *Gavrilovic v Croatia* ICSID Case No ARB/12/39 Award (26 July 2018) para 432.

Filippo Fontanelli, *Procedural Requirements for Administrative Limits to Property Rights in the International Law on Promotion and Protection of Foreign Investments* In: *Procedural Requirements for Administrative Limits to Property Rights.* Edited by: Martina Conticelli And Thomas Perroud, Oxford University Press. © Filippo Fontanelli 2022.
DOI: 10.1093/oso/9780198867586.003.0014

exhausting them. The domestic lawfulness of state measures cannot prejudge their lawfulness under international law.

I. Is there any constitutional provision or convention concerning land expropriation in the traditional sense (ie the forced transfer of ownership ordered for reasons of general interest) in the cases provided for by the law, and with provisions for compensation? If not, please elaborate.

IIL is constitutionally and historically concerned with expropriation, including expropriation of land. Indeed, contemporary IIL has evolved from customary guarantees against the expropriation of foreigners' property.[4] IIL treaties protect foreigners from acts of states that observe the Calvo doctrine (which defers all disputes to the local courts)[5] or the principles of the New International Economic Order movement of the 1960s and 1970s[6] (including the state's prerogative to nationalise private property, providing partial compensation or none at all).[7]

Virtually all IIL documents require expropriation to be lawful (ie fairly administered, non-discriminatory, serving a public interest, and accompanied by compensation)[8] and prescribe the necessary features of compensation (ie prompt, at full market value, and transferrable).[9] Through arbitration, expropriated individuals can seek compensation as a remedy.

For investors faced with lawful or unlawful expropriation, the end game is comparable: compensation. States might pay it willingly, during a lawful expropriation process, or upon a tribunal's order, as reparation for unlawful conduct.[10] More importantly, what counts as expropriation in the first place is still controversial, especially when the state has effected no formal taking, and so-called regulatory expropriation is alleged.[11]

[4] KJ Vandevelde, 'The Political Economy of a Bilateral Investment Treaty' (1998) 92(3) AJIL 621, 633.

[5] W Shan, 'Is Calvo Dead?' (2007) 55(1) AJCL 123; R Dolzer, 'New Foundations of the Law of Expropriation of Alien Property' (1981) 75(3) AJIL 553; K Lipstein, 'The Place of the Calvo Clause in International Law' (1945) *22* Br Yearb Int Law 130.

[6] V Ogle, 'State Rights against Private Capital: The "New International Economic Order" and the Struggle over Aid, Trade, and Foreign Investment, 1962–1981' (2014) 5(2) Humanity: An International Journal of Human Rights, Humanitarianism, and Development 211.

[7] FV Garcia-Amador, 'The Proposed New International Economic Order: A New Approach to the Law Governing Nationalization and Compensation' [1980] Law Am 1.

[8] 2012 US Model BIT, art 6(1).

[9] ibid art 6(2).

[10] A distinction exists when reparation includes other elements such as future profits and moral damages. Sometimes, to remedy a wrongful act, the state must pay more than the full market value at the time of the expropriation owed in case of lawful expropriation. *ADC Affiliate Limited and ADC & ADMC Management Limited v Hungary* ICSID Case No ARB/03/16 Award (2 October 2006) paras 484 ff; *Tidewater Investment SRL and Tidewater Caribe CA v Venezuela* ICSID Case No ARB/10/5 Award (13 March 2015) paras 135–42.

[11] SR Ratner, 'Compensation for Expropriations in a World of Investment Treaties: Beyond the Lawful/Unlawful Distinction' (2017) 111(1) AJIL 7. See IIL Case 11 below.

II. Is there any constitutional provision or convention concerning limitations to property rights in the broad sense? If not, please elaborate.

Limitations to property rights are the precise focus of IIL instruments. Roughly, IIL protects foreign investors from unfair encroachments on their businesses. Investors are bestowed contingent rights, like the protection against nationality-based discrimination. Furthermore, they enjoy non-contingent rights that local laws cannot diminish: eg the right to full-market compensation for expropriation; fair treatment from state authorities; protection against external threats; and the freedom to transfer currency and proceeds. Recent instruments contain guidelines to distinguish between compensable expropriatory measures and non-compensable measures which only incidentally affect property rights and their enjoyment.[12] Brazil, a newcomer to the IIL game, drafted treaties that go further and only provide protection against direct expropriation.[13]

III. How are competences regarding expropriation distributed among different levels of government (ie in regional, federal, or confederal states)?

IIL governs any act attributable to the state. Under general international law, acts of local and central governments are equally imputable to the state and must therefore comply with its international obligations.[14]

IV. Please include a brief description of the procedure, listing the formal acts necessary for an expropriation. What is the relationship between urban planning procedures and expropriation? When is an environmental impact assessment needed?

IIL does not dictate a procedure for expropriation but sets the conditions for its lawfulness and the compensation's features. Acts different from formal expropriation, including the denial or withdrawal of building permits, might qualify as indirect expropriation or as breaches of fair and equitable treatment (FET).[15] Investors

[12] 2012 US Model BIT, Annex B. The distinction is notoriously difficult, and conceptually slippery. R Higgins, *The Taking of Property by the State: Recent Developments in International Law, Recueil des Cours, Hague Academy in International Law*, vol 176 (Martinus Nijhoff 1982) 259, 331.

[13] Brazil–India BIT (2020, not in force), art 6.3; Brazil–Ecuador BIT (2020, not in force), art 7.5.

[14] *ADF Group Inc v USA* ICSID Case No ARB (AF)/00/1 Award (9 January 2003) para 166; *Grand River Enterprises Six Nations v USA* UNCITRAL Objections to Jurisdiction (20 July 2006) para 1. Conversely, the state (not its subdivisions) is the correct respondent. *Cable Television v St Kitts and Nevis* ICSID Case No ARB/95/2 Award (13 January 1997) para 2.25.

[15] *ECE v Czech Republic* PCA Case No 2010-5 Award (19 September 2013) para 4.764.

must observe local laws, including urban planning rules.[16] Their investments must be made lawfully, and a breach of urban planning regulations can entail the loss of IIL-based protection, or lead tribunals to consider the state measures legitimate rather than expropriatory or unfair. The investor's failure to carry out an environmental impact assessment required by domestic law might determine the investment's illegality or the state measure's lawfulness.[17] Conversely, state authorities might have to follow procedures (eg compulsory onsite surveys), failing which the expropriation is void.[18] State measures encroaching on an investor's assets are tested for fairness, and expropriation measures must evince a public purpose and be capable of promoting it.[19] In the context of environmental measures, therefore, an environmental impact assessment by the state or the evaluation of the investor's assessment can affect the review of the state acts.

V. What are the consequences of a court finding that an expropriation is unlawful on the grounds of substance and/or of process? Is it merely annulled, or are there other consequences, for example the award of damages?

In case of unlawful or indirect expropriation (including through regulatory measures), investors are owed compensation. Depending on the nature of the investment damaged or expropriated, the damages can include either solely investment expenditures and the value of the assets lost, or also future profits. Theoretically, tribunals could order specific performance (for instance, the restitution of the assets);[20] but, in ISDS, reparation is predominantly through monetary compensation.[21]

VI. Is there any difference between expropriation and nationalisation?

In IIL, 'expropriation' and 'nationalisation' are interchangeable. Another conceptual distinction occasionally emerges in connection with indirect expropriation. States often claim that, without the title's formal transferral revealing their confiscatory intention, there is no expropriation.[22] Mostly, tribunals discount the importance of the

[16] *Biloune v Ghana* 95 ILR 183, 207–10; *Metalclad v Mexico* ICSID Case No ARB(AF)/97/1 Award (30 August 2000); *Desert Line v Yemen* ICSID Case No ARB/05/17 Award (6 February 2008); *Mamidoil v Albania* ICSID Case No ARB/11/24 Award (30 March 2015).

[17] *Cortec v Kenya* ICSID Case No ARB/15/29 Award (22 October 2018) paras 385–87; *Blusun v Italy* ICSID Case No ARB/14/3 Award (27 December 2016) para 275; see also Understanding of the ECT Contracting Parties, art 19(1)(i).

[18] *Olin v Libya* ICC Case No 20355/MCP Award (25 May 2018) para 162.

[19] *Metalclad* (n 16) para 106; *Tecmed v Mexico* ICSID Case No ARB (AF)/00/2 Award (29 May 2003) paras 124–32.

[20] *Al-Bahloul v Tajikistan* SCC Case No V064/2008 Award (8 June 2010) para 47.

[21] Tribunals cannot order a respondent to change its laws or withdraw its acts; compensation is the remedy of choice. See *RWE v Spain* ICSID Case No ARB/14/34 Jurisdiction, Liability and Certain Issues of Quantum (30 December 2019) paras 681, 685.

[22] *SPP v Egypt* ICSID Case No ARB/84/3 Award (20 May 1992) para 163.

state's intention, and regard the measure's impact and design as most (but not exclusively) decisive.[23] Conversely, not all measures affecting foreign investments' value are expropriatory. The difficulty lies in demarcating execution of legitimate general policies (with incidental effects on investors' profits and assets) from illicit interferences (requiring states to make the investors whole).

VII. Notes on the Questionnaire

For ease of analysis, all scenarios are assumed to fall under IIL's reach. Specifically, all dispossessed individuals are foreign investors (*ratione personae*) and all affected assets are investments or pertain to one (*ratione materiae*). *Ratione temporis*, IIL applied when the state acted.

A word about remedies. Under general international law, states can expropriate, and IIL subjects this right to procedural requirements and compensation. Likewise, states can regulate, subject to the IIL's obligation of behaving equitably.

Investment tribunals cannot annul domestic acts,[24] but they can find them incompatible with IIL. Litigating investors almost invariably seek monetary damages, not the measures' annulment or *restitutio in integrum* (for instance, the restitution of a licence withdrawn). If tribunals requested states to take specific actions, they would encroach on their sovereign regulatory powers; in any event, if states refused to comply, the order would be unenforceable.[25]

ISDS differs from domestic judicial review of administrative acts in another respect. International tribunals do not review *de novo* administrative decisions. They can examine state measures' rationale, design, procedural record, and impact, but only to assess their compliance with standards of procedural and substantive fairness. A tribunal reviewing the decision to foreclose mining projects in an area of cultural and historical importance for indigenous tribes noted: '[I]t is simply not this Tribunal's task to become archaeologists and ethnographers and to draw a definitive conclusion as to the location of the Trail of Dreams.'[26] Tribunals 'need not be satisfied that they would have made precisely the same decision as the regulator in order for them to uphold such decision.'[27]

Therefore, arbitrators typically afford a 'high level of deference'[28] to domestic authorities' decisions.

[23] *Armas v Venezuela* PCA Case No 2013-03/AA473 Award (26 April 2019) paras 279–81; *Glamis Gold v USA* (NAFTA, UNCITRAL) Award (8 June 2009) para 355.
[24] *LG&E v Argentina* ICSID Case No ARB/02/1 Award (25 July 2007) para 87.
[25] *Arif v Moldova* ICSID Case No ARB/11/23 Award (8 April 2013) para 571.
[26] *Glamis Gold v USA* (n 23) para 779.
[27] *Invesmart v Czech Republic* (UNCITRAL, ad hoc) Award (26 June 2009) para 501.
[28] *SD Myers v Canada* (UNCITRAL, NAFTA) Partial Award (13 November 2000) para 261.

PART III
CASES

15
Cases

Martina Conticelli and Thomas Perroud

I. Questionnaire

A. Case 1: The requirement to state reasons in expropriations

Mr Banks is the owner of a piece of land located next to an area where public works are to be carried out. The competent authorities notify Mr Banks of the decision to expropriate his property without providing any reason for seizing his land rather than the neighbouring properties. Mr Banks challenges the legitimacy of the expropriation on the grounds that, following careful examination by the competent authorities, any finding/relevant factor taken into account in the selection of Mr Banks' property should be provided in the statement of reasons.

Would the court endorse Mr Banks' reasoning? If so, would the court annul the disputed decision?

B. Case 2: An expropriation without notice

Mr Burns is the owner of a residential area chosen as the site for a medical facility in Springfield. Initially, the competent authority proposes to purchase Mr Burns' property. After extensive negotiations to reach an agreement and following Mr Burns' refusal to sell, the authority expropriates the area without formally notifying him of its intentions. Mr Burns then challenges the expropriation, alleging that due process requirements were not respected since he received no formal notice of the

Martina Conticelli and Thomas Perroud, *Cases* In: *Procedural Requirements for Administrative Limits to Property Rights*. Edited by: Martina Conticelli And Thomas Perroud, Oxford University Press. © Martina Conticelli and Thomas Perroud 2022.
DOI: 10.1093/oso/9780198867586.003.0015

expropriation and, consequently, was given no opportunity to be heard during the procedure.

Would Mr Burns be successful? If so, would the court annul the disputed decision?

C. Case 3: Participation and due process in urban planning

Mrs Sheraton obtained a permit to build a new hotel under the current urban plan in a tourist area located near the city of Belleville. One year later, the local authorities amend the urban plan, altering the use of the area in question and modifying its designation from commercial to residential. Mrs Sheraton challenges the revised urban plan in court, arguing that no information was given regarding the start of the procedure of amendment.

Would the court uphold the view that participatory requirements should be respected in amending urban planning acts? In the affirmative, what would the consequences of failing to do so be?

D. Case 4: Due process in urgent requisitions

Following violent occupation by workers in the course of a strike, a local authority commands the immediate, although temporary, requisition of a hydroelectric power plant for serious reasons of public order.

The company management challenges the order before the competent court on the grounds that its assets have been adversely affected and unduly restricted by the measures adopted by the local authority in the absence of any formal notice before the requisition.

Would the Court give weight to the 'grave public necessity' argument in considering a possible restriction to due process requirements; that is, the absence of prior notice? Or would the court emphasise the restriction of the company's rights? If the court were to endorse the applicant's claims and annul the contested measure, would the affected company be entitled to damages?

E. Case 5: A constructive expropriation

The city of Metropolis orders the occupation of private lands, including a part of Miss Busy's property, to carry out urgent public works for the renovation and maintenance of a highway.

After three years of occupation of the land, the works are not carried out and the land is not used, but the owner is still prevented from using her land.

Would Miss Busy have any means of getting her property back? Could the failure to comply with the works schedule constitute grounds for the annulment of the order restricting property rights? Could such a failure also be grounds for damages?

F. Case 6: The public interest of a private hospital

Miss Nightingale is given notice that her property has been selected for the construction of a new private hospital.

However, the notice does not include any mention of the public interest of this project.

Can Miss Nightingale challenge the decision and, if so, how? Would the competent authority annul the disputed decision?

G. Case 7: Local pressure against a nudist beach

Mr Baywatch has a licence to run the sun umbrella and chair services on Paradise beach. Following Mr Baywatch's decision to set aside a part of the beach for nudists, which met with disapproval from the local population, the competent authority withdraws Mr Baywatch's licence. Formally, the authority withdraws on the ground of an alleged breach of the terms of the licence by Mr Baywatch, stating that he wrongfully left the beach unattended. Substantially, the decision can be regarded as being a response to local opposition to nudism.

Would Mr Baywatch be able to challenge the authority's decision on the grounds of an inaccurate representation of the facts? Would the court be willing to annul the disputed decision?

H. Case 8: Cultural heritage

Miss Lucky has a charming mansion in Gotham, where she keeps a small art collection. One day, she discovers that, unbeknownst to her, her collection comprises a genuine portrait of Batman painted by the Joker. While she is preparing to sell it at a foreign auction, the public authorities declare the portrait to be part of the cultural heritage of Gotham.

What will the consequences of this declaration be? Might Miss Lucky be entitled to compensation in the event of a restriction of her property rights? Could she challenge the decision? If so, would the competent court be willing to annul the disputed decision?

I. Case 9: Acoustic pollution: exceeding the sound limits

Mrs Owner owns and lives in a property close to the site chosen for the construction of an airport and connecting railway system.

Although the impact assessment carried out before construction did not indicate any problems in the area where Mrs Owner's land is located, once the airport is fully operational, Mrs Owner is disturbed by permanent noise. Noise abatement procedures laid down by the competent authority prove insufficient, and the property no longer appears to be suitable for habitation.

Is Mrs Owner entitled to challenge the impact assessment? Could Mrs Owner ask for and obtain expropriation? If the answer is negative, could she lodge a claim for compensation or seek another remedy?

J. Case 10: A new urban planning act

Belleville City council enacts its new urban planning act, according to which Miss Busy's property is chosen for public use, namely for the construction of a bus station.

The competent authorities then expropriate Miss Busy's land and begin working on the area. After one year, the urban planning act is quashed, but the public works go on.

Miss Busy challenges the expropriation on the grounds that it is no longer justified by the planning act.

Would Miss Busy be entitled to challenge the expropriation on these grounds? What remedy would be available to Miss Busy, considering that she has been deprived of her property and that the works for the bus station have already started?

K. Case 11: Regulatory taking

Mr Mad Hatter bought fifty acres of land near the Belle Coast in order to create a tourist resort. He complied with the building regulations and conserved the natural zones. One year after opening, the competent authorities decide that the Belle Coast is an area of exceptional natural value and proceed to regulate public access, considerably restricting entry to the zone and the activities authorised therein.

What remedies are available to Mr Mad Hatter in this scenario? Could he seek annulment of the disputed decision and/or ask for damages? Would the result be different if Mr Mad Hatter were a foreign investor?

II. Case 1: The Requirement to State Reasons in Expropriations

A. Belgium

David Renders, Luca Ceci, Caroline Delforge, and Kevin Polet

In the situation described, Mr Banks is the owner of a piece of land located near a site where public works are to be carried out. The competent authority wishes to expropriate it. The expropriation decision—which, under Belgian law (as indicated in the chapter by D Renders, L Ceci, C Delforge, K Polet, 'Procedural Requirements for Administrative Limits to Property Rights in Belgium', in this volume) does not yet cause the transfer of ownership—of which Mr Banks received notification does not, in his view, mention the elements justifying the choice of his land rather than another.

The Belgian courts, when seized with an action against an expropriation decision, may have to address both substantive and formal defects.

- With regard to *substantive defects*, it should be recalled that under Belgian law, any expropriation—regardless of the competent authority—must be based on a public purpose.[1]

However, when the decision to expropriate is challenged on the grounds that there is, allegedly, no public purpose, the prerogative of the Belgian courts is limited to a review of legality, regardless of any review of appropriateness.[2] This implies that the court cannot substitute its own assessment of the public purpose for that formulated by the authority issuing the decision to expropriate, which has discretionary power of appreciation. Only manifest errors in the assessment may therefore be sanctioned.[3]

The question of whether the court seized of an action may examine the choice of the parcel expropriated by the competent authority falls within this context. The Belgian courts may censor the choice of the expropriated parcel of land only when this choice constitutes a manifest error of assessment.[4]

In practice, a decision on whether the authority has committed a manifest error of assessment in the choice of the expropriated parcel of land involves a case-by-case examination of each case.

To cite an example, it has already been ruled that:

> the mere fact that a storm basin may be built in any other location or positioned differently is not in itself likely to jeopardise the public purpose, as long as the expropriated

[1] Belgian Constitution, art 16.

[2] O Wéry, 'L'expropriation pour cause d'utilité publique: chronique de jurisprudence (2000-2014): Première partie' [2014] Journal des Tribunaux 773, 779.

[3] ibid.

[4] ibid; M Pâques, L Donnay, and C Vercheval, 'La cause d'utilité publique' in D Renders (ed), *L'expropriation pour cause d'utilité publique* (Bruylant 2013) 227–45, in particular 238–42.

> persons do not prove that there is a disproportion between the intended expropriation and the purpose pursued.[5]

A decision relying on a manifest error of assessment is unlawful.

- With regard to *formal defects*, it must be emphasised that the decision to expropriate constitutes a unilateral administrative act of individual scope subject to an obligation of formal motivation.[6] This means that the act must state the legal and factual grounds on which it is based. The statement of the reasons on which the act is founded must be adequate.

On this matter, the Belgian Court of Cassation has ruled that:

> [i]n the field of expropriations, the motivation must indicate why the expropriation is necessary, which implies that the motivation must be based on real facts, that a reasonable relationship between the planned expropriation and the intended purpose must be deduced from it and that, depending on the case, it must be clear that the political options chosen have been evaluated.[7]

The reasons given for the decision to expropriate does not necessarily have to be long, however.[8] There is also no obligation for the authority to specify the reasons for its motivation.

Failure to comply with the obligation to state the formal reasons for the act renders the decision to expropriate unlawful.

In this case, Mr Banks believes that the decision to expropriate is unlawful because it should mention all the elements justifying the choice of his land rather than another person's land.

Since all the legal and factual reasons underlying the decision to expropriate must, in principle, be mentioned, the decision should therefore be considered unlawful.

On the contrary, unless it can be shown that the authority committed a manifest error of appreciation, which cannot be ascertained from the wording of the case, the decision to expropriate should not be censured on the sole ground that other parcels of land could have been expropriated.

B. France

Emma Guernaoui

Mr Banks argues that the administration's decision to expropriate his property is illegal because it was not motivated. The litigation therefore focuses on the failure to

[5] Civil court of Arlon (28 November 2006) RG No 06/123/A, cited by Wéry (n 2) 779 (free translation).

[6] Act 'on the formal motivation reasoning of administrative acts' (29 July 1991; publication in the Belgian Official Gazette on 12 September 1991). In scholarship see Wéry, 'L'expropriation pour cause d'utilité publique' (n 2) 775; D Renders, S Ben Messaoud, and S Ganty, 'Les acteurs de l'expropriation' in Renders (ed) (n 4) 205–208, in particular 124–27.

[7] Court of Cassation (1st Chamber) (3 February 2000) *Aménagement-Environnement* (2001) 324. From the same perspective see Court of Cassation (11 September 2003) *Pasicrisie* (2003) 1380.

[8] Wéry (n 2) 777.

state reasons for the expropriation decision, known as a 'declaration of public utility' in French law.

It is therefore necessary to analyse the nature of these declarations in order to determine whether they are subject to an obligation to state reasons. These declarations of public utility (governed by Articles L121-1 to L122-7 of the Expropriation Code) are decrees 'of a non-regulatory nature and not creating rights' following the constant jurisprudence of the *Conseil d'État*, which holds that they are 'specific decisions'.[9] This means that these declarations are not subject to the law of 11 July 1979 on giving reasons for administrative acts. It is consequently not a defect in the form of the declaration if no reasons are given.

Mr Banks could base his request on Article L1221-2 of the Expropriation Code, mentioning: 'The act declaring the operation to be in the public interest is accompanied by a document setting out the reasons and considerations justifying its public interest.'

Unfortunately for the petitioner, the analysis of case law testifies to an extremely narrow interpretation of this provision. The reasons could not be considered as a condition of the external legality of the declaration of public utility. The *Conseil d'État* has thus ruled that:

> The act declaring the public interest is accompanied by a document setting out the reasons and considerations justifying the public interest nature of the operation; that these provisions, which require that the author of the act, once his decision has been taken, provide the public with additional information explaining the reasons and considerations on which it is based, cannot be interpreted as imposing an additional obligation concerning the form of this act; that, consequently, the absence of a visa for such an information document, intended for the public, has no influence on the legality of the contested decree.[10]

This leads the scholarship to consider that 'the legal consequences attached to the insufficiency or absence of such a document are more than reduced'.[11]

Consequently, the lack of reasons for the declaration of public utility cannot be a valid reason for the administrative courts to overturn this specific decision.

The petitioner should instead challenge reasons of the public inquiry prior to the declaration of public utility, which is a preliminary stage in which he or she must normally participate. It is defined in these terms:

> The purpose of the public inquiry is to ensure public information and participation, as well as the consideration of the interests of third parties during the preparation of the decisions likely to affect the environment mentioned in article L 123-2. The observations and proposals received during the investigation period are taken

[9] CE, Decision of 29 April 1994, Association Unimate, Nos 112910 and 115044. *AJDA* 1994, 400 and 367, chron C Maugüé and L Touvet.

[10] CE, Decision of 15 November 2006, Société Placoplâtre et Commune de Vandières, Nos 285658, 285799, and 291022, Rec, Tables 908.

[11] J Betaille, 'The Contribution of Law to the Effects of Public Participation: Taking into Account the Results of Participation' (2010) 2 Revue Juridique de l'Environnement 197.

into consideration by the project owner and by the authority competent to take the decision.[12]

The absence of a justification for the operations carried out constitutes a reason for the irregularity of the investigation. Thus, Mr Banks should consider challenging the legality of this preliminary phase if he has not been questioned or even informed of an explanatory notice of the operations being undertaken. Therefore, the absence of an impact study will lead to the cancellation of the declaration of public utility.[13]

C. Germany

Foroud Shirvani

The expropriation of Mr Banks' property must be substantively and procedurally lawful. As a written administrative act, the decision of the expropriation authority must be reasoned.[14] The duty to state the reasons for administrative acts follows from the rule of law.[15] The administrative act must contain all essential factual and legal reasons which led the authority to its decision.[16] If the reason is missing, the administrative act has a procedural error and is formally unlawful.

How detailed the reasoning must be depends on numerous factors, such as the level of knowledge of those affected or the number of individual problems to be resolved. In this respect, the authority must present the factual and legal situation in a way that enables the person concerned to verify the correctness of the factual basis and the legal conclusions.[17] If a fundamental right is affected, as is the case here with regard to the fundamental right to property under Article 14 GG, the requirements for the content and scope of the reasoning increase.[18]

If the authority has not sufficiently complied with its obligation to state reasons, the expropriation measure is unlawful and must be annulled by the court. In particular, Mr Banks was not informed why his property, and not his neighbour's property, was to be expropriated. This could constitute a lack of reasoning according to the criteria mentioned. However, it is possible to remedy the error by providing for a statement of the reasoning.[19] The lack of reasoning can be remedied in court up to the last instance of fact.[20] If the error is remedied, the court will dismiss the action.

[12] Expropriation Code, art L 123-1.

[13] CE, Decision of 16 April 1982, Ministre de l'Industrie C/Commune d'Aubagne, Rec T 684.

[14] VwVfG, § 39 sec 1 sentence 1.

[15] P Tiedemann, '§ 39' in J Bader and M Ronellenfitsch (eds), *BeckOK VwVfG* (50th edn, CH Beck 2021) para 2.

[16] VwVfG, § 39 sec 1 sentence 2.

[17] VGH Kassel, NVwZ-RR 2006, 776 (779).

[18] Tiedemann (n 15) para 26.

[19] VwVfG, § 45 sec 1 No 2, sec 2; U Battis, '§ 113' in U Battis, M Krautzberger, and R-P Löhr, *Baugesetzbuch: Kommentar* (14th edn, CH Beck 2019) para 2.

[20] VwVfG, § 45 sec 2.

D. Italy

Silvia Mirate

The case concerns the relationship between the expropriation procedure and the use of administrative discretion by the public administration.

The expropriation has to be based on a motivated public interest that needs to be indicated by the expropriating authority within the declaration of public utility. Therefore, the answer to the case involves a brief analysis of Italian case law concerning the use of discretionary power in expropriation decisions and the related need of a specific or more general motivation.

The expropriation procedure, starting from the issuance of the pre-established constraint for expropriation, which is the result of the evaluation of the need of territorial planning by the competent authority and the declaration of public utility that expressly states the general interest in the execution of the public work or public intervention involves a high level of discretion exercised by the public administration.

As administrative case law has repeatedly highlighted, in the expropriation for public utility the identification of the area where a public work is to be located constitutes a technical-discretionary choice of the administration, which cannot be subject to judicial review, except for obvious profiles of irrationality or abnormality.[21]

In the Italian judicial system, a dispute concerning an expropriation order itself (for example, for incompetence or for lack of motivation in the deed) and any consequential claim for damages comes under the administrative jurisdiction, while any judgments regarding only the adequacy of the compensation awarded falls within the jurisdiction of the ordinary judge.

The administrative judge can review the lawfulness of the expropriation decree (and of the expropriation procedure that led to the issue of this order), but cannot verify the merit of the administrative decision. The administrative decision to expropriate involves both a discretionary power and an evaluation of merit. While the exercise of the discretionary power has to be based on its compliance with the legal requirements, the evaluation of merit relates to the appropriateness and benefit of a particular choice; it is not a legal choice and therefore is totally exempt from judicial review.

The administrative courts have often stated that administrations are granted extensive discretion in territorial planning, and that expropriation is based on city-planning choices which are evaluations of merit and not subject to judicial review, except in cases where they are affected by factual errors, procedural violations, abnormal irrationality, or are in conflict with particular situations that have given rise to qualified expectations.[22] Therefore, urban-planning choices do not have to be supported by a specific motivation that considers the aspirations of the private owners unless these subjects have legitimate expectations arising from particular situations, such as

[21] See eg TAR Toscana, Sec I (2 January 2018) No 9.

[22] See TAR Lombardia Milano, Sec IV (28 May 2018) No 1344; TAR Lombardia, Brescia, Sec I (30 March 2020) No 252.

pre-existing private agreements with the expropriating administration.[23] The declaration of public utility does not need a specific motivation either, as it is a consequence of the approval of the final project implementing the planning choice.[24]

Applying these solutions to this case, it is important to note that the public administration has a wide discretion in choosing whether to expropriate Mr Banks' property instead of his neighbour's. Moreover it is a choice that does not contain only a technical discretion, but also an evaluation of merit, not subject to the control of the administrative judge. Providing reasons for the necessity to use Mr Banks' land instead of neighbouring properties is not an obligation for the public administration. A specific motivation on the choice of that particular area is not necessary. The burden of motivation that has to be fulfilled by the administration when planning the territory may be fulfilled by indicating the general criteria underlying the choices made, and not by specifying a particular reason such as the selection of one parcel of private land instead of another. The only exceptions are related to the existence of a special legitimate expectation that the private owner might have, for example, on the basis of a previous urban-planning agreement (but this is not the case in Mr Banks' situation).

The administrative decision on the planning choice can be reviewed by the administrative court only in the event of factual errors, procedural violations or abnormal irrationality, but it does not seem that Mr Banks' challenge involves any of these. So the court cannot endorse Mr Banks' reasoning and cannot annul the expropriation decision only on the basis of the lack of reasons for the selection of the private property.

E. The Netherlands

Jacques Sluysmans and Nikky van Triet

Under Dutch law an expropriation as indicated above would have to be based on Article 11.6 Environment and Planning Act, that is, an expropriation aimed at the development of an environment plan. Therefore, the actual expropriation should be preceded by an irrevocable environment plan designating the land for, in this example, public works. The discussion as to whether the envisaged public works ought to be carried out on a neighbouring plot instead of on the property of Mr Banks is a discussion that would have to be held in the environment plan procedure. It thus falls outside of the competence of the court in an expropriation case to rule on this issue.

F. Poland

Inga Kawka and Łukasz Kozera

In the Polish legal order, expropriation of immovable property may be carried out when public purposes cannot be pursued in a way other than a removal or a limitation of rights to immovable property and such rights cannot be acquired by means

[23] See eg TAR Puglia, Lecce, Sec III (6 July 2018) No 1109.
[24] Cons Stato, Sec IV (25 September 2014) No 4824.

of a civil law agreement.[25] This view is supported by both Article 21(2) of the Polish Constitution and Article 112(3) of the IPMA. These regulations provide for the principle of expropriation subsidiarity and recommend prioritisation of mildest forms of administrative interference. Administrative law solutions should be resorted to only after attempts at concluding relevant civil law agreements. In the legal circumstances at hand, no such attempt has taken place: the authorities did not declare their intention to purchase the land, nor did they propose any negotiations; further, no appropriate expropriation proceedings were launched preceded by relevant notices. Thus, formal flaws occurred in the case, which later resulted in procedural ones: no administrative hearing was held; Mr Banks and persons who might have enjoyed rights in rem to the land were deprived of their right of defence; the compensation amount was not set, nor a method of its calculation.

However, the gravest procedural flaw is a breach of Article 107 of the CAP, which provides that the decision should include a factual and legal justification from which it should transpire why Mr Banks' property should be subject to expropriation. In it, the authorities should have provided a detailed description of the facts and evidence on which they based their decision, as well as reasons why other facts and circumstances were deemed irrelevant. Moreover, Article 107 of the CAP spells out that *lex specialis* regulations can extend the scope of the justification due, just like in the case of expropriation decisions issued pursuant to Article 119 of the IPMA, which should include, inter alia, a precise indication of the purpose for which the immovable property is expropriated. The very object of the expropriation must be related to that purpose and indicated precisely by means of invoking the property number(s) in the court-kept land and mortgage register, as well as other cadastral data. The decision served on Mr Banks clearly lacks a so-formulated statement of reasons.

Here, a vital aspect should be mentioned related to the lots adjacent to the land being expropriated. This is that, the legislator has provided special protection for the neighbours in cases of an existing risk of losses or any inconveniences that may occur as a result of expropriation or land development different that current at a later date. In such cases, the expropriation decision includes the establishment of necessary easement on them as well as the obligation to construct and maintain appropriate facilities preventing such events or circumstances. The obligation to construct and maintain appropriate facilities is incumbent on the party applying for expropriation, in practice the state treasury or a local government unit.[26]

Returning to the conclusion of Mr Banks' case, it should be noted that a major breach of material law has taken place, as well as a blatant violation of procedural law, which result in absolute reasons for appeal and must lead to the ascertainment of the invalidity of the decision issued by an appellate body or an administrative court. In the case discussed here, one could also contemplate an application for the resumption of

[25] A Łukaszewska, 'Artykuł 112' in J Szałuchowicz, M Krassowska and A Łukaszewska (eds), *Gospodarka nieruchomościami: Komentarz* (LexisNexis 2003) 314; M Horoszko and D Pęchorzewski, *Gospodarka nieruchomościami: Komentarz* (CH Beck 2010) 326–27; T Woś, *Wywłaszczanie nieruchomości i ich zwrot* (LexisNexis 2011) 25–45.

[26] More extensively on other legal limitations of using immovable property: IPMA, art 124.

the decision issued as it might have been a result of an obvious blunder on the part of the administrative body.

G. Portugal

Rui Guerra da Fonseca

The location of the land—'*beside an area*'—suggests Mr Banks might have been inconvenienced only with the temporary occupation of his property by machinery and other supporting uses serving the public works that were being carried out. When these ended so would the occupation of Mr Banks' land. This possibility is contemplated in the Portuguese Code of Expropriations (CE) (Article 18)[27] as a possible effect of the 'public utility declaration' [dup]. In this case, the expropriation would be disproportionate and without cause.[28]

In any case, the 'public utility declaration', being an administrative act, must expressly give reasons and grounds regarding why and what the land is for (Article 13/1 of the CE, and Article 152 of the Administrative Procedure Code (CPA). This is actually a constitutional right vis-à-vis all administrative acts (Article 268/3 of the Portuguese Constitution).

The reasons given in the dup must clearly identify the general interest that justifies the taking of the property (reasons of fact and grounds of law: Article 153/1 of the CPA). This reasoning does not have to explain in principle why other pieces of land are not needed. But the situation might be exceptionally awkward: for instance, if in regular circumstances such an expropriation would affect other pieces of land, then an explanation must be given for the abnormality of taking only Mr Banks' property. This would be the only way for Mr Banks to be able to discuss equality issues in this case.

Mr Banks could challenge the legality of the expropriation in terms of substance (disproportionality considering that a mere temporary occupation would suffice) but also considering the violation of legal rules about the completion, transparency and non-contradiction of the reasons given for the dup. These are two different aspects of legality in terms of administrative law and process.

Focusing on the latter, it is plausible that an administrative court would endorse Mr Banks' view and, consequently annul the decision (dup). In fact, according to our Administrative Supreme Court, in an expropriation procedure (and also in general terms) giving reasons means describing the reasons which determined the decision, clarifying for the recipient the motives that were determined. Some perspectives actually consider that the decision should be declared null (never having been effective) on the basis that giving reasons is a fundamental right and the declaration of nullity is the (stronger and) correct consequence (Article 161/2 al d) of the CPA).

[27] And also in the Code of Public Procurement for public works (art 351).

[28] See Decision of Supreme Administrative Court, Pr 01089/04.9BESNT 0600/18 (27 November 2019). Also, Decision of Supreme Administrative Court, Pr 045899 (29 November 2006): if there is free area in a certain piece of land to build accessibly price housing for social purposes, the expropriation of a part of the land in which there are inhabited buildings violates the principle of proportionality.

However, it has to be taken into account that the procedure of expropriation is complex, beginning with a decision to expropriate which must itself contain reasons of general interest justifying the expropriation and the identification of lands and owners (Article 10 of the CE). This is to say that the dup may refer to other procedural documents when giving reasons, namely documents that the owners already have knowledge of.

In short, Mr Banks has the right to be given reasons for the expropriation and the lack of these might determine the illegality of the former; but the decision (dup) has to be considered, for this purpose, in the context of the procedure.

H. Spain

Luis Arroyo Jiménez and Dolores Utrilla Fernández-Bermejo

The court most likely would uphold Mr Banks' claim and invalidate (annul) the declaration of the need to expropriate, which is the single-case administrative decision determining the rights or assets to be expropriated (Article 15 LEF). This administrative decision is challengeable in court. This clarification is far from trivial, since the original version of the 1954 LEF (passed during the Franco regime) did not subject such decision to appeal pursuant to Articles 22(3) and 126(1). Nevertheless, this rule precluding the judicial appeal must be deemed repealed by the 1978 Constitution, which provides for the right to an effective judicial protection in Article 24(1). This fundamental right prevents any kind of administrative action from escaping judicial review.[29]

The duty to give reasons as to the choice of the rights or assets to be expropriated is not specifically laid down in the LEF. However, it stems from the general duty to give reasons, ie the duty to state the grounds or reasoning for a decision, applicable to any administrative acts restricting individual rights or interests (Article 35(1) LPAC). These reasons can be stated in the actual administrative decision or otherwise be included in duly referred reports, legal opinions, or technical documents within the administrative file (Article 88(6) LPAC). The explanation of the grounds that justify the relevant administrative action is necessary in order for the courts to review public authorities' activity, as well as for the party concerned to be able to submit any relevant claims, comments, or evidence.[30]

As for the declaration of the need to expropriate, the assets to be addressed by the reasoning can be inferred from Article 15 LEF, which is worded as follows: '[the expropriated rights or assets] should only be those strictly necessary to fulfil the purposes of the expropriation' and, if appropriate, those 'essential for expected extensions of the works or the further advancement of any other purpose to be fulfilled'. The case law does not require a comprehensive line of reasoning; it suffices sufficiently and aptly to set out the reasons leading to the projected administrative decision.[31] The scope of

[29] STS of 8 April 1992 (RJ 2632); of 9 March 1993 (RJ 1672), and of 30 September 1996 (RJ 5134).

[30] STS of 12 April 2012 (Rec 5651/2009).

[31] STS of 31 May 2012 (Rec 621/2011), of 28 June 2010 (Rec 3821/2006), of 9 July 2010 (Rec 1/2008), and of 8 October 2010 (Rec 5/2008).

the statement of reasons will depend on the complexity of the selection of the rights or assets to be expropriated. It could be a brief overview, without any detailed considerations, if the choice of seized property is simple. However, it will have to include a more in-depth explanation if so required by the circumstances of the case.[32] In any event, the expropriation of Mr Banks' property without providing any grounds for taking his land instead of the neighbouring properties certainly breaches the duty to give reasons.

A declaration of the need to expropriate giving insufficient reasons or none at all as to why the rights or assets were eligible for expropriation could be invalidated (annulled) by a court of justice. Nevertheless, it is worth differentiating between three types of flaws or defects in administrative acts under Spanish law. First, an act can be rendered null and void (*nulidad absoluta*) if it is seriously flawed; full invalidation is left for the most serious defects, which are expressly laid down by the law. There is no way to remedy this invalidity, and it can be declared at any time. A declaration of the need to expropriate giving no—or insufficient—reasons does not qualify as a defect giving rise to full invalidation (Article 48 LPAC). Secondly, administrative acts can also qualify as 'voidable' (*anulabilidad*), which is the type of illegality provided for by default. These defects can be remedied by the lapse of time or otherwise if the flaws are rectified (Article 48(1) LPAC). Generally, lack or insufficient reasons of the declaration of the need to expropriate will render it voidable. The third category of defects is that of formal or procedural flaws not leading to invalidity as long as they do not render the party concerned defenceless—ie deprived of legal protection[33]—for instance, because the party otherwise gained knowledge of the reasons underlying the public authority's expropriation decision. In sum, Mr Banks' claim for annulment could be upheld if he demonstrates that the lack of reasons actually undermined his chances of defending his ownership rights; for instance, by precluding him from learning the reasons why the expropriating authority considered his property the best suited to fulfil the public purpose at hand than the neighbouring properties.

I. Sweden

Patricia Jonason

Nothing in the law explicitly requires that the decision of expropriation as such has to provide reasons why one property has to be expropriated rather than other properties. However, Mr Banks could borrow arguments from Section 12, Chapter 2 of the Expropriation Act according to which 'Expropriation permits shall not be granted, if the purpose should be suitably satisfied otherwise'. The preparatory works mention that when the property concerned by the application for expropriation is not the only one that is adequate with regard to the purpose of the expropriation the 'guiding principle should be that the alternative that causes the least damage should be chosen'.[34] The preparatory works also say that 'the applicant does not need to show that it is

[32] STC 37/198.
[33] STS of 4 April 2012 (Rec 3406/2010).
[34] Prop 1972:109, 218 (Preparatory work).

excluded to move the plant to another location but only that specific reasons speak for the alternative selected'.[35] However, giving the fact that: 'It may only be in purely exceptional cases that the intentions of the municipality are questioned',[36] it does not seem likely that Mr Banks' complaint will be successful.

If the court finds that Section 12, Chapter 12 of the Expropriation Act has been infringed, then the court would quash and probably remand the decision.

J. Ukraine

Halyna Dovhan

The court would annul the challenged decision due to the legislative requirement for reasoning in cases of decisions on expropriation.

In Ukraine, the forced alienation of land plots involves two obligatory stages: pre-trial and at trial. The decision on redemption should be taken prior to forced alienation per se, (Articles 7 and 15 of the Law of Ukraine 'On alienation').[37] If the owner disagrees with it, this enables executive authorities or local self-government bodies to file a suit before an administrative court requesting forced alienation (Articles 1 and 15 of the Law of Ukraine 'On alienation').

The decision on redemption should contain reasons, taking into account that redemption and subsequent forced alienation are possible only on the grounds of public needs or public necessity. Therefore, these grounds should be laid down and clarified in the primary decision taken by executive authorities or local self-government bodies. The law states that use of the alienated land plot is admissible only for the purposes for which it was forcibly alienated, so the accent is on the targeted usage (Articles 4(5) and 18(3) of the Law of Ukraine 'On alienation').

The Law of Ukraine 'On alienation' provides that a claim to forced alienation of a land plot will be admissible if a plaintiff proves that the construction, capital renovation, and reconstruction of assets that are planned to be placed on the land plot in question are impossible without the termination of the property right over the land plot (Article 16 (2) of the Law of Ukraine 'On alienation'). One of the principles of the forced alienation of land plots is that it can be carried out if the placement of such assets on another land plot will directly cause a substantial financial loss or will inflict negative ecological consequences on a given territorial community, society, or state (Article 4 of the Law of Ukraine 'On alienation'). Hence, the reason for the choice of the land plot in question should be clearly explained in the decision.

In administrative cases on the unlawfulness of decisions, actions, or the inactivity of the competent authorities, the burden of proof of the lawfulness of their decision, action, or the inactivity is on the respondent (Article 77(2) of the Code of Administrative

[35] ibid.

[36] ibid.

[37] Law of Ukraine 'On the alienation of land plots, other Real Property Assets located on them which are private property for the public needs or on the grounds of public necessity' (17 November 2009) https://zakon.rada.gov.ua/laws/show/1559-17 (accessed 5 May 2021).

Proceedings of Ukraine).[38] Thus, the competent authority should provide reasons for taking Mr Banks' land in particular rather than the neighbouring properties during the court examination.

As stated in the Resolution of the Supreme Court of Ukraine of 5 March 2020, reasonableness is an obligatory element in a decision (action, inactivity) by the competent authority and should be ascertained by the administrative court.[39] Case law shows that courts annul decisions on redemption or do not endorse claims for forced alienation if there is a lack of reasonableness. As a rule, besides national legislation, the case law of the European Court of Human Rights (ECtHR) is used to substantiate such cases. According to the Code of Administrative Proceedings of Ukraine, administrative courts apply the principle of the rule of law, taking into consideration the case law of the ECtHR (Article 6(2)). For example, in the Resolution of the Supreme Court of 13 February 2019 and in the Decision of the First Appellate Administrative Court of 4 November 2019, the *Tregubenko v Ukraine* case was cited.[40] As noted in *Tregubenko v Ukraine*:

> [a]ny interference with property must also satisfy the requirement of proportionality. As the Court has repeatedly stated, a 'fair balance' must be struck between the demands of the general interest of the community and the requirements of the protection of the individual's fundamental rights, the search for such a fair balance being inherent throughout the Convention. The Court further observes that the requisite balance will not be struck where the person concerned bears an 'individual and excessive burden' (§ 53).[41]

While applying Article 1 to Protocol No 1 to the European Convention on Human Rights, both courts used the three elements proportionality test.

K. The United Kingdom

Emma Waring

Mr Banks seeks to challenge the legitimacy of the expropriation on the grounds that inadequate reasons have been provided for the decision to purchase his land compulsorily. The Secretary of State is obliged by the Inquiries Procedure Rules to provide notification of his decision and the reasons for the decision in writing.[42] The House of Lords considered the adequacy of reasons (in a planning, rather than a compulsory

[38] Code of Administrative Proceedings of Ukraine (6 July 2005) https://zakon.rada.gov.ua/laws/show/2747-15 (accessed 5 May 2021).

[39] Resolution of the Supreme Court of Ukraine of 5 March 2020 in the case No 640/467/19 https://reyestr.court.gov.ua/Review/88062082 (accessed 5 May 2021).

[40] Resolution of the Supreme Court of Ukraine of 13 February 2019 in the case No 874/4/17 https://reyestr.court.gov.ua/Review/79791148 (accessed 5 May 2021); Decision of the First Administrative Appellate Court of 4 November 2019 in the case No 850/8/19 https://reyestr.court.gov.ua/Review/85423801 (accessed 5 May 2021).

[41] Judgment in *Tregubenko v Ukraine* of 2 November 2004 https://zakon.rada.gov.ua/laws/show/980_355#Text (accessed 23 May 2021).

[42] CP(IP)R 2007, r 19(1).

purchase order (CPO) context) in *South Bucks DC v Porter (No 2)*, where Lord Brown stated:

> The reasons for a decision must be intelligible and they must be adequate. They must enable the reader to understand why the matter was decided as it was and what conclusions were reached on the 'principal important controversial issues', disclosing how any issue of law or fact was resolved. Reasons can be briefly stated, the degree of particularity required depending entirely on the nature of the issues falling for decision … The reasons need refer only to the main issues in the dispute, not to every material consideration … Decision letters must be read in a straightforward manner, recognising that they are addressed to parties well aware of the issues involved and the arguments advanced. *A reasons challenge will only succeed if the party aggrieved can satisfy the court that he has genuinely been substantially prejudiced by the failure to provide an adequately reasoned decision* [emphasis added] (*South Bucks DC v Porter (No 2)* [2004] 1 WLR 1953, 1964 (Lord Brown)).

Despite the planning context of the case in which this statement was made, even in a CPO case much depends on the context in deciding whether or not Mr Banks' claim will be successful. For example, more detailed reasoning would be required if the Secretary of State disagreed with the inspector about the decision to expropriate Mr Banks' land. Most decisions by the Secretary of State that follow an inspector's advice will still require an adequate explanation of the ultimate decision,[43] and should be communicated clearly so that they are easily comprehensible without the need for members of the public to seek legal advice to decipher them.[44] The failure to provide any reasons at all would be unusual. It would be open to Mr Banks to argue that his claim for judicial review should be granted permission since the lack of reasons provided for the choice of property indicate that the full case could not have been fairly expressed to the Secretary of State, as in *W H Gibbs Ltd v Secretary of State for the Environment*.[45]

Under section 23 ALA 1981, 'persons aggrieved', which includes people whose property is directly affected by the CPO,[46] as well as people who appeared at a public inquiry or objected to the CPO, can challenge a CPO within six weeks of its confirmation. Section 23 ALA 1981 provides two statutory grounds for questioning the validity of a CPO: (i) that the authorisation of the order is not empowered to be granted under the ALA 1981 (ie that the authorisation is ultra vires);[47] or (ii) that a 'relevant requirement' of the ALA 1981 or the Tribunals and Inquiries Act 1992 has not been complied with.[48] Arguments about the merits of a decision to confirm a CPO are inadmissible and any challenge must relate to errors of law. The absence of any reasons for a decision may form a basis for challenging the decision on the basis of unreasonableness or a failure of natural justice.

[43] *Dover District Council v Campaign to Protect Rural England (Kent)* [2018] 1 WLR 108.
[44] *Horada v Secretary of State for Communities and Local Government* [2016] EWCA Civ 169 [57].
[45] *W H Gibbs Ltd v Secretary of State for the Environment* (1973) 229 Estates Gazette 103.
[46] *Turner v Secretary of State for the Environment* (1973) 28 P&CR 123.
[47] ALA 1981, s 23(1).
[48] ibid s 23(2).

It is also possible to challenge a decision not to confirm a CPO, or a decision by an acquiring authority to implement a confirmed CPO, by way of judicial review applying normal public law principles. In the event that Mr Banks is successful in challenging the decision via judicial review, the court has the power to exercise its discretionary powers under section 24 ALA 1981. These include: (i) the power to grant interim relief suspending the CPO or provisions of it (eg those relating to Mr Banks' property) whilst the final determination occurs; and (ii) the power to quash the CPO being challenged, or particular provisions of it (eg those relating to Mr Banks' property) where substantial prejudice has been caused. It is also possible for the court not to quash the CPO itself, but instead to quash the decision to confirm the CPO. This saves the Secretary of State the time and money that would otherwise be required to start again at zero, but instead retaining the validity of the CPO and only requiring the decision to confirm the CPO to be retaken. If Mr Banks' claim succeeds it would be highly unusual for the court to deny a remedy, but it is worth noting that the powers under section 24 ALA 1981 are discretionary rather than automatic.

L. The United States

Ilya Somin

In general, if a taking is for a 'public use' and is properly authorised by state or federal legislation, the government need not provide a rationale for taking a given property rather than a neighbouring one. The government is required, in most cases, to explain what the condemned property will be used for and cannot condemn the property for no purpose at all or for entirely speculative purposes.[49] But it does not have to provide evidence that the condemnation of the tract in question was necessarily preferable to taking neighbouring land.

However, under the doctrine of 'necessity', some states do require that the government prove that the condemned property is needed to effectuate the purpose for which the property in question is taken, even if the government need not prove that it is a better site for it than some other location.[50]

[49] See eg *Cincinnati v Vester* 281 US 439, 447–48 (1930) (holding that 'private property could not be taken for some independent and undisclosed public use'); *State ex. rel. Sharp v 0.62033 Acres of Land*, 110 A 2d 1, 6 (Del Super Ct 1954), *aff'd* 112 A 2d 857 (Del 1955) (holding that '[t]he doctrine of reasonable time prohibits the condemnor from *speculating* as to *possible* needs at some *remote* future time') (emphasis in the original); *Alsip Park Dist v D & M Partnership*, 625 NE2d 40, 45 (Ill App Ct 1993) (holding that '[I]f the facts' in a condemnation proceeding 'established that … [the condemnor] had no ascertainable public need or plan, current or future for the land, defendants [property owner] should prevail'); *Mayor of the City of Vicksburg v Thomas* 645 So 2d 940, 943 (Miss 1994) (holding that property may only be condemned for transfer to 'private parties subject to conditions to insure that the proposed public use will continue to be served'); *Krauter v Lower Big Blue Nat Res Dist*, 259 NW2d 472, 475–76 (Neb 1977) (holding that a condemning agency must have a present plan and a present public purpose for the use of the property before it is authorised to commence a condemnation action … The possibility that the condemning agency at some future time may adopt a plan to use the property for a public purpose is not sufficient).

[50] For an overview of relevant jurisprudence see RC Byrd and LJ Oswald, 'Necessity as a Check on State Eminent Domain Power' (2009) *102* U Pa J Const L99.

M. International investment law

Filippo Fontanelli

Failure to state reasons can determine a measure's wrongfulness under international investment law (IIL). Unlike some domestic systems,[51] IIL does not require specifically administrative authorities to give reasons for their acts.[52] However, the formal lack of ostensible reasons can reflect substantive problems, like arbitrariness, lack of *reasonableness*, or unjustifiable motivations.[53] If these problems emerge, the measure might breach the standards on fair and equitable treatment (FET) and expropriation.

Discrimination could arise if Mr Banks is treated less favourably than other local or foreign investors 'in like circumstances'.[54] Non-discrimination is one condition for lawful expropriation,[55] so allegations of differential treatment might point to a breach.[56] Alternatively, the mere lack of reasons might cast doubts on the compliance of the expropriation with minimum due process guarantees. Lack of reasons can signal or dissimulate a substantive irregularity.[57] Discrimination or arbitrariness could entail a violation of the FET standard,[58] in particular its guarantee of due process, making the expropriation unlawful: '[i]n assessing whether there has been ... a breach of due process, it is relevant that the Guatemalan administration entirely failed to provide reasons for its decisions'.[59]

If domestic law requires that restrictive measures provide reasons, their absence would constitute a domestic irregularity that could influence the determination of international wrongfulness. Measures breaching domestic law are more evidently lacking in procedural propriety.[60] Furthermore, conduct holding the rule of law in open disregard can be wrongful under an autonomous customary standard:

> [since] the decision of the local executive body impeding implementation of construction by the investor ... was adopted 'in violation of the procedures established by the

[51] G della Cananea, 'Equivalent Standards under Domestic Administrative Law: A Comparative Perspective' in F Ortino and others (eds), *Investment Treaty Law: Current Issues Volume II* (BIICL 2007) 149–66; G della Cananea, *Due Process of Law Beyond the State: Requirements of Administrative Procedure* (OUP 2016) 61–81.

[52] J Hepburn, 'The Duty to Give Reasons for Administrative Decisions in International Law' (2012) *61*(3) ICLQ 641.

[53] *Tecmed v Mexico* ICSID Case No ARB (AF)/00/2 Award (29 May 2003) para 123; *Bear Creek v Peru* ICSID Case No ARB/14/21 Award (30 November 2017) para 387. See Michael Reisman's characterisation of a host state's measure: '[t]he absence of a clear public purpose for the measure is disturbing and reinforces the suspicion that the measure was essentially private'. *Railroad Development Corporation v Guatemala* ICSID Case No ARB/07/23 Reisman's Second Opinion (11 March 2011) para 7.

[54] US Model BIT, arts 3, 4. Other IIL instruments speak of 'similar circumstances'.

[55] ibid art 6(1)(b).

[56] *Saint-Gobain v Venezuela* ICSID Case No ARB/12/13 Decision on Liability and the Principles of Quantum (30 December 2016) para 396.

[57] *Lemire v Ukraine* ICSID Case No ARB/06/18 Decision on Jurisdiction and Liability (14 January 2010) paras 309–16, 328.

[58] *AIG v Kazakhstan* ICSID Case No ARB/01/6 Award (7 October 2003); *Elettronica Sicula SpA (ELSI)* (Judgment) [1989] ICJ Rep 15, paras 123–31.

[59] *TECO v Guatemala* ICSID Case No ARB/10/23 Award (19 December 2013) para 457.

[60] *Bear Creek* (n 53) para 413 (the domestic constitutional court had found the state measure illegal for lack of reasons); *TECO* (n 59) para 457.

> current legislation', this Tribunal records a finding that the taking (by measures tantamount to expropriation) was arbitrary, in wilful disregard of due process of law and the series of acts [in the relevant period] were shocking to 'all sense of juridical propriety'.[61]

Not every formal irregularity, including lack of reasons, entails necessarily a breach of due process.[62] Conversely, abundant reasons can signal that authorities followed due process.[63] Ultimately, procedural breaches hardly matter per se under IIL: tribunals cannot annul domestic acts and only award remedies if economic harm occurs. For this reason, tribunals will not sanction breaches of due process that occurred but were remedied[64] or that did not cause damage.[65]

Missing, contradictory, or insufficient reasons preclude or hinder the review of the state measure's reasonableness on the merits and, in turn, its lawfulness under IIL.[66] The presence of reasons—and their validity—is crucial to determining whether the state measures are expropriatory or plainly licit.[67] Even when the reasons are not apparent, the measure might be lawful if it was, in fact, based on valid reasons.[68] Tribunals must therefore examine in substance the validity or veracity of the reasons, whether publicly stated or not; false or unsupported reasons can shed light on the substantive irregularity of the state measure.[69]

[61] *AIG* (n 58) para 10.5.2. The quote is from *ELSI* (n 58).

[62] *Thunderbird v Mexico* Award (26 January 2006) UNCITRAL, para 200; *AES v Hungary* ICSID Case No ARB/07/22 Award (23 September 2010) para 9.3.40: 'The standard is not one of perfection.'

[63] *Thunderbird* (n 62) para 198.

[64] *United Utilities v Estonia* ICSID Case No ARB/14/24 Award (21 June 2019) para 870.

[65] *IGB v Spain* ICSID Case No ARB/12/17 Award (14 August 2015) para 185.

[66] *Lemire v Ukraine* (n 57) para 311; *Rumeli v Kazakhstan* ICSID Case No ARB/05/16 Award (29 July 2008) para 618; *Crystallex v Venezuela* ICSID Case No ARB(AF)/11/2 Award (4 April 2016) para 584.

[67] *Gold Reserve v Venezuela* ICSID Case No ARB(AF)/09/1 Award (22 September 2014) para 667.

[68] *Genin v Estonia* ICSID Case No ARB/99/2 Award (25 June 2001) paras 370–71; *South American Silver v Bolivia* PCA Case No 2013-15 Award (30 August 2018) para 558.

[69] *Quiborax v Bolivia* ICSID Case No ARB/06/2 Award (16 September 2015) paras 208–15.

III. Case 2: An expropriation without notice

A. Belgium

DR, LC, CD, and KP

In the context of the case in question, a public authority offers to buy Mr Burns' property located in a residential area for the purpose of building a medical facility.

Negotiations between the two parties have been unsuccessful.

The public authority then decides to expropriate Mr Burns' property without warning him and thus without allowing him to participate in the procedure.

As indicated in the chapter by Renders, L Ceci, C Delforge, K Polet, 'Procedural Requirements for Administrative Limits to Property Rights in Belgium' in this volume, when a public authority wishes to expropriate, Belgian law requires it to obtain a decision allowing the expropriation. This decision takes the form of a motivated expropriation decision, which must at the very least be notified to its addressees.

It should also be recalled that the adoption of the decision allowing expropriation must be preceded by an administrative phase. In some cases, this phase allows the expropriated owner to express him/herself and requires the public authority to organise a public inquiry or to obtain a prior opinion from advisory bodies.[70] The form of the administrative phase generally depends on specific regulations and is thus variable.

Lastly, if an amicable agreement cannot be reached, the public authority must initiate a legal action in order to expropriate. The court will assess the legality of the decision allowing the expropriation and will consequently grant—or otherwise—the forced transfer of ownership. This will not be admissible if the expropriated owner does not take part in the procedure.

Belgian law makes Mr Burns' situation very unlikely as the forced transfer of ownership may only be granted pursuant to a judicial decision. This would entail Mr Burns being notified of the expropriation in the course of legal proceedings, and he would be able to challenge the decision authorising the expropriation before a court.

B. France

EG

Mr Burns is the owner of a residential area chosen as the site for a medical facility in Springfield. Initially, the competent authority proposes buying Mr Burns' property. After a long negotiation to reach an agreement, following Mr Burns' refusal to sell, the authority expropriates the area without sending him a formal notice. Mr Burns then challenges the expropriation alleging that no due process requirements were respected since he was not sent any formal notice about the expropriation, and consequently, he was not given any chance to be heard in the procedure.

Would Mr Burns be successful? If so, would the court annul the challenged decision?

[70] See in particular K Polet, 'La régionalisation de la procédure judiciaire d'expropriation sous la Sixième réforme de l'Etat: les prémices d'une réforme souhaitable?' (2014) 3 Administration publique 474.

Expropriation may be the result of negotiation between the administration and the expropriated party. Should no amicable agreement be reached, expropriation may be carried out if certain preconditions are met. These include a public inquiry conducted by an independent investigating commissioner responsible for leading an impartial impact study. The expropriated party must be heard and informed of the outcome of this preliminary phase.

The primary purpose of this phase prior to expropriation is to inform the expropriated party and the general public of the reasons justifying the expropriation.

The public and the people who have been expropriated must therefore be informed and heard if they wish to make remarks concerning the purposes of the project being pursued. In this sense, the so-called '*Grenelle II*' law of 12 July 2010 and the decree of 3 August 2016 establishing Article L123-1 of the Environmental Code provides that:

> The purpose of the public inquiry is to ensure that the public is informed and involved, and that the interests of third parties are taken into account during the preparation of the decisions likely to affect the environment mentioned in article L 123-2. The observations and proposals received during the inquiry period are taken into consideration by the project owner and by the authority competent to take the decision.

On the one hand, Mr Burns could base his claim on the fact that he did not participate in this preliminary phase. The administrative courts ensure that the expropriator has not withheld information that is crucial to the expropriated party. Access to available information is therefore a vital element in the pre-trial phase.[71]

On the other hand, if he has indeed been heard but not individually notified of the declaration of public utility justifying the expropriation, his request will not be founded. The declaration of public utility must be accompanied by 'sufficient publicity' involving, in particular, a posting in the municipal office opening a two-month period for appeal.[72] However, no individual notification is required if sufficient publicity is given.[73]

In this regard, Mr Burns will not be able legitimately to challenge the declaration of public utility if the preliminary investigation phase is handled correctly and if the requirements relating to the publicity of the declaration of public utility have been respected.

C. Germany

FS

The expropriation presupposes that the person applying for the expropriation has made a serious but unsuccessful effort to acquire the land to be expropriated by a

[71] CE, Decision of 3 April 1981, Ministre de l'Equipement et de l'Aménagement du territoire C/ Association des propriétaires de la région soustonnaise et autres, No 162, Rec T 773.

[72] CE, Decision of 18 November 1964, Sieur Marchand *AJDA* (1965) II 157.

[73] CE, Decision of 8 June 1998, Groupement foncier agricole du domaine de la Cabanne, 1079 *AJDI* (1998).

private contract.[74] If no acquisition by a private contract takes place, the expropriation procedure is initiated by setting a date for an oral hearing with the parties involved to reach an agreement on expropriation and compensation. The owner must also be summoned to this hearing.[75] At the oral hearing, the expropriation authority must extensively discuss the relevant facts and the legal questions. The expropriation authority must give the parties involved sufficient time to reason their objections and applications.[76] The lack of date for the oral hearing and the lack of summons constitute procedural errors which could lead to the annulment of the expropriation decision.[77]

D. Italy

SM

In the expropriation procedure some procedural requirements are similar to the requirements provided by the Italian Administrative Procedure Act No 241/1990, such as the communication of the commencement of the procedure or the participation of the private owner and of other interested parties. According to Article 7 of the Act: 'Provided there exist no impediments deriving from the need to conduct a procedure particularly swiftly, the commencement of a procedure shall be communicated ... to the parties who will be directly affected by the final measure.' The notice is important for the purpose of enabling participation in the expropriation procedure which may consist in the right to inspect the documents relating to the procedure and to present documents and written arguments, which the authority has the duty to evaluate provided that they are pertinent to the object of the procedure (Article 10 of Act No 241/1990).

Administrative case law regularly states that the private owner of an area intended for expropriation must be guaranteed, by means of a formal communication of the notice of commencement of proceedings, the opportunity to intervene in the proceedings and to present their observations on the attribution of the expropriation constraints, before the declaration of public utility and, therefore, the approval of the final project.[78] In the absence of the formal notice about the commencement of the expropriation procedure, the owner is entitled to challenge the legitimacy of the expropriation. The administrative court can annul the contested expropriation decree because the lack of the notice has as a final consequence the non-expropriation of the land. Nevertheless, in several judgments the Council of State and the administrative tribunals recognised an exception to the formal notice whenever knowledge of the beginning of the procedure has intervened anyway. The communication of the commencement of the procedure, aimed at promoting procedural participation, is not

[74] BauGB, § 87 sec 2 sentence 1.

[75] ibid § 108 sec 1.

[76] H-J Dösing, '§ 108' in W Spannowsky and M Uechtritz (eds), *BeckOK BauGB* (51st edn, CH Beck 2020) para 14.

[77] H Dyong and T Groß, '§ 108' in W Ernst, W Zinkahn, W Bielenberg, and M Krautzberger, *Baugesetzbuch: Kommentar* (CH Beck 2020) para 22.

[78] See Cons Stato, Sec IV (11 November 2014) No 5525.

necessary where the interested party already had knowledge of the administrative procedure and has actually taken part in it.[79]

Moreover, failure to communicate commencement of the procedure does not affect the final provision, if the content of this is bound and cannot be changed on the basis of any comments from the private party. In this regard, we might also recall the provision of Article 21-*octies*, according to which 'an administrative measure shall not be voidable on the grounds of failure to communicate the commencement of a procedure if the authority shows at trial that the content of the measure could not have been other than that actually adopted'. But this rule cannot apply in the expropriation procedure. The final expropriation order must be considered unlawful if the communication of the commencement of the procedure is missing, provided that the participation in the procedure by the private owner might be useful in directing the exercise of the discretionary power by the public administration and in any case in order to allow the owner to be heard in the procedure.

In this case, Mr Burns is right to allege that no due process requirements were respected, since he was not informed of any formal notice about the expropriation, and consequently he was not given any chance to be heard in the procedure. The Court will annul the expropriation decree because the lack of a formal notice means a violation of the right of participation in the expropriation procedure that the owner must always be able to exercise. The lack of an agreement on the purchase of the area by the public administration cannot be seen as a fact from which derives the exception about the knowledge of the beginning of the procedure. The negotiation and Mr Burns' decision not to sell his residential land cannot be considered as a prerequisite for knowing about the beginning of the expropriation procedure. The private owner was not in a position to know in advance the will of the administration to carry out the expropriation. The communication of the commencement of the procedure was therefore necessary to allow an effective participation in the procedure that was necessary for Mr Burns to assert his property right faced by the exercise of the discretionary power of the expropriating administration.

E. The Netherlands

JS and NvT

According to Articles 16.33c and 16.33d Environment and Planning Act a property owner (and also those who may have other rights regarding the property) should receive (written) notice of both the draft decision and the final decision to expropriate. The court—which has to acknowledge every expropriation decision by a public authority—will in all cases review whether this notice has been properly given, but of course a property owner may bring this to the attention of the court herself. In such a case the court must rule that not all the required formalities have been met. This, however, does not necessarily mean that the expropriation decision has to be annulled. The court would generally assess whether the fact that the owner did not

[79] See Cons Stato, Sec III (9 April 2018) No 2148; Cons Stato, Sec IV (4 June 2013) No 3086; TAR Lombardia, Milano, Sec IV (7 February 2013) No 373.

receive a proper and timely notice has actually resulted in a disadvantage for that owner. If the answer is affirmative, the question would be whether this disadvantage can be repaired in the court proceedings. If that is the case, there might be no need for annulment. An example of this is the case where the property owner complains that there has been no serious effort from the side of the public authority to acquire their property through negotiations. Although this argument was—due to the lack of prior notice—not brought forward (and therefore not explicitly taken into account) in the procedure leading to the expropriation decision, it may perfectly well be assessed (in first instance) by the court without any (evident) disadvantage to the position of the property owner.

F. Poland

IK and ŁK

In Mr Burns' case, there was clearly an attempt at effecting expropriation given the public purpose referred to in Article 6(6) of the IPMA, ie a public healthcare facility. Initially, the public authority proceeded correctly; that is, it approached Mr Burns with a land purchase proposal, and even carried out relevant negotiations with him.[80] Then, however, it committed a number of formal flaws resulting in breaches of both material and procedural law.

After inconclusive negotiations, an administrative body has no grounds yet to start expropriation as it is now obliged to set for the owner a deadline of two months to conclude an agreement on the matter being subject to the negotiations. It is only after the lapse of that deadline with no effect that expropriation proceedings may be initiated. This must be done by a notice served on the parties, the proceedings being launched on the service day. The public body should conduct an administrative hearing and let the parties express their positions in the case, as well as collect witness testimonies, consider expert opinions and ensure a maximum concentration of evidence. All this allows for the materialisation of both the principle of directness and that of contradictoriness in administrative proceedings. Finally, the outcome of the proceedings is announced publicly by means of a notice, prior to which the parties must be notified of the method, date, and form of the notification.[81] The expropriation decision contains a verdict on the compensation. In principle, the issuance of a separate decision on expropriation, with one on compensation only following it, is inadmissible.[82] Non-compliance with these principles constitutes a serious breach of law.[83]

[80] Negotiations are not held if the object of expropriation is immovable property with unregulated legal status, that is such in the case of which it is not possible to ascertain its owners or persons who are entitled to other rights in rem related to it. See also M Szalewska, *Wywłaszczenie nieruchomości* (TNOiK 2005) 198 ff.

[81] CAP, arts 49 and 49a. The most common form is the Public Information Bulletin. In case of many parties (more than twenty), the method and date of the decision promulgation may also be effected by means of a public announcement.

[82] Exceptions to this rule are established by art 129(5) of the IPMA.

[83] IPMA, arts 112–118. See also A Jakubowska, *Ustawa o gospodarce nieruchomościami z komentarzem* (INFOR 2010) 99.

After its public announcement, the decision issued does not have to be served *ex officio*, yet on a party's request the authority makes a copy of the decision accompanied by a statement of reasons and sends it. The decision itself must meet the formal requirements of Article 107(1–3) of the CAP and additionally contain the elements provided for in Article 119(1) of the IPMA. This means that the most important aspect of the decision is not the very resolution as such but also its factual and legal justification. In case of expropriation decisions, they should among other things, indicate the ascertainment of purposes for which the immovable property is expropriated and the definition of the object of expropriation.

In Mr Burns' case, most of the procedural principles referred to above have been disregarded. One could conclude, in general that only the purpose for which the expropriation was to be carried out actually existed. Apart from that, the administrative body began the stage of negotiations. When Mr Burns failed to agree, the authority, without respecting the two-month deadline, launched expropriation proceedings without notifying him of the fact. Then, the body failed to respect a number of procedural and material law provisions by conducting flawed expropriation proceedings, which instead of a hearing was principally conducted in chambers. Finally, the body delivered an administrative decision for Mr Burns that failed to meet the formal requirements as it did not contain a statement of reasons related to the factual and legal circumstances, a calculation of the compensation or a relevant instruction. In the circumstances, both a second-instance body and the administrative court should repeal the expropriation decision. Furthermore, if Mr Burns appealed belatedly due to the absence of the relevant instruction while the decision was already valid, he would have the right to seek the ascertainment of its invalidity.[84]

G. Portugal

RGdF

In this particular case, Mr Burns' success might depend (partially) on the type of expropriation in question—normal or urgent—due to the procedural differences between them. There is no doubt, however, that if the medical facility to be built were a public hospital, there was a justifying constitutional reason of general interest governing the expropriation.[85]

If the expropriation was a normal one, then the negotiations with the owner to reach an agreement to buy the land (a civil law contract) is mandatory (Article 11 of the CE). Before the petition of 'dup' is sent to the competent government level, such an attempt must take place, and the entity promoting the expropriation shall present its proposal to the owner according to the amount deemed fair by an expert (Article 11/1 and 2). But if the expropriation is urgent this attempt to buy the land is not mandatory

[84] More on the invalidity of expropriation decisions and the need to remove them from the legal order of a democratic state: judgment of the Supreme Administrative Court of 30 November 1999, V SA 876/99, LEX No 50137.

[85] See Portuguese Constitution, art 64/3 al b), incumbent on the state to assure a rational and efficient nationwide coverage by health facilities (namely hospitals and health centres) and human resources.

(Article 11/1). In principle, it can still take place if the responsible entity wishes to do so (it might prevent an expropriation!), but only if it does not impair the urgency of the procedure.

The negotiation should not be overly long, however: Mr Burns would only have twenty calendar days, after receiving the proposal, to accept it or make a counter-proposition (Article 11/5). After that, the expropriation procedure follows its course (Article 11/6). In any case, Mr Burns refused to sell (it is not said if he considered the whole issue unfair, or if he simply disagreed with the amounts).

If the authority expropriated the area, this can only mean that a 'dup' was issued, but not notified to Mr Burns. He confuses this aspect with not being given a chance to be heard, but these are actually distinct (but connected) legal problems.

The 'dup' must be notified to the owner of the land—in this case, Mr Burns—and to other persons with legal interests, and it must also be published in the official journal of the Republic (*Diário da República*). Both the notification and publication are requisites for the effectiveness of the 'dup', being—as it is—an administrative act (Articles 158 and 160 of the CPA). This means that the prototypical effects of that act will not produce themselves. So, all the things that the 'dup' entitles the expropriator to do, cannot actually be done, because there is no entitlement. The consequence is the illegality of what happened after that.

It is debated whether Mr Burns would have the right to be heard, as he claims. In procedural terms, this hearing ('*audiência previa*') would take place shortly before the 'dup' as the last chance for the owner to present an argumentation to try to stop or change the mind of the public administration regarding expropriation. The CE does not contemplate this procedural moment. So, there are two different positionings regarding this. The case law of the Supreme Administrative Court refuses that possibility because it is not expressly laid down in the CE.[86] Doctrine tends to go the opposite way: the subsidiary application of the CPA to the expropriation procedures and acts (Articles 13/1 and 98/1 of the CE, and Article 2 of the CPA) determines the application of that right to be heard before the final administrative decision (Article 121 of the CPA). Moreover, it is again a fundamental right (Article 268 of the Portuguese Constitution). This right to be heard at this point could not be consumed by the negotiations that took place earlier between the owner and the public administration, not only because both moments involve different aspects,[87] but also because they may take place before different entities (the hearing is always before the authority competent to issue the 'dup', but the negotiations are with the beneficiary of the expropriation, and they can be different entities).

However, if the expropriation is urgent the authority competent to issue the 'dup' may dispense with the hearing (by application of article 124/1 al. *a)* of the CPA).[88] Then again, the urgency of the expropriation is determined by the 'dup' as one of its prototypical effects when the competent government level wants to use that option.

[86] See Decisions of Supreme Administrative Court, Pr 36854 (4 October 2001); Pr 46819 (12 December 2002).

[87] See F Alves Correia, *Manual de Direito do Urbanismo, vol 2* (Almedina 2010) 382.

[88] In this particular matter the case law of the Supreme Administrative Court makes sense (although it is contradictory vis-à-vis other decisions that consider the expropriation procedure a special one to which the CPA does not apply): see Decision of Supreme Administrative Court, Pr 01844/02 (27 February 2008).

So, if those effects do not produce themselves because the 'dup' is not effective, the same goes for the characterisation of that particular expropriation as urgent, and consequently there could be no dispensation of the hearing on the grounds of urgency.

Probably, Mr Burns would have success in the Portuguese Administrative Courts of law, and subsequent steps or decisions would be invalid—due to the ineffectiveness of the 'dup'—but it would in principle be possible to repeat the procedure from the notification of the 'dup' to Mr Burns on, finally, giving him the chance to be heard.

H. Spain

LAJ and DUFB

This is a complex issue due to the regulation of the expropriation procedure under Spanish law. The purpose of the first stage of the procedure is to select the rights and assets eligible for expropriation. Public authorities shall identify and describe the rights and assets to be taken (Article 17 LEF). This list is not individually notified to the owners; rather, it is published in an official journal (Article 18 LEF). Any party is entitled to submit comments within fifteen days, in order to rectify any inaccurate descriptions, as well as to challenge the suitability of the selected rights or assets with respect to the public purpose of the expropriation (Article 19 LEF). However, at this early stage of the procedure, owners are not individually notified yet. Following the submission of comments, the relevant public authority shall issue the declaration of the need to expropriate within twenty days. The latter is a formal administrative act accurately listing and describing the rights and assets to be seized, as well as the owners' and right holders' identities, who have the right to receive an individual notice (Article 20 LEF). This is in line with the general rule that due notice must be given of any administrative decisions and acts interfering with concerned parties' rights and interests (Article 40 LPAC). Accordingly, the Supreme Court has reiterated the need to notify the party concerned individually of the said declaration of the need to expropriate.[89]

Mr Burns would only be entitled to an individual notification of the administrative decision to expropriate his rights or assets at this stage of the procedure. This has drawn severe disapproval even in the judiciary,[90] but ultimately has been upheld by the Constitutional Court.[91] Although this might seem unsatisfactory, Article 22 LEF makes up for it by providing for a special administrative appeal that can be filed by the expropriated party against the declaration of the need to expropriate. This appeal must be filed within ten days, and—crucially—it has the power temporarily to stay the effect of the challenged act. Accordingly, the expropriating authority will be unable to continue with the next stages of the expropriation procedure—and thus will not be able to seize the property—until the appeal is settled. There is a twenty-day time period to adjudicate the appeal. Through this appeal, Mr Burns will not only be entitled: (i) to rectify any misstated

[89] STS of 11 July 2000, of 24 April 2003, of 20 September 2006, of 21 April 2009, of 17 February 2010, and of 14 November 2011.

[90] See eg Order of 11 of June 2015, of the regional High Court of Castilla-La Mancha, asking the Constitutional Court to declare this unconstitutional by means of an exception of unconstitutionality (*cuestión de inconstitucionalidad*).

[91] Constitutional Court Order no 63/2016 of 15 March.

information regarding the rights and assets subject to expropriation; but also (ii) to challenge the suitability thereof for the public purpose pursued by the expropriation procedure, whilst suggesting other more appropriate goods. Mr Burns will have the right to submit comments throughout the appeal procedure. If the relevant public authority dismisses the appeal, Mr Burns will be entitled to bring a judicial claim to challenge the said declaration of the need to expropriate (Article 25 LJCA).

Therefore, the due process right to be heard is not exercised during the approval of the declaration of the need to expropriate, where public authorities need not give individual notice to the expropriated owner. Rather, the exercise of the right to be heard takes place at a later procedural step initiated by the filing of an appeal after the expropriating authority has duly notified the party concerned of the above-mentioned declaration. Failure to notify will trigger the invalidity of any subsequent administrative action, including the setting of fair compensation and the seizure of property, which could be rendered invalid (annulled) by a court of justice. More specifically, subsequent administrative acts will be subject to full invalidation.[92]

This is the consequence of two rules. On the one hand, Article 47(1)(e) LPAC provides that any administrative acts 'issued in blatant disregard of the legally established procedure' will be fully invalidated (*nulidad absoluta*). The case law has widened the scope of this rule so as to cover cases where the relevant authority, despite managing some sort of procedure, has omitted essential steps.[93] In particular, according to Article 125 LEF, the declaration of the need to expropriate qualifies as a 'substantial requirement' within expropriation procedures. This makes total sense, considering that giving notice of this declaration allows the expropriated owner to make her views known and to enforce her ownership rights in the context of expropriations. On the other hand, in Mr Burns' case the declaration was actually adopted, the procedural flaw being that the expropriating authority has failed to notify him of it. Nevertheless, any administrative act that must be duly notified according to the law will only be legally effective upon notification (Article 39 LPAC). Thus, a non-notified act of expropriation will have no legal effect.

In conclusion, failure to notify the declaration of the need to expropriate individually will render any subsequent acts fully invalid (null and void) on the grounds that an essential procedural step was omitted, exactly as if the administrative decision had never been adopted. This is why, under Article 125 LEF, Mr Burns may seek to regain possession of his property before a civil court, as if the administrative act had never existed. In case Mr Burns does challenge any subsequent administrative decisions (Article 25 LJCA), administrative law courts would invalidate them (Article 71(1)(a) LJCA). They would also rule that the judgment take effect from before the unlawful administrative action, taking back all administrative action so that the expropriating authority could duly notify the expropriated owner, thereby allowing him to challenge the suitability of the property subject to expropriation through an administrative appeal (Article 71(1)(b) LJCA).

[92] STS of 21 April 2009.

[93] STS of 2 October 2013 (Proceeding no 5719/2010), and of 4 July 2016 (Proceeding no 1106/2015). J García Luengo, *Las infracciones formales como causa de invalidez del acto administrativo* (Iustel 2016) 41–45.

I. Sweden

PJ

In expropriation cases as in other cases the rule is that the party, in this case the property unit owner, has to be heard before the matter is decided.

This rule is to be found in the Administrative Procedure Act (*Förvaltningslagen* 2017: 900).[94]

According to section 25 of this Act: 'Before a public authority[95] takes a decision in a case it shall, unless it is obviously unnecessary, notify the party of all material of importance to the decision and give the party the opportunity to comment on the material within a specified time.' The question that arises in the current case is whether, with regard to the long negotiation to reach an agreement that preceded the expropriation decision, it can be considered that the so-called obligation of communication and the associated obligation to provide the party with an opportunity to be heard have become 'obviously unnecessary'. If this is the case, the court will not endorse Mr Burns' arguments.

If the court, on the contrary, arrives at the conclusion that the obligation of communication was not 'obviously unnecessary' and that therefore a violation of a legal rule—section 25 of the Administrative Procedure Act—has occurred, the question to be raised is whether the infringement of this procedural rule could have had an impact on the outcome of the case. Here too, the occurrence of the long negotiation could point to the conclusion that the fact that Mr Burns has not been heard—an infringement of a procedural rule—has not had an impact on the outcome of the decision.[96] On the one hand, under these circumstances the possibility of Mr Burns being successful and having the decision quashed would be almost non-existent.

On the other hand, the court might consider that this kind of formal failure constitutes a serious flaw and could then quash the decision.

[94] Interestingly, the Expropriation Act that preceded the current Act stated that the property owner and others who may have suffered loss from the expropriation should be afforded the opportunity to comment on whether it was particularly inconvenient that the intended land was abandoned or leased, if other suitable land could be used with less inconvenience and if there were any other comments regarding the results of the application. See Prop 1972:119, 282 (Preparatory work).

[95] This rule applies, according to the letter of the law, to 'public authorities' (*förvaltningsmyndighet*), which means in the context of expropriation the County Administrative Board or other subordinate authorities. The rule also applies, according to the preparatory works, when the government—which is not formally a public authority—takes decisions within the expropriation field. See Prop 1972:119 (n 34) 282.

[96] In practice, the two steps become one only in this kind of case. See eg RÅ 1996 ref 28 concerning an urban plan and where a decision was quashed and remanded through legal review. The right to be heard was not unnecessary, the court said, and an infringement of a procedural rule had occurred. The court did not pronounce itself in an autonomous manner on the question of whether 'an error in the procedure' had occurred 'which may have had an impact on the result', while it explicitly reminded in the judgment that the legal review encompasses the review of whether 'an error in the procedure may have had an impact on the result'.

J. Ukraine
HD

According to Ukrainian legislation, the construction of a medical facility is neither a ground for land plot redemption nor a reason for its forced alienation (Articles 7 and 15 of the Law of Ukraine 'On alienation').[97] The Constitution of Ukraine provides that no one shall be unlawfully deprived of their right to property. The Land Code of Ukraine provides that executive authorities and local self-government bodies cannot intervene in the enjoyment of an owner's property rights to a land plot without a court decision (Article 154).[98] Furthermore, the Land Code of Ukraine provides that if an act violates a person's right to own, enjoy, or dispose of a land plot, it will be invalidated, and damage caused by such an act must be fully indemnified by the authority issuing the act (Article 155). Thus, the court will surely annul the challenged unlawful decision, and Mr Burns will be awarded damages.

The Law of Ukraine 'On alienation' requires formal notification during the process of forced alienation of a plot of land. There must be a written notification regarding the decision, which should be sent or delivered to the owner of the land plot within five days of its adoption, but no later than three months before redemption (Article 10(2)). As noted in the decision of the Kyiv Circuit Administrative Court, a lack of written notice and nonreceipt by the owner should be treated as rendering the enacted decision unlawful due to procedural infringement and the conditions of its enactment. It restricts the owner's rights to express his consent or disagreement with the redemption.[99]

It is worth mentioning that a similar case was considered by the Supreme Court in Ukraine composed of a panel of judges of the Administrative Court of Cassation in 2018.[100] Upon application by the communal enterprise 'SportResurs', Lviv City Council as a local self-government body handed down a decision on redemption because of the initiative to build a stadium. But the City Council failed to inform the owner of the land plot directly. Instead, the applicant, which is the communal enterprise, sent the notification on its behalf. Having received the owner's rejection to sell a land plot, Lviv City Council filed a suit before the Lviv Appellate Administrative Court requesting a decision on a forced alienation but gained no satisfaction. Thus, Lviv City Council brought an action before the Supreme Court. The Supreme Court upheld the prior decision noting that, first, building the

[97] Law of Ukraine 'On the alienation of land plots and other real property assets located on them which are private property for the public needs or on the grounds of public necessity' (17 November 2009) https://zakon.rada.gov.ua/laws/show/1559-17 (accessed 5 May 2021).

[98] Land Code of Ukraine (25 October 2001) https://zakon.rada.gov.ua/laws/show/2768-14 (accessed 5 May 2021).

[99] Decision of Kyiv Circuit Administrative Court of 21 December 2019 in case No 320/2287/19 https://zakononline.com.ua/court-decisions/show/86585798 (accessed 5 May 2021).

[100] Resolution of the Supreme Court of 20 March 2018 in case No A/9901/1/17 876/7/17/ https://protocol.ua/ua/vs_kas_primusove_vidchugennya_zemli_ta_ob_ektiv_neruhomosti_moge_buti_zastosovane_lishe_yak_vinyatok_za_umovi_dotrimannya_vstanovlenoi_protseduri_ta_poperednogo_i_povnogo_vidshkoduvannya_ih_vartosti_(vs_kas_a_9901_1_17_876_7_17_20_03_18)/ (accessed 5 May 2021).

stadium was not included on the list of grounds for the redemption and forced alienation. Secondly, it observed that the notification was not delivered by the legally prescribed person (paragraphs 22, 24).

K. The United Kingdom

EW

A number of notices have to be provided under the Acquisition of Land Act (ALA) 1981. First, the ALA 1981 requires that a notice must be placed for two successive weeks in one or more newspapers that are local to the area where the designated land is sited. The notice must provide details about the order, describe the land and the purpose for which it is being acquired, indicate where locally a copy of the order and map of the land can be viewed, specify a period of at least twenty-one days for objections to the order and specify how objections can be made.[101] Additionally, a notice must be fixed on a conspicuous object on or near the land detailed in the order, such as a lamp post.[102] Additionally, the acquiring authority must serve a notice on every 'qualifying person', which would include Mr Burns since he owns the affected land.[103] Again, as with the notice to be placed in local newspapers, the notice served on Mr Burns should have stated the effect of the CPO, given notice that it is being submitted for confirmation and provide details about how and when objections can be made. A notice is served under the ALA 1981[104] where it is delivered or left at Mr Burns' last known address, or posted by registered post or recorded delivery to that address. If no one lives on the land then a copy of the notice can normally be left on the land or near it.[105]

Mr Burns' case would depend on whether or not he could persuade the court that he had not had notice of the plan, so much would depend on the precise facts. In the event that the authority can demonstrate that it published the notice in local newspapers, placed a notice on or near the affected land, and sent a notice to Mr Burns, he would not have a case even though he had not actually read the notice. In the event that the authority had not provided notice before the CPO was confirmed, the failure to provide notice could be challenged under the section 23 ALA 1981 grounds (discussed in case 1 above) and would be likely to be quashed. In practice, it is highly unlikely that a notice would not be sent; it is more likely that Mr Burns failed to read the notice sent to him.

Additionally, it is open to Parliament to relax publicity measures for planning purposes. The Town and Country Planning (Development Management Procedure, Listed Buildings and Environmental Impact Assessment) (England) (Coronavirus) (Amendment) Regulations 2020 came into force on 14 May 2020 and supplement

[101] ALA 1981, s 11(2).
[102] ibid s 11(3).
[103] ibid s 7(1).
[104] ibid s 6(1).
[105] This is not possible where the owner, tenant, or occupier is a local authority, statutory undertaker (ie utilities company), or the National Trust.

existing statutory rules governing planning applications until 31 December 2020. The regulations temporarily amended notice requirements to allow for the use of social media and communication by electronic means in order to communicate the notice to people likely to have an interest in a planning application, for example.

L. The United States

IS

Mr Burns would prevail. State and federal law in the US virtually always requires advance notice of a condemnation,[106] although the exact details of how much notice and in what form vary. But a total failure to provide notice is clearly illegal, and thus the condemnation of Mr Burns' property would be rejected by a state or federal court.

M. International investment law

FF

State measures adopted without notice and without allowing the addressees to submit their views might be procedurally defective and breach the due process standard. A condition of expropriation's lawfulness is compliance with due process.[107] Assuming that the other conditions are met (ie Springfield offered to pay full compensation promptly and the medical destination of the facility is genuine), the expropriation's review revolves around its procedural regularity.

States must conduct a fair and predictable process 'based on the application of duly adopted laws'.[108] Mr Burns could plausibly make a due process claim, since 'reasonable advance notice and a fair hearing'[109] are among the 'basic legal mechanisms' required:

> ['d]ue process of law', in the expropriation context, demands an actual and substantive legal procedure for a foreign investor to raise its claims against the depriving actions already taken or about to be taken against it. Some basic legal mechanisms, such as *reasonable advance notice, a fair hearing* and an unbiased and impartial adjudicator to assess the actions in dispute, are expected to be readily available and accessible to the investor to make such legal procedure meaningful. In general, the legal procedure must be of a nature to grant an affected investor a reasonable chance within a reasonable time to claim its legitimate rights *and have its claims heard*. If no legal procedure

106 See eg Federal Rule of Civil Procedure 71.1 (outlining requirements for federal takings).

107 Occasionally, due process is not an expropriation's feature, but the investor must be able 'to establish promptly by due process of law ... the legality of the expropriation'. See *Guaracachi v Bolivia* PCA Case No 2011-17 Award (31 January 2014) para 439, contrasting UK–Bolivia BIT (due process precondition) and US–Bolivia BIT (*post facto* right to recourse).

108 *AIG v Kazakhstan* ICSID Case No ARB/01/6 Award (7 October 2003) para 10.5.1.

109 *Kardassopoulos v Georgia* ICSID Case No ARB/05/18 Award (3 March 2010) para 397.

> of such nature exists at all, the argument that 'the actions are taken under due process of law' rings hollow.[110]

Tribunals cannot void administrative measures, even if clearly unlawful under domestic law; they can only ascertain their legality under IIL. Domestic legality can factor in that assessment,[111] especially if a treaty provision refers to it.[112] Conversely, municipal law might be so inadequate that an international wrongdoing can occur even if the process observed it.[113]

Mr Burns would not primarily challenge the measure's nullity under domestic law, but the absence of any recourse for challenging it.[114] The determination must be made 'in the light of the facts established in [the specific] case';[115] that a viable process exists under domestic law in the abstract is not enough, if it is in effect unavailable.

Conversely, if Mr Burns had had a viable opportunity to challenge the decision after receiving the letter, his case of due process violations for lack of notice and impossibility to be heard would be weaker, as these irregularities would not have deprived him altogether of the right of recourse.[116] Due process includes the availability of recourse, but resorting to local courts is not an arbitration precondition; unless the claim alleges denial of justice, to commence or exhaust a local lawsuit is not required.[117]

The investor's failure to attempt reversal of an irregular administrative decision, however, is relevant when under review are the causal link between the state measure and the damage suffered[118] or the compliance with due process of domestic law remedies.[119] Moreover, if the investor claims that the administrative irregularities constitute denial of justice, a finding of breach is unlikely 'when further remedies or avenues of appeal are potentially available under municipal law'.[120]

[110] *ADC Affiliate Limited and ADC & ADMC Management Limited v Hungary* ICSID Case No ARB/03/16 Award (2 October 2006) para 435 (emphasis added). On reasonable notice see also *Vestey v Venezuela* ICSID Case No ARB/06/4 Award (15 April 2016) para 307; *Tecmed* (n 53) para 173.

[111] *Olin v Libya* ICC Case No 20355/MCP Final Award (25 May 2018) para 171.

[112] *Tenaris v Venezuela I* ICSID Case No ARB/11/26 Award (29 January 2016) para 494.

[113] *Vestey v Venezuela* (n 110) para 305.

[114] *von Pezold v Zimbabwe* ICSID Case No ARB/10/15 Award (28 July 2015) para 499; *Bear Creek* (n 53) para 446; *Quiborax* (n 69) paras 221, 226; *Kardassopoulos* (n 109) para 404.

[115] *ADC* (n 110) para 438; *Tza Yap Shum v Peru* ICSID Case No ARB/07/6 Award (7 July 2011) paras 223–39.

[116] *Railroad v Guatemala* (n 53) para 221.

[117] *Inmaris v Ukraine* ICSID Case No ARB/08/8 Award (1 March 2012) para 302; *Abengoa v Mexico* ICSID Case No ARB(AF)/09/2 Award (18 April 2013) para 626.

[118] *Generation Ukraine v Ukraine* ICSID Case No ARB/00/9 Award (16 September 2003) para 20.30: 'expropriation is doubtful in absence of a reasonable not necessarily exhausted effort by the investor to obtain correction'.

[119] *South American Silver* (n 68) para 585.

[120] *Corona v Dominican Republic* ICSID Case No ARB(AF)/14/3 Award (31 May 2016) para 248.

IV. Case 3: Participation and due process in urban planning

A. Belgium

DR, LC, CD, and KP

In this case, the local authorities decide to amend a land use plan, altering the use of an area and modifying it from commercial to residential use.

Mrs Sheraton challenges the revised land use plan and complains to the authorities, that no information was given about the beginning of the amending procedure.

To the best of our knowledge, in Belgian law, the provisions concerning the revision of urban planning acts always require the organisation of public consultations.[121]

The Council of State should decide whether the public consultation during the revision of urban planning acts is a formality of an 'essential' nature or not.

In Belgian law, a formality is considered 'essential' when it is instituted only in the interest of the citizen, or in the interest of both the citizen and the administration.[122] If this formality has not been accomplished or is unlawful, the Council of State should quash the act.[123]

However, the breach of an essential formality can lead to the act being quashed only if the violation of the essential formality may have had an influence on the outcome of the decision in question, or if it has deprived the applicant of a guarantee.[124] In other words, the applicant must show an interest in invoking the violation of the formality at issue, which is called 'interest to the ground'.[125]

The Council of State has already stated that public consultation during the review of urban planning acts is an essential formality.[126] As a consequence, the Council of State could consider that public consultation (including that concerning Mrs Sheraton) during the revision of the land use plan at issue is an essential formality.

Furthermore, Mrs Sheraton could argue that she has been deprived of a guarantee by not being consulted, as she owns a building in the area altered by the review of the land use plan concerned. Moreover, as public consultation serves to provide the authority with all the elements necessary to rule on the revision of an urban planning act, the applicant can argue that this consultation could have influenced the decision in question.

On these grounds, the Council of State should quash the challenged decision.

121 For example, the Code of Territorial Development, arts D.II.47 and D.VIII.5 (20 July 2016; publication in the Belgian *Official Gazette* on 14 November 2016); Brussels Code for Town and Country Planning, art 25 (9 April 2004; publication in the Belgian *Official Gazette* on 26 May 2004). See also D Renders, *Droit administratif général* (3rd edn, Larcier 2019) 344–46.

122 Renders, *Droit administratif général* (n 121) 326–27.

123 ibid 327; Council of State, *sa Trabeka* No 8.177 of 7 October 1960.

124 Coordinated Acts 'on the Council of State', art 14, §1, sub 2 (12 January 1973; publication in the Belgian *Official Gazette* on 21 March 1973).

125 Renders (n 121) 636; Council of State, *Thomas* No 239.832 of 9 November 2017; Council of State, *Tipold* No 242,814 of 26 October 2018.

126 Council of State, *Everaert and Others* No 226.813 of 19 March 2014; Council of State, case *SA Iteco* No 218,445 of 13 March 2012.

If Mrs Sheraton wishes to halt the effects of the revised land use plan during the time needed for the Council of State to review it, she could decide to lodge a request of stay before the court. In order to request the suspension of this decision, the applicant will have to demonstrate that the case has become too urgent to be dealt with during the annulment procedure.[127]

B. France

EG

Mrs Sheraton is obliged to comply with the local urban plan to carry out the construction of her hotel. This is a provision under Article L153-54 ff, taken up in Article L122-5 of the New Expropriation Code. It is therefore acknowledged that the declaration of public utility cannot be valid if it is not in conformity with the local urban plan.

Furthermore, it should be noted that the local urban plan cannot be valid without following two key steps to involve the public. Upstream, a 'preliminary consultation' phase must be carried out. It aims to inform and involve local residents and associations in developing the plan as quickly as possible.[128] Indeed, after its modification, the 'preliminary consultation' must take place when the project is in the process of development without yet being decided. It aims for the authority to decide on the project's objectives while making available to the public the documents needed to make the decision. In addition, the environmental public inquiry[129] takes place later in the Constitution of the local urban plan project. It allows all residents to participate in the decision-making process. Its objective is to consider all the project's environmental consequences and inform third parties of these consequences.

The relevant question of law is whether an amendment to the local urban plan can be made after authorization has been granted. The legal answer is quite explicit. Revision of the local urban plan is a procedure detailed in the Urbanism Code. The public inquiry is the second phase that takes place after the deliberation of the revision project.[130] This inquiry must gather the opinions of the public. The applicant appears to be the first person justified in submitting her observations, given the impact that a modification of the rules could have on her construction project. Thus, in the absence of a public inquiry, the new modifying plan is vitiated by a procedural defect because all the steps were not respected. As a result, the new local urban plan will be cancelled, and the old one will remain in force for the claimant's benefit.

It therefore appears that Mrs Sheraton is legally entitled to continue building her hotel since she has received due authorization. In conclusion, the granted building permit cannot be questioned because of the appearance of new urban planning rules.

[127] Coordinated Acts 'on the Council of State', art 17 (12 January 1973; publication in the Belgian *Official Gazette* on 21 March 1973).

[128] Urbanism Code, art L 103-2.

[129] ibid art L 120-1.

[130] ibid art L 103-3.

C. Germany

FS

According to the Federal Building Code, the public must be involved when a land-use plan is amended.[131] The public must be informed as early as possible about general aims and purposes of planning, different solutions for the redesign or development of an area and expected effects of the planning. The public must be given the opportunity to comment on and discuss the plan.[132] The draft of the land-use plan must be publicly displayed for a period of one month. The place and duration of the display must be announced in advance in the usual local manner.[133] Violations of this requirement can generally not be ignored and lead to the nullity of the land-use plan.[134] The lack of involvement of Mrs Sheraton is a procedural violation that can be challenged before the court. If the city violates public participation, the state supervisory authority can also be involved in the procedure.

D. Italy

SM

Article 13 of the Italian Administrative Procedure Act No 241/1990 provides the scope of application of the rules on participation in administrative proceedings, as described in the previous Articles (7 to 12). It states that the provisions on participation 'shall not apply to public administrative action that is directed towards the issuance of measures having a … planning or programming function. Such measures shall continue to be governed by the specific rules regulating their framework'. Therefore, the specific discipline of the sector must be considered for planning proceedings. In the case of urban planning the procedure is ruled by DPR No 327/2001, Consolidated Law on Land Expropriation, where there are specific provisions for each kind of proceeding (ie town regulatory plan, housing plan, landscape plan, production centre plan, etc). The discipline is also integrated by the specific rules given by the regions, which can provide more guarantees for the participation in the regional planning proceedings through their own legislation.

In this framework administrative case law has stated that the formal notice ruled by Article 7 of Act No 241/1990 does not apply to the planning procedure.[135]

The purpose is to remove from participation, and in any case from the free availability of the private parties, the object of the administrative activity aimed at issuing regulatory, general, and administrative planning acts.

[131] BauGB, §§ 1 sec 8, 3.
[132] ibid § 3 sec 1 sentence 1.
[133] ibid § 3 sec 2.
[134] ibid § 214 sec 1 sentence 1 No 2.
[135] See eg Cons Stato, Sec IV (24 November 2014) No 5819; Cons Stato, Sec IV (15 September 2014) No 4679; TAR Lazio, Roma, Sec II (12 March 2015) No 4115; TRGA Trento, Sec I (5 December 2012) No 358.

However, the administrative courts recognise the exception for owners directly affected by the location of public works, or in any case of subjects with different positions, in respect of which there is an obligation for individual communication of the initiation of the urban-planning procedure by the public administration.[136]

Some scholars believe, moreover, that the above-mentioned Article 13 does not prevent the administration from admitting a participation of the type envisaged for individual proceedings also with respect to the procedures for 'the issue of regulatory, general administrative, planning and programming acts': more simply, it would exclude that in these cases the administration 'is required to guarantee' such participation.[137]

In any case the specific discipline of urban-planning procedure (the fundamental Urban Planning Act of 1942) provides for a participation in the observations/oppositions, which intervene when the planning instrument has already been decided, although not formally adopted. The observations/oppositions are written arguments provided as a function of guarantee and collaboration. For the administration there would be only the obligation to examine them and to indicate, even in summary and cumulative form, the reasons for their possible non-acceptance because they are in contrast with the interests and general considerations on which the plan was created.

However, administrative judges do not always say that the omission of participatory activities infringes the entire process of the urban-planning approval. Sometimes, especially where the effective participation of the interested party in the procedure does not prove to have been prevented, the omission has been declassified to a mere non-vitiating irregularity (in line with the widespread attitude of case law on the interpretation of Article 7 of Law No 241/1990), observing that the applicants had not suffered any concrete reduction in their prerogatives for procedural participation.[138]

The participation of the private party in the urban-planning proceeding does not necessarily mean the possibility to apply for judicial review before the administrative courts. Case law often states that the so-called '*vicinitas*', ie the situation of a stable connection existing between the property of the applicant and the area affected by the contested provision, is not in itself sufficient to form the basis of an interest to appeal against the planning decisions.[139] The applicant must demonstrate that the planning choices affect, in some way, the enjoyment or the market value of their property.

In urban planning the decisions adopted by the public administration are an evaluation of merit, and therefore they are not reviewed by the administrative judge. The judicial review can be referred only to cases of errors of fact or abnormal irrationality, so that even the destination given to the individual areas does not need a specific reason, unless particular situations have not created expectations in favour of subjects whose positions appear worthy of specific consideration. But case law denies that a specific expectation can derive from the different previous urban destination of the same area,

[136] TAR Sardegna, Sec II (7 June 2010) No 1415; TAR Lombardia, Milano, Sec II (24 February 2010) No 452.

[137] See A Travi, 'Accordi tra proprietari e comune per le modifiche al p.r.g. e oneri esorbitanti' (2002) V Foro It 274.

[138] TAR Lombardia (n 22) No 2153.

[139] See above all Cons Stato, Sec IV (16 July 2015) No 3579.

with respect to which the administration has extensive discretion, being able to make changes for the worse with respect to the interests of the owner, who has only a generic expectation to maintain the previous more advantageous urban destination.[140] For the lawfulness of new planning choices, an individual reason for each individual area is not then required of the public administration in order to justify the specific suitability of the planning decision to meet public needs.

In applying these rules to the case, it might be said that Mrs Sheraton was not in a position to receive a formal notice about the beginning of the planning procedure to change the use of the area (from commercial to residential) where her hotel should have been located. However, she could participate in the procedure in order to make objections or to offer observations, had the proceeding still been ongoing when she was informed about it.

From the point of view of the standing and the consequent judicial review, Mrs Sheraton can apply to the administrative judge asking for the protection of her participatory rights, and above all for the annulment of the planning decision and compensation for damages that the change in the use of area might cause to her property. She can be considered as an applicant being in a situation of stable connection existing between the property of the applicant and the area affected by the contested provision, but she has to demonstrate how the new planning choice could affect the market value of her hotel under construction in the area concerned.

Nevertheless it is highly unlikely that the administrative tribunal would find an abnormal irrationality in the decision taken by the administration on the new destination of the area. And, as we have already said, given a different previous urban destination of the area, this does not provide for the applicant any particular expectation that might justify a more extensive judicial review of the reasons provided by the administration on the choice of the new urban destination of the area where Mrs Sheraton's hotel was to have been located.

E. The Netherlands

JS and NvT

On the preparation procedure for an urban plan (an environment plan under the Environment and Planning Act), the so-called 'uniform public preparatory procedure' (section 3.4 General Administrative Law Act) is applicable.[141] This means that the administrative authority makes a draft decision available for inspection by any party during a prescribed period. Before making the draft decision available for inspection, the administrative body has to notify the public about the draft decision in (eg) free local papers.[142] The notification states when and where the draft decision can be inspected, who can express an opinion ('*zienswijze naar voren brengen*') and how they can express that opinion.[143]

[140] See eg Cons Stato, Sec IV (29 December 2014) No 638.
[141] Spatial Planning Act, art 3.8, and in the future art 16:30 section 1 Environment and Planning Act.
[142] General Administrative Law Act, art 3:12.
[143] ibid arts 3:11, 3:15 and 3:16.

Because of the far-reaching consequences of zoning plans (and environment plans), the reach of the notification needs to be as large as possible. This means that the notification of the draft decision also has to be published in the *Government Gazette* and be accessible online. In the case of a zoning plan, opinions can be expressed by any party. The final decision also has to be published online and in the *Government Gazette*.[144]

From the previous it follows that there is no individual right to be notified about changes in the zoning plan. It is a person's own responsibility to be informed about possible changes. This means that in the event that the administrative authority has followed the procedure as prescribed by the General Administrative Law Act, the Spatial Planning Act and the Spatial Planning Decree, Mrs Sheraton cannot successfully refer to participatory requirements.

If the prescribed participatory requirements are not met (which does not include individual notification), this can lead to the annulment of the zoning plan. Such a procedural defect however does not necessarily lead to annulment.[145] For annulment of the zoning plan (or environmental plan), it will have to be argued that there are substantial defects.

For the sake of completeness (because there are quite a number of cases dealing with this question), we point out there is also not an obligation for administrative authorities to provide an opportunity to express opinions on a preliminary zoning plan ('*voorontwerpbestemmingsplan*').[146] This requirement does not follow from the General Administrative Law Act, The Spatial Planning Act or the Spatial Planning Decree. This requirement will also not follow from the Environment and Planning Act.

F. Poland

IK and ŁK

Mrs Sheraton obtained a permit for building a hotel in a tourist area located near the city of Belleville under the current urban plan, which the Polish legislator calls the 'spatial development plan'. Such issues as land purpose or the concept and urban layout are merely one aspect of the spatial development plan.[147] The competent authorities for its adoption are commune councils, the legal basis being the Spatial Planning and Development Act (SPDA) of 27 March 2003 (JoL of 2003, No 80, item 717, as amended).[148] Regrettably, not all Polish communes have adopted spatial development plans, or if they have, such plans do not cover their entire territory but only individual districts or areas. In the case of the latter, a zoning decision for specific property must

144 Spatial Planning Act, art 3.8. This requirement will probably soon change due to the Electronic Publication Act, under which local authorities will have to publish their decisions regarding environmental and planning law in the official journal of the relevant local authority. See www.officielebekendmakingen.nl (accessed 26 February 2021).

145 Procedural defects can be disregarded, based on General Administrative Law Act, art 6:22.

146 See eg Council of State (18 December 2019) ECLI:NL:RVS:2019:4347, para 4.2, and Council of State 5 June 2019, ECLI:NL:RVS:2019:1836, para 3.2.

147 E Czekiel—Świtalska, 'Urbanistyka a miejscowy plan zagospodarowania przestrzennego w Polsce' in (2016) XLIV Teka Komisji Urbanistyki i Architektury PAN Oddział w Krakowie 329.

148 The spatial development plan has the status of a bye-law.

be obtained before a building permit is applied for. It is on the basis of that decision that the future investor produces an architectural design and applies for a building permit. The most desirable scenario is a valid spatial development plan in force as this is a guarantee of the full enforceability of the building permit decision issued on its basis. Once it is legally valid, it has the status of an acquired right and so starting the construction on the conditions and within the timeframe specified in such a decision one has the right to complete it and release the building for use. This is the legal situation in Mrs Sheraton's case. This does not take away from her the rights related to her possible participation in the procedure or amending the spatial development plan. Importantly, the local plan, has the status of a by-law, hence the ascertainment of its invalidity will remove it from the system of legal transactions yet will not invalidate its past consequences.

Returning then to Mrs Sheraton's procedural position, one should conclude that she undoubtedly has a legal interest to seek the repealing of the resolution on amending the urban plan. That interest, however, does not consist in the inability to build the hotel and release it for use as planned but focuses instead on the will to restore the previous urban planning order, which must have surely been more attractive in terms of tourism and nature than the residential estates planned. If the planning procedure did not include the public consultation aspect, and in particular the administrative authority failed to make the plan available to the public and to allow it to submit comments and conclusions under Article 18 in connection with Article 17(9) of the SPDA, such a failure would be an absolute ground for an appeal. Even if the voivode exercising the control function oversaw such a failure, an administrative court would surely have reasons for repealing the local plan resolution. And in the case of its being in force, one could demand that its invalidity be ascertained due to a blatant breach of law.

Furthermore, if in the circumstances, due to the amendment of the local plan, Mrs Sheraton's use of her property or its part has become impossible or significantly limited in the manner or for the purpose practised thus far, she can demand from the commune: compensation for the loss actually incurred or purchase of the entire property or its part.[149] If, due to the adoption of the local plan or its amendment, the value of the property has decreased and the owner is selling it and has not exercised the rights specified above, she can demand from the commune compensation equal to the decrease in her property's value. Her claims could also be met by means of the commune offering the owner or perpetual usufructuary replacement property in a location of his/her interest. Once such a replacement agreement has been concluded under civil law, the claims in question expire.

G. Portugal

RGdF

Participation in procedures to do with uses of land, planning and urban planning is a general right guaranteed by Articles 6/2 and 49 of the Law of Public Policy for Land,

[149] SPDA, art 36.

Planning and Urban Planning (LPPSPU),[150] with access to information in the possession of the public authorities. But the case in hand is not only a matter of participation: it involves the loss of (other) rights, and not only the impossibility of exercising procedural rights.

Classification and reclassification of soils is a planning option and it defines its uses (Article 10/3 and 4 of the LPPSPU) at an intermunicipal or municipal level (Articles 20/1 and 43). In Portuguese law, like in so many other legal orders, urban plans are municipal. Municipal urban plans can be of three kinds (main municipal plans, plans of urbanisation, and detailing plans). These plans are all mandatory for both public authorities and private parties (Article 46).

According to Article 17/1 of the LPPSPU, the sacrifice of pre-existing rights which are legally solid can only take place where the law or plans (which are administrative norms or regulations) so permit and compensation is provided. Even if technicalities can be discussed regarding the meaning of 'pre-existing rights' and 'legally solid' rights, the same Article 17/3 is very clear, establishing that, regardless, there must be compensation for every sacrifice imposed on land proprietors that has an equivalent effect to an expropriation ('sacrifice expropriation').

This rule is reaffirmed and detailed in Article 171 of the Land Planning Instruments Law[151] (LPIL): the sacrifice of pre-existing and consolidated rights—like the ones resulting from a building licence—imposed on proprietors by urban plans must be fairly compensated by indemnity when another kind of compensation is not possible (for instance, building capacity rights). This must be explained.

Planning and programming the use of land is a public obligation (Article 8/2 al a) of the LPPSPU). For reasons of general interest, public authorities must make options regarding the uses of land (public and private), and those options many times limit the possibilities that a certain land provides at a certain moment. In other words, private owners are sometimes confronted with changes in the possible uses of their land: a land that had building capacity might lose it because public authorities consider, from a certain moment on, it is part of a natural reserve or it is due to be used for a public infrastructure. These possibilities must be accepted as a price or risk of societal living. Accordingly, even if indemnities due to this changes tend to be subject to strict conditions (if not exceptional) and time limits.[152]

Regardless, these restrictions imposed by plans have an equivalent effect to an expropriation: they do not transfer ownership of the land to a third party, but they deprive or diminish its owner of the possibilities of use. That is why they are called 'expropriations of sacrifice', or 'plan expropriations', or 'substantial expropriations',[153] which are perfectly admissible in Portuguese law and recognised by the Constitutional Court[154] and the Administrative Supreme Court.[155]

[150] See Law 31/2014 of 30/05.

[151] See Decree-Law 80/2015 of 14 May 2015.

[152] See LPPSPU, arts 171/4 and 5.

[153] See Alves Correia (n 87) 132; FP Oliveira, *Regime Jurídico dos Instrumentos de Gestão Territorial* (Almedina 2012) 484.

[154] See Decisions of the Constitutional Court 341/86, 131/88, 184/92, 262/93, and—most relevant for the situation in question—329/99 and 517/99. On this case law see Alves Correia (n 87) 137–38.

[155] See Decision of the Supreme Administrative Court, Pr. 0996/06 (15 October 2014).

This issue is related to an important debate on whether the *ius aedificandi* (the right to build) is inherent to the property right, or if it is instead attributed by public authorities through plans (regulations) and other administrative decisions (the latter is the thesis supported by constitutional and administrative case law, and also the one with wider doctrinal acceptance).[156]

But when building rights have already been attributed not only in general terms by a plan but also adjudicated by a licence—an administrative act or concrete decision—their restriction following an alteration of the plan is much more evident. Actually, the 'change of plan'—so to speak—has the implication of revoking Mrs Sheraton's prior permit, eliminating a right to build a hotel that she had unequivocally acquired. Restrictions on private property are subject to a fair compensation (Article 62 of the Constitution and Article 4/3 of the LPPSPU). And so would the deprivation suffered by Mrs Sheraton: she would have a right to an indemnity calculated according to the CE, and also compensation for the costs she would have had exercise her (previous) right (for instance, architectural drawings that she had to pay for and other expenses) (Article 171/2, 6, and 7 of the LPIL).

The LPIL establishes a complex net of participatory rights when public authorities want to introduce changes to these plans (Articles 118, 119). Many aspects depend on the type of change. In any case, the public authorities have initiate the procedure and provide information to citizens, allowing suggestions and other interventions (Article 88). There is a period of public discussion, duly publicised, for no less than thirty or twenty working days (depending on the type of plan), and afterwards the town hall must consider all aspects brought to its attention, namely restrictions of rights, and answer them specifically (Article 89). These participatory rights also derive from the CPA as a general set of procedural rules (Articles 98 ff).

So it is fair to say that Mrs Sheraton's case should have been considered if only proper procedure had been followed. The courts would uphold the view that participatory requirements should have been respected, and consequently would find for the illegality of the amendment of the plan. Its previous version would thus have to be maintained as a consequence of the nullity of the changes.

There is no specific interim procedure to stop the urban plan revision in order to protect participatory requirements. General interim instruments allowed by the administrative justice legislation are available, but it is questionable if a provisional suspension of this kind of procedure would be given by the courts (only in a very creative mood might this happen).

H. Spain

LAJ and DUFB

The court would uphold Mrs Sheraton's claim. Under Spanish law, it is on autonomous regions to regulate urban plan approval and amendment procedures, so there

[156] See Oliveira (n 153) 484. For an example of the minoritary thesis see J Reis Novais, 'Ainda sobre o *ius aedificandi* (... mas agora como problema de direitos fundamentais)' in *Estudos Jurídicos e Económicos em Homenagem ao Prof. Doutor António de Sousa Franco* (Coimbra edn 2006) 493 ff.

are different procedures depending on the region. Nonetheless, these procedures must comply with minimum participatory requirements stemming from the right to participate in administrative rule-making (Article 105(a) CE). The definition of these requirements falls within the national legislature's competence, and thus they are applicable across the country. On the one hand, Article 4(2)(c) TRLSRU requires all regional pieces of legislation to secure citizens' rights to be informed about and participate in urban planning. On the other, under Article 5(e) TRLSRU, all citizens are entitled to participate effectively in urban planning approval and amendment procedures; they also have the right to receive a reasoned response to their comments by the relevant public authorities. All regional urban planning legislation has implemented these rights by means of (i) public consultation procedures open to anyone and (ii) hearings for affected landowners.

According to long-standing case law,[157] heavily contested in recent scholarly works,[158] urban plans qualify as administrative rule-making. Under Spanish law, administrative rules contrary to applicable legislation are always null and void; this breach can neither lead to voidability nor be considered a fault not leading to invalidity (Article 47(2) LPAC). Accordingly, any violations related to mandatory participation or consultation procedures will always render the plan fully invalid, there being no chance to rectify this fault or for it to be remedied by the lapse of time.[159] This due process violation does not only occur if the consultation procedure is not initiated, but also where the relevant public authority substantially amends the plan with respect to the draft submitted for public consultation.[160] The modification of the Belleville urban plan is thus fully invalid (null and void).

With regards to interim relief, Spanish law enables judicial authorities to order interim measures. More specifically, courts have jurisdiction to stay all urban plans as soon as appealed against if the implementation or enforcement thereof could deprive the appeal of its lawful purpose (Articles 129 to 136 LJCA). However, preparatory acts issued whilst the planning procedure is still ongoing are only subject to appeal if: (i) they directly or indirectly settle the merits of the case; (ii) prevent the procedure from moving forward; or (iii) render the party concerned defenceless or irreparably undermine rights or interests (Article 25(1) LJCA). Otherwise, the party concerned would generally be able to challenge the final act ultimately approving or amending the plan, on the grounds that the violation of due process rights renders the plan invalid. Therefore, as a general rule, the parties will be unable to seek interim relief vis-à-vis interim or preparatory procedural acts, and thus the administrative procedure intended to modify the plan will not be interrupted as an interim measure. Conversely, upon the plan's approval, Mrs Sheraton will be entitled to file the relevant appeal against, it and the competent court may stay the plan's legal effect until it rules on the merits.

[157] STS of 8 May 1968 (RJ 2548); of 26 January 1970 (RJ 229), of 4 November 1972 (RJ 4692), and of 27 March 1991 (RJ 2226).

[158] L Parejo Alfonso, 'La actuación administrativa, a caballo entre normación y simple ejecución y el caso e la planificación y el plan' (2020) 1 Revista de Derecho Público: Teoría y Método 30.

[159] STS of 10 May 2011 (Rec 2072/2007), of 28 September 2012 (Rec 1009/2011), of 12 May 2015 (Rec 1920/2013), and of 27 November 2015 (Rec 831/2014).

[160] STS of 27 February 2014, of 19 January 2016, and of 3 February 2016.

I. Sweden

PJ

Changing the use of an urban plan from commercial to residential would require a new plan. The answers below, however, concern a case where an urban plan has been amended.

The first questions to be answered are whether the consultation is formally a part of the procedure to draft an urban plan and if the consultation was a necessary element of the current procedure. The answers are affirmative.

Indeed, according to section 11, Chapter 5 of the Building and Planning Act (2010:900) the municipality has to consult known property unit owners when drafting an urban plan, except when the draft 'is not of importance (*saknar betydelse*) to them', (section 11 2 st, Chapter 5, Building and Planning Act). In the current case, the draft was of importance for Mrs Sheraton so she had the right to be consulted.

The Building and Planning Act states the manner in which the notification of the consultation procedure has to take place: According to section 11d, Chapter 5: 'a notice shall be posted on the municipal notice board and entered in a local newspaper'.[161]

The next questions to be answered are whether the decision to amend a plan is subject to appeal and if Mrs Sheraton is entitled to appeal against the changes made to the urban plan. Here too the questions may be answered in the affirmative. First, amendments to urban plans constitute decisions that may be appealed against (according to section 2.3, Chapter 13 of the Building and Planning Act)

Secondly, Mrs Sheraton is entitled to lodge an appeal against the decision. Indeed, if the law states that '[a] decision to ... amend ... an urban plan ... may only be appealed by the party who has submitted written comments before the end of the review period that have not been satisfied', which is not the case with Mrs Sheraton who was not even offered the possibility of participating in any consultation procedure, the law also lays down exceptions: this requirement 'does not apply if ... the appeal is based on the fact that the decision has not been brought in due order'. Mrs Sheraton should be able to base her right to appeal on this procedural failure.

The final question is whether the court, which is the Land and Environmental Court in this case.[162] The court quashes the decision if it is "in breach with a legal rule". The decision shall not be quashes however if it is evident that the failure has no importance for the outcome.[163]

[161] 'It must be stated in the announcement

1. the area of the detailed plan;
2. if the proposal deviates from the general plan;
3. where the proposal is available and how long the consultation period is;
4. that anyone wishing to comment on the proposal should do so during the consultation period; and
5. to whom comments on the proposal should be made.'

[162] Section 2a, Chapter 13 of the Building and Planning Act.

[163] According to section 17, Chapter 13 of the Building and Planning Act.

J. Ukraine
HD

Taking into account the breach of the procedure for the adoption of city planning documentation, the court would uphold the claims declaring amendments to the urban plan illegal and annulling them.

According to the Law of Ukraine 'On the Regulation of City Planning Activity', adoption of city planning documentation on the local level without public discussion is forbidden (Article 21(2).[164] The Order of Conducting Public Hearings for the Consideration of Public Interests during the Development of City Planning Project Documentation on the Local Level envisages that materials on the consideration of public opinion are an inalienable part of the documentation.[165]

In order to stop the revision of the urban plan, Mrs Sheraton can include such a claim in her legal action, or the court could decide on its own initiative. According to the Code of Administrative Proceedings of Ukraine, when an individual administrative act is annulled, the court can oblige the competent authority to perform concrete acts in order to renew the claimant's rights, freedoms, or interest for the protection of which the case was brought (Article 245(3)).

As an example of case law concerning a breach of participatory requirements in urban planning, the following judgment might be mentioned: Resolution of the Supreme Court of 30 January 2020 in case No 127/17274/17.[166]

K. The United Kingdom
EW

In the English context, Mrs Sheraton has been granted the equivalent of planning permission to build a new hotel, under the current urban plan. The applicable legislation will depend on whether or not she has already built the hotel. Once planning permission has been approved, a local authority has no power to withdraw that permission unilaterally without paying compensation. Planning permission may be *revoked* under section 97 of the Town and Country Planning Act 1990 (TCPA 1990) before building works start. Section 97 TCPA 1990 is framed broadly, but applied restrictively where:

[164] Law of Ukraine 'On the regulation of city planning activity' (17 February 2011) https://zakon.rada.gov.ua/laws/show/3038-17 (accessed 5 May 2021).

[165] Order of conducting of public hearings for the consideration of public interests while drafting of city planning documentation on the local level (25 May 2011) https://zakon.rada.gov.ua/laws/show/555-2011-%D0%BF (accessed 5 May 2021).

[166] Resolution of the Supreme Court of 30 January 2020 in the case No 127/17274/17 https://reyestr.court.gov.ua/Review/87297258 (accessed 5 May 2021).

(1) If it appears to the local planning authority that it is expedient to revoke or modify.
  a. any permission ... to develop land granted on an application made under this Part, or
  b. any permission in principle granted by a development order,
  the authority may by order revoke or modify the permission to such extent as they consider expedient.
(2) In exercising their functions under subsection (1) the authority shall have regard to the development plan and to any other material considerations.
(3) The power conferred by this section may be exercised
  a. in the case of planning permission that relates to the carrying out of building or other operations, at any time before those operations have been completed;
  b. in the case of planning permission that relates to a change of the use of any land, at any time before the change has taken place.
(4) The revocation or modification of planning permission for the carrying out of building or other operations shall not affect so much of those operations as has been previously carried out.

If there is an objection to a revocation order, as here with Mrs Sheraton, section 98(1) TCPA 1990 provides that an order under section 97 'shall not take effect unless it is confirmed by the Secretary of State'. In practice, it is rare for a revocation order to be submitted to the Secretary of State, with only three such orders submitted and one confirmed from 2009 to 2016.[167] Mrs Sheraton could challenge the validity of an order under section 97 TCPA 1990 by making an application to the High Court, within six weeks of the order's confirmation.[168]

Planning permission may only be revoked before any building works or change of use has been completed. Where planning permission is revoked or modified under section 97 TCPA 1990, compensation is payable under section 107 TCPA 1990 if the claim is made within the time and manner prescribed by regulations under the Act.[169] Compensation will be payable under section 107 TCPA 1990 where a person interested in the land has: (i) incurred expenditure in carrying out work which is rendered abortive by, the revocation or modification; or (ii) has otherwise sustained loss which is directly attributable to the revocation or modification.[170] Compensation may include more than the depreciation in market value of the land and could include future profits.[171]

167 Planning Permission: Written question—28113 answered on 2 March 2016. See https://www.parliament.uk/written-questions-answers-statements/written question/commons/2016-02-23/28113 (accessed 26 February 2021).

168 TCPA 1990, s 288(3).

169 Regulation 12 of the Town and Country Planning General Regulations 1992 requires a claim under s 107 TCPA 1990 to be in writing and served by delivery at the authority's offices, or posted within twelve months of the date of the decision to which the claim relates.

170 TCPA 1990, s 107.

171 *R v Bassetlaw DC, ex p Oxby* [1998] PLCR 283.

Where building works or a change of use have *already* occurred, the local authority may instead consider powers to make a 'discontinuance order' under section 102 TCPA 1990. This provision states that:

> (1) If, having regard to the development plan and to any other material considerations, it appears to a local planning authority that it is expedient in the interests of the proper planning of their area (including the interests of amenity)—
> a. that any use of land should be discontinued or that any conditions should be imposed on the continuance of a use of land; or
> b. that any buildings or works should be altered or removed,
> they may by order—
> i. require the discontinuance of that use, or
> ii. impose such conditions as may be specified in the order on the continuance of it, or
> iii. require such steps as may be so specified to be taken for the alteration or removal of the buildings or works, as the case may be.

The Secretary of State must confirm an order under section 102 TCPA 1990.[172] Again, compensation would be payable to Mrs Sheraton on the terms set out in section 115 TCPA 1990, where a discontinuance order has been made under section 102 TCPA 1990. Section 115 TCPA 1990 requires that any claim for compensation should be made in the prescribed manner and timescale, and that the local authority must pay compensation where a person has suffered loss because of a discontinuance order. Section 115 TCPA 1990 refers to losses caused by the depreciation of land values, disturbance, or by expenses incurred in complying with the order.

In the UK context, it is possible that Mrs Sheraton's property may be covered not by general planning permission, but under a local development order (LDO). This is a type of order used by a local authority to grant planning permission to specific types of development within a defined area. A planning authority can revoke a LDO at any time.[173] If a local planning authority wants to modify a LDO then reconsultation may be required but this is not always necessary so Mrs Sheraton's claim will be highly fact-specific.[174] Section 108 TCPA 1990 (as amended by section 189 of the Planning Act 2008) provides for compensation to be payable where planning permission granted by a LDO is withdrawn, so Mrs Sheraton could claim for compensation even if she cannot prevent the change in use from being implemented. If the planning authority has given at least twelve months' notice of the proposed revocation of the LDO, then compensation is not normally payable, but if development work started before a notice of revocation was published, compensation will be payable unless the LDO itself permits developments begun to be completed.[175]

[172] TCPA 1990, s 103.
[173] TCPA 1990, s 61A(6).
[174] HM Government Planning Practice Guidance, 'Can Local Development Orders Be Revoked and Modified? See https://www.gov.uk/guidance/when-is-permission-required#paragraph_082 Paragraph: 082 Reference ID: 13-082-20140306, 6 March 2014 (accessed 26 February 2021).
[175] TCPA 1990, s 108(3D).

It is also possible that Mrs Sheraton's property may be covered not by general planning permission, or a LDO but instead be covered by a neighbourhood development order (NDO).[176] The Localism Act 2011 strengthened the idea of neighbourhood planning at a more local level, allowing communities to influence the development of local areas and encourage community participation. NDOs can be prepared by parish or town councils and then submitted to the local authority for consideration. They can only be challenged at particular points during the process of making an NDO. The time limits for challenging a NDP under section 61N TCPA 1990 are rigid and the Court of Appeal confirmed in *R (Oyston Estates Ltd) v Fylde Borough Council*[177] that the court has no discretion to extend time, in the way that it normally could under the Civil Procedure Rules (CPR) rule 3.1(2)(a), when a Part 54 CPR claim for judicial review is made. The time limits under section 61N are statutorily fixed and minimise the uncertainty and unpredictable nature of any challenge, thus preventing a waste of time and resources in the final stages of the process when the local planning authority has made a decision or taken action.

Once an NDO is in force, as it appears with Mrs Sheraton's situation, it can be revoked by the Secretary of State[178] or by the planning authority with the consent of the Secretary of State.[179] An NDO may be revoked even after permitted developments have begun[180] and such developments may be completed, unless completion is prohibited by the revocation order itself. Planning authorities may modify a NDO if they consider that the modification does not 'materially affect any planning permission granted by the NDO'[181] but consent from the parish council or neighbourhood forum that initiated the NDO in the first place is required before the modification can take place.[182] The Neighbourhood Planning (General) Regulations 2012 (NPGR 2012) require that a modification to a NDO must be published on the planning authority's website and notice should be given to people previously notified during the making of the NDO.[183] The validity of NDOs can be challenged by judicial review within six weeks of the decision being published.[184]

L. The United States

IS

There is no federal constitutional 'participatory requirement' of this type. However, some state and local governments do require opportunities for citizen comment and

[176] s 61E(2) TCPA 1990.
[177] *R (Oyston Estates Ltd) v Fylde Borough Council* [2019] EWCA Civ 1152.
[178] TCPA 1990, s 61M(1).
[179] ibid s 61M(2).
[180] ibid s 61L(7).
[181] ibid s 61M(4A).
[182] ibid s 61M(5).
[183] Neighbourhood Planning (General) Regulations 2012/637, reg 30.
[184] TCPA 1990, s 61N(1).

participation in amendments of urban planning.[185] Some scholars have advocated more extensive public involvement in eminent domain planning and proceedings.[186]

Urban planning procedures vary greatly by state. But, as a general rule, a plan cannot come into force until state-mandated procedural requirements have come into force.

M. International investment law

FF

Investors occasionally invoke their right to participate in public decision-making processes (as opposed to the mere right to receive notification and provide views), but restrictions of this right are rarely sufficient to ground IIL breaches. Tribunals have denied that customary law grants participation rights,[187] so specific IIL guarantees must be examined. More commonly, the question arises whether stakeholders other than investors,[188] who might be affected by the investment's operation or the public measures that support it, should have been involved, to grant 'social licence' to the investment.[189]

As explained, tribunals conduct a holistic review of state conduct for compliance with due process (a requirement of expropriation's lawfulness and a fair and equitable treatment (FET) manifestation).[190] Tribunals applying the FET standard can examine 'whether due process has been denied to the investor',[191] and consider whether the investor had participatory rights. Participation matters, for instance, in connection with assessment or audits performed by authorities, which culminate in administrative sanctions or other adverse acts.[192] The investor's exclusion from the public decision-making process is not a decisive hallmark of a violation of FET per se and could be justified under national security[193] or public order.[194]

For instance, an investor complained that the decision-making process of a Decree reducing the price paid to electricity generators did not involve them in the review.[195]

[185] For an overview see AS Lemar, 'Overparticipation: Designing Effective Land Use Public Processes' Fordham Law Review (forthcoming) https://papers.ssrn.com/sol3/papers.cfm?abstract_id=3786306 (accessed 21 April 2021). See also I Somin, *The Grasping Hand: Kelo v City of New London and the Limits of Eminent Domain* (rev edn, University of Chicago Press 2016) ch 1 (describing Connecticut procedures used in the *Kelo* case).

[186] See eg M Heller and R Hills, 'Land Assembly Districts' (2008) *121* Harv L Rev 1465; D Becher, *Private Property and Public Power: Eminent Domain in Philadelphia* (Oxford University Press 2014) 234–35. For an overview and critique of such proposals see ibid 219–21.

[187] *Guaracachi* (n 107) para 439.

[188] This second aspect does not pertain to the scenario, but might be relevant when states ask investors to consult the local communities. A failure to comply can be invoked as reason for subsequent restrictive measures. See s II.7.

[189] *Pac Rim v El Salvador* ICSID Case No ARB/09/12 Amicus curiae brief, Center for International Environmental Law (20 May 2011); *Gran Colombia Gold v Colombia* ICSID Case No ARB/18/23 Notice of Arbitration (25 May 2018) para 77.

[190] On due process see *Yukos v Russia* PCA Case No 2005-04/AA227 Final Award (18 July 2014) para 1583.

[191] *Lemire v Ukraine* (n 57) para 284.

[192] *Bosh v Ukraine* ICSID Case No ARB/08/11 Award (25 October 2012) para 214.

[193] *CC/Devas v India* PCA Case No 2013-09 Award on Jurisdiction and Merits (25 July 2016) para 416.

[194] See IIL Case 4 below.

[195] *AES* (n 62) para 9.3.58.

The tribunal noted the investor's failure to make comments before the Decree's adoption, petition an individual price review thereafter, or challenge it in local courts. Moreover, the authorities considered the investor's comments after the Decree. The tribunal assessed the process overall:

> [t]he several procedural shortcomings in Hungary's implementation of the price decrees are [not] sufficient to constitute unfair and inequitable treatment.... In short, while [the host State's] consultations with Claimants on the Prices Decrees may not have been optimal, they do not amount to a culpable 'failure to consult properly' as alleged.[196]

When the applicable obligation lists due process as a feature of post-expropriation remedies (rather than of the expropriation process itself), the lack of prior participation cannot establish a breach if the state subsequently provides a fair opportunity of contestation:

> [the applicable BIT] does not impose upon the expropriating State an obligation to assess the value of compensation through a process in which the expropriated national or company must necessarily participate ... Rather, the investor's recourse, if it disputes the valuation performed by the expropriating State, is to seek review through procedures made available in that State's internal law ... or to submit the matter to international arbitration ...[197]

Pre-expropriation participation, in these cases, is not a valid cause of action, as the state has no duty to 'establish "legal recourse" to call into question the "legality" of a decision that has not yet been made'.[198]

In another case, the tribunal found the state's decision not to invite the investor to meetings with protestors against a mining plan 'politically plausible'.[199] However, a breach of due process was found in failure to contact or consult the investor in subsequent preparation of the decree blocking its business.[200]

Ultimately, the right to participate in the authorities' deliberation is just one intimation of due process. Its denial alone does not prejudge whether the administrative decision is lawful, but can influence that determination.

196 ibid paras 9.3.66; 9.3.70.
197 *Guaracachi* (n 107) paras 439–40.
198 *South American Silver* (n 68) para 584.
199 *Bear Creek* (n 53) para 380.
200 ibid para 446.

V. Case 4: Due process in urgent requisitions

A. Belgium

DR, LC, CD, and KP

In the case in question, a local authority orders the requisition of a hydro-electric power plant for 'serious reason of public order' following aggressive occupation by strikers.

The company owning the power plant challenges this decision on the grounds that the requisition was executed with no formal notice.

In Belgian law, requisition can be defined as a measure through which the authority can take temporary possession of, or use, an asset.[201]

The requisition must—in principle—be based on a legal provision and be justified by exceptional circumstances.[202]

Unlike expropriation, requisition does not imply that the owner is completely and permanently deprived of his property, nor does it entail the payment of an indemnity, unless the legal provision on which the requisition is based authorises it.[203]

A Belgian law of 15 May 2007 on civil security[204] could be applied in the case at hand, and more specifically Article 181, paragraph 1, according to which:

> The minister or his delegate can, during interventions executed in the frame of the missions referred to in Article 11, in the absence of public services available and necessary means, proceed to the requisition of persons and assets that he finds necessary. The mayor, the commander of the area and, by delegation, the officers have the same power during interventions executed in the framework of their missions.[205]

The general missions of the operational civil security services—referred to in Article 11 of the above-mentioned law[206]—include 'the rescue of persons and assistance to persons in dangerous situations, as well as the protection of their properties'.[207]

[201] On the concept of requisition see especially C Cambier, *Droit administrative* (Larcier 1968); M-A Flamme, *Droit administratif*, vol 2 (Bruylant 1989) 354; O Wéry, 'L'appropriation des biens immeubles par les pouvoirs publics: le vieux (et dangereux?) concept de la réquisition remis au goût du jour' [2001] Administration publique 26; P Bouvier and others, *Eléments de droit administratif* (Larcier 2013) 262–65; T Ceder, 'Les pouvoirs de réquisition du bourgmestre. Bourgmestre, ordre public et réquisition: un triptyque inconciliable?' (2006) 4 Revue de droit civil 3.

[202] Ceder (n 201) 5–7.

[203] Wéry (n 201) 33, 34, and 37.

[204] Act 'on civil security' (15 May 2007; publication in the Belgian *Official Gazette* on 31 July 2007).

[205] Act 'on civil security', art 181, § 1 (15 May 2007; publication in the Belgian *Official Gazette* on 31 July 2007; free translation).

[206] Act 'on civil security', art 11 (15 May 2007; publication in the Belgian *Official Gazette* on 31 July 2007).

[207] Act 'on civil security', art 11, § 1, 1° (15 May 2007; publication in the Belgian *Official Gazette* on 31 July 2007).

The execution of this power of requisition is regulated by a Royal Decree of 25 April 2014, which sets the scope and forms of requisition as well as the indemnities due to those affected by it.[208]

If the court before which the decision is challenged considers that the case at hand falls within the scope of the law of 15 May 2007, it would observe that this law provides that, in the event of grave emergency, the requisition may be ordered verbally[209] and thus without formal notice.

The court should then control whether, in the case in question, circumstances of grave emergency justified the absence of formal notice and whether the requirements set by the Royal Decree of 25 April 2014 have been met.

If the court deems that a case of grave emergency justified the absence of formal notice and that the requirements set by the Royal Decree of 25 April 2014 have been met, the requisition should be considered lawful. When the requisition ends, the applicant should receive an indemnity, based on the provision of the afore-mentioned Royal Decree.[210]

If the court considers that there has been no grave emergency justifying the absence of formal notice, it should quash the challenged decision or grant refusal to enforce it whether the applicant decides to bring the case before the Council of State or an ordinary court. In addition, the court might consider that the local authority is at fault under Articles 1382 ff of the Belgian Civil Code, and could grant the applicant compensation if the company suffered damages.

However, unlike the case explored in point 4, if the court deems that the law of 15 May 2007 cannot be applied in the case at hand, it might acknowledge that the requisition is legal as a 'police requisition', a concept inspired by French law.[211]

The Belgian court has in fact already deemed that local authorities can order a requisition with no legal provision authorising it explicitly, in order to ensure public order when there is no other choice and when the situation is one of specific and grave emergency.[212] However, this opinion is not unanimous, and the case law is rare and old.[213]

The court should then verify whether, in the case at hand, there is a specific and grave emergency justifying a 'police requisition'.

If the court holds that the case at hand is one of specific and grave emergency, the requisition must be considered lawful. However, the applicant may attempt—under Article 1 of Protocol No 1 to the European Convention on Human Rights—to demonstrate that there has been disproportionate interference with its right to property and to claim damages.[214] Indeed, when there is disproportionate interference with the

208 Royal decree 'on the modality of the power of requisition referred to in Article 181 of the Act of 15 May 2007 on civil security' (25 April 2014; publication in the Belgian *Official Gazette* on 27 November 2014).

209 ibid art 4, § 1, sub 2.

210 Royal decree 'on the modality of the power of requisition referred to in Article 181 of the Act of 15 May 2007 on civil security', arts 8 and 9 (25 April 2014; publication in the Belgian *Official Gazette* on 27 November 2014).

211 See Ceder (n 201) 10–14.

212 Court of Cassation (6 December 1858) *Pasicrisie*, 1859, I, 30; Civil Court of Termonde (29 July 1896) *Pasicrisie*, 1896, III, 304. See also other decisions mentioned by Ceder (n 2): Liège Court of Appeal (12 April 1919) *R.A.*, 1920, 102 ff; Ghent Court of Appeal (15 February 1922) *R.A.*, 1922, 343; Liège Court of Appeal (18 December 1940) *Pasicrisie*, 1941, II, 76.

213 Ceder (n 2) 12–14.

214 Wéry, (n 201) 37.

right to property, the European Court of Human Rights (ECtHR) has stated that the owner concerned may be entitled to compensation.[215]

If the court finds no specific and grave emergency, it should quash the challenged decision or allow refusal to enforce the decision, regardless of whether the applicant decides to bring the case before the Council of State or an ordinary court. In addition, the court might consider that the local authority is at fault under Articles 1382 ff of the Belgian Civil Code and award the applicant company damages.

B. France

EG

French law provides a framework for the requisition regime, which can concern both movable property and persons. This faculty enjoyed by the administration allows it to face emergencies in order to preserve the general interest. The requisition is generally justified because it is supposed to preserve 'the general needs of the Nation'. The act of requisition is therefore, in essence, an act that derogates from ordinary law. On the one hand, it is an act of coercion, and on the other hand, an act that infringes on individual rights and freedoms.

The persons targeted by an act of requisition must de facto submit to the orders of the local or national public authority on pain of penal sanctions. The case at hand is of a civil nature because it concerns a hydro-electric power station owned by a private company. The requisition is of a civil nature, whose regime differs from the military requisitions, and in these words governed by the Code of Defence: 'In times of peace, failure to comply with measures legally ordered by a public authority is punishable by imprisonment for one year and a fine of 4,500 euro.'[216] Guarantees for the injured party accompany this procedure. Among other things, formal requirements are imposed, as well as an indemnity to the attention of the person subject to the requisition.

The case presented is not exceptional and concerns most civil requisitions: it is related to an aggressive occupation and, more broadly, strikes. Given the urgency, the public authority deciding to requisition the hydro-electric plant does not directly notify the company of its decision. This may, a priori, justify the company's request before the administrative court. On the one hand, the requisition order constitutes an act of constraint, which must be a written act and notified to its addressee.[217] On the other hand, it must be accompanied by reasons if it is issued by the prefect, who is indeed a local authority.[218] Lastly, the object of the requisition is supposed to be specified and detailed with regard to its nature, duration, and quantity, so that the addressee of the requisition understands the nature of the order addressed to him.[219]

[215] *Chassagnou and Others v France* App no 25088/94 (ECtHR, 29 April 1999); *Alatulkkila and others v Finland* App no 33538/96 (ECtHR, 28 July 2005); *Anonymos Touristiki Etairia Kritis v Greece* App no 35332/05 (ECtHR, 21 February 2008); *Hermann v Germany* App no 9300/07 (ECtHR, 26 July 2012); Constitutional Court, case No 55/2012 of 19 April 2012; Court of Cassation (24 June 2010) *Pasicrisie*, 2010, 2004.

[216] Defence Code, art L 2236-2.

[217] Defence Code, art L 2213-4 of the.

[218] General Code of Local Authorities, art L 2215-1, 4°.

[219] ibid art L 2214-1, 4°.

In this case, none of these conditions of formality seems to have been respected by the public authority. Indeed, this is without taking into account the jurisprudential appreciation of these requirements. It appears that the urgency can justify order being provisionally formulated orally[220] before being subsequently confirmed in writing. The case law has therefore largely attenuated this requirement to make it extremely limited in practice. The very essence of requisitions is to deal with emergencies. In conclusion, the company's request will probably be rejected on this basis.

Lastly, suppose the administrative courts consider the requisition ordered by the local authority not to have been justified by the emergency and contrary to the principle of proportionality. In that case, the company may hold the state liable because it should have refrained from acting.[221] The company can then claim damages.[222] It should be noted, however, that this only happens very rarely because the urgency 'to rule on the basis of a purely subjective assessment'[223] leads judges to be generally favourable to decisions taken by the administration.

C. Germany

FS

The requisition of the hydro-electric power plant could constitute a measure taken by the police authorities. The police authorities are responsible for protecting public safety or public order. According to police law, an object can be seized by the police to avert a current danger to public safety or order.[224] This means that the police take possession of an object by excluding other people from any interference.[225] This can also involve immovable property, such as land and buildings.[226] The seizure of an object constitutes an encroachment on the right of property under Article 14 section 1 GG and therefore requires a balancing of the interest of the state to seize the object with the property right of the person concerned.[227] The interest of the state is to ensure the water supply. This interest can justify the temporary seizure of the hydro-electric power plant.

Prior to the seizure, the company must principally be given the opportunity to be heard in order to raise any objections.[228] However, a hearing may be omitted if an

220 CE, Decision of 5 March 2015, Chavat, Rec 62.

221 This form of accountability is now the norm, although it was not initially the case. At first, during the nineteenth century, the irresponsibility of the state was justified by the adage that 'the king can do no wrong'. It was necessary to wait for a decision of the *Tribunal des Conflits*, in 1873, to engage the responsibility of the state for the first time. Professor Léon Duguit described this revolutionary turn in these words: 'The State is not a power that commands, a sovereignty; it is a cooperation of public services organized and controlled by the governors.'

222 CE, Decision of 4 February 2015 No 369224.

223 J Rivero, 'Le droit positif de la grève dans les services publics d'après la jurisprudence du Conseil d'État' (1951) 14 DS 595.

224 cf eg BayPAG, art 25 No 1 lit a).

225 R Senftl, 'Art 25 PAG' in M Möstl and T Schwabenbauer (eds), *BeckOK Polizei- und Sicherheitsrecht Bayern* (15th edn, CH Beck 2020) para 8.

226 ibid para 12.

227 ibid para 7.

228 VwVfG, § 28 sec 1.

immediate decision appears to be necessary in the public interest.[229] This may be the case if there is an acute danger to the public water supply.

Thus, the seizure of the hydro-electric power plant in the case of an acute danger to public safety is in principle permitted. The hearing of the company can only be omitted in exceptional cases. If the court considers the seizure to be unlawful, the company is entitled to claims under state liability law. In such a case, compensation for unlawful sovereign interference with the right of property is possible ('*Anspruch aus enteignungsgleichem Eingriff*').

D. Italy

SM

Requisition is the legal act by which a person is deprived of their rights of possession (and sometimes ownership) of an asset. In other words, it is a measure by which the public administration, in the exercise of expropriation powers, temporarily or definitively withdraws the enjoyment of an asset, movable or immovable, by reason of superior public interest, with compensation.

The power to requisition private assets for serious public need has been recognised since Article 7 of Law No 2248/1865, annex E, (still in force), which introduced a power of dispensation, with respect to the principles of the legal system and today also of the Constitution itself, having, as an inevitable presupposition, the existence of an extraordinary and unpredictable public need, which would be impossible to tackle through ordinary proceedings.

Urgent requisitions are generally provided for in Article 835 of the Italian Civil Code. It states that: 'When serious and urgent public, military or civil needs arise, the requisition of movable or immovable property may be ordered. The owner is due a fair compensation. The requirements concerning requisitions are determined by special laws'.

In Italian law, expropriation and requisition are two different expressions of the power of the public administration over private assets (and rights).'

Unlike expropriation, requisition is linked more to an urgent need. This is the reason why the requisition procedure, having to serve the protection of an urgent interest, is much faster and less guaranteed than that of expropriation.

Requisition can be ordered by the prefect or the mayor with a contingent and urgent order for reasons of public security (the power of the mayor is based on Article 50, § 5, of Legislative Decree No 267/2000, the so-called Consolidated Law of Local Public Authorities; the authority of the prefect is more general and derived from the provision of Article 7 Law No 2248/1865, mentioned above).

Requisitions are exceptional measures with no specific discipline: the main principles (and guarantees) are provided for by administrative case law.

A distinction is made between 'requisition in property' and 'requisition in use'.

[229] ibid § 28 sec 2 No 1.

The first concerns only movable property and has definitive effects; the second can also affect real estate and has effects limited to the time necessary for the use of the asset. The requisition in use concerns the use of the property, while leaving ownership unchanged.

The case concerns a requisition in use of a hydro-electric power plant for serious reasons of public order. As administrative case law has regularly pointed out, the requisition in use of private property is, by its nature, a decision of an extraordinary nature which distorts the natural order of legal relationships, and is adopted on the basis of contingencies that can only be faced with exceptional measures.[230] Given their extraordinary nature, the requisition orders for the use of private property must be adopted through an emergency proceeding that does not provide a formal notice and the consequent participation of the private owner of the asset subject to the requisition. However, the courts impose the respect of certain requirements by the public administration in order to create the least damage to the private property.

First of all there must be the need to urgently use exceptional measures to safeguard general interests that would otherwise not be protectable and to fix a term for the effectiveness of the requisition order. The impossibility of using ordinary remedies must however derive from reasons unrelated to the will of the public administration and must not be attributable to its negligence.

In this case, the use of the requisition of the plant must be considered legitimate to avoid interruption of an indispensable public service for the community and to prevent the occurrence of events capable of compromising public order and safety. However, the management of the company can challenge the order before the court in order to review the decision on the grounds of the lawfulness of the reasons for the requisition and its compliance with all the requirements mentioned above. It does not seem possible for the applicant to claim a lack of participation, as usually provided for in the ordinary procedure, such as for land expropriation. If the administrative court, however, decides to quash the requisition order on the basis of the lack of the relevant requirements (ie an incorrect evaluation of the urgency and the contingency of the measure, negligence by the public administration, the lack of a term for the validity of the order, etc), it can also award a compensation resulting from the illegitimate requisition of the private property.

E. The Netherlands

JS and NvT

Temporary restriction in the Netherlands in such cases is only possible under the Requisition Act ('*Vorderingswet*'). This is a so-called emergency act, under which—in certain extraordinary circumstances—through a requisition decision, someone's property right can be (temporarily) taken away. The requisition can be applied to (movable and immovable) property and proprietary rights. The requisition procedure takes place under administrative law; the amount of compensation to be awarded however is decided

[230] See eg Cons Stato, Sec IV (9 July 2002) No 3823.

upon by the civil courts. There is a statutory obligation to award damages (if there is any damage, Article 15 subsection 1 Requisition Act).

A requisition decision can only be made on the level of the central government (namely by the Minister concerned). Local authorities cannot make such a decision. The decision is made without input from the owner and without prior notice. The publication of the decision happens by post or hand delivery to the owner[231] and in this case will also need to be sent to the mayor of the municipality in which the building stands.[232]

The owner cannot appeal against the requisition decision, only against the amount of damages awarded.

F. Poland

IK and ŁK

The factual circumstances taking place at the hydro-electric power plant show that it may be necessary to restrict the right of property use in emergency situations. Undoubtedly, the occupation strike staged by the workers, which resulted, or could have resulted, in a blackout in a specific area is one such situation. In Poland, neither the electric power producer nor supplier must be a public entity. However, the market is regulated and enterprises operating on it are subject to a number of administrative duties and restrictions.[233] It should be noted that a power plant or a water dam may be a piece of the 'critical infrastructure' referred to in Article 3(2)(a) of the Emergency Management Act of 26 April 2007.[234] It should be understood as systems, as well as their constituent functional structures linked with one another, including buildings, facilities, installations and roads of key importance for the security of the state and its citizens and serving to ensure the efficient functioning of public administration bodies as well as institutions and enterprises. If the strike resulted in a crisis, that should be understood as a situation exerting a negative impact on the level of the security of persons, property on a large scale or the environment, causing significant restrictions in the operation of competent public administration bodies due to their inadequate powers and means.[235]

Given the above, Article 126(1) of the IPMA provides, among other things, that in case of force majeure[236] or an urgent need to prevent the occurrence of a major

231 Requisition Act, art 9.

232 ibid art 9 subs 2.

233 Energy Law Act of 10 April 1997, JoL 2019.755. See further W Pyzioł and A Walaszek-Pyzioł, *Prawo energetyczne: Komentarz* (Wydawnictwo Prawnicze Lexis Nexis 1999).

234 Uniform text: JoL 2019.1398.

235 ibid art 3(1).

236 See Supreme Court judgments: of 9 July 1962, I CR 54/62, LEX No 106473; of 26 August 1992, I PRN 36/92, LEX No 13282; of 11 February 1997, II CKN 78/96, LEX No 55387; of 16 January 2002, IV CKN 629/00, LEX No 54332; of 4 September 2004, IV CKN 420/01, LEX No 146450; Supreme Court resolutions: of 24 November 2000, III CZP 37/00, LEX No 44005; of 13 December 2007, III CZP 100/07, LEX No 322091; G Bieniek, *Komentarz do kodeksu cywilnego: Księga trzecia. Zobowiązania*, vol 1 (Lexis Nexis 2002) 371; A Łukaszewska, 'Artykuł 126' in J Szachułowicz and others (eds), *Gospodarka nieruchomościami: Przepisy i komentarz* (Wydawnictwo Prawnicze LexisNexis 2003) 351; P Wojciechowski, 'Artykuł 126' in P Czechowski (ed), *Ustawa o gospodarce nieruchomościami: Komentarz* (Wolters Kluwer 2015).

damage, the county head, or *starost*, performing a government administration task, grants, by means of a decision, a permission to temporarily requisition property for a period not exceeding six months, counting from the requisition day. An urgent need suggests extraordinary circumstances as reasons for the threat, such as catastrophes or breakdowns of appliances or networks. The essence of this condition is an unforeseeable situation or state necessitating instantaneous rapid action in order to prevent the occurrence of a major damage; additionally, the issuance of the decision should be also based on reliable information that supports the need for immediate action.[237]

In application-triggered proceedings, the decision is issued without delay, yet not later than within seven days counting from the application submission day. Pursuant to paragraph 2 of the provision referred to above, the decision is instantly enforceable. Additionally, Article 126(5) of the IPMA provides that should the urgent need to prevent a threat or damage make it impossible to submit an application for the issuance of a temporary property requisition decision, the owner shall be obliged to make the property available in order to prevent such circumstances. The obligation to make property available is subject to administrative enforcement. The entity that has requisitioned the property applies for the issuance of that decision within three days following the requisition day. The decision can be issued not later than six months after the day of property requisition.[238]

Given the factual circumstances of the case and the provisions of law referred to above, one should conclude that the company that owns the hydro-electric power plant has no grounds for securing a ruling on the invalidity of the administrative decisions issued. Yet it can seek relevant compensation. Additionally, in order to prevent excessive use of the solutions provided for in Article 126(5) of the IPMA, the legislator foresees administrative-law penalties. They are imposed in case of a failure on the part of the entity that requisitioned the property to submit an application within three days. Performing a government administration task, the starost, by means of a decision, imposes a fine of PLN 5,000 per each day of delay, counting from the day after the day when the application submission deadline lapsed. The *starost* will also impose a penalty if a property requisition itself has taken place yet not conditions justifying it. This provision is undoubtedly a certain guarantee for the property owner that urgent situations will be duly examined and analysed.

G. Portugal

RGdF

The requisition is tantamount to an expropriation in the sense that it affects property rights in a way that impedes the use (fully or partially) of the assets in question. That is why Portuguese law regulates both of them, expropriation and requisition, in the same law: the CE (Articles 80 and ff are about requisition). But requisition does not

[237] See the judgment of the Supreme Administrative Court of 5 February 2009, I OSK 301/08, LEX No 515988; the judgment of the Provincial Administrative Court in Wrocław of 9 December 2010, II SA/Wr 555/10, LEX No 755652.

[238] Ł Strzępek, *Ograniczenie praw rzeczowych w drodze wywłaszczenia* (Wyższa Szkoła Humanitas 2016) 36 ff.

have an unified legal framework in Portuguese law. Besides the CE, there is other legislation about requisition, and sometimes they overlap, giving raise to various issues and doubts. To name the main ones, Decree-Law 637/74 of 20/11, sets the principles of civil requisition; Law 20/95, of 13/07, sets the legal discipline of mobilisation and requisition for reasons of national defence; Decree-Law 153-A/90, of 16/05, sets the discipline for requisition of sports infrastructures.[239]

The requisition presented to us in this case could have many meanings or objects. It would surely fall upon the building of the power plant which had been occupied. But serious reasons of public order would surely have to do with the need of keeping the power plant working normally, and for that the building itself would not be enough: all other goods pertaining to the service would be needed (fuel, stationary, light and heavy machinery, etc.), and also employees (without these the plant would not be able to operate, unless other ones were brought in).

All this renders requisition complex. Article 80/1 of the CE allows the requisition of buildings, including commercial and industrial establishments, but it is not clear if this permission extends to persons (employees), or if, for that, the law on civil requisition should be used as well. On the other hand, it is also not clear if this would imply an intervention on the management of the plant (the nature of this enterprise is not known, but even if it was a private corporation, the Constitution allows a public intervention at management level, for instance, appointing temporarily one or all the members of the board—Articles 83 and 86/2).

In any case, this requisition could not be 'commanded' by a local authority (municipality). If the procedure of the CE was to be followed, the local authority could ask the government (the minister responsible for the sector) to determine the requisition, and then a resolution of the Council of Ministers would have to recognise the need for the requisition and only after this could the competent minister decide upon it (Articles 81, 82, and 83). Only the government can decide because requisitions can only take place in cases of urgent necessity when general and national reasons are involved. So, there is no requisition on case of mere local needs. In the present case, the power plant could of course be nationally and not only locally important. But this centralisation of/on government powers also happens with the other legal frameworks of requisition.[240]

The company should have been heard before the decision of requisition, and the entity which is asking for the requisition must offer the government proof of prior negotiations with the proprietor and why they failed (Articles 83 al d) and 85/6 of the CE). Not doing so is a procedural illegality which could determine the annulment of the requisition (which is an administrative act) by the courts. The urgency of the requisition could determine that the government would dispense with the prior hearing

[239] In the context of the COVID-19 crisis, the state of emergency was declared by the Presidential Decree 14-A/2020 of 18 March. The governmental Decree 2-A/2020 of 20 March established the measures of execution of the Presidential Decree, among which are possibilities of requisition, by the Minister of Health, of various industries, factories, and facilities of every nature (including health facilities), along with all kinds of goods and services necessary to fight the crisis in hand (art 19). There is also a general (and again, partially overlapping) provision regarding civil requisition (art 27).

[240] In the autonomous regions of Azores and Madeira, this power belongs to the regional governments, not to the central government of the Republic.

of the company (Article 124/1 al a) of the CPA), but this particular option requires a specific justification. The courts could uphold it, but they would have to overcome an argument: the requisition can only take place in situations of 'urgent need' (Article 80/1 of the CE) and even in this case the CE demands the prior hearing. So, only the strongest situation of need, it seems, would authorise 'urgency upon urgency' to infringe that rule of the CE. A declaration of state of administrative necessity would be considered as a strong recognition of such a need to overlook procedural rules (Article 3/2 of the CPA).

H. Spain

LAJ and DUFB

In the so-called civil requisitions (as opposed to military ones), public authorities may implement measures that entail 'destruction, effective damage or private property seizures', only 'on serious grounds of public order or public security, or in the face of epidemics, floods or other emergencies' (Article 120 LEF). Property can be seized without any prior declaration of the need to expropriate. However, the expropriated owner will have the right to seek compensation in an amount calculated under the rules established by the LEF regarding the expropriation's fair compensation. Civil requisitions are thus a specific type of expropriation defined by the lack of a prior administrative procedure as well as by the fact that compensation is calculated once the effects of the seizure are over.[241] Thus, Article 120 LEF strikes a fair balance between two competing constitutional principles: the rights to private property and to be heard in expropriation procedures (Article 33(3) CE), on the one hand, and the obligation to safeguard public order, public security, and public health (Article 103(1) CE), on the other.

A paradigmatic example of civil requisitions is that provided for in the Spanish legislation on constitutional states of emergency according to Article 116 CE. Under Article 11 LOEAES, in case of formal declaration of the so-called 'state of alarm' (*estado de alarma*), which is an exclusive prerogative of the Spanish government that can be exercised only in extraordinary circumstances, it is possible 'to carry out temporary requisitions of all types of goods and to impose obligatory personal services', either by the administrative decree declaring the state of alarm or by successive ones issuing on its basis. This is what has happened recently, in the context of the pandemic caused by the coronavirus outbreak. Pursuant to Art. 8 of Royal Decree No 463/2020, declaring the COVID-19 state of alarm:

> the competent delegated authorities—ie, a limited number of Ministers—may agree, *ex officio* or at the request of the Autonomous Regions or local entities, to carry out temporary requisitions of all types of goods necessary for the fulfilment of the purposes set out in this Royal Decree.

[241] STS of 25 April 1997 (Rec 6217/1992).

If the act providing for the seizure is under appeal, the court should basically verify two aspects under Article 120 LEF. First, if there are 'serious grounds of public order' as invoked by the relevant public authority. The court would thus have to decide whether the public body has appropriately subsumed the facts of the case under the applicable provision, taking into account that legal provisions include undetermined legal concepts. Public authorities enjoy certain scope of appreciation for the interpretation thereof, often allowed by judges unless in certain cases, such as manifest error or lack of reasons.[242] The second aspect to be examined by the court is whether the adopted measure fulfils the principle of proportionality, ie if the measure is a suitable, necessary, and strictly reasonable—proportionate *stricto sensu*—means to achieve the aims—ie to tackle the serious public order-related issue. On the contrary, courts are not entitled to impose additional procedural steps other than those laid down in the applicable legislation. Otherwise, the court would be interfering with the balance between competing constitutional principles stricken by the Parliament.[243]

If, in the view of the deciding court, the relevant seizure was lawful, the court will instruct the expropriated owner to seek fair compensation for expropriation within an administrative procedure (Article 120 LEF). Conversely, if the court considers that there were no serious grounds of public order that may justify the seizure—or otherwise that such seizure was unreasonable—it will declare it invalid (Article 71(1)(a) LJCA). If this were the case, the court will restore the status quo prior to the unlawful administrative decision (Article 71(1)(b) LJCA). If such reinstatement was *de facto* impossible or unfeasible, or if there was loss or damage, the judgment will declare the owner's right to receive compensation for public authority liability (Article 71(1)(d) LJCA). The mere administrative decision's invalidation or annulment does not allow on its own to hold public authorities liable, being necessary that the decision be manifestly illegal.[244] Nonetheless, given the deference granted to public authorities regarding the scrutiny over the fulfilment of Article 120 LEF requirements, which entails that the act will only be invalidated in case of lack of reasons or manifest error by the issuing public authority, one could assume that there will be no difference regarding the scope of protection granted by an annulment or compensation.

I. Sweden

PJ

The Civil Protection Act (*Lagen om skydd mot olyckor* 2003:778) allows for the kind of intervention described in the above-mentioned case.

Indeed, section 2 of Chapter 6 (entitled *Interference with another's right*) allows public authorities to

[242] E García de Enterría and T-R Fernández, *Curso de Derecho administrativo*, vol 1 (Thomson-Civitas 2017) 503–510.

[243] STS of 10 December 2018 (Rec 3781/2017).

[244] See L Arroyo Jiménez and D Utrilla Fernández-Bermejo, 'Procedural Requirements for Administrative Limits to Property Rights in Spain' in this volume, section V. STS of 17 February 2015 (Rec 2335/2012), and of 26 October 2011 (Rec 188/2009).

> block or evacuate areas, use, remove or destroy property and other interference with another's right, insofar as the intervention is justifiable in view of the nature of the danger, the damage caused by the intervention and the circumstances in general

when 'danger to life, health or property or damage to the environment cannot be conveniently prevented in any other way'.

The court would take into consideration the existence of 'a substantial public or individual interest' which 'requires immediate notification of the decision' and set aside the mechanisms guaranteeing due process such as the obligation for communication and the right to express itself as allowed by the Administrative Procedure Act (section 25).

The company management has the right to lodge an appeal against the decision. The decision nevertheless applies even in the event of appeal (section 4, Chapter 10 of the Civil Protection Act).

The Act entitles the parties whose rights have been infringed to receive damages (section 7, Chapter 7).

J. Ukraine

HD

Under the Civil Code of Ukraine there are two grounds for requisition. The first includes natural calamity, accident, epidemic, epizootic, and other emergencies. Forced alienation in such cases is admissible only for the purpose of public necessity. And there should be advance and full reimbursement to the value of the property. The second ground covers conditions of martial law or a state of emergency. In this case reimbursement can be made after the requisition has taken place. Thus, the main difference between these two grounds is the time of the reimbursement: before or after requisition. Regarding the first ground, however, the Civil Code contains an explicit condition, namely that a forced alienation should be imposed on the basis and in the way established by law (Article 353(1)).[245] Nevertheless, up to now, there is no specific law dealing with the requisition procedure in Ukraine. This entails uncertainty in the legal regulation of requisition. In fact, the lack of a specific law on requisition makes its application on the first ground impossible.[246]

As noted by specialists in civil law, requisition is an unjudicial (administrative) order of forced alienation. It is treated as the primary form of property rights' acquisition because of its forced character, namely the importance of the sole will of the state as the property's acquirer. According to the doctrinal interpretation of the legal norms of the Civil Code of Ukraine concerning requisition according to the first ground, it may be applied only by the state authorities.[247]

[245] Civil Code of Ukraine (16 January 2003) https://zakon.rada.gov.ua/laws/show/435-15 (accessed 5 May 2021).

[246] V Bobrika, I Spasibo-Fateeva, and O Banasko (eds), *Civil Code of Ukraine. Scientific and Practical Commentary*, vol 5 (Strajd 2011) 249.

[247] ibid 241.

There is no unambiguous answer as to which argument the court would take into account: grave public necessity or violation of the procedural rules.

The Code of Administrative Proceedings of Ukraine provides that while examining cases the judge should ascertain whether the decisions have been adopted proportionally, namely observing the proper balance between any adverse effects on the rights, liberties or interests of persons and the purpose that the decision pursues (Article 2(2)). A competent authority has to prove the lawfulness of its decision, action, or inaction (Article 77 of the Code of Administrative Proceedings of Ukraine).[248] Therefore, the burden of proof lies with the local authority.

If we can assume that this situation happened during a state of emergency, the Law of Ukraine 'On transfer, forced alienation or seizure of property under the legal order of martial law or state of emergency' would be applied. Under this law, forced alienation of property has to be recorded in a special act signed by the owner of the property. If the owner is absent, this act can be prepared without his involvement, but he has a right to known about the act later. A copy of the act has to be handed to the owner, who will acknowledge receipt (Article 7).[249] If the court gives weight to the restriction of company's rights, this legal norm could be used as one of the arguments. If the court annuls the requisition, the local authority will have to indemnify damages. The Code of Administrative Proceedings of Ukraine establishes that damages can be awarded if the court recognizes an individual act as unlawful and, as a result of it, the court will quash it (Article 245(2)). The Constitution of Ukraine provides that everyone has a right to reimbursement at the expense of the state or local self-government bodies for material and moral damage caused by illegal decisions, actions, or the inactivity of public authorities, local self-government bodies, or their officials while exercising their powers (Article 56).[250]

If the court emphasizes grave public necessity, it will have to be ascertained whether the local authority has exercised proportionality. In Ukraine, the practice of the ECtHR is applied as the source of law.[251] As the ECtHR noted:

> It may also be relevant whether it would have been possible to achieve the same objective by less invasive interference with the applicant's rights and whether the authorities examined the possibility of applying these less intrusive solutions (OAO Neftyanaya Kompaniya Yukos v. Russia, §§ 651-654; *Vaskrsić v. Slovenia*, § 83).[252]

[248] Code of Administrative Proceedings of Ukraine (6 July 2005) https://zakon.rada.gov.ua/laws/show/2747-15 (accessed 5 May 2021).

[249] Law of Ukraine 'On transfer, forced alienation or seizure of property under the legal order of martial law or state of emergency' (17 May 2012) https://zakon.rada.gov.ua/laws/show/4765-17 (accessed 5 May 2021).

[250] Constitution of Ukraine (28 June 1996) https://zakon.rada.gov.ua/laws/show/254%D0%BA/96-%D0%B2%D1%80 (accessed 5 May 2021).

[251] Law of Ukraine 'On the enforcement of judgments and application of practice of the European Court of Human Rights' (23 February 2006) https://zakon.rada.gov.ua/laws/show/3477-15 (accessed 5 May 2021).

[252] *Guide on Article 1 of Protocol No 1 to the European Convention of Human Rights* (31 August 2020) 26–77 https://www.echr.coe.int/Documents/Guide_Art_1_Protocol_1_ENG.pdf (accessed 5 May 2021).

K. The United Kingdom

EW

Fairness is normally context specific in English administrative law. It is possible that the normal expectation that notice should be given before requisitioning land could be overridden by urgent considerations, such as public health or national security.[253] In English law, the temporary possession of land has historically been difficult, unless it involves a wartime requisition. This situation is due to change when sections 18 to 31 of the Neighbourhood Planning Act 2017 (NPA 2017) comes into force. The NPA 2017 introduces a new power under section 18 enabling acquiring authorities to take temporary possession of land, either by agreement or compulsorily. The power can only be exercised in situations where the acquiring authority already has a power compulsorily to acquire land permanently. Even under the NPA 2017 at least three months' notice of the intended entry must be given under section 20. Additionally, the land must be identified, the purposes described, and the period for which land will be temporarily possessed stated.

In the circumstance in this case, it is more likely that the authority would base its temporary requisition on other legislative powers. The Civil Contingencies Act 2004 (CCA 2004) Part I provides for emergency regulations to be made where they are appropriate for the purpose of 'preventing, controlling or mitigating an aspect or effect of the emergency'.[254] An emergency is defined as 'an event or situation which threatens serious damage to human welfare in a place in the United Kingdom; an event or situation which threatens serious damage to the environment of a place in the United Kingdom; or war, or terrorism, which threatens serious damage to the security of the United Kingdom'.[255] The situation with the hydro-electric plant could fit within section 1(2)(e) CCA 2004, which defines an event threatening damage to human welfare as one where there is disruption 'of a supply of money, food, water, energy or fuel'. Here, the occupation of the hydro-electric plant could be said to disrupt the supply of energy.

Under the CCA 2004, emergency regulations can include any provision of the kind that could be made by Act of Parliament including 'providing for or enabling the requisition or confiscation of property, with or without compensation'.[256] There is no need to consult Parliament or to obtain its approval before emergency regulations come into effect, but a senior minister must lay them before Parliament as soon as possible. The regulations will lapse after seven days unless both Houses of Parliament approve them. Where the regulations are approved, they will lapse after thirty days[257] but the government can pass further regulations to renew their effect.[258] The CCA 2004 provides for consultation with devolved administrations in Scotland, Northern Ireland, and Wales but even here the minister can disapply a requirement to consult due to

[253] *Council of Civil Service Unions v Minister for the Civil Service* (GCHQ case) [1985] AC 374.
[254] Civil Contingencies Act 2004 (CCA 2004), s 23(1).
[255] ibid s 1.
[256] ibid s 22(3)(b).
[257] ibid s 26(1).
[258] ibid s 26(2)(a).

urgency[259] and a failure to consult devolved administrations does not affect the validity of the regulations.[260]

It is worth noting that the workers occupying the premises could potentially challenge an order on the grounds that CCA 2004 emergency regulations may not 'prohibit or enable the prohibition of participation in, or any activity in connection with, a strike or other industrial action'.[261] However, here the company rather than the striking workers wish to challenge the order. It would be open to the company to challenge the regulations, but where emergency regulations have been approved by Parliament, the courts are likely to accept a restriction on due process requirements because of the Parliamentary scrutiny involved and the CCA 2004 context. The CCA 2004 cannot amend or abridge the Human Rights Act 1998 (HRA 1998), which incorporates the European Convention on Human Rights into domestic law. It would therefore be possible for the courts to strike down any emergency regulations where these contradict protections secured by the HRA 1998.[262] However, the rights secured by the HRA 1998 are relative and can be interfered with where the government believes that this is proportionate and necessary for a public purpose.

The company could try relying on administrative principles of fairness and argue that the requirement for notice has been interfered with. However, it seems likely that the urgent need to secure energy supplies would justify overriding a requirement for notice. Administrative law principles of fairness are context specific and are

> not immutable ... What fairness demands is dependent on the context of the decision ... [and an] essential feature of the context is the statute which creates the discretion, as regards both its language and the shape of the legal and administrative system within which the decision is taken.[263]

The GCHQ case[264] provides useful support for this approach. Here, there had been an established tradition of consultation with Trade Unions before changes were made to Civil Servants' employment terms and the government was challenged when, without consultation, it abolished the right of civil servants to belong to trade unions. The House of Lords held that whilst fairness would normally have required consultation, this was outweighed by national security justifications.

It is possible that the hydro-electric plant could have been temporarily requisitioned under the Electricity Act 1989 (EA 1989). This statute provides for the Secretary of State to give 'requisite or expedient' directions for the purposes of 'preserving the security of buildings or installations used for, or for the purposes connected with, the generation, transmission or supply of electricity'.[265]

[259] ibid s 29(4)(a).
[260] ibid s 29(4)(b).
[261] ibid s 23(3)(b).
[262] ibid s 30(2).
[263] *R v Secretary of State for the Home Department, ex parte Doody* [1994] 1 AC 531, 560 (Lord Mustill).
[264] *Council of Civil Service Unions v Minister for the Civil Service* [1985] AC 374.
[265] EA 1989, s 96(1)(a), (6).

Additionally, the Secretary of State can give directions to mitigate 'the effects of any civil emergency which may occur'.[266] The Secretary of State should consult with a 'licence holder' or any person authorised to generate[267] or supply[268] electricity before giving directions, but no notice period is set out. It is also open to the Secretary of State to require that no information be disclosed about the event where the parties involved are notified that disclosure is 'against the interests of national security'.[269]

L. The United States

IS

In many situations, the occupation or even destruction of private property by law enforcement as part of an operation to prevent crime or maintain public order is considered an exercise of the 'police power' and therefore not a taking requiring compensation.[270] The case described above would probably qualify as such a situation.

The exact boundary between exercises of the 'police power' and takings are disputed, and some experts argue that the distinction should be abolished, or at least that the scope of 'police power' actions not requiring compensation should be significantly narrowed.

Outside the context of law enforcement, government occupation and destruction of property for purposes of addressing an emergency, is sometimes treated as a compensable taking, particularly if the property in question was not itself the source of the threat to the public, but was rather damaged or destroyed in order to mitigate a danger emanating from elsewhere. For example, the US Court of Claims recently ruled that the deliberate flooding of part of the city of Houston to prevent greater flooding elsewhere, during a massive hurricane, is a taking requiring compensation.[271]

M. International investment law

FF

Urgent measures taken without prior notice and ostensibly aimed at the protection of public order can be admitted under IIL, depending on several factors.

In the scenario, the government appears to provide full protection and security (FPS) to the investment. Since 'a State has a duty to protect aliens and their investment against unlawful acts committed by some of its citizens',[272] the state must exercise due

[266] ibid s 96(1)(b). For these purposes, 'civil emergency' means any natural disaster or other emergency, which in the opinion of the Secretary of State is or may be likely to disrupt electricity supplies under s 96(7) EA 1989.
[267] ibid s 4(4).
[268] ibid s 4(4).
[269] ibid s 96(5).
[270] See eg *Lech v Jackson* 719 Fed Appx 711 (10th Cir 2019).
[271] *In re Upstream Addicks & Barker* 146 Fed Cl 219 (Ct Cl 2019).
[272] *Amco v Indonesia* ICSID Case No ARB/81/1 Award (20 November 1984) para 172.

diligence in protecting the investor's property from escalating violence, including the aggression of employees.[273] In the *Elettronica Sicula* case,[274] local authorities requisitioned a plant after the owners, who planned to liquidate their business, started dismissing employees who had already occupied the factory. The requisition did not deprive the owners of their right to control the business. As this right had already lapsed due to the state of insolvency, there was effectively no longer any right to expropriate.[275]

The obligation to protect, if realised by seizing the property (either to protect it, or to evict the illegal occupants), also entails the subsequent obligation to restore the property to the investor's control when the requisition is no longer necessary:

> [E]gypt violated its obligation under Article 2(2) of the IPPA to accord Wena's investment 'fair and equitable treatment' and 'full protection and security' ... there is substantial evidence that Egypt was aware of EHC's intentions to seize the hotels and took no actions to prevent EHC from doing so. Moreover, once the seizures occurred, both the police and the Ministry of Tourism took no immediate action to restore the hotels promptly to Wena's control.[276]

If the requisition is, in effect, temporary and does not deprive the investment of its value, it cannot constitute expropriation. The investor could seek compensation alleging the breach of fair and equitable treatment (FET) if the requisition—even if purportedly designed to protect it—unduly encroaches on the investment, for instance by limiting the investor's right to due process. In principle—see above IIL, Case 2—due process is an element of FET and prior notice is expected.

In this scenario, the measure's urgency and the invocation of 'grave public necessity' point to two possible (although related) defences:

(a) the measure's reasonableness/proportionality in the circumstances, to avert a FET breach; or
(b) a higher-order justification invoking the state of necessity or public order considerations, accepting that a breach might have occurred, but was justified.

Under (a), the tribunal could accept the state's view that the urgent need to prevent social unrest dispensed with the requirement of prior notice. In *Bear Creek*, the tribunal upheld the state's view that it was unnecessary to involve the investor in governmental meetings with the protesters that had been 'undisputedly organized to deal with the social unrest' caused by the investor's plan.[277] While this choice interfered with the investor's due process right of participation,[278] public order justified it. Due process review is performed holistically and one administrative irregularity is not

[273] *Noble Ventures v Romania* ICSID Case No ARB/01/11 Award (12 October 2005) para 164–166; *Pantechniki v Albania* ICSID Case No ARB/07/21 Award (30 July 2009) paras 71–84.
[274] *ELSI* (n 58) p 15.
[275] ibid para 76.
[276] *Wena v Egypt* Award (8 December 2000) para 84.
[277] *Bear Creek* (n 53) para 380.
[278] IIL Case 3.

always fatal: the tribunal will determine if the lack of notice harmed the investor irreversibly or, instead, the investor's rights were safeguarded because the state acts could be challenged in local courts.

Conversely, an urgent confiscation of the investment, motivated by the investor's alleged wrongdoing (ie transporting goods without a permit), was not considered justified by public order. Even if the allegations had been established, the requisition was disproportionate and amounted to expropriation in light of its method and duration:

> [e]l Tribunal encuentra gravemente desproporcionado que esa alegada infracción pudiera dar lugar a una acción militar de la envergadura de la mencionada, [including] a la intervención total en las operaciones de la empresa infractora, a la sustitución de sus administradores y al decomiso de la totalidad de sus inventarios.[279]

Under (b), the International Court of Justice in *ELSI* observed that treaty guarantees cannot be construed so widely as to remove the state's power to adopt public order measures.[280] General international law provides for necessity as a circumstance precluding wrongfulness,[281] but it does not spare states from compensating the damage caused by the excused conduct.

Investment tribunals have generally held that customary international law accepts the 'that a deprivation can be justified if it results from the exercise of regulatory actions aimed at the maintenance of the public order'.[282] Inevitably, tribunals must determine in each case whether 'particular conduct by a state "crosses the line" that separates valid regulatory activity from expropriation'.[283]

Recent treaties include general exceptions inspired by the Articles XX and XXI of the WTO General Agreement on Tariffs and Trade (GATT).[284] Article XXI, in particular, provides that the GATT does not bind states adopting measures necessary to protect public order and public security. For instance, a recent IIL instrument provides that: 'Rien dans le présent accord ne peut être interprété comme une limitation à une Partie d'adopter ou de mantenir des mesures visant à preserver sa sécurité nationale ou l'ordre public.'[285] If the applicable treaty contains a similar exception, the state's conduct is not excused but simply licit, and no duty of compensation can arise.

[279] *Armas v Venezuela* PCA Case No 2013-03/AA473 Award (26 April 2019) para 345; see also *OI European Group v Venezuela* ICSID Case No ARB/11/25 Award (10 March 2015) para 518.

[280] *ELSI* (n 58) para 74.

[281] International Law Commission Articles on State Responsibility, art 25.

[282] *Saluka v Czech Republic* (UNCITRAL, ad hoc) Partial Award (17 March 2006) para 254.

[283] ibid para 264.

[284] See more recently C Henckels, 'Scope Limitation or Affirmative Defence? The Purpose and Role of Investment Treaty Exception Clauses' in L Bartels and F Paddeu (eds), *Exceptions in International Law* (OUP 2020).

[285] Brazil–Morocco BIT (2019, not in force), art 12.1.

VI. Case 5: A constructive expropriation

A. Belgium

DR, LC, CD, and KP

In the context of the case in question, the city of Metropolis orders the occupation of a part of Miss Busy's property, in order to carry out urgent public works for the renovation and maintenance of a motorway.

However, after three years of occupation of the applicant's property, the works have not been carried out, and Miss Busy complains to the city of Metropolis that she is still prevented from using her property.

Several forms of interference with the right to property must be distinguished in Belgian law.

Interference could take the form of expropriation based on public purpose—in the strict sense—which implies a transfer of property and the obligation to follow a specific procedure, as described in the chapter by D Renders, L Ceci, C Delforge, K Polet, 'Procedural Requirements for Administrative Limits to Property Rights in Belgium' in this volume. In this case, under Article 16 of the Belgian Constitution, a '*fair compensation paid beforehand*' must be paid to the owner who has been deprived of his right to property.

In addition, as also mentioned in the chapter referred to above, the case law has sometimes acknowledged that severe forms of interference with the right to property might be seen as an expropriation—qualified as 'expropriation in fact'[286]—and that the conditions required for expropriation in the narrow sense must be respected. Therefore, owners deprived of their right to property must be awarded compensation.

Lastly, there are situations where interference with the right to property is based on a legal provision and does not imply a transfer of property. In this case, the owner can still use his or her property, albeit only in part.

Then there is the question of public servitude, which does not fall within the scope of Article 16 of the Belgian Constitution.[287] In effect, under Article 544 of the Belgian Civil Code, the legislator can establish limits to the right to property if this is in the public interest. No compensation is granted in this case.[288]

When a public servitude is created with regard to a given property, the concerned owner has, in principle, no right to compensation, unless the text on which the public servitude is based allows it.[289]

[286] See especially M Denys, 'De la quasi-expropriation ou de l'indemnisation des interdictions de bâtir' [1983] Journal des Tribunaux 405; O Wéry, 'L'appropriation des biens immeubles par les pouvoirs publics' (n 201) 34–37; D Lagasse, 'L'indemnité et la quasi-expropriation' in D Renders (ed), *L'expropriation pour cause d'utilité publique* (n 4) 565–604.

[287] Lagasse (n 286) 599.

[288] ibid 567, 568.

[289] ibid 583.

However, if, according to Article 1 of Protocol No 1 to the European Convention on Human Rights, the public servitude in question creates a disproportionate interference with the right to property, the European Court of Human Rights has ruled that the owner concerned may be entitled to compensation.[290] Based on this case law, the Belgian Court has also already established that public servitudes may imply a right to compensation.[291]

In the case at hand, Miss Busy's property is occupied by the city of Metropolis. There is thus no transfer of property, and it is not an expropriation for public purposes in the narrow sense.

Therefore, if Miss Busy decides to challenge the interference with her right to property, the court should first ascertain whether the applicant can still use her property.

If the court considers that Miss Busy has been entirely deprived of the right to use her property, it might find that the limits set by the city of Metropolis are severe and thus represent de facto expropriation.

It should then consider that the conditions required for expropriation in the narrow sense ought to have been complied with and that Miss Busy is entitled to an indemnity.

If the court deems that Miss Busy can still use her property, it should examine whether the measure adopted by the city of Metropolis is based on a legal provision allowing occupation of the applicant's property.

If there is no legal basis allowing the occupation of the applicant's property, the court would have to quash the challenged decision or allow refusal to enforce it regardless of whether Miss Busy decides to bring the case before the Council of State or an ordinary court. In addition, the court might consider that the city of Metropolis is at fault under Articles 1382 ff. of the Belgian Civil Code, and could grant the applicant compensation if she suffered damages.

If the measure taken by the city of Metropolis is based on a legal provision allowing the limitation of Miss Busy's right to property, the court should consider that this interference is a public servitude entailing no compensation, unless the text on which the public servitude is based allows it.

If no compensation is granted, Miss Busy could attempt to demonstrate disproportionate interference with her right to property. The court should then examine whether there is a balance between the interference and the aim pursued by the measure. In the event of imbalance, the applicant may be entitled to compensation.

Under Belgian law, Miss Busy's property would not be returned to her, nor could she request the annulment of the decision of the city of Metropolis arguing that the authority has failed to comply with the works schedule. She could only claim for damages within the above-mentioned limits.

[290] *Chassagnou and Others v France* (n 215); *Alatulkkila and Others v Finland* (n 215); *Anonymos Touristiki Etairia Kritis v Greece* (n 215); *Hermann v Germany* (n 215); Constitutional Court, case No 55/2012 of 19 April 2012; Court of Cassation (24 June 2010) *Pasicrisie*, 2010, 2004.

[291] Constitutional Court, case No 55/2012 of 19 April 2012. See also the principles stated by the Court of Cassation regarding compensation for interference with the right to property: Court of Cassation, 24 June 2010, *Pasicrisie*, 2010, p 2004.

B. France

EG

Miss Busy has had her property taken over by the public authority to renovate and maintain a highway. This constitutes a reason of public interest because these roads benefit all public users. In this case, it seems that the administration has neither started the works nor made use of the land taken from the owner. The work is aimed at re-establishing the railroad tracks and is intended to be temporary. It is not necessary to resort to expropriation to undertake them. As such, the claimant would like to regain possession of her property. She is trying to apply for a 'retrocession' of her property.

We are therefore in a situation of precarious occupation of the private domain by the administration. This occupation—supposed to stop—dispossesses the plaintiff of her property. An indemnity is thus provided to compensate the latter. However, the administration has not started the work for three years. The occupation is thus illegal because the occupation is no longer justified:

Any decree which authorises studies or a temporary occupation is expired by right if it is not followed by execution within six months of its date.[292]

Lastly, the claimant will be able to regain full use of her property rights, also receiving an indemnity because the administration did not respect the legal deadline for undertaking the work.

C. Germany

FS

The legal basis for the measure against Miss Busy is questionable. If the private property were to be expropriated at a later date, Miss Busy could be dispossessed in advance of the expropriation ('*vorzeitige Besitzeinweisung*').[293] Otherwise, the 'occupation' could constitute a seizure under police and security law. The preconditions for the intervening measure vary, depending on the legal basis on which the measure is based. The precondition of the '*vorzeitige Besitzeinweisung*' is that the immediate execution of the project is urgently required for reasons of public good.[294] A seizure under police law can be carried out to avert a current danger.[295]

Regardless of its legal requirements, the measure must be compatible with the constitutionally guaranteed right to property. The fundamental right to property ensures the holders of the right the freedom to act within the sphere of property rights and thereby guarantees them an independent way of life.[296] The fundamental property

[292] Article 9 of the Law of 29 December 1892 relating to the damage caused to private property through the execution of public works.

[293] cf eg EEG NW, §§ 37 sec 1, 38 sec 1.

[294] cf eg ibid § 37 sec 1 sentence 1.

[295] cf eg PolG NW, § 43 No 1.

[296] BVerfGE 97, 350 <370f>; 115, 97 <110>.

right protects the freedom to dispose of the property freely and to use it freely.[297] A three-year occupation without carrying out the intended works could be a disproportionate interference with the guaranteed right of property. Miss Busy is impaired by the 'occupation' in her right to use the property. Any interference with the property must be proportionate, ie it must not unreasonably burden the owner.[298] The interference with Miss Busy's property was justified by the urgency of the public works for the renovation of a highway. Necessary public works for the renovation of a road may certainly constitute a legitimate purpose for the interference with the right of property. However, since the public work has not yet begun even after a long period of time, it is doubtful whether there is a legitimate purpose at all. Moreover, the interference with Miss Busy's property would also have to be necessary in order to carry out the work. However, since no work is being carried out on the occupied land, it is also questionable whether the occupation is necessary to repair the road.

Miss Busy can challenge this in court and require her possession to be restored. The court will probably classify the encroachment on the property as disproportionate and therefore unlawful. If the interference with the property is unlawful, Miss Busy is entitled to claims under state liability law. This includes the claim of compensation because of unlawful sovereign interference with the right of property. The claim does not require the fault of the authority. Furthermore, a claim for public liability pursuant to § 839 BGB in conjunction with Article 34 GG regarding the breach of an official duty is possible because the competent officials violated their duty to act lawfully. This claim requires that the officials be at fault.

D. Italy

SM

Constructive expropriation is one of the main topics for the Italian legal system on the limitations of property rights.

Under the constructive expropriation rule ('*accessione invertita*' or '*occupazione acquisitiva*'), the public authorities would acquire ownership of the land from the outset before formal expropriation if, after taking possession of the land and irrespective of whether such possession was lawful, the works in the public interest were carried out.

This particular mechanism for constructive expropriation was created by the Court of Cassation, sitting as a full court, in the judgment of 16 February 1983, No 1464.

Constructive expropriation has allowed the public administration to take possession and ownership of lands without respecting the formal procedure of expropriation. Compensation, that is to say damages for the deprivation of the land, was due to the owner in consideration of the loss of ownership caused by the unlawful taking of possession, but originally such compensation could not exceed the amount due with a formal expropriation.

[297] cf BVerfGE 104, 1 <11>; 143, 246 para 228; H-J Papier and F Shirvani, 'Art 14' in T Maunz and G Dürig, *Grundgesetz, Kommentar* (CH Beck 2020) para 146.

[298] cf BVerfGE 122, 374 <391 and 392>; P Axer, 'Art 14' in V Epping and C Hillgruber (eds), *BeckOK Grundgesetz* (45th edn, 2020) para 85.

In several judgments[299] the ECHR condemned Italy because the constructive expropriation rule did not comply with the peaceful enjoyment of private possessions safeguarded by Article 1 of Protocol No 1 ECHR. The constructive expropriation resulted in arbitrary outcomes depriving litigants of effective protection of their rights. The occupation of private land in order to carry out building work that took place without an expropriation order and without compensation infringed Article 1 of Protocol No 1 ECHR.

The Italian legislator modified the original discipline several times in order to adapt it to the ECHR requirements. Nowadays the rule is provided in Article 42-bis of the Expropriation Act (DPR No 327/2001), according to which the authority which uses a property for public-interest purposes, modified in the absence of a valid and effective provision for expropriation or declaring the public utility, may order that it be acquired, not retroactively, and that an indemnity be paid to the owner for monetary and non-monetary damage, the latter forfeit calculated as ten percent of the market value of the asset.

The acquisition provision, indicating the circumstances that led to the undue use of the area and, if possible, the date from which it began, is specifically motivated in reference to the current and exceptional reasons of public interest that justify the issue, evaluated comparatively with the opposing private interests and highlighting the absence of reasonable alternatives to its adoption.

In this case, Miss Busy was deprived of her property without a lawful expropriation proceeding. The public administration occupied the private land for urgent public works, without the ordinary guarantees, such as the formal notice and above all the declaration of public utility that is the fundamental condition for carrying out a correct procedure until the issue of the expropriation order.

Case law currently states that whenever there has been an error in the expropriation procedure, the private owner can make a claim for compensation. More specifically, in the case of occupation by the administrative authority in the lack of a formal expropriation procedure and of an irreversible transformation of the land for the realisation of public works, the private owner can have the property back or alternatively ask for damages for the loss of the asset, commensurate with the market value of the land.[300]

Miss Busy can therefore challenge the order restricting her property right, by asking the administrative judge for restitution of the land or compensation for damages (in the event restitution is no longer possible, because it has, for example, been irreversibly transformed). The failure to comply with the works schedule and to continue the procedure of constructive expropriation can be a well-founded reason to ask for the quashing of the occupation order.

Nevertheless this solution must consider the above-mentioned discipline of Article 42-bis of the Italian Expropriation Act. According to this provision the public administration always has the power to change the situation and to order the acquisition of the private land, occupied for reasons of public interest and modified in the absence of a valid and effective measure of expropriation or declaration of public utility. In

[299] See especially judgment ECtHR (17 May 2005) *Scordino v Italy* App no 43662/98 (ECtHR, 17 May 2005) and the following judgment for the application of Article 41 (ECtHR, 6 March 2007) *Scordino v Italy*.
[300] See above all Cons Stato, Sec II (28 November 2019) No 8119.

this case, the owner will only be entitled to a compensation for monetary and non-monetary damage (the latter paid as ten per cent of the market value of the asset).

It is therefore possible that the city of Metropolis may decide to acquire Miss Busy's property under the provision of Article 42-bis. This can also take place more than three years after the occupation of the land, because the above-mentioned article does not provide a deadline for the acquisition order. The public administration can always acquire the property for reasons referring to the current and exceptional reasons of public interest that justify this choice, comparatively evaluated with the opposing private interests and in the absence of reasonable alternatives. If the administrative judge recognises the lawfulness of the public choice for the acquisition of the private property, Mrs Busy can only receive compensation as provided for by Article 42-bis of the Expropriation Act.

E. The Netherlands

JS and NvT

Article 11.21 Environment and Planning Act becomes relevant when the expropriation took place, but the plans for which the expropriation took place are not carried out in time, or at all, or properly. This is the case if the plans are abandoned or are amended to such a degree that the original plan has all but disappeared. In those cases, the expropriated party can claim the property back, or claim additional compensation. In this way, Article 11.21 Environment and Planning Act protects owners against expropriations that in hindsight were unnecessary or carried out too early.[301]

This claim can only be made by the former owner of the property, ie the expropriated party themselves. Furthermore, the article is only applicable in cases of expropriation. If the property in question has been sold to prevent expropriation, the former owner cannot reclaim the property,[302] unless the sale took place within the expropriation proceedings, for instance because an additional offer from the expropriating party was accepted.[303] Parties can of course also contractually stipulate that Article 11.21 is applicable to the sale. This article enables the expropriated party under certain conditions to compel the expropriating party to expropriate the whole of the real estate property in question. There is no fixed time limit for a claim ex Article 11.21 Environment and Planning Act, although it would appear safe not to let the general civil law time limit for prescription (twenty years) elapse before the claim.

The former owner can claim the property back if—as a result of causes that could have been addressed by the expropriating party—(i) the expropriating party did not make a start on the works for which expropriation took place within three years after the expropriation judgment attained res judicata; (ii) if the works were discontinued for more than three years; (iii) if it may be inferred from other circumstances that the works will probably not be carried out. If one of these situations applies, the expropriating party must offer the expropriated party the property in its current state. The

[301] Supreme Court (7 December 1979) *NJ* 1980/290 (*Van Hensbergen/The Hague*).
[302] See Supreme Court (7 December 1979) *NJ* 1980/290 (*Van Hensbergen/The Hague*).
[303] Supreme Court (19 December 2003) *NJ* 2004/408 (*Zillikens/Limburg III*).

expropriated party is then obligated to return the compensation they received for this property. If the expropriating party does not make this offer, the expropriated party can enter a claim ex Article 11.21 Environment and Planning Act by summons. The claim can consist either of the return of their former property or additional compensation. If returning the property is not possible because the expropriating party no longer owns the property, the judge may not order the expropriating party to pay additional compensation if that has not been claimed.[304] In order to enter the claim successfully, the situation must be such that the expropriating party could have taken steps to address the causes of the delay (and that there is thus a certain degree of culpability). The expropriating party must set out why these steps could not have been taken.

The article gives rise to the question whether the works in question, although adapted, still count as the works for which expropriation took place. According to the Supreme Court, small adaptations are allowed. The Supreme Court takes a fairly broad view of the works for which expropriation took place. As long as the goal for which expropriation took place remains the same, the works are considered the same. In general, changes with implications for the amount of compensation or the permissibility of the expropriation can be qualified as significant changes.

The timeliness of the works also raises questions. The Supreme Court holds that it is not sufficient to apply for the relevant building permits. In order to come to the conclusion that a start has been made with the realisation of the works, some kind of physical work must have been carried out.[305] This start need not necessarily be made on the expropriated property itself. If the works are being realised over a larger area, it is sufficient if a start has been made somewhere in this area.[306]

There is no case law concerning the situation in which the works have not been carried out for more than three years, or in which there are 'other circumstances' as discussed above.

If the property is successfully reclaimed, the former owner must repay the compensation they received, or rather that part that corresponds to the value of the property at the time of the expropriation, including the compensation for the devaluation of the remaining part of the property.[307] If the value of the property has since decreased, the amount of compensation that must be repaid is decreased by the same amount. If the value of the property has since increased, on the other hand, the surplus benefits the former owner.

The additional compensation that can be claimed ex Article 11.21 Environment and Planning Act also raises some questions. It is clear that this compensation is not the amount that corresponds directly to the value of the expropriated property, but instead corresponds to the sacrifice that the former owner was forced to make.[308] Case law shows that the additional compensation is calculated by

[304] Supreme Court (18 June 1971) *NJ* 1971/454 (*Assies/Roden*).
[305] Supreme Court (3 December 1965) *NJ* 1966/161 (*Assies/Roden I*).
[306] Supreme Court (5 April 1978) *NJO* 1978/5 (*Amsterdam/Koster*).
[307] Supreme Court (20 July 1999) *NJ* 2000/61 (*Bakkeren/Rotterdam*).
[308] EJ Snijders-Storm and JS Procee, 'Terugvordering op Grond van Artikel 61 Onteigeningswet; Stand van Zaken' in EWJ de Groot and RD Harteman (eds), *Bijzonder Geschikt voor het Werk* (IBR 2012) 127.

subtracting the compensation received for the actual value from the current value of the property.[309]

F. Poland
IK and ŁK

Pursuant to Article 6(1) of the IPMA, public purposes include public roads and various types of tasks and works related to them. They include activities actually linked to demarcating land for roads, their construction as well as other construction works concerning maintenance of roads and related infrastructure. The legislator considers all this as public purposes. Given the above, it is possible to restrict Miss Busy's rights to use the property on the basis of an expropriation decision.

The Article 136 of the IPMA provides for a prohibition of using expropriated property for purposes other than those specified in the expropriation decision. The observance of that rule is guaranteed by the obligation to return expropriated property, if it has become redundant for the public purpose for which it was expropriated. The property return obligation is a special guarantee to ensure that expropriation is not used beyond indispensable needs related to the attainment of public purposes.[310] The statutory conditions of the redundancy of property for the purpose specified in the expropriation decision have been laid down in Article 137 of the IPMA, as failure to meet the deadline for the start of the pursuance of a public purpose as well as a lapse of the deadline set for the end of its attainment. These deadlines are—respectively—seven and ten years after the day when the property expropriation decision became final. Miss Busy may demand that the property be returned, if no construction works have been done despite the lapse of seven years after the day when the property expropriation decision became final, or if despite the lapse of ten years after the day when the property expropriation decision became final the purpose of the renovation and maintenance of the motorway was not attained.[311] Redundancy consists in the fact that the purpose of the expropriation is not, and has not been, actually pursued or attained, which is obvious in Miss Busy's case. In the circumstances, she could retrieve her property, yet only after the lapse of the deadlines specified above. The compensation issue, however, would have been settled originally, ie already in the expropriation decision.

A property use limitation can also result from the Public Roads Act (PRA). A public road managing authority may exercise its right to access property adjacent to a roadway, should it find it necessary to perform its tasks related to the maintenance and protection of public roads (Article 21(2)(1)). Apart from exercising its access right, the managing authority can organise a temporary passage through land adjacent to a roadway for the period when the road is not passable (Article 21(2)(2)). Contrary to most legal provisions that give administration competences as regards expropriation,

[309] Supreme Court (18 June 1971) *NJ* 1971/454 and Court of Appeal Arnhem (30 January 2007) ECLI:NL:GHARN:2007:AZ9810.

[310] Supreme Court judgment of 15 February 2002, III CKN 543/00, LEX No 381365.

[311] Supreme Administrative Court judgment of 4 September 2003, II SA/Gd 1552/00, LEX No 298527.

the said Article 21(2) of the PRA does not provide for an authority to issue an administrative decision. As the legal result of the actual actions is restricting rights in rem to land property, the activities listed in Article 21(2) should be perceived as material/technical. An obvious fault of the provision is the absence of a set maximum time limit when a public road managing authority can restrict rights in rem to property adjacent to a roadway. That authority loses its competences in that regard once the conditions that justified the introduction of the restrictions cease to exist and the road manager should immediately start restoring the pre-restriction state.

Actions by road managing authorities are subject to legality control by administrative courts. For that to happen, Miss Busy should call on the public road administration body to remove the breach of law (Article 52(3) of the Act on proceedings before administrative courts, (APAC)). Once the reply which does not take into account her legal interest has been served on Miss Busy, she can appeal against the action by the road manager before an administrative court. Controlling the actions taken pursuant to Article 21(2) of the PRA, the court is obliged to check whether the road managing authority was entitled to introduce the restrictions. Ruling in favour of the petitioner, the court can repeal the action in question or ascertain its ineffectiveness (Article 150 of the APAC).

The public authority whose body performed the action restricting the right to use property adjacent to a roadway is obliged towards the owner for any damage resulting from such action (Article 21(3) of the PRA).

Restricting the property use right may also be necessary in emergency situations. Article 126(1–5) of the IPMA provides that in case of force majeure or an urgent need to prevent the occurrence of a major damage, the starost, performing a government administration task, grants, by means of a decision, a permission to temporarily requisition property for period not exceeding six months, counting from the requisition day. If either of the conditions referred to in Article 126(1–5) of the IPMA has been met in Miss Busy's case, the restriction on her ownership right would be justified. Moreover, after six months Miss Busy would be entitled to use her property again. After the period for which property is requisitioned has lapsed, the entity that requisitioned the property is obliged to restore it to its previous state.

Miss Busy would also be entitled to compensation for making her property available and possibly for any damage resulting from the property requisition under Article 126(3) of the IPMA. This includes both the value of the damage sustained and an amount equivalent to the lower value of the property. The fact that the planned works did not actually start, and the public purpose was not attained does not have any bearing on the existence of the compensation right.

G. Portugal

RGdF

The occupation of neighbouring lands is allowed by Article 18 of the CE as an effect of the 'dup' when it is necessary for works to be carried out on the expropriated parcels thereof. It is an accessory of the expropriation because most of the time the end pursued can only be achieved through building or rebuilding works that claim for the temporary back-up use of surrounding lands (for machinery, warehousing, installation of cranes, etc). The occupation is subject to a special procedure: the proprietor must be notified fifteen days in advance and has the right to demand a previous inspection '*ad perpetuam rei memoriam*' to establish the characteristics and elements of the land that might be relevant regarding compensation. The proprietor is entitled to damages calculated in general terms (there are no special criteria for this in the CE, contrary to what happens to expropriations, strictly speaking).

But the occupation of Miss Busy's land is a particular situation: it is not associated with an expropriation. In fact, the city of Metropolis only wants to carry out urgent public works for the renovation and maintenance of a highway. In Portuguese law, Article 8 of the Law 34/2015, of 27 April (Statute of Roads in the National Road Network), allows both the urgent expropriation of lands which are needed for the construction, conservation or exploitation of roads, and also the mere occupation of neighbouring third-party lands when necessary for roadworks. These disjunct possibilities clearly show that occupation and expropriation can take place separately, as long as the former follows the procedure in the CE (Article 8/2 of the Law 34/2015).[312]

Moreover, the Code of Public Procurement also allows the occupation of neighbouring third-party lands when necessary for public works (Article 351). Indeed, it would be a major obstacle for public works if this possibility did not exist. We should remember that roads are public property (Article 84 of the Constitution) which needs to be maintained and taken care of. And for this most of the time the public powers have to contract private parties to do so; but they remain responsible for the conditions of the works, namely, promoting the necessary procedures regarding the occupation of neighbouring lands.

Article 13 of the CE contains complex rules regarding the expiry of the 'dup'. One of these rules — Article 13/7 — was designed specifically with road building in mind: in the case of continuous works[313] expiry cannot be invoked after the works have been initiated in any place of the line, except if the works have been suspended or are interrupted for more than three years.

When the occupation is associated with an expropriation that rule is protective of the proprietors of the occupied lands: because the 'dup' expires, and with it the expropriation effect, the same happens with the occupation that the 'dup' permitted as one its effects. But what about when there is no 'dup' and no expropriation as in the present case? Various hypotheses can be envisaged, namely associated with the term of a public contract for works of this kind (such a prolonged stop would certainly have consequences at that level, with effects on the occupation). But this would always be uncertain. It is perfectly acceptable to use a principle of analogy and apply the rule of

312 All this is applicable to highways because they are part of the National Road Plan (Decree-Law 222/98, of 17 July, lastly by Decree-Law 182/2003, of 16 August) which is the object of application of the Law 34/2015.

313 A work is continuous if it has a linear geometrical configuration and if, by its nature, can occur in different phases according to a global and coherent plan (art 5/3 of the CE).

Article 13/7 of the CE to these kinds of situations: because there is in fact an analogy regarding the protection of the proprietor.

So Miss Busy could approach the administrative courts claiming for the expiry of the occupation permit (or as subsidiary its annulment for subsequent lack of cause) and also for damages.

H. Spain

LAJ and DUFB

The broad notion of expropriation under Spanish law[314] covers temporary seizures or occupations that do not entail any transfer of property, but rather the deprivation of the right to use the asset during a given time period (Article 1(1) LEF). These temporary occupations can be justified on grounds of construction, repair or maintenance of works or public facilities declared of public utility, such as roads (Article 108(2) LEF). This type of expropriation is conducted under a streamlined procedure, and it gives rise to compensation for the expropriated owner's loss of profit, for any property loss or damage, and for any costs incurred to restore the property to its original condition (Articles 111 to 123 LEF).

Assuming that the temporary occupation was legally determined, recovery of the land by Miss Busy could only take place if she exercised her right to reverse the expropriation on the grounds that it failed to fulfil its intended purpose (*reversión*). Nevertheless, the expropriated party is only entitled to reversal in the events expressly provided in the law, which cannot be extended by judicial authorities, since the right of reversal does not stem from the constitutional right to property (Article 33 CE); rather, it is a statutory right.[315] There are two particularly remarkable grounds for reversal. First, expropriation can be reversed if the works have not yet commenced within five years following seizure of the expropriated property (Article 154(3)(b) LEF). Secondly, expropriation will be reversed if, having commenced the works, these were suspended for more than two years for reasons attributable to the public authorities or the private beneficiary of the expropriation (Article 154(3)(c) LEF). Miss Busy's case does not fall under any of these scenarios, because the works have not commenced and there has only been a 3-year delay. Therefore, she will have to wait another two years to exercise her right of reversal.

As for expropriations that entail the transfer of property, exercising the right of reversal entails reciprocal restitution, following a re-appraisal of the property: (i) if the occupation or seizure exceeded two years; or (ii) if the property has undergone changes in its physical condition or legal status (Article 54 LEF). Therefore, the expropriated owner will reimburse the fair compensation that she previously received. Compensation for liability would only be payable if the expropriated party had a right to reversal, yet it was impossible to carry out due to

314 See Arroyo Jiménez and Fernández-Bermejo (n 244) section I.

315 STC 166/1986, 141/2014, and 43/2015.

a physical transformation or a change in legal status of the expropriated right or asset (Articles 66 REF and 121 LEF).[316] Regarding temporary occupations like that affecting Miss Busy, which does not involve the transfer of property, reversal only allows the expropriated party to regain possession of the asset and to seek compensation for any loss or damage caused by public authorities. Such compensation will be calculated under the general public law rules on non-contractual liability (Articles 106(2) CE and 32 LRJSP), and taking into account the amount previously received as fair compensation for expropriation.

I. Sweden

PJ

The question can be answered with the help of three different legal bases, depending on the more concrete aspects of the case in question.

(1) If the situation as described in the above-mentioned case is not an emergency case, the provisions regarding road operation (*drift av väg*) according of the Roads Act (*Väglagen* 1971:948) apply.
In this case the decision to establish a road plan (which contains inter alia a map of the road and the land that has to be taken) ceases to apply five years after the year in which the decision entered into force if 'the stretch of the road has not become clearly marked on the ground, and road construction has not begun' (section 18a). Furthermore, 'If there are special reasons, the period of validity may be extended by a maximum of two years'.
In the above-mentioned case, the public authority deciding on the occupation is still respecting the time frame laid down in the Roads Act.

(2) If the situation as described in the above-mentioned case is one of emergency and the public works consist of creating a temporary road, another provision from the Roads Act applies. Section 36 states:

> If a road cannot be used without risk of an accident due to work in progress or as a result of landslides or flooding or for any other reason, the County Administrative Board may, on the request of the road holding authority, decide that the right of use to land or other space for a temporary road shall be granted for the time such a road is needed as a result of the obstacle.

There are possibilities to lodge an appeal against the decision before the Government and also to receive damages (section 63).

(3) Another legal ground applicable in the case (with consideration to emergency) would be the Civil Protection Act.[317] See under Sweden, Case 4.

[316] STS of 28 March 1979 and of 3 March 2017 (Rec 2702/2015).
[317] Prop 2002/03:119, *Reformerad räddningstjänstlagstiftning* (Preparatory work).

J. Ukraine

HD

Prior to forced alienation of a plot of land, the competent authority has to propose its redemption to the owner. The owner should give an answer within one month of notification. If the owner does not consent to it, the competent authority is entitled to file a suit with the administrative court asking for forced alienation.

If it is assumed that Miss Busy did not agree with the redemption, or the suit was filed by the competent authority to the court, and the proceeding has been ongoing for three years while the public works were already started, the solution could be the following.

The first question is to ascertain the legal basis for the beginning of such works on the private land plot taking into account the fact that the land plot still belongs to Miss Busy.

Miss Busy could challenge this act. The burden of proof lies on the competent authority adopting such an act. The Code of Administrative Proceedings of Ukraine provides that damages can be awarded if the court recognises that an individual act is unlawful and, as a direct consequence, the court will quash it. In such a case the ground for the annulment will be the unlawfulness of the act restricting property rights.

Miss Busy can also bring a negatory action (*actio negatoria*). The Civil Code of Ukraine provides the right of the owner to bring a negatory action citing obstacles to the right of use of his or her property (Article 391).

A similar legal provision is set forth in the Land Code of Ukraine. Here, the owner of the land plot has a right to demand the removal of any infringements of his rights on land and compensation for damages (Article 152(2)).

As the Grand Chamber of the Supreme Court has stated, while a person is the owner of real estate, namely the right of property is still registered in this person's name, he or she has the right to bring a case before the court citing the obstacle to the right of use and right of disposal of this property.[318]

According to the Civil Code of Ukraine, any unlawful legal act issued by a state authority or local self-government body which violates the owner's rights must be annulled in court. The owner could demand reinstatement (restoration of the prior situation that existed before the adoption of unlawful act). If the last is impossible, the owner has the right to claim damages for moral and material damages (Article 393).

K. The United Kingdom

EW

The occupation of land without a licence is a trespass and in the absence of consent or statutory power, Metropolis could be sued for trespass or Miss Busy could bring an

[318] Ruling of the Grand Chamber of the Supreme Court of 4 August 2018 in case No 653/1096/16-ц https://reyestr.court.gov.ua/Review/75296538 (accessed 5 May 2021).

action for the recovery of land and any damages would be assessed on the basis of a nominal licence fee.[319] Here, it appears that an order exists but it is worth noting that in English law there are very few situations where temporary possession of land in this way is legally justified. Part II of the Neighbourhood Planning Act 2017 (which is not yet in force) gives authorities that have a power to acquire land compulsorily a power to take temporary possession of land with a right to compensation for the affected owner. A minimum of three months' notice of intended entry must be given before temporary possession can be taken. The notice must specify the period for which the land is to be possessed[320] and the power has to be exercised within three years if authorised by a compulsory purchase order (CPO), or five years if authorised by a development consent order (DCO). An owner can issue a counter-notice limiting the period of temporary possession to twelve months for a dwelling or part of a dwelling, or six years for other situations. The acquiring authority has twenty-eight days in which it can decide to accept the counter-notice and possess the land for the limited period, or withdraw the notice of intended entry, or purchase the owner's interest in the land outright as though it were a normal compulsory purchase.

In the absence of the Neighbourhood Planning Act 2017 provisions being in force, Metropolis would normally have exercised its compulsory purchase powers as an acquiring authority and compulsorily purchased Miss Busy's land permanently. Once they had finished with the land, Metropolis would then have been free to sell the land at market value or it may have agreed to return the land to Miss Busy (often for lower upfront compensation). Where the land has been compulsorily purchased, Miss Busy would not have a claim based on the failure of the works to take place, but she could make a claim for the property to be sold to her in the event that Metropolis no longer needed the land.[321]

Another option, if Miss Busy's land has been occupied rather than subject to a CPO, would be for Miss Busy to ask for her land to be acquired by agreement. A highway authority has discretion under section 246 of the Highways Act 1980 to obtain land by agreement where this will mitigate 'any adverse effect' on the surroundings of a highway being constructed or improved, or which it is proposed will be constructed or improved.[322] Miss Busy would be eligible as a resident owner-occupier for compensation to be paid; the compulsory power of acquisition must be begun before the date on which the highway or improved highway is first open to public traffic, which would appear to be satisfied here given that the improvements have not yet started.[323] It is possible for the highways authority to either pay compensation for the depreciation in value caused by the highway activities, or compensation for acquisition of the affected land.

[319] *National Provident Institution v Avon County Council* [1992] EG 56.

[320] Neighbourhood Planning Act 2017, s 20.

[321] Department for Levelling Up, Housing and Communities, *Guidance on Compulsory Purchase Process and the Crichel Down Rules* (July 2019) https://assets.publishing.service.gov.uk/government/uploads/system/uploads/attachment_data/file/1071500/CPO_guidance_-_with_2019_update.pdf (accessed 19 May 2022); *Charlesworth v Crossrail Ltd* [2018] EWHC 915 (Admin).

[322] Highways Act 1980, s 246(1), as amended by the Planning and Compensation Act 1991.

[323] Highways Act 1980, s 246(3).

Unfortunately, Miss Busy would struggle to challenge the CPO authorising the occupation of land in the High Court under section 23 of the Acquisition of Land Act 1981 because this procedure has very strict time limits. An application under section 23 may only be brought within six weeks of the confirmation of the CPO being first published. Section 25 of the Acquisition of Land Act 1981 prevents a CPO being questioned in any legal proceedings other than a section 23 procedure, but it is open to the courts to question the decision to make the CPO in judicial review under Part 54 of the Civil Procedure Rules. Again, claims for judicial review have very strict time limits and applications must be made promptly and no later than three months after the grounds arise (which will normally equate to the decision to confirm a CPO).

In the absence of any authorising legislation and means of redress, it appears that the occupation of the land for so long could amount to an excessive interference with Miss Busy's right to the 'peaceful enjoyment' of her possessions in breach of A1P1 of the ECHR. Given the delay in implementing the scheme it does not appear that there is a sufficient public interest involved that would justify the interference with Miss Busy's possessions in this way. The tripartite test in *Sporrong v Lönnroth* provides the classic formulation in deciding whether an interference with property is: (i) a general interference with possessions; (ii) a deprivation of possessions; or (iii) a control on the use of those possessions. As is well known, the payment of compensation is normally expected in deprivation situations, unless there are exceptional circumstances justifying the non-payment of compensation.

Controls of use do not normally carry with them a requirement that compensation should be paid unless the 'fair balance' test requires compensation.[324] The line between deprivation and control of use is significant but the 'distinction is not always obvious'.[325] The UK Supreme Court commented in a case involving environmental controls affecting a fishing licence, that the 'distinction between expropriation is neither clear-cut, nor crucial to the analysis'[326] in the particular case where the owner had been deprived of 95 per cent of their right to fish. The severity and disproportionate impact on the applicant in that case meant that a fair balance had not been struck and the absence of compensation meant that the interference was unlawful under A1P1, despite the state's wide margin of discretion especially in imposing necessary environmental controls.[327] Here, the authority does not appear to have given any thought to Miss Busy's situation and the impact of their actions appears to have fallen unfairly on her leaving her with no meaningful use or control over the land. From an A1P1 perspective this would appear to be an unwarranted deprivation, which should be compensated.

[324] *Hutten-Czapska v Poland* (2007) 45 EHRR 4 [167]; *Trailer and Marina (Leven) Ltd v Secretary of State for the Environment, Food and Rural Affairs* [2005] 1 P&CR 495 [58].
[325] *R (Mott) v Environment Agency* [2018] 1 WLR 1022.
[326] ibid 1033 [32].
[327] ibid 1034 [37].

L. The United States

IS

The permanent physical occupation of private property by the government is almost always a taking requiring compensation.[328] Some states have laws allowing property owners to regain condemned property if it is not used for the 'public use' that supposedly justified the taking within a certain period of time after the condemnation takes place.

M. International investment law

FF

In this scenario, the question focuses on the remedy available: in particular, whether a tribunal could order the restitution of the lands occupied or the payment of damages, in light of the delay in public works. That the land is merely occupied rather than expropriated is irrelevant, since clearly 'the practical and economic use of the Property ... was irretrievably lost, notwithstanding that [the investor] remained in possession of the Property'.[329] As explained above, restitution is, theoretically, one method of reparation in international litigation, but it is rarely sought or granted. Investors can seek compensation for expropriation. Expropriation must always occur against compensation, so a failure to compensate Ms Busy would provide her with a cause of action irrespective of the delay in the works.

Conversely, if she had already been paid compensation,[330] it should be determined whether the delay might render the expropriation unlawful retroactively and, if so, whether this would warrant a request for damages higher than the amount previously received.

On the first issue (a supervening cause of unlawfulness), the investor could argue that the delay reveals a lack of genuine urgency and, in turn, that the expropriation had no valid public purpose (see IIL Case 7). The authorities' delay per se could also be questioned for breach of due process, but ultimately the investor must demonstrate to have suffered unfair harm. In *Unglaube*, the tribunal considered the authorities' delay in processing a request to change the destination of a land a breach of fair and equitable treatment (FET) in principle, but the investor had failed to establish the causal link between the delay and the damage asserted.[331]

The chances of a successful claim (under expropriation or FET) increase if the delay breaches domestic law. For instance, Costa Rican law requires that property expropriated must be dedicated to the designated public purpose within ten years;

328 The leading precedent on this point is *Loretto v Teleprompter Manhattan CATV Corp* 458 US 419 (1982).

329 *Santa Elena v Costa Rica* ICSID Case No ARB/96/1 Award (17 February 2000) para 81.

330 Obviously, if the state had paid no compensation in the first place, Ms Busy would have always had a cause of action for unlawful compensation, irrespective of the subsequent quashing of the urban land act.

331 *IGB* (n 65) 187.

afterwards, owners can recover it from the state. In 1995, Costa Rica passed a law creating a national marine park and providing for a gradual process of expropriation of the lands contained therein. The authorities commence the expropriation process only in 2003, and took five years to complete it. The domestic illegality of the process, which also local courts acknowledged, was noted by the tribunal as evidence of the expropriation's unlawfulness under the applicable treaty.[332] Normally, delays in the expropriation process are challenged as straightforward breaches of the requirement to provide compensation 'without delay'.[333] However, even if compensation had occurred in some form, the delay might still be relevant in the plea for unlawfulness of the process, with a different amount of damages to be sought, as explained below.

On the second issue (the convenience of investor–state dispute settlement), Ms Busy's incentive to launch arbitration depends on whether unlawful expropriation warrants a higher amount of compensation than she has (or should have) already received; if so, tribunals could award successful claimants with the difference. Certainly, tribunals can make an award of compound interest to account for the time during which the investor has suffered from the unlawful measure.[334] More fundamentally, some tribunals have noted a difference between compensation as a requirement for lawful expropriation and compensation as a remedy for unlawful expropriation:

> [c]ompensation for a lawful expropriation is fair compensation represented by the value of the undertaking at the moment of dispossession and reparation in case of unlawful expropriation is restitution in kind or its monetary equivalent.[335]

Essentially, payment of the fair market value of the land is sufficient for lawful expropriation, while, for unlawful expropriation, the state must make a payment corresponding to the value of the asset as if expropriation had not occurred. Therefore, if, at the time of the award the value is higher than it was at the time of expropriation, the investor is owed the higher amount.[336]

[332] *Unglaube v Costa Rica* ICSID Case No ARB/08/1 Award (16 May 2012) para 219.
[333] *Funnekotter v Zimbabwe* ICSID Case No ARB/05/6 Award (22 April 2009) para 75.
[334] *Santa Elena* (n 329) paras 104–105.
[335] *Tidewater Investment SRL and Tidewater Caribe CA v Venezuela* ICSID Case No ARB/10/5 Award (13 March 2015) para 145.
[336] *ADC* (n 110) para 497.

VII. Case 6: The public interest of a private hospital

A. Belgium

DR, LC, CD, and KP

The competent authority adopted a decision to expropriate Miss Nightingale's property for the construction of a new private hospital.

The expropriation decision notified to Miss Nightingale—which, under Belgian law as indicated in the chapter by D Renders, L Ceci, C Delforge, K Polet, 'Procedural Requirements for Administrative Limits to Property Rights in Belgium' in this volume, does not have the effect of transferring ownership—does not contain, in her view, any details relating to the public purpose of the project.

The Belgian courts, when seized with an action against an expropriation decision, may have to address both substantive and formal defects.

- With regard to *substantive defects*, it should be recalled that under Belgian law, any expropriation—regardless of the competent authority—must serve a public purpose.[337]

When the decision to expropriate is challenged on the grounds that there is allegedly no public purpose, courts must scrutinise the purpose pursued by the expropriation. The notion of public purpose is interpreted broadly by Belgian courts.[338] The mere fact that the expropriation is carried out for the benefit of a private entity does not, in itself, suffice to exclude the existence of a public purpose.[339] The existence of a public purpose is, in effect, recognised in situations where the use that the private entity makes of the expropriated property contributes to a public purpose, or even contributes to the social good.[340] However, an expropriation cannot be carried out on the initiative of a private company with the sole aim of promoting its exclusive interests.[341]

In this sense, the Belgian Council of State has already ruled, with regard to an expropriation carried out in view of an urban development project involving the creation of a shopping centre in the town centre, that:

> the fact that the expropriation plan allows a private initiative project to be carried out does not mean, from the outset, that it would not serve a public purpose, nor that it would be intended solely to satisfy a property developer to the detriment of the citizens or private and public interest.[342]

337 Belgian Constitution, art 16.

338 Constitutional Court, case No 129/2012 of 25 October 2012.

339 Wéry, 'L'expropriation pour cause d'utilité publique' (n 2) 778; Pâques, Donnay, Vercheval (n 4) 212.

340 Wéry (n 2) 778; Pâques, Donnay, and Vercheval (n 4) 212.

341 Justice de Paix of Huy (13 novembre 2000) *CDPK*, 2001, 208.

342 Council of State, case *Galeyn*, No 225.735 of 6 December 2013. In the same perspective see Constitutional Court, case No 143/2018 of 18 October 2018.

Determining whether expropriation pursues a public purpose requires a case-by-case examination by the courts, evaluating the concrete circumstances of each case. However, when faced with a challenge to a decision to expropriate, the prerogative of the Belgian courts is limited to a review of legality with no review of suitability.[343] This implies that the court cannot substitute its own assessment of the public purpose for that made by the authority issuing the decision to expropriate, which has a discretionary power of appreciation. Only manifest errors of assessment may therefore be sanctioned.[344]

- With regard to *formal defects*, it must be emphasised that the decision to expropriate constitutes a unilateral administrative act of individual scope whose reasons must be given.[345] This means that the act must state the legal and factual grounds on which it is based. The statement of reasons on which the act is founded must be adequate.

On this, the Belgian Court of Cassation has ruled that in the field of expropriations, the reasons given must indicate why the expropriation is necessary, which implies that they must be based on real facts, that a reasonable relationship between the planned expropriation and the intended purpose must be deduced from it and that, depending on the case, it must be clear that the political options chosen have been evaluated.[346]

The motivation of the decision to expropriate does not, however, necessarily need to be long.[347] There is also no obligation for the authority to specify the reasons for its motivation.

Failure to comply with the obligation to state the formal motivation of the act makes the decision to expropriate unlawful.

In the present case, Miss Nightingale considers the decision to be unlawful because it does not contain any statement concerning the public purpose of the project.

Under Belgian law, Miss Nightingale's view seems justified: all the legal and factual reasons underlying the decision to expropriate must be mentioned in the *instrumentum* of the act.

Since the decision to expropriate does not mention all the reasons underlying it, it should be censured by the court seized.

However, the court seized should carry out only a marginal review as regards to the public purpose of the project. Unless it can be shown that the authority made a manifest error of assessment—which cannot be determined from the wording of the case—it should not be possible to quash the decision to expropriate on the sole ground that it regards the construction of a private hospital.

343 Wéry (n 2) 779.

344 ibid.

345 Act 'on the formal motivation reasoning of administrative acts' (29 July 1991; publication in the Belgian *Official Gazette* on 12 September 1991). In scholarship see Wéry (n 2) 775; Pâques, Donnay, and Vercheval (n 4) 205–208, in particular 124–27.

346 Court of Cassation (1st Chamber) (3 February 2000) *Aménagement-Environnement*, 2001, 324. In the same perspective see Court of Cassation (11 September 2003) *Pasicrisie*, 2003, 1380.

347 Wéry (n 2) 777.

B. France

EG

First of all, it seems important to note that Miss Nightingale wishes to challenge the act of declaration of public utility that she has received. The question of law raised is a priori whether the lack of motivation for this act justifies its annulment before the administrative judge.

However, according to the case concerning Mr Banks (France, Case 1), this act is 'neither regulatory nor individual' and cannot be annulled on the grounds of failure to state reasons. Moreover, according to the *Conseil d'Etat*, the statement of reasons that is supposed to accompany the declaration of public utility is merely accessory. It thus appears that an action for excess of power against this act would not allow Miss Nightingale to block the expropriation of her property solely because it is not reasoned.

On the other hand, the applicant could formulate her request by arguing that the construction of a private hospital does not pursue an aim of general interest. Indeed, an expropriation to build a private hospital could legitimately arouse suspicion. The administration may be engaging in misuse of power, which means that it would use its power to serve interests directed against the common good. In French administrative law, the misuse of power constitutes one of the means of internal legality opening a petition in excess of power.[348]

It would be erroneous to drastically oppose the private and the public logics because they are becoming increasingly intertwined. If the general interest was historically the prerogative of public action, it must be noted that private actors are now imposing themselves as determining and major relays to whom missions of general interest are entrusted and delegated. In this way, it is less easy to grasp the contours of the misuse of power insofar as private actors can effectively work for the general interest if they respond to the missions that the administration entrusts to them.

In this case, it appears that the construction of a private hospital pursues the goal of improving the health system. This ultimately constitutes a reason legitimising an expropriation. This case is classically recognised in case law as evidenced by this formulation of the *Conseil d'Etat*:

> The fact that the project only concerns private health establishments is not such as to make it lose its character of general interest, whereas these establishments may be associated with the operation of the public hospital service by virtue of agreements concluded in accordance with the terms and conditions set out in the Public Health Code.[349]

[348] It is a remedy which 'is open even without text and has the effect of ensuring, in accordance with the general principles of law, the respect of legality' and tends to overturn an administrative decision (CE Ass, Decision of 17 February 1950) Dame Lamotte, No 86949).

[349] CE, Decision of October 2005, Sté du Tertre Rouge, No 069125.

In this sense, even if the construction of this hospital offers a 'direct and certain' advantage to the private company, this is not sufficient to cancel the declaration in itself. All the more so if the motive pursued is an improvement of the public service for its users.[350] The administrative court will therefore have to use a precious tool to establish its judgment, namely the theory of the balance sheet-cost-benefit, one that requires courts to take into account all the aspects of an operation—both negative and positive—in order to assess public utility:

> An expropriation operation can only be legally declared to be in the public interest if the harm to private property, the financial cost, the social disadvantages, the threat to the protection and enhancement of the environment, and the possible harm to other public interests that it entails are not excessive in relation to the interest that it presents.[351]

The likelihood of Miss Nightingale having the expropriation set aside is low because, although court control has been greatly enhanced,[352] annulments in these cases are still relatively infrequent.

C. Germany

FS

The expropriation must be carried out in a procedure that is legally established, in order to ensure that all essential legal and factual issues are considered, especially the rights of the affected owner.[353] The legal procedure also stipulates that the purpose of the expropriation must be stated in the expropriation decision.[354] In German law, however, the declaration of the public interest is not an independent procedural step in the expropriation procedure. A formal error therefore only exists if Miss Nightingale was not informed of any purpose at all.

[350] In this respect, it is worth noting this decisive ruling in the establishment of this standpoint: 'If the deviation of the road in question provides the company "Automobiles Peugeot" with a direct and certain advantage, it is in accordance with the general interest to satisfy both the needs of public traffic and the requirements of the development of an industrial complex which plays an important role in the regional economy in CE, Decision of 20 July 1971, Ville de Sochaux, No 80804, *AJDA* 227 (1972).'

[351] CE Ass, Decision of 28 May 1971, Ministre de l'Equipement et du logement C/ Fédération de défense des personnes concernées par le projet actuellement dénommé 'Ville nouvelle Est', No N° 78825.

[352] See in particular the following analysis: 'While the administrative judge originally only verified the "general usefulness" of the project, according to the formula of government commissioner Pierre Josse, the theory of the cost-benefit balance (CE Ass, Decision of Mai 28, 1971, Ministre de l'Equipement et du logement C/ Fédération de défense des personnes concernées par le projet actuellement dénommé "Ville nouvelle Est", No N° 78825) drawn by Guy Braibant, reflected the deepening of its control. Today, this litigation is sometimes summarized, on the side of external legality, as a vain and painful litany of procedural means and, on the side of internal legality, as the venerable balance sheet that has long received the anointing of the Major judgments' in C Nicolas and Y Faure, 'News from the Public Utility Judge, Commenting CE Decision of July 9, 2018, Commune de Villiers-le-Bâcle et autres' [2018] AJDA 1661.

[353] Axer (n 298) para 112.

[354] EEG NW, § 30 sec 1 No 3.

Furthermore, the undertaking is only substantively lawful if the expropriation is necessary in the particular case for the public good and the expropriation purpose cannot be achieved in any other reasonable way.[355] Private projects can also be in the public interest and thus serve the public good. The construction of a hospital will generally be in the public interest, as it ensures healthcare. But the special needs of healthcare must require the construction of the hospital on Miss Nightingale's property in particular. The measure could be disproportionate if healthcare is already sufficiently guaranteed in the area, or if another plot of land is evidently more suitable, for example because of better accessibility.

As a legal remedy, Miss Nightingale has the option to sue before the administrative court. Since the public interest, that justifies the expropriation, does not have to be specifically declared in German law, the court will probably not annul the expropriation, as far as no further objections are given.

D. Italy

SM

According to Article 11 of the Expropriation Act, the owners of areas subject to expropriation must receive notification from the moment of the approval of the urban planning element that resulted in this expropriation. Within five years of the application of the expropriation constraint, the public administration has to issue the declaration of public utility. This declaration is the formal document where the public administration has to demonstrate the public interest in the completion of the public work or intervention.

The declaration of public utility can derive from the approval of the final project of a public work or the approval of other items of urban planning, such as the detailed plan, the development plan, the recovery plan, the reconstruction plan, the area plan (Article 12 of the Expropriation Act).

The declaration of public utility constitutes a sub procedure of the expropriation procedure and can be challenged independently since it produces an immediately harmful effect.

It is preceded by the formal notice of the commencement of the procedure and is always necessary for the expropriation procedure to be valid.

In the Italian legal system, the use, occupation or irreversible transformation of private land by the public administration in the absence of a declaration of public utility cannot be considered as a valid expropriation, to the extent that any dispute between the private owner and the administration comes under the ordinary rather than administrative jurisdiction. In this case, of so-called encroaching occupation, the ordinary judge can order the return of the asset to the private owner or, if this is not possible, compensation for damages.[356]

[355] ibid § 4 sec 1.

[356] See above all TAR Campania, Salerno, Sec II (13 September 2019) No 1580; TAR Sardinia, Sec II (9 February 2019) No 106; Cass Civ, Sec I, Ord (23 May 2018) No 12846.

In this case, Miss Nightingale received formal notice of the expropriation procedure, but this notice does not mention any reference to the existence of a declaration of public utility.

On this matter, a distinction has to be made between two hypotheses: if the failure to refer to the public utility is due only to a formal defect in the notice, but in reality the declaration of public utility exists, or, instead, if this declaration is completely lacking and this is why the notice is not indicated.

In the first case, Miss Nightingale can challenge the formal notice and ask the administrative judge to quash the decision. However, we have to consider that the public administration could issue a new notice of the commencement of the expropriation procedure, provided there is still time to complete the expropriation procedure (normally the deadline is indicated in the declaration of public utility, or otherwise it can be five years, according to Article 13 of the Expropriation Act).

In the second case, Miss Nightingale is entitled to appeal to the ordinary judge for compensation, because without the declaration of public utility the procedure is not valid.

In any case, it is important to note that the public administration can always decide to apply the provision of Article 42-bis of the Expropriation Act on the unentitled use of an asset for public interest purposes. According to this article, the authority that uses private land for purposes of public interest, modified in the absence of a valid and effective declaration of public utility, can order that it be acquired, non-retroactively, into its unavailable assets and that compensation be paid to the owner for the loss suffered. Such an acquisition measure can also be adopted by the public administration during the judicial proceeding on the quashing of the previous expropriation procedure decision, such as the formal notice on the commencement procedure.

E. The Netherlands

JS and NvT

As mentioned previously the Dutch system works in such a way that the (possible) grounds for expropriation are laid down in the law, in the Environment and Planning Act. The (by far) most common ground for expropriation is expropriation aimed at the development of an environment plan (or a comparable decision regarding zoning). Once such a zoning decision has been taken by the competent public authority and, if challenged, the public interest of the envisaged project has again further been upheld by the court(s) as already enshrined in the relevant zoning decision, it is a given in the subsequent expropriation procedure, and therefore in that procedure no longer up for (serious, meaningful) debate.

F. Poland

IK and ŁK

Pursuant to Article 21(2) of the Polish Constitution, expropriation may be allowed solely for public purposes. In Article 6 of the IPMA, the legislator defines more precisely the manifestations of the pursuance of public purposes. Consequently, it provides a list of public purposes, yet not of a *numerus clausus* nature but open-ended, so indicating that separate acts of law can specify other public purposes. The construction and maintenance of non-public healthcare facilities (a private hospital) is not among the public purposes defined in Article 6(6) of the IPMA, which concerns public healthcare facilities, or in any other act of law.

The definition for what public purpose property is expropriated must be provided for precisely in the expropriation decision (Article 119(1)(1)), even more so as a public purpose is of key importance when assessing the admissibility of property return.[357] Further, the institution of expropriation belongs to the domain of public law and covers primarily an enforced removal of property for the benefit of the state treasury or another public-law entity. At the same time, private-law regulations that provide for a transfer of the right of ownership, even against the will of the entitled party, to another person yet not the state treasury should not be treated as expropriation.[358]

As things stand, Polish legislation does not include a legal basis for property expropriation in order to build a private hospital. Miss Nightingale can then lodge an appeal. In expropriation cases, the *starost's* decision may be appealed before a provincial governor (*voivode*). The appeal decisions ending second-instance administrative proceedings can be contested before provincial administrative courts. Proceedings before administrative courts are double-instance and one can lodge a cassation appeal or a complaint before the Supreme Administrative Court.[359] Administrative courts do not rule on the merits of the case but uphold or repeal contested administrative decisions in entirety or part, referring them back for re-examination by the competent administrative bodies.[360]

G. Portugal
RGdF

The need for Miss Nightingale's property is determinant in its expropriation: in fact, there is no way to build a new hospital without depriving Miss Nightingale of all the uses and rights the normal proprietor is entitled to, and we must assume the whole land is needed, or such a proportion of it that it renders the remaining part unusable.

The notice received by Miss Nightingale would be the decision of expropriation—which is actually a decision to request the exercise of the power of expropriation directed to the competent authority (normally, the Government). This request is

[357] Supreme Administrative Court judgment of 9 December 2010, I OSK 235/10, LEX No 745185; J Szachułowicz, *Gospodarka nieruchomościami* (Lexis Nexis 2005) 208; P Wojciechowski, 'Artykuł 119' in P Czechowski (ed), *Ustawa o gospodarce nieruchomościami: Komentarz* (Wolters Kluwer 2015) https://sip.lex.pl/#/commentary/587659374/456814 (accessed 29 March 2020).

[358] CC judgments: of 29 May 2001, K 5/01, OTK 2001/4/87; of 21 June 2005, P 25/02, OTK-A 2005/6/65; of 21 December 2005, SK 10/05, OTK-A 2005/11/139; of 11 September 2006, P 14/06, OTK-A 2006/8/102; P Wojciechowski, 'Article 112' in *Ustawa o gospodarce nieruchomościami: Komentarz* (Wolters Kluwer 2015).

[359] The systemic place of administrative courts is determined by the followings acts of law: The Polish Constitution (arts 10, 45, 77–79, 165(2), 166(3), and 173–187), Act of 25 July 2002 on the system of administrative courts, JoL of 2019, item 2167, as amended, Act of 30 August 2002 on proceedings before administrative courts, JoL of 2019, item 2325, as amended.

[360] Administrative court proceedings are governed by arts 45 ff of the APAC.

governed by Articles 10 and 12 of the CE: it is the first formal moment of the expropriation procedure and it must be notified to the proprietor. According to Article 10/1 al a), the justifying public reason for the expropriation is actually the first element to be mentioned in the request. The absence of that mention might be a simple procedural error that can be corrected or it might reveal a deeper problem: the inexistence per se of a justifying public interest for expropriation. Let us concentrate on the latter which seems to be the problem in hand.

According to the Constitution (Article 62) and the law (Article 1 of the CE), an expropriation can only occur for reasons of *public* interest, a public end—for the benefit of the whole community—which can prevail over legitimate property rights. There is a certain fluctuation of expressions (public interest, general interest, among others)[361] which, however, does not reflect any conceptual crisis. Only for public ends is an expropriation possible. This means that a private or non-state actor cannot be the beneficiary of an expropriation.

But the CE seems to open an exception: according to Article 14/5, some private companies may request the acknowledgement of a public interest regarding the expropriation of lands necessary to build, amplify, reorganise, or reconvert their units of production or access. In these situations, the power to issue the 'dup' lies with the minister responsible for that particular sector, and the company requesting the expropriation must guarantee the existence of funds to pay for the necessary indemnities.

What private actors are we (exceptionally) talking about? Some companies that have licences to search and explore for minerals (quarries), and companies involved in the exploitation of dams for the production of electricity, are examples; as are associations and foundations to which a special statute of public utility is recognised (not companies, strictly speaking); and public corporations or companies with a private statute.[362] The complexity nowadays of the network of public/private bodies/entities involved in public functions tends to blur clear-cut distinctions in this and other fields.

In any case, when truly private actors are involved it seems that legality demands express and specific rules stating the possibility of their involvement in expropriation procedures as beneficiaries.[363] Portugal, as in other continental nations, has been progressively distancing itself from a period (nineteenth and early twentieth centuries) when the specific causes of public interest should be listed by law. For the last four decades, the public interest in expropriations has consisted of a general clause which is to be made concrete by (high) administrative power, usually at the governmental level. This flexibility of the principle of legality is a general issue nowadays. But when it comes to expropriation, the clause of general *public* interest is still a limitation that has to be fulfilled. In Portuguese law, a rule that would cover the possibility in question is not known.

361 See Alves Correia (n 87) 191.

362 See Alves Correia (n 87) 191.

363 A similar instrument to expropriation is 'forced selling' and this actually has private parties as beneficiaries. 'Forced selling' exists, for instance, in urban planning for situations when proprietors refuse to rebuild or to take care of their property when it would be necessary to provide effectiveness to a certain plan (art 160 of the LPIL; arts 62 and 63 of Decree-Law 307/2009, of 23 October). The sale takes place at a public auction. The—constitutionally questionable—forced selling must be contemplated in a specific legal rule.

So, if the request for expropriation actually originated a 'dup', an administrative court of law should annul it—or perhaps better—declare its nullity.

H. Spain

LAJ and DUFB

Article 33(3) CE allows for the expropriation of rights or assets 'on justified grounds of public utility or social interest'. While the first concept relates to an activity of public interest carried out by a public authority, the second one relates an activity of public interest carried out by a private beneficiary. Therefore, the fact that an expropriation is conducted to build private infrastructure does not necessarily entail that it be considered unconstitutional, insofar as there is a prior statement declaring that such private infrastructure pursues a public purpose.[364]

According to Article 9 LEF, a prior formal statement declaring that a given right or asset must be considered 'of public utility' or 'of social interest' is a precondition for any expropriation (see Part I, Question 4 above). As a general rule, this declaration must be specific and provided in a statutory provision (Article 11 LEF). However, there are some exceptions. First, generic statements of public purpose enshrined in a piece of legislation are allowed for abstract categories of activities or services as long as they are subsequently further defined for each specific case (Article 10 LEF). Secondly, concerning expropriations of real estate intended to implement public works and public service plans (urban planning, road plans, hospitals, etc) the statement of public utility or social interest is deemed implied following the approval of the relevant plan (Article 10 LEF). Thus, the requirement that a prior declaration (of social interest, in the case at hand) be issued would only be met if public authorities had previously enacted a hospital construction plan providing for the building of the disputed hospital.

Failure to mention the declaration of public utility or social interest in the administrative expropriation decision is not grounds for invalidity if such statement previously existed and met the aforesaid requirements. Otherwise, the declaration of the need to expropriate Miss Nightingale's property will be fully invalid (null and void) according to the abovementioned general invalidity framework, since the declaration of public purpose is a necessary condition required for the administrative procedure to be triggered. Article 47(1)(e) LPAC provides that any administrative acts 'issued in blatant disregard of the legally established procedure' will be fully invalidated. This invalidity can be declared within an administrative procedure, following an administrative appeal against the declaration of the need to expropriate, or within judicial proceedings following a judicial appeal before administrative law courts against the decision to dismiss the prior administrative appeal. Also, the affected owners may bring claims to recover the possession of their seized property before civil law courts. These are called 'writs to regain possession', and they are governed by Article 125 LEF.

[364] D Utrilla Fernández-Bermejo, *Expropiación forzosa y beneficiario privado* (Marcial Pons 2014) 67–100.

I. Sweden
PJ

There is no formal declaration regarding public interest per se in the Swedish legal system. However, expropriation must be based on one of the purposes listed in the Expropriation Act, which themselves have been chosen by the legislator in consideration of their public interest. In Miss Nightingale's case, the relevant ground/purpose for expropriation would be section 10, Chapter 2 of the Expropriation Act according to which 'expropriation may be made to meet the need for space for a building, premises or other facility for activities that the state, a municipality, a region or a municipal association has to cater for or that is otherwise of significant importance to the state or the locality or a certain population group'.
This ground encompasses among others the possibility to expropriate for a hospital.[365]

J. Ukraine
HD

The construction of hospitals is not covered by the notion 'public needs' or 'public necessity' (Articles 7 and 15 of the Law of Ukraine 'On alienation').[366] Thus, redemption and forced alienation of a plot land could not be carried out for this purpose.

Both the Constitution of Ukraine (Article 41(4) and the Civil Code of Ukraine (Article 321)) provide for the inadmissibility of the unlawful deprivation of the right to property. Under the Constitution, everyone must be guaranteed the right to challenge the decisions, actions, or the inactivity of public authority, local self-government bodies, officials, and officers (Article 55) in court.

The procedure for challenging this decision depends on the entity that issued it. If the act has been passed by local self-government bodies and officials, Miss Nightingale will need to file a suit with the administrative court.[367] Instead, an act promulgated by local state administrations could be challenged before the superior body or the administrative court.[368]

So, Miss Nightingale can definitely challenge this decision by filing a lawsuit with the administrative court claiming the unlawfulness of this act and asking to have it annulled. The competent authority will annul the decision.

An example from case law concerning the groundless forced alienation of land plots is the Resolution of the Lviv Appellate Administrative Court of 14 April 2016.[369]

[365] Prop 1972:109, 276.

[366] Law of Ukraine 'On the alienation of land plots and other real property assets located on them which are private property for public needs or on the grounds of public necessity' (17 November 2009) https://zakon.rada.gov.ua/laws/show/1559-17 (accessed 5 May 2021).

[367] Law of Ukraine 'On local self-government' (21 May 1997 https://zakon.rada.gov.ua/laws/show/280/97-%D0%B2%D1%80 (accessed 5 May 2021).

[368] Law of Ukraine 'On local state administrations' (9 April 1999) https://zakon.rada.gov.ua/laws/show/586-14 (accessed 5 May 2021).

[369] Resolution of Lviv Appellate Administrative Court of 14 April 2016 in the case No CK-876/1/14 https://reyestr.court.gov.ua/Review/57258520 (accessed 5 May 2021).

Among other arguments, the court carried out a three-criteria proportionality assessment according to Protocol No 1 to the European Convention of Human Rights. In addition, *Tregubenko v Ukraine* and *Fedorenko v Ukraine* were also used.

K. The United Kingdom

EW

An acquiring authority *must* demonstrate a compelling case for the use of compulsory purchase powers as directed by the Government's *Guidance on Compulsory Purchase and the Crichel Down Rules*.[370] The justification should be stated in the notice sent to Miss Nightingale and since it has not been, she may make an objection in writing to the compulsory purchase order (CPO), which will be considered in one of three ways: written representations; public local inquiry; or at a hearing.[371] Miss Nightingale could also argue that there will be an infringement of A1P1, since this states that private property may be taken where there is a compelling case in the public interest.[372]

In the event that no compelling public interest is found but the CPO still goes ahead, Miss Nightingale could challenge the CPO in the High Court[373] on the grounds that the decision is unreasonable given that the decision-maker has failed to take into account a relevant matter.[374] It would also be open to Miss Nightingale to challenge the decision to make the CPO in an application for judicial review under Part 54 of the Civil Procedure Rules. An application for judicial review must be made promptly within three months of the grounds arising and permission must be sought first, before the court will hear any substantive claim. In the *Margate Town* decision the Court of Appeal noted that a CPO 'should only be made where there is a compelling case in the public interest'[375] and that the 'draconian nature of the order will itself render it more vulnerable to successful challenge on *Wednesbury/Ashbridge* grounds unless sufficient reasons are adduced affirmatively to justify it on the merits'.[376] In the event that the Secretary of State did not consider whether the public interest was engaged in this CPO the court will quash the decision as an error in law, unless the court is satisfied that the decision-maker would have made the same decision nonetheless.[377]

It is worth noting that there is nothing inherently wrong with an acquiring authority using its powers of compulsory acquisition to benefit a private company, such as a hospital provider. Section 226(1) of the TCPA 1990 provides local authorities with broad

370 *Margate Town Centre Regeneration Co Ltd v Secretary of State for Communities and Local Government* [2013] EWCA Civ 1178.

371 Planning and Compulsory Purchase Act 2004, s 13A.

372 *R (Clays Lane Housing Cooperative Ltd) v Housing Corporation* [2005] 1 WLR 2229.

373 ALA 1981, s 23.

374 *Associated Picture Houses v Wednesbury Corp* [1948] 1 KB 223; *Bolton MBC v Secretary of State for the Environment and Greater Manchester Waste Disposal Authority* [2017] PSTR 1091.

375 *Margate Town Centre Regeneration Co Ltd v Secretary of State for Communities and Local Government* [2013] EWCA Civ 1178, [17].

376 ibid, quoting Slade LJ in *DE Rothschild v Secretary of State for Transport* (1988) 57 P&CR 300.

377 *Margate Town Centre Regeneration Co Ltd v Secretary of State for Communities and Local Government* [2013] EWCA Civ 1178, [17], referring to *Simplex GE (Holdings) Ltd v Secretary of State for the Environment* [1988] 3 PLR 25, 42.

powers to acquire land compulsorily where the authority is satisfied that the expropriation will facilitate the carrying out of development, redevelopment or improvement on or in relation to the land. The expropriation should contribute to the promotion or improvement of the economic well-being, social well-being or environmental well-being of the local area. Additionally, section 226(4) TCPA 1990 explicitly states that it is 'immaterial by whom the local authority propose that any activity or purpose ... be undertaken or achieved (and in particular the local authority need not propose to undertake an activity to achieve that purpose themselves)'. The involvement of a private hospital in the scheme is therefore not problematic in the English context and would not be grounds for a successful challenge.

L. The United States

IS

This is another issue that varies by state. However, in general the government must indicate some sort of public use that will be served by a taking, and also show how it is authorised by statute. In many states, private facilities that promote 'economic development' or other similar public benefits—including the provision of services such as health care—qualify as 'public uses' under the state constitution and statutory law.[378] In such a state, a taking for a hospital would be permissible, so long as proper procedures were followed.

M. International investment law

FF

In this scenario, at stake is the absence of a reference to public interest in an expropriatory measure. As discussed previously, this deficiency can undermine the measure's alignment with due process but is unlikely to suffice for a finding of breach—IIL is concerned with substance more than form.

The investor could argue that the lack of indication of public interest either (a) reveals the absence of a genuine public interest in the measure or (b) is harmful per se. In the latter case, the failure to mention the public interest, irrespective of whether there is one, arguably contradicts the duty of transparency and prevents further scrutiny and contestation on the merits—since it is impossible to gauge the measure's necessity and proportionality. Both arguments would ultimately regard the substantive alignment between the state act and the common good. The applicable test is of substantive (not formal) regularity: a generic reference to 'public utility services [and] societal needs' can be sufficient indication of public purpose, if the measure genuinely maps onto a public goal.[379]

[378] For overview of relevant state law see Ilya Somin, *The Grasping Hand:* Kelo v City of New London *and the Limits of Eminent Domain* (University of Chicago Press 2015) ch 5.

[379] *CC/Devas* (n 193) para 413.

A public declaration of the measure's purpose increases the transparency and accountability of governmental action. An identified goal permits ascertaining whether alternative measures—equally effective but less restrictive—could have been taken instead.[380] For Miss Nightingale, knowing the expropriation's purpose would facilitate contestation: for instance, if the state owned sufficient unbuilt land nearby, the confiscation would have been unnecessary to achieve the goal of building the hospital. Only by disclosing the public purpose is it possible to gauge the effectiveness of the state measure against its intended goal:

> [a] defence that an expropriation was undertaken 'for a public purpose related to the internal needs of [the] Party' requires—at least—that the Respondent set out the public purpose for which the expropriation was undertaken and offer a prima facie explanation of how the acquisition of the particular property was reasonably related to the fulfilment of that purpose.[381]

The relevant issues arising in both scenarios are fully discussed elsewhere: the duty to state reasons (IIL Case 1), the right to challenge administrative acts (IIL Case 2), and the hypothesis of insufficient or insincere reasons (IIL Cases 4 and 7).

[380] *British Caribbean Bank v Belize* PCA Case No 2010-18/BCB-BZ Award (19 December 2014) para 245. See also *Vestey* (n 110) para 298.
[381] *British Caribbean Bank* (n 380) para 241.

VIII. Case 7: Local pressure against a nudist beach

A. Belgium

DR, LC, CD, and KP

In the context of the case in question, a public authority has granted Mr Baywatch a licence allowing him to run umbrella and chair services on Paradise Beach.

Mr Baywatch decided to set aside a part of the beach for nudism which, according to the authority, represents a breach of the terms of his licence. The authority thus decides to withdraw Mr Baywatch's licence.

The authority's decision is in fact a response to local pressure against nudism.

Belgian law establishes several types of administrative contracts, amongst which concessions for services and public domain granted in concession.

On the one hand, the concession for services can be described as:

> [a] contract concluded in writing and for pecuniary interest by which one or several awarding authorities entrust to one or several service providers the execution and management of services—other than works ... and where the consideration for the provision of services consists either solely in the right to exploit the services or in this right together with payment.[382]

On the other hand, public domain granted in concession can be described as:

> [a]n administrative contract by which the awarding authority allows a user either to temporarily and exclusively occupy a parcel of public land, or to use a parcel of public land for a specific purpose—which is not its primarily purpose—in a sustainable manner but on a precarious and revocable basis, and, in principle, for a licence fee.[383]

In principle, Belgian law permits a public authority to terminate such contracts unilaterally on grounds of public interest. In such cases, the public authority must compensate the other party for all damages linked to the termination of the contract,[384] unless the contract states otherwise.

The authority's decision to terminate the contract unilaterally could, in any case, be challenged before the competent court.

The case at hand seems to involve both a concession of services and, provided that the beach belongs to the public authority, a concession of the public domain.

In both cases, Mr Baywatch could challenge the motivation of the decision to unilaterally terminate the concession in court. The court should consider this decision illegal, as it is based on inaccurate factual grounds.

[382] Act 'on concession contracts', art 2, 7°, b) (17 June 2016; publication in the Belgian *Official Gazette* on 14 June 2016; free translation).

[383] D Renders, *Droit administratif général* (n 121) 430 (free translation).

[384] ibid 437–38 and 573–74.

An ordinary court could not make this decision disappear from the legal system. Indeed, this faculty is not conferred to the ordinary court under Belgian law. However, based on Article 159 of the Belgian Constitution, the court could refuse to apply this unlawful decision.

B. France
EG

Mr Baywatch attempts to annul an administrative decision against him, aiming to block the establishment of a nudist area on the public domain that he occupies. It is a question of analysing whether the local administration can effectively and unilaterally revoke authorisation of privative temporary occupation of its public domain.

Firstly, it should be noted that this occupation is by nature temporary. Furthermore, it is deemed to be 'precarious and revocable',[385] which means that the beneficiary does not exercise any rights over the public domain, which is the exclusive property of the public authority. By the same token, the beneficiary is obliged to act in accordance with the authorisation from which he benefits, under penalty of having it withdrawn, without compensation, by the administration.

In this case, this is the argument put forward by the local authority, which claims that Mr Baywatch left the beach unattended in order to justify its withdrawal—if one considers that this was part of the obligations incumbent on Mr Baywatch under the authorisation granted to him.

In this sense, the decision could be tainted by an error of fact if the alleged facts are materially inaccurate. This would be the case, for example, if Mr Braithwaite had fulfilled all his obligations, such as the supervision of the beach or its regular maintenance. This seems to be the case, as the decision seems unfounded and not motivated by the administration. Therefore, the administrative judge must analyse *in concreto* the direct, material and specific prejudice that can affect a beneficiary in the hypothesis that the revocation of the authorisation is unfounded. In this case, this is indeed the case: although Mr Baywatch only benefits from an authorisation of occupation that does not create property rights—he exercises a service activity—the administration is obliged to factually justify its withdrawal. Mr Baywatch can therefore claim an indemnity even if he will no longer be able to enjoy his previous authorisation. This is the object of the established case law of the *Conseil d'État* when the administration engages its responsibility for fault. The judge will therefore have to establish the 'prejudices alleged by the company … relating to the consequences of the withdrawal of the permission which could give rise to a right to compensation'.[386] Mr Baywatch will benefit from the error committed by the administration by receiving compensation even though the administration had a much more effective alternative to put an end to this activity. Indeed, the administration can legally revoke an authorisation to occupy the public domain before its term 'for reasons of general interest',[387] which

[385] General Code of Public Property, art L 2122-2.
[386] CE, Decision of 29 March 1968, Ville de Bordeaux, No 68946.
[387] CE, Decision of 1 February 1980, ORTF, No 09908.

seem to be characterised in this case as pressure is exerted locally to bring this activity to an end.

C. Germany

FS

Mr Baywatch holds a licence for a beach chair and parasol service at Paradise Beach, which also includes the duty to supervise the beach. If Mr Baywatch takes legal action against the withdrawal of the licence, the court will investigate the facts *ex officio*. The court is not bound to the arguments of the parties, but it can take into consideration their knowledge and information when clarifying the facts.[388] The court must therefore investigate whether the reason for the withdrawal stated by the authority is in fact given or whether it is an alleged reason that does not justify the withdrawal of the licence. If the court does not investigate at all, this can be a procedural error. The withdrawal of a licence for exclusively political motives is unlawful on grounds of substance. It is an error of discretion if the authority includes reasons that have no material connection to the withdrawal of a licence. Furthermore, any misconduct by Mr Baywatch, such as a possible violation of the duty to supervise, would first have to be addressed by the authority before the licence is withdrawn as a final step. This is required by the principle of proportionality.

D. Italy

SM

In the Italian legal system, temporary concessions from the state have to conform to the public interest to which they respond; and public interest consists in the particular use of a public good if and to the extent that it complies with the former; the precarious nature of this use is related to the subjugation to the power of withdrawal exercised by the granting administration. The withdrawal of an administrative decision can take the legal form of voidability or revocation.

One of the most important forms of withdrawal decisions is revocation, provided for by Article 21-*quinquies* of Act No 241/1990. This is an instrument of decision-making aimed at the removal, with *ex nunc* (from now) efficacy (and, therefore, not retroactive), of a decision of lasting efficacy, following a new (and different) evaluation of the public interest in the conservation of its effectiveness. The conditions for the revocation are: (1) the occurrence of reasons of public interest; (2) the change in the actual situation (unforeseeable at the time of the adoption of the provision); and (3) a renewed (and different) evaluation of the original public interest (except for the authorising measures or assigned economic advantages). The power to revoke a concession is therefore discretionary and implies the use of discretionary power by the competent authority.

[388] VwGO, § 86 sec 1 sentences 1 and 2.

With specific reference to the maritime state concession, such as the beach concessions that concern a parcel of public land, a widely discretionary power is acknowledged by case law.

In the concession, the competent public authority subtracts the good from the common use and makes it available to certain subjects (so-called particular use). The contrary provision, which revokes the concession, must be supported by a reasonable motivation regarding the changes that may have occurred in the actual situation, or by reasons for which a situation, unchanged up to that moment, should be considered and evaluated differently, with respect to the assessment made at the time the concession was issued.

The use of the state maritime concession in a manner that is different from what was established (for example, in the case of illegal occupation of public spaces) clearly justifies revocation. The revocation of the administrative authorisation issued for the operation of a bathing establishment where the authorised activities are carried out against urban planning and building regulations is, for example, fully lawful.

We might also recall the specific provision of Article 47 of the Navigation Code (RD No 327/1942), which provides the reasons for the revocation of the concessionaire, and indicates among these the failure to fulfil the obligations deriving from the concession.

Administrative case law has pointed out that this kind of revocation is a sanctioning and discretionary decision that has to be adopted by the public administration after a preliminary evaluation in order to take into account not only the seriousness of the failure to fulfil the obligations deriving from the concession, but also the overall behaviour of the concessionaire in carrying out the concession.[389] The decision must be taken in consultation with the interested party and it can be considered lawful only if the factual analysis at the basis of this decision is effective and appreciable.[390]

Accordingly, in the case concerning Mr Baywatch, he can be considered able to challenge the decision of the authority, complaining about the lack of a correct factual analysis at the basis of the revocation of the licence. The administrative judge can verify the fairness of such an analysis, and if absent can quash the contested decision.

Moreover, another aspect can be considered as regards the motivations of the decision, because it can be viewed as being a response to local pressures against nudism. The administrative judge could also review the effectiveness of the withdrawal to see if the decision to revoke is in reality unjustified on the basis of the non-observation of the obligations deriving from the concession, but is actually based on the evaluation of reasons of different public interest.

The administrative courts apply a case-by-case reasonableness and proportionality test on the decision to revoke a maritime concession, which must be reasonably justified on the existence of a public interest that is prevalent in comparison with the legitimate expectation of the private subject based on decades of use of the area.[391] The revocation of a concession must be supported by a reasonable motivation in order for

[389] See eg Cons Stato, Sec V (3 April 2018) No 2072; Cons Stato, Sec VI (8 May 2014) No 2356.

[390] TAR Sicily, Palermo, Sec I (19 March 2020) No 659; TAR Tuscany, Florence, Sec III (4 October 2010) No 6428.

[391] See eg Council of State, Sec V (3 April 2018) No 2072.

any changes that have occurred in the factual situation, or the reasons why a situation, unchanged up to that point, to be considered and assessed differently to the assessment made at the time of the granting of the concession.

In this respect the judge will be able to verify if there were actually other reasons that justified the revocation of the concession by the public administration, quite different from the justification given regarding Mr Baywatch's behaviour in leaving the beach unattended. If so, they can quash the revocation decision for a contradictory motivation and a misrepresentation of facts which the decision was formally based upon by the competent authority.

E. The Netherlands

JS and NvT

Mr Baywatch could argue the decision is made contrary to the principles of proper administration, more specifically a breach of the principle of due care, the duty to give reasons, and/or the principle of proportionality.[392] However, whether this argument will move the court to quash the contested decision remains to be seen.

A decision by an administrative authority has to maintain a balanced weighing of interests. Whether Mr Baywatch will be able to convince the court to quash the decision will depend on the reasoning of the decision and more specifically the balancing of interests that has taken place in the making of that decision. In the event the decision is well-reasoned and Mr Baywatch actually has left the beach unattended (in which case there is no actual inaccurate factual analysis) and the administrative authority is allowed to withdraw his licence on that basis, the decision will stand up in court. The fact that the actual reasoning behind the withdrawal of the licence differs from the reason given in the withdrawal is not enough to quash the decision if the decision is well-reasoned.

F. Poland

IK and ŁK

The rules on managing immovable property owned by the state treasury and local government units are laid down in the IPMA. Its Article 25(1) indicates the commune's executive authority in managing its real estate resources. The executive body of the commune is a single-person authority, the commune head or town or city mayor, depending on the type and size of the commune.

Further, in case of the sale, placing in perpetual usufruct, use, rental, or lease of property located within the technical belt (an area directly adjacent to a seashore forming a zone of mutual direct impact of sea and land, designed to maintain the shore so that it complies with the safety requirements and environmental protection standards), it is required to obtain consent of the territorially competent maritime administration

[392] General Administrative Law Act, arts 3:2 and 3:4.

authority (Maritime Office director).[393] Under such rules, the beach could be rented out to Mr Baywatch for his economic activity of beach gear (chairs and umbrellas) rental. Under Polish legislation, no licence is required for such an activity. The rental agreement with Mr Baywatch may be cancelled, renounced, or terminated in compliance with the provisions of the Civil Code.

Rental for the purpose of his economic operation does not entitle Mr Baywatch to defining beach use rules as beaches and rules for using them are regulated by local government. Under Articles 37 and 38 of the Water Law Act (WLA),[394] the commune head (and so also the town or city mayor) keeps a list of bathing sites and applications for entering them onto the list, organises bathing sites and prepares drafts of the commune assembly's resolutions related to the list of bathing sites. There exist no legal provisions, however, that would serve straightforward regulations on establishing nudist beaches or delineating their borders. The legislation commonly in force, including bye-laws, does not prohibit or allows for establishing nudist beaches.

G. Portugal

RGdF

As in most countries, such a use of the beach, which is public property (maritime public domain, to be more precise), would require a permit: a licence (administrative act) or a concession (public contract). This kind of use—*umbrella parasol and chair services*—would probably require a licence (Article 60/1 als d) and e) of the Law 58/2005, of 29 December, known as Water Law WL),[395] which would be effective for a maximum period of 10 years (Article 67/2 of the WL).[396] So, assuming that Mr Baywatch had in fact (and in strict legal terms) a licence, all the following steps must take into account the legal demands for such an administrative act.

The termination of Mr Baywatch's licence is not an expropriation properly speaking, and is not a similar or close concept. Nevertheless, it consists in an act of will coming from administrative powers (we will soon see of what sort) with a 'taking' effect: Mr Baywatch will lose 'property' in a broad sense, since it will negatively affect his business, which will have at the least to change location, but will almost certainly be lost. He will keep the property rights over the removable goods (like the chairs and parasols), but any infrastructure he might have built will be lost with no compensation.[397]

393 IPMA, art 19(2)(1).

394 Water Law Act of 20 July 2017, JoL of 2020, item 310, as amended; P Szuwalski, 'Art. 14' in *Prawo wodne: Komentarz do wybranych przepisów* (System Informacji Prawnej LEX 2019).

395 Last amended by Law 44/2017 of 19 June.

396 The concession, on the other hand, can be effective for a maximum period of seventy-five years, and gives the private party rights that the licence does not (art 68 of the WL). On the differences between both legal concepts in this context see M Assis Raimundo, 'Título de utilização e exploração do domínio público marítimo' in R Guerra da Fonseca and M Assis Raimundo (eds), *Direito Administrativo do Mar* (Almedina/ICJP—CIDP 2016) 136 ff.

397 See art 69 of the WL. It would be different only if the termination of the licence before its time would happen for the protection of hydric resources or other unforeseen circumstances (arts 69/6 and 7 of the WL). In the situation in question, Mr Baywatch would actually have to pay himself for the removal of any infrastructure he might have built, since he has the obligation of leaving the land as it was before (art 34 of the Decree-Law 226-A/2007, of 31 May—Hydric Resources Use (HRU)).

So, Mr Baywatch will be deprived of the rights inherent to his business, and he will have damages arising from his loss. Considering the scope of 'property rights' that our Constitutional Court considers protected by Article 62 of the Constitution, this is an administrative decision with an expropriatory effect.[398]

Portuguese law allows naturism, on beaches and in camps, but subjects it to licence (Law 92/88 of 13 August): it is for the municipalities to license certain beaches as nudist areas, and this can happen on their own initiative or on that of naturist associations (Article 3 and 8 of the Law 53/2010 of 20 December, which regulates the practice of naturism and the creation of such spaces). Naturism is, however, rather bureaucratic when it comes to the licensing procedure. Of course, these beaches can have services, but their licensing supposes the prior classification of the corresponding beach, or the concurrence of the owner in a service already present on that beach: if the owner opposes, the beach cannot be licensed for naturism (Article 9 of the Law 53/2010).

Although the beach where Mr Baywatch's had his services was not a naturist one, it is questionable whether his licence could be revoked on the grounds of favouring nudism (Articles 56 onwards of the WL, and 32 of the Decree-Law 226-A/2007 do not offer a clear answer to this).

Anyway, the administrative decision under analysis does not seem to be flawed by *inaccuracy of its factual analysis*: the facts were clear and the public authorities made no mistake about them. What happened was that such a decision was biased and deviated.[399] Bias can be analysed from a subjective perspective—to not favour A to the detriment of B, or to not harm A to favour B—or from an objective perspective—consider the relevant facts: all the relevant facts and only the relevant facts. The case in question calls for the second perspective: public authorities considered irrelevant facts in the face of the law (the community disapproval) and invented or inflated other facts (leaving the beach unattended) due to the difficulty in fulfilling the legal grounds for revocation. Moreover, the decision was deviated: because the public authorities used their power to pursue an end which was not the one that justified its legal attribution. In fact, the power to revoke the licence was not granted to them to resolve issues of the *local population being discontent*.

But would the courts be willing to decide for Mr Baywatch? Let us hope so: it would be disproportionate to cancel his licence.

[398] The Constitutional Court includes in the concept of 'property' rights as different as estate rights, salaries, rights over bonds and other titles, intellectual rights, etc: actually any rights of 'ownership', pretty much as in other legal orders in Europe, and also the USA. Among others see Decision of the Constitutional Court 139/2004 of 10 March.

[399] The classification of the causes of invalidity changes from domestic order to domestic order for legal-cultural reasons, though many times they do not have such different meanings. Deliberately, here, words are chosen/used to transmit in English the closest idea to the Portuguese legal reality (without worrying about approximating it to any foreign system: namely, to one of the anglophone systems simply because we are writing in English).

H. Spain

LAJ and DUFB

It must be taken into account that, under Spanish law (Article 132 CE), beaches qualify as publicly-owned land subject to a specific public law regime. The conditions and limits on revocation or withdrawal depend on the type of licence held by Mr Baywatch—hereinafter, also referred to as the licensee—either an administrative permit or an administrative concession.[400]

If the licensee has a right to use the beach with the deployment of movable property—such as umbrellas and chairs—or detachable facilities, the licence would be an administrative permit, and the competent public authority may revoke it unilaterally. This revocation will not give rise to compensation, given that the grounds for revocation are either (i) non-compliance with the permit conditions, or (ii) the permit:

> [a] being incompatible with the general conditions subsequently approved, [b] causing damage to the public good, [c] preventing the use of the area for activities with greater public interest or [d] undermining the public use (Articles 92(2) LPAP and 55 LC).

Since the case at hand involves a permit, public authorities would have been required to evidence that Mr Baywatch wrongfully left the beach unattended, thereby breaching his obligation under the permit conditions. However, the revoking public body could also have approved new general conditions precluding nudism. In this last scenario, it would have also been entitled to revoke the permit unilaterally without any compensation.

Conversely, if Mr Baywatch had a right to use the beach (i) carrying out works, (ii) with fixed installations, or (iii) otherwise for a time period exceeding four years, the licence would not have been a permit but an administrative concession, which could be withdrawn in case of non-compliance by the licensee, or reversed—bailed out or terminated in advance—at the public authority's discretion in exchange for compensation payable to the licensee (Articles 100(d) LPAP and 78(1)(i) LC). In the latter case, the relevant public authority would not need (i) to justify that Mr Baywatch left the beach unattended or (ii) to approve new rules in order to revoke the permit. However, compensation for investment losses would be due.[401]

Particularly regarding Mr Baywatch, the grounds for the permit's withdrawal were non-compliance with his obligation to monitor the activities taking place

[400] F López Menudo, 'Títulos habilitantes para la utilización de los bienes y derechos demaniales: Tipología y régimen' in C Horgué (ed), *Régimen patrimonial de las Administraciones públicas* (Iustel 2007) 193–233; L Parejo Alfonso, 'El régimen de la utilización de los bienes y derechos de dominio público: Autorizaciones y concesiones demaniales' in C Chinchilla (ed), *Comentarios a la Ley 33/2003, del Patrimonio de las Administraciones Públicas* (Civitas 2004) 433–74.

[401] JF Mestre Delgado, 'La extinción de las autorizaciones y concesiones demaniales' in C Chinchilla (ed), *Comentarios a la Ley 33/2003, del Patrimonio de las Administraciones Públicas* (Civitas 2004) 491–520.

on the beach. The competent public authority should have evidenced this breach within a specific administrative procedure leading to a revocation decision. Mr Baywatch's judicial appeal against the decision to revoke his permit could be based on an incorrect assessment of the facts. Generally, courts carry out a careful scrutiny of public authorities' assessment of the factual background, and such factual assessments are fully subject to judicial review. Courts show no deference to public authorities when examining whether the facts triggering the application of administrative provisions occurred, regardless if the relevant administrative provision gives authorities discretionary powers.[402] Courts do carry out a less stringent scrutiny regarding complex technical assessments—within the so-called margin for technical discretion—upon verifying that the public authority's factual assessment is not manifestly incorrect.[403] However, the factual assessment of whether the beach was left unattended is not covered by this exception. In the case at hand, judicial review would be full, and Mr Baywatch could produce any evidence to prove that he did not breach the permit conditions.

I. Sweden

PJ

Legally Mr Baywatch is party to a contract of general lease (*lägenhetsarrende*) with the local authority according to Chapter 8 of the Land Code (*Jordabalken* 1970:994).

The question is therefore one of a breach of a contract. According to the Land Code, mediating lease disputes are to be heard first by the competent Regional Tenancy Tribunal (*arrendenämnd*). The decision of the tribunal may be appealed before a court of appeal.

J. Ukraine

HD

According to Ukrainian legislation, no licence is required for this type of activity (to offer beach services) (Article 7 of the Law of Ukraine 'On licensing of types of economic activity').[404] Under the Land Code of Ukraine, beaches are considered to be municipal property (Article 83(4)).[405] The Law of Ukraine 'On the lease of land' establishes that local councils are the lessors of municipal property (Article 4(4)).[406] A lease contract can be dissolved by mutual content. At the request of one of the parties, the

[402] STS of 17 June 1989 (RJ 1989732), of 22 December 1990 (RJ 19900183), of 2 April 1991 (RJ 1991278) and of 14 April 1992 (RJ 1992038).

[403] STS of 14 July 2000 (Rec 258/1997), and of 12 February 2020 (Rec 3226/2016).

[404] Law of Ukraine 'On the licensing of types of economic activity' (2 March 2015) https://zakon.rada.gov.ua/laws/show/222-19 (accessed 5 May 2021).

[405] Land Code of Ukraine (25 October 2001) https://zakon.rada.gov.ua/laws/show/2768-14 (accessed 5 May 2021).

[406] Law of Ukraine 'On the lease of land' (6 October 1998) https://zakon.rada.gov.ua/laws/show/161-14 (accessed 5 May 2021).

lease contract can be terminated before time only by means of a court order (Article 31 of the Law of Ukraine 'On the lease of land'). The leaseholder is obliged to use the land plot according to the purpose stated in the contract. If the leaseholder neglects this duty, another party can file a suit to the court initiating the early termination of the contract (Article 32 of the Law of Ukraine 'On the lease of land'). The same provision is provided for in Article 141 of the Land Code of Ukraine.

As the Grand Chamber of the Supreme Court held, cases concerning the dissolution of economic contracts by parties which are also parties in the dispute must come under the jurisdiction of the economic courts (§ 4.22.).[407]

If we assume that Mr Baywatch runs services on Paradise Beach by virtue of a lease contract, the local council would have to apply to the economic court in order to terminate the contract early, citing misuse of the beach. If the lease contract includes a condition providing the necessity to use the beach according to its purpose constituting the essential provision of the lease contract, the local council's claim will be upheld by the court, since Mr Baywatch has not respected this provision. In this case the appellate court will not annul the decision.

An example from case law concerning the misuse of land plots: a ruling of the Civil Chamber of the Supreme Court of Ukraine of 23 December 2015.[408]

K. The United Kingdom

EW

It is possible for local byelaws made by a local council to prohibit public nudity in a particular area (eg Hampstead Heath in London). However, nudity in public per se is not an offence in English law, if there is no intention to cause alarm or distress and where there is no sexual context to the nudity. In the given case, it does not appear that a local byelaw prohibiting public nudity on Paradise Beach exists, since if it did the authority would have grounded their decision clearly on this breach by Mr Baywatch. There is also no indication that a criminal offence related to nudity has occurred. The local discontent, on its own, is not therefore a relevant consideration that the authority should have had in mind when revoking Mr Baywatch's licence. Decision-makers are required to take account of factors that are relevant to their statutory power and to ignore irrelevant factors.[409] Additionally, the authority has erred in failing to consider relevant considerations such as the legality of public nudity in the absence of a bye-law condemning this, or a criminal offence having occurred. Mr Baywatch could seek judicial review of the decision to revoke his licence.

The courts try to strike a balance between administrative certainty and guarding against arbitrary decisions. The court will need to decide whether the irrelevant consideration of public discontent about nudism played a substantial or significant

[407] Ruling of Grand Chamber of Supreme Court of Ukraine of 6 February 2019 in case No 911/1357/18 https://reyestr.court.gov.ua/Review/79834975 (accessed 5 May 2021).

[408] Ruling of the Civil Chamber of the Supreme Court of Ukraine of 23 December 2015 in case No 6-2271цс15 https://reyestr.court.gov.ua/Review/54688916# (accessed 5 May 2021).

[409] *Hanks v Ministry of Housing and Local Government* [1963] 1 QB 999, 1020.

part in the authority's decision-making thus rendering it irrational and liable to being quashed. This will be a matter of evidence and may be difficult to prove. If the authority's decision was based substantially on the nudism then their decision to revoke Mr Baywatch's licence is likely to be invalid and quashed. However, where the irrelevant consideration was only one aspect of the decision and did not exert a substantial or significant effect on the decision-making, the court will normally allow the decision to stand. If the authority would in any event have revoked Mr Baywatch's licence (because he had wrongfully left the beach unattended), whether or not nudism had occurred, then the court is likely to allow the decision to stand.

L. The United States

IS

This will vary based on the laws of the state or locality in question, and perhaps also on the specific terms of the licence. It is not an issue controlled by the Takings Clause of the Fifth Amendment and its state constitutional counterparts.

M. International investment law

FF

Sometimes, tribunals find that the host state, under the cover of measures ostensibly taken to pursue public goals (eg fiscal assessment,[410] fight against money-laundering,[411] administrative fines,[412] regulation of key economic sectors,[413] widening public access to food[414]), effectively schemed to hurt or seize the investment.

More often, even if the state is not accused of covertly taking the investments, the grounds of its measures are contested. Investors can successfully challenge adverse administrative acts—typically refusals to issue a licence or permit—alleging the inaccuracy of the reasons stated therein, sometimes arguing that the real motives are different and illicit (eg political pressure, discrimination, persecution).[415]

For instance, a tribunal examined a state's justification for terminating a concession on grounds of harm to public interest. Since the only plausible reasons adduced were formal irregularities, the tribunal concluded that the state termination process had occurred 'under a cloak of formal correctness allegedly in defense of the rule of law, in fact for exacting concessions unrelated to the [allegations of irregularity]'.[416] Assessing the grounds for termination, the tribunal also noted that some of the irregularities had

[410] *Yukos* (n 190) para 1581.
[411] *Casinos Austria v Argentina* ICSID Case No ARB/14/32 Decision on Jurisdiction (29 June 2018) paras 53, 244.
[412] *Armas* (n 279) para 345.
[413] *British Caribbean Bank* (n 380) para 240.
[414] *Vestey* (n 110) para 300.
[415] *Tethyan v Pakistan* ICSID Case No ARB/12/1 Decision on Jurisdiction and Liability (10 November 2017) para 1366.
[416] *Railroad* (n 53) para 234.

been known and tolerated—if not caused—by the authorities, and hinted therefore at acquiescence and clean hands when rejecting the false motives.[417]

Similarly, an investor contested the merits of the reasons attached by the administration to its denial of environmental clearance for an underwater dredging venture.[418] Among other things, the challenge made a purely substantive point, noting the administration's failure to recognise that loggerhead turtles live in shallow waters and cannot be affected by the dredging. Concurrently, the investor could allege that the denial was 'arbitrarily dictated to facilitate the career ends of a high State official'.[419]

In *Bear Creek v Peru*, a tribunal found that the ostensible reasons of a governmental decree blocking mining works 'for the purpose of safeguarding the environmental and social conditions' were insufficient[420] and fabricated post facto.[421] There had been opposition by indigenous communities, and the tribunal reviewed whether the restrictive measures were justified by looking at the grievances of the protestors and evaluating whether they were meritorious in light of the investor's conduct.[422] Ultimately, the tribunal disregarded the professed reasons and observed that the restrictive measure 'was taken to placate controversial political opposition'.[423]

In *South American Silver v Bolivia*, a comparable analysis lead to the opposite outcome. The tribunal assessed the alleged reasons behind the State's intervention, citing the need to end social conflicts and restore peace in the area of an extractive project. The tribunal confirmed the existence of genuine public security concerns—for which the investor was largely responsible and which the investor failed to resolve[424]—and agreed that the expropriation was necessary and proportionate in light of its accompanying reasons.[425]

In a case relating to a national park's creation, the investor took issue with its environmental and cultural rationales, questioning the veracity of the underlying motives:

> [a] primary objective of the Park is to protect the Salto Baiguate, or Baiguate Waterfall. However, the Salto Baiguate falls some three kilometers outside the boundaries of the national park ... the Decree indicates that the Park is intended to protect local walnut trees. However, there appear to be no walnut trees on Jamaca de Dios, in either Phase 1 or Phase 2.159 ... Not surprisingly, given these pretexts, the Respondent has refused to provide the technical study, if one exists, that should have been done to support the creation of the Park.[426]

[417] ibid para 235.
[418] *Odyssey v Mexico* (NAFTA, UNCITRAL) Notice of Arbitration (5 April 2019) para 100.
[419] ibid para 94.
[420] *Bear Creek* (n 53) para 388.
[421] ibid para 431.
[422] ibid para 401: '[t]he issues for the present Tribunal are whether the unrest was caused by or can be attributed to Claimant and whether Respondents action depriving Claimant of the rights it had been granted ... was legally justified'.
See also *Abengoa* (n 117) paras 670–71.
[423] *Bear Creek* (n 53) para 432.
[424] *South American Silver* (n 68) para 562.
[425] ibid para 577.
[426] *Ballantine v Dominican Republic* PCA Case No 2016-17 Amended Statement of Claims (4 January 2017) paras 132–34.

State conduct after the impugned measure is also relevant. While the stated purpose might be acceptable in principle, the state's subsequent failure to pursue it might be 'evidence that the measure was not taken in furtherance of such purpose'.[427] Subsequent conduct, therefore, can retrospectively reveal which professed goals were just window-dressing[428]—for instance, if the state builds a business venture based on the investor's representations, after finding them unsatisfactory.[429] However, that the expropriated investment was put to public use is insufficient evidence of the original public purpose of the taking.[430]

States are ambivalent about explaining their action with public or political pressure. Public contestation might be cited to confirm that state measures served an urgent societal need. Conversely, acknowledging external pressure casts doubt on the measure's reasonableness or proportionality, if they seem to flow from political capture rather than conscientious planning. Tribunals entertain allegations of illegitimate motives only if necessary (eg corruption, desire for personal gain, political tactics); the review of measures that are ultimately unlawful for breach of proportionality or due process need no additional scrutiny for secret purposes.[431]

427 *Vestey* (n 110) para 296.

428 A case in point is *von Pezold* (n 114) paras 502–503, in which the tribunal rejected the argument that the expropriation sought to right historical wrongs, as the land was not subsequently distributed to the disadvantaged population.

429 *Tethyan* (n 415) para 1370.

430 *Siag & Vecchi v Egypt* ICSID Case No ARB/05/15 Award (1 June 2009) paras 429–33.

431 *Inmaris* (n 117) para 303; *Quiborax* (n 69) para 243; *Kardassopoulos* (n 109) para 392.

IX. Case 8: Cultural heritage

A. Belgium

DR, LC, CD, and KP

In the context of the case in question, the authorities have declared a portrait belonging to Miss Lucky to be part of Gotham's cultural heritage.

Miss Lucky cannot therefore sell the portrait in a foreign auction as planned.

In Belgian law, several texts ensure the protection of movable cultural heritage.[432] The protected movable heritage is recorded in a list or inventory created according to the provisions of the text protecting it.

The protection of movable heritage implies several forms of interference with the owner's right to property. For example, rules of conservation may be imposed,[433] the sale of the property has to comply with a specific procedure,[434] and the protected property may not be moved without authorisation.[435]

This interference with the right to property does not imply a transfer. Therefore, it is not an expropriation for which the payment of a 'fair compensation paid beforehand' based on Article 16 of the Belgian Constitution can be granted.

This form of interference is, according to Belgian law, a public servitude, which does not, in principle, envisage any right to compensation unless the text on which the public servitude is based allows it.[436] In effect, in Belgian law, the legislator can, as

[432] See, for example, Act 'on the national cultural heritage' (16 May 1960; publication in the Belgian *Gazette* on 5 August 1960); Act 'on conservation of monuments and sites', Articles 17–20 (7 August 1931; publication in the Belgian *Gazette* on 5 September 1931); Decree of the French Community 'regarding the French Community's cultural heritage and cultural property' (11 July 2002; publication in the Belgian *Gazette* on 24 September 2002); Decree of the Flemish Community 'on protection of movable cultural heritage of outstanding interest' (24 January 2003; publication in the Belgian *Gazette* on 14 March 2003); Decree of the Brussels Region 'regarding the Brussels Region's cultural heritage and cultural property' (25 April 2019; publication in the Belgian *Gazette* on 17 May 2019).

[433] Decree of the French Community 'regarding the French Community's cultural heritage and cultural property', Article 11 (11 July 2002; publication in the Belgian *Gazette* on 24 September 2002); Decree of the Flemish Community 'on protection of movable cultural heritage of outstanding interest', Article 8 (24 January 2003; publication in the Belgian *Gazette* on 14 March 2003); Decree of the Brussels Region 'regarding the Brussels Region's cultural heritage and cultural property', Article 17 (25 April 2019; publication in the Belgian *Gazette* on 17 May 2019).

[434] Decree of the French Community 'regarding the French Community's cultural heritage and cultural property', Articles 10 and 21 (11 July 2002; publication in the Belgian *Gazette* on 24 September 2002); Decree of the Flemish Community 'on protection of movable cultural heritage of outstanding interest', Articles 12-18 (24 January 2003; publication in the Belgian *Gazette* on 14 March 2003); Decree of the Brussels Region 'regarding the Brussels Region's cultural heritage and cultural property', Article 20 (25 April 2019; publication in the Belgian *Gazette* on 17 May 2019).

[435] Decree of the French Community 'regarding the French Community's cultural heritage and cultural property', Article 7 (11 July 2002; publication in the Belgian *Gazette* on 24 September 2002); Decree of the Flemish Community 'on protection of movable cultural heritage of outstanding interest', Article 11 (24 January 2003; publication in the Belgian *Gazette* on 14 March 2003); Decree of the Brussels Region 'regarding the Brussels Region's cultural heritage and cultural property', Articles 18, 21, and 22 (25 April 2019; publication in the Belgian *Gazette* on 17 May 2019).

[436] Lagasse (n 286) 583.

established in Article 544 of the Belgian Civil Code, set up limits to the right to property in the public interest and without any right to compensation.[437]

However, if, according to Article 1 of Protocol No 1 to the European Convention on Human Rights, the public servitude causes disproportionate interference with the right to property, the European Court of Human Rights has ruled that the owner concerned may be entitled to compensation.[438] Based on this case law, the Belgian Court has also already considered that public servitudes may entail the award of compensation.[439]

In the case at hand, if the portrait in question falls within the scope of a text protecting it as movable cultural heritage, Miss Lucky must accept the forms of interference with her right to property provided by the text. For example, the text could provide that the portrait cannot be sold in a foreign auction.

The applicant could request compensation if this is provided for in the text protecting the portrait.[440]

If the text grants no compensation, Miss Lucky could try to demonstrate disproportionate interference with her right to property. The court should then examine whether there is a balance between the interference and the aim pursued by the measure. In the event of imbalance, the applicant may be entitled to compensation.

Miss Lucky could also decide to challenge the public authorities' decision to protect the portrait before the Council of State.

The court should then ascertain whether the decision to protect the portrait is lawful and specifically whether it is based on a text allowing the portrait to be protected and whether the procedure provided for in this text is lawful.

If this is the case, the court should reject the applicant's claim. If not, the court should quash the decision to protect the portrait.

B. France

EG

Miss Lucky owns a work of art that the City of Gotham has decided to classify as part of its cultural heritage. The latter designates all the works and monuments with such a historical and cultural value that they should remain on the national territory. Such a notion is easily explained by the particular sensitivity that each person has for his or her own culture: 'If the impact of national borders comes from cultural differences between countries, then we must find a border effect in

[437] ibid 567, 568.

[438] *Chassagnou and Others v France* (n 215); *Alatulkkila and Others v Finland* (n 215); *Anonymos Touristiki Etairia Kritis v Greece* (n 215); *Hermann v Germany* (n 215); Constitutional Court, case No 55/2012 of 19 April 2012; Court of Cassation (24 June 2010) *Pasicrisie*, 2010, 2004.

[439] Constitutional Court, case No 55/2012 of 19 April 2012. See also the principles stated by the Court of Cassation regarding compensation for interference with the right to property: Court of Cassation, 24 June 2010, *Pasicrisie*, 2010, p 2004.

[440] Generally, in the form of subsidies.

the exchange of cultural goods, which can then become a kind of 'tracer' of cultural preferences.'[441]

Therefore, the question is to determine whether Miss Lucky enjoys full ownership of a work of significant national cultural value. If so, this will authorise her to sell it to a foreign person.

The Heritage Code governs the law applicable in this matter. The state has a right of pre-emption over cultural property, initially resulting from the law of 31 December 1921 and modified on 10 July 2000. Thus, according to Article L123 of the Code, it is understood that:

> The State may exercise, on any public sale or private sale of cultural property carried out under the conditions provided for in article L 321-9 of the Commercial Code, a right of pre-emption by the effect of which it is subrogated to the successful bidder or the buyer.

In this sense, it can legally claim the repurchase of the Batman painting that Miss Lucky wishes to sell, given that paintings are part of cultural heritage. The state is therefore entitled to subrogate itself to the right of the foreign buyer who was party to the private sale.

In this case, the right of pre-emption is not in conflict with Miss Lucky's right of ownership. However, Miss Lucky can express her dissatisfaction. The classification of her painting as part of the state's cultural heritage is made according to a decree of the Ministry of Culture after consultation with the Higher Commission for Historical Monuments. This administrative decision could be the object of a legal challenge in excess of power because the qualification of 'cultural good' would be erroneous. In the absence of a precise definition of what can legitimately be considered as 'cultural property', it seems unlikely that the claim will be received favourably since the painting is linked with the history of the city and—more broadly—the country.

The applicant can contest the sale of her pre-empted property if she feels that the sale was not made at a fair price.

Thus, two options are open to her. On the one hand, she can act in tort against the auctioneer before the judicial courts. Indeed, the auctioneer has the specific obligation not to estimate the value of a cultural good at a low price. He may therefore have committed a fault by estimating the value of the painting at too low a value. Moreover, the applicant could also bring an action to have the sale contract cancelled. The auctioneer must indeed be particularly careful in his estimation, by being surrounded by experts, during his estimation. If this is not done seriously, the sale contract will be void, and the former owner will be able to regain possession of her property.

Finally, as a piece of cultural heritage, the Batman painting will have to be put up for public auction, and the representatives of the state will legitimately enjoy a right of pre-emption over foreign buyers. The estimated value of the work must still have been correctly established.

441 Ministry of Culture—DEPS, 'International trade flows of cultural goods and services: determinants and issues' (2007) *1*(2) Culture Studies 1.

C. Germany

FS

Since the picture is supposed to be a cultural property, the Cultural Property Protection Act ('*Kulturgutschutzgesetz*') is applicable in German law. Under this act, national cultural property as a part of the cultural heritage is subject to protection against removal from the national territory.[442] Cultural property is 'national cultural property' if it is listed in a register of cultural property of national significance.[443] This requires an official registration procedure, which is initiated *ex officio* or upon the request of the owner.[444] The initiation of the registration procedure entails a ban on the export of the cultural property as long as the decision on the registration has not yet become incontestable.[445] However, the owner of the cultural property must be heard in the registration procedure.[446] This has not been done in the present case. The registration procedure therefore has a procedural error and can be challenged in court.

The entry in the register of cultural property of national significance constitutes an encroachment on the fundamental right to property. It is not an expropriation under Article 14 section 3 GG, but a determination of content and limits of property under Article 14 section 1 sentence 2 GG. The entitled person is not deprived of the property, but is restricted in the power of its use and disposition. The owner of a cultural property listed in the register of cultural property of national significance is not compensated, but given tax concessions.[447] Only in the event of a sale due to economic hardship a fair settlement may be granted.[448]

D. Italy

SM

According to Italian Law (Cultural Heritage Code, Act No 42/2004), the identification procedure for cultural heritage is a ministerial procedure (a national-level procedure, not local).

For private property and for that of commercial companies, formal notification of a declaration of cultural interest is required.

The superintendent ('*sovrintendente*': an associate office of the Ministry of Cultural Heritage) initiates the procedure for the declaration of a cultural interest for the item in question, also backed by a motivated request of the region and any other interested territorial entity, giving notice to the owner, possessor or holder in whatever capacity.

[442] KGSG, § 5.
[443] ibid § 6 sec 1 No 1.
[444] ibid § 14 sec 1 sentence 1.
[445] ibid § 21 No 1.
[446] ibid § 14 sec 3 sentence 2.
[447] ibid § 12 sec 1.
[448] ibid § 12 sec 2.

The notification contains the elements of identification and evaluation of the asset arising from the first investigations, the indication of the effects of the declaration, as well as the indication of the term, in any case not less than thirty days, for the presentation of any observations.

The owners or holders of the property, within a time period set by the superintendency but not less than thirty days, may take part in the administrative procedure by sending the superintendent any observations, written submissions and documents to illustrate circumstances deemed relevant for the issuing of the final provision. After the terms of the procedure established by Article 2 of the Administrative Procedure Act No 241/1990 (thirty days or a different time established by ministerial rules), the superintendency proposes to the regional secretariat (the regional office of the Minister of Cultural Heritage) the issuance of the decree of cultural interest on the basis of the documentation transmitted.

Pending the issuing of the decree, the assets are in any case subject to protection, and therefore cannot be modified in any way without the authorisation of the superintendency.

Within 120 days of the communication to the interested parties, the regional secretariat, if it accepts the proposal of the superintendency, issues the decree of declaration of cultural interest. This decree, accompanied by the scientific report, photographic documentation and cadastral plan, is notified to the owners or holders and to the competent municipality.

This in short is the procedure for the recognition of an asset as an element of cultural heritage.

In this case, Miss Lucky can first of all exercise her participatory right in the procedure. The participation in the proceeding makes it possible to ascertain circumstances and elements suitable for an exact evaluation of the relevance of the asset to be subject to a cultural heritage restriction and possibly, if the conditions are met, to cause the administration to withdraw from its erroneous decision. Miss Lucky could therefore challenge the cultural heritage decree before the administrative court for any procedural defect, and the court could quash the contested decision if it finds that the procedural violation could affect the content of the final decision. And, in this case, the applicant may be entitled to compensation for damages.

The situation will be different if there are no procedural violations and the cultural heritage decree is well founded and completely lawful.

The portrait is therefore lawfully declared as cultural heritage and this recognition determines a series of constraints for the owner.

According to the rules of the Cultural Heritage Code (Article 20), cultural heritage assets cannot be destroyed, damaged or used for purposes that are not compatible with their historical or artistic character or that might harm their conservation.

Miss Lucky, as the owner of an element of cultural heritage, is required to keep the portrait. The use of it, which must be compatible with its historical or artistic character, is not unlimited. The constraint also serves to avoid damage or destruction of cultural heritage through improper use.

Every intervention on the property must be approved in advance by the competent authority and can be performed only once authorisation has been obtained.

Miss Lucky cannot export the portrait abroad without the prior authorisation of the Ministry of Cultural Heritage.

Any change of ownership or possession (sale, exchange, inheritance, donation, etc) must be notified to the competent administration. If Miss Lucky wants to sell the portrait, the state can exercise the right of first refusal: the state can buy it for the same sum that she intended to derive from the sale.

The discipline in the Cultural Heritage Code imposes said constraints to the property with the consequent obligations and limitations on the use of the asset without providing any allowance for the owner. Miss Lucky is therefore not entitled to compensation for the lawful restriction of her property due to the legal recognition of the portrait as an element of cultural heritage.

E. The Netherlands

JS and NvT

In this case the Heritage Act applies. The Heritage Act has multiple articles regarding the protection of cultural objects. In the case of private ownership, there are 'Rules regarding designation as a protected cultural object or protected collection' (*Aanwijzing van cultuurgoed en verzameling*). The Minister of Education, Culture, and Science has the authority (ex officio) to designate objects that meet certain (open) criteria as 'protected'.[449] Protected objects cannot—inter alia—be sold, moved, put up for auction, or be encumbered without notification to the Inspectorate of Public Sector Information and Heritage (*Inspectie Overheidsinformatie en Erfgoed*).[450]

For six weeks after the notification, no action is allowed without the permission of the Public Sector Information and Heritage or the Minister. During those six weeks, the Minister can state objections against an intended action. If those objections have merit, the intended action is not allowed.[451] The objections can only be based on the danger of loss of cultural heritage. The objections need to be published in the *Government Gazette*.[452]

Within six weeks of publication, possible buyers of the protected cultural object can report to the minister. The ministers gives the notifications of the possible buyers to the owner. After the six-week period, the objections of the minister are considered to be an offer to buy the protected cultural object. This offer stands for three months.[453] The owner and the state can then negotiate about the price and other conditions. In the event the negotiating parties do not reach an agreement, the price is determined by the Court of The Hague.[454]

[449] Heritage Act, art 3.7.

[450] ibid art 4.4.

[451] ibid art 4.6.

[452] ibid art 4.9.

[453] ibid art 4.10 subs 4.

[454] The decision of the court on the price may only be appealed before the Supreme Court: ibid art 4.14 subs 4.

The minister only compensates expenses which have been incurred without purpose due to objections made on the grounds of Article 4.6.[455]

In some cases, appointment of an object cannot take place without the permission of the owner (Article 3.9, mainly if the owner is the maker of the cultural heritage or the heir of the maker). This does not seem to be the case with Miss Lucky. The court therefore will not annul the decision based on the argument that Miss Lucky's property rights are being restricted.

F. Poland

IK and ŁK

The Act on the protection and care of historical monuments (PCHMA)[456] lays down precise regulations on possible restrictions and removals of their ownership. The goal of the protective measures taken by public administration bodies is to prevent all phenomena that could lead to damaging historical monuments or their complete destruction (loss). Protection covers works of art, including paintings, that are historical monuments defined by the PCHMA as immovables and movables, their parts or units, made by man or related to human activity and constituting testimony to a past epoch or event, retention of which lies in public interest due to their historical, artistic or scientific value (Article 3(1) of the PCHMA).

The Polish legal system does not provide for the issuance of decisions indicating that a given object is a piece of cultural heritage and the basic form of historical monument protection is an entry into the register of historical monuments. Under Article 10(1) of the PCHMA, applications for an entry into the register of movable historical monuments should be made by the owner of such a monument. In principle, such an entry could be made exclusively on Miss Lucky's request. The provincial historical monument conservator can issue an *ex officio* decision to enter a movable historical monument in the register only by way of exception, in case of a justified suspicion that the said monument could be destroyed, damaged or illegally moved abroad, or that a historical monument of exceptional historical, artistic or scientific value could be moved abroad (Article 10(2) of the PCHMA).[457] Given that Miss Lucky wanted to sell the portrait in a foreign auction, the basis for an *ex officio* entry into the historical monument register could be the suspicion that the historical monument could be illegally moved abroad.

The decision on the entry into the historical monument register is a constitutive one. On its basis, a specific object is covered by a legal form of protection by the historical monument conservator (Article 7(1) of the PCHMA), which translates, inter alia, into restricting ownership entitlements of the holder of such an object.[458] As a

455 ibid art 4.16.

456 The Act of 23 July 2003 on the protection and care of historical monuments, JoL of 2020, item 282.

457 K Zalasińska and K Zeidler, *Wykład prawa ochrony zabytków* (Wydawnictwo Uniwersytetu Gdańskiego 2015) https://sip.lex.pl/#/monograph/369383074/306086 (accessed 2 April 2020).

458 M Cherka and others (eds), *Ustawa o ochronie zabytków i opiece nad zabytkami: Komentarz* (LEX 2010).

consequence, due to the entry of the painting into the register, it would be Miss Lucky who would be obliged to obtain the permits referred to in Article 36(1) of the PCHMA, eg concerning the performance of works and examination, or a permanent transfer of a historical monument, in violation of the tradition-sanctioned decor of the interior where the historical monument is. It would be also possible, for instance, to make the painting covered by a permanent prohibition to move it abroad (Article 51(4) of the PCHMA). Moreover, pursuant to Article 50(4)(1) of the PCHMA, should it not be possible to remove any of the above-mentioned actual and direct threats to the movable historical monument entered in the register, such a monument may be taken over by the provincial historical monument conservator to be owned by the state Treasury, for the purpose related to culture, education or tourism, against compensation reflecting its market value. The said transfer is effected by means of an administrative decision.[459]

The other form of protection that Miss Lucky's painting could be covered by is its entry onto the Heritage Treasure List. That requires meeting the same conditions as the entry into the register (the recognition of a movable item as a work of man or related to human activity and constituting a testimony to a past epoch or event, retention of which lies in public interest due to its historical, artistic or scientific value) and, additionally, of one the very precise criteria stemming from Article 14a of the PCHMA (the criteria refer to the age or economic value of the historical monument expressed in euros). Moreover, the entry onto the List is conditional upon the recognition of its particular value for cultural heritage. The Heritage Treasure List is a more rigorous form of protection of historical monuments than the register because the possibility of an *ex officio* entry is not made conditional upon the occurrence of a risk of the monument's destruction, damage or transfer abroad but upon its value in terms of national heritage. The entry onto the Heritage Treasure List also entails further-reaching restrictions of the right of ownership. The PCHMA, in particular, establishes rules for storage of the historical monuments entered onto the Heritage Treasure List (Article 37(i) of the PCHMA), imposes the obligation—and not the possibility, as is in the case for historical monuments entered into the register—to issue a decision on securing such a historical monument by its temporary requisition until the risk of its destruction, damage, theft, loss or illegal transfer abroad has been removed. Further, if such a risk cannot be removed (being permanent), the minister competent for culture and protection of national heritage is obliged to take over the historical monument by means of a decision, to be owned by the state treasury, for the purpose related to culture, against compensation reflecting its market value.

The decision concerning the entry of a movable historical monument into the historical monument register or onto the Heritage Treasure List is issued in compliance with the procedure regulated in the CAP. Consequently, Miss Lucky can resort to measures of appeal and lodge a complaint before an administrative court. What is more, an entry into the register, and by its virtue onto the List, of an object that is not

[459] P Gwoździewicz, 'Ograniczenia prawa własności zabytków' (2009) 9 Roczniki Administracji i Prawa 111.

a historical monument, constitutes a blatant breach of law in the meaning of Article 156(1)(2) of the CPA.[460]

Miss Lucky can also lodge a complaint before a provincial administrative court, after having first called upon the authorities to remove the breach of law (see Article 52(3) of the APAC), ie the very entry into the register. That would be possible in such circumstances as: the entry having been made despite the absence of a relevant legal basis (ie in the absence of a relevant decision); the entry not having been removed despite the issuance of a decision to remove the entry pertaining to that monument from the historical monument register; the contents of the entry significantly differing from the contents of the decision constituting the basis for it.[461]

G. Portugal

RGdF

Normally, owners do as they please with their property. But if civil law systems usually consider that property has a certain kind of social function, some goods go beyond that: they can be tagged of general interest and accordingly suffer additional limitations on their use by their owners. The portrait of Batman owned by Miss Lucky found itself placed in that realm due to its being declared cultural heritage. Those limitations are equivalent to a 'removal' in the sense that they 'remove' from the owner possibilities that otherwise they would have regarding the use of the asset. So Miss Lucky would want to know: after the declaration of the portrait as *cultural heritage*, would she still be able to sell it, export it, lend it (domestically or abroad), put it in a warehouse if she no longer wants it on the wall? Because all this was possible before, and are legitimate actions vis-à-vis other paintings she has.

In Portugal, according to Article 2/1 and 2 of the Law 107/2001 of 8 September (Basis for the Policy of Cultural Heritage and its Protection and Valorisation, BPCHPV), the cultural heritage integrates all those assets that bear valuable witness to civilisation or culture and so must be protected and appreciated (reflecting values of memory, antiquity, authenticity, originality, rarity, singularity). This is a follow-up of the constitutional right to the enjoyment of cultural heritage (Article 78 of the Constitution and Article 7 of the BPCHPV).

Articles 14 ff of the BPCHPV regulate the classification of goods that must be considered cultural heritage. The classification is issued in different categories and with different concepts and potential consequences. But it always involves limitations for the owners.

The classification is a decision of the public authorities (an administrative act) subject to due process (Articles 18 and 23 onwards of the BPCHPV; the procedure is regulated in a very detailed manner by Decree-Law 148/2015 of 4 August, which also details the rights and duties of private owners of movable goods considered *cultural heritage*).

[460] Judgment of the Supreme Administrative Court of 26 September 1996, I SA 558/95, LEX No 143870.
[461] Cherka (ed), Antoniak, Elżanowski, Wąsowski (n 458).

Even if the classification is 'light', owners have special duties regarding conservation and facilitating public access (unless public access is incompatible with the personal rights of the owners, such as when a portrait is in their living room) (Article 21 of the BPCHPV). For instance, selling and other forms of transmitting must be reported (Article 36 of the BPCHPV) and the state has the right of first refusal (Article 37 of the BPCHPV). There are other obligations, such as communicating the change of location of a portrait (Article 57 of the BPCHPV). Export and shipping are among the activities with more intense regulation and limitations (Articles 64 and ff. of the BPCHPV).

Disregarding these rules is sanctionable and might even constitute a crime (Articles 100 ff).

Article 20/al *d)* of the BPCHPV[462] determines the right to damages when the classification prohibits or severely restricts the usual utilisation of the asset. This last concept—'usual use of the good'—is debatable. It certainly calls for knowing what the owner usually does with the asset. But in the present case the situation is a little more complex: because selling at a foreign auction is an acceptable use (in normal circumstances, before classification) but it is certainly a 'single act use'. So, it is a 'normal' use, but not an 'usual' one.

Nevertheless, Miss Lucky already had a definite expectation that she would sell, so she suffers a negative patrimonial consequence. Miss Lucky remains the proprietor of the portrait, so it can be argued that her damage is virtual. But the fact is that she will not be able to sell at her own volition (namely, abroad) and that from now on she has duties of conservation that did not exist prior to the classification. So it seems that Miss Lucky should be entitled to damages.[463]

Miss Lucky has the right to challenge the decision (Article 9 of the BPCHPV, and also in general terms as in the face of any other administrative act). But if the portrait actually meets the criteria to be classified (and the courts would only be able to cancel that if the administrative reasoning was grossly lacking legal basis or in clear violation of principles), then only due to procedural illegalities would Miss Lucky have grounds.

H. Spain

LAJ and DUFB

The Spanish legal framework applicable to the protection of artwork revolves around two main aspects. First, protection of cultural heritage is both on the state and on the seventeen autonomous regions' hands. This is why there are different legal frameworks depending on whether the asset qualifies as national or regional heritage. Below is an analysis of the national framework laid down in the LPH. Secondly, the notion of historical heritage can be applied to various categories of assets (Article 1 LPH) subject to different protection regimes based on each category's social function. The most

[462] See also Decree-Law 148/2015, art 26/1 al c).

[463] Another possibility (that must not be set aside) is for Miss Lucky to have a right to be expropriated (the expropriation of movable goods that constitute cultural heritage is a possibility according to article 91 of the CE).

important goods are the so-called assets of cultural interest (*bienes de interés cultural* or BIC) so declared by statute or administrative decision (Article 9 LPH).

An asset being declared a BIC triggers a convoluted preservation, protection and conservation legal framework. Within this framework, it is worth highlighting the following set of obligations incumbent on owners; failure to fulfil these obligations could lead, inter alia, to a compulsory expropriation of the relevant asset, as well as to administrative—or even criminal – sanctions: (i) any transfers or relocations of these assets must be duly registered (Article 13(1) LPH); (ii) owners must facilitate administrative inspections of the assets, and they must also encourage that they be publicly displayed or exhibited (Article 13(2) LPH); (iii) owners must appropriately safekeep or guard the assets and ensure that they are preserved in good condition (Article 36(1) LPH); (iv) their use cannot jeopardise the underlying purposes that justify the protection thereof, so certain use restrictions apply (Article 36(2) LPH); (v) any export of these assets requires a prior administrative authorisation (Article 29 LPH); and (vi) full disclosure in case of transfer or auction of the assets is required, where public authorities will retain rights of first refusal on these goods (Article 38 LPH).

In terms of Article 33(2) CE, these provisions define the content of the right to property of this category of assets in view of their social function.[464] Thus, neither laying down these obligations and requirements in proportional statutory provisions, nor the imposition thereof on specific owners by means of single-case administrative decisions in accordance with the applicable law give rise to compensation. In other words, as opposed to the right to property of other goods, the right to own an asset of cultural interest does not allow for exporting the good with no prior authorisation or for inappropriately preserving the asset. Therefore, the definition of these obligations and prohibitions, as well as their imposition by means of an administrative decision declaring a BIC are no expropriation of the owner's property rights nor is the owner entitled to any compensation.

Owners of assets subject to protection regimes are eligible for tax benefits provided in the applicable legislation (Articles 67 to 74 LPH). These include deductions and exemptions on various taxes, such as personal income, corporate income, inheritance tax and wealth tax. These tax advantages are aimed at facilitating compliance by the owners with their obligations and requirements, insofar as fulfilment thereof is in the public interest. However, these tax benefits do not qualify as compensation for expropriation or damages. This is evidenced by the fact that their extent is not based on the loss sustained by the owner, who has no right that her assets' value remain unchanged prior and after they are declared BICs.

However, in addition to triggering the application of the relevant protection regime, the declaration of a given asset as BIC might indirectly deprive the owner of other property rights related to the protected asset, thereby giving rise to potential compensation. For instance, this is the case with the BIC declaration of a historical building located on a plot which, up to the BIC declaration and subject to the applicable urban planning provisions, could be torn down. The obligation to preserve the building declared as a BIC does not give rise to compensation, since it is a proportional

[464] See Arroyo Jiménez and Fernández-Bermejo (n 244) s II. JM Alegre Ávila, *Evolución y régimen jurídico del patrimonio histórico* (Ministerio de Cultura 1994).

limitation on the right of property lawfully stemming from the good's social function. Nevertheless, the BIC declaration entails loss of profit, ie the profit to be made by the owner following the construction of a new building. Accordingly, the inability to exercise his right to build a new and profitable building amounts to loss or damage to be compensated by public authorities.[465]

Challenging the declaration of an asset as a BIC is unproblematic as long as the decision has been made by administrative authorities, as is most often the case. The owner may file the relevant administrative or judicial appeals against the administrative act providing for the BIC declaration (Articles 112 LPAC and 25(1) LJCA). In any event, public authorities enjoy a wide scope of technical discretion inherent to the declaration of an asset as BIC, so there will be a deferential judicial review in this respect.[466] Usually, judicial authorities will simply verify that any factual assessments be correct and that formal and procedural requirements be met. In Miss Lucky's case, there are no apparent arguments to question that the decision to subject the artwork to a protection regime—which, as the BIC declaration, restricts the possibility to sell the piece abroad—is lawful.

The available legal remedies differ if the declaration is issued in a parliamentary piece of law—this is more uncommon—since the Spanish judiciary has no jurisdiction to review the constitutionality of laws or acts passed by the legislature. This power is exclusively held by the Constitutional Court, and individuals have no legal remedies available to bring a direct appeal before this Court against Parliamentary action. The only way to challenge a BIC declaration laid down in a Parliamentary piece of law is to bring a judicial appeal against any administrative acts implementing the BIC legal regime, in order to persuade the court that the statutory provision including the BIC declaration is unconstitutional. If the appellant succeeds, the court could make a reference to the Constitutional Court to rule on the provision's constitutionality by submitting an exception of unconstitutionality (*cuestión de inconstitucionalidad*) (Article 163 CE).

I. Sweden

PJ

In the Swedish context there is a need for special permission to remove from the country cultural objects which may be assumed to have existed in Sweden for at least 75 years and which may be of great importance to the cultural heritage (section 1, Chapter 5 (entitled *Protection against the export of certain older cultural objects*) of the Historic Environment Act (*Kulturmiljölagen*, 1988:950).

It is possible to lodge an appeal before the administrative court if the authority in charge of delivering a permit issues a refusal (section 15, Chapter 5 of the Historic Environment Act).

[465] STS of 15 December 2010 (Rec 1336/2009).

[466] STS of 29 July 2007 (Rec 5742/2001) and of 15 November 2011 (Rec 761/2010).

Neither the state nor the authority in charge of delivering a permit has the obligation to buy or otherwise compensate for the refusal.[467]

J. Ukraine
HD

In Ukrainian legislation two concepts are considered in this context: cultural heritage and cultural assets. The first covers immovable monuments (Articles 1, 2 of the Law of Ukraine 'On the protection of cultural heritage')[468] while the second has a much broader meaning including pictures as well as other assets (Article 1 of the Law of Ukraine 'On the export, import, and return of cultural assets').[469]

Public authorities are not entitled to declare private property (for example, a picture in a private collection) as cultural assets on their own initiative.

However, if the owner intends to move (transport, take abroad, or transfer) the picture across the border, (s)he is obliged to file an application asking for a permit. After filing the application, an obligatory state opinion on this object has to be given. If the owner refuses the expert opinion, this will amount to a waiver on moving the object across the border. Depending on the conclusion of the state expert, the asset (for example, a picture) will be allowed to cross the border, or not. The owner must be informed in writing (Article 15 of the Law of Ukraine 'On the export, import, and return of cultural assets').

According to the rules of state expert assessment of cultural assets, the expert can recommend adding the asset to the State Register of National Cultural Heritage (para 9).[470] It will be added to the register without the owner's consent (Article 13 of the Law of Ukraine 'On the export, import and return of cultural assets').[471]

Consequently, the asset will not be allowed to cross the border. The Law of Ukraine 'On the export, import, and return of cultural assets' provides that cultural assets included in the State Register of National Cultural Heritage, the National Archival Fund and the Museum Fund of Ukraine may not be removed from Ukraine (Article 14).

According to the Civil Code of Ukraine, the peculiarities of exercising property rights over national, cultural and historical assets are established by law (Article 319 (8)).[472] Regarding cultural assets, the only law concerning them is Law of Ukraine 'On the export, import and return of cultural assets'.

[467] See https://www.raa.se/app/uploads/2016/07/Broschyr_utforsel_webbversion.pdf (accessed 1 March 2021).

[468] Law of Ukraine 'On the protection of cultural heritage' (8 June 2000) https://zakon.rada.gov.ua/laws/show/1805-14#Text (accessed 5 May 2021).

[469] Law of Ukraine 'On the export, import, and return of cultural assets' (21 September 1999) https://zakon.rada.gov.ua/laws/show/1068-14 (accessed 5 May 2021).

[470] Rules of State expert assessment of cultural assets approved by order of the Cabinet of Ministers of Ukraine on 26 August 2003 https://zakon.rada.gov.ua/laws/show/1343-2003-%D0%BF (accessed 5 May 2021).

[471] Law of Ukraine 'On the Export, Import and Return of Cultural Assets' (21 September 1999) https://zakon.rada.gov.ua/laws/show/1068-14 (accessed 5 May 2021).

[472] Civil Code of Ukraine (16 January 2003) https://zakon.rada.gov.ua/laws/show/435-15 (accessed 5 May 2021).

Compensation for restriction of property rights over cultural assets is not provided for under this law.

As mentioned in the decision of the Constitutional Court of Ukraine in a case regarding conformity with the Constitution of Ukraine of the provisions of the Law of Ukraine 'On the transfer of the art collections of joint-stock company "Gradobank" into State property' (16 October 2008) the right to private property is not absolute, due to some constitutional and legal limits set out in Articles 13(3), 41(7) of the Constitution of Ukraine. According to these, property may not be used to the detriment of society.[473] As stressed in the decision, one of the grounds for the special legal regime regarding property rights relating to certain objects is their cultural value.

The legal status of objects recognised as national cultural heritage does not interfere with the owner's rights to own, enjoy and dispose of his or her property.

Under the Constitution of Ukraine, the state must ensure the preservation of objects of cultural value (Article 54(5).[474]

If we assume that the portrait is declared to be of cultural value as the result of the state evaluation conducted while preparing the documents needed for taking the picture abroad, the situation will be the following. If the picture is added to the State Register of National Cultural Heritage, it will not be permitted to send the work abroad. In this case, Miss Lucky will not be entitled to compensation because this limitation is not treated as a restriction of her property rights but as coming under a special regime provided for the cultural assets. Taking into account the legitimate goal of such a prohibition (preservation of cultural assets), there are no legal grounds for compensation. In any case, Miss Lucky has the right to challenge the decision.

If the picture is not on the register, she will be given a certificate confirming the right to take the picture abroad.

K. The United Kingdom

EW

In England, the export of cultural goods and antiques over a certain age and value,[475] whether by individuals or institutions, is governed by an export control regime[476] operated by the export licensing unit at Arts Council England.[477] Declaring an item to

[473] Decision of the Constitutional Court of Ukraine in case about conformity with Constitution of Ukraine of provisions of Law of Ukraine 'On the Transfer of the Art Collections of Joint-Stock Company "Gradobank" into State Property' (16 October 2008) https://zakon.rada.gov.ua/laws/show/v024p710-08 (accessed 5 May 2021).

[474] Constitution of Ukraine (28 June 1996) https://zakon.rada.gov.ua/laws/show/254%D0%BA/96-%D0%B2%D1%80 (accessed 5 May 2021).

[475] Export of Objects of Cultural Interest (Control) Order 2003 SI 2003/2759 prohibits the export of 'any objects of cultural interest manufactured or produced more than 50 years before the date of exportation except for postage stamps, birth, marriage, death certificates, and letters relating to the personal affairs of the exporter of their spouse, and goods that are the personal property of a manufacturer and their spouse or widow/widower, unless the Secretary of State has granted an export licence'.

[476] Export Control Act 2002.

[477] Arts Council, *UK Export Licensing for Cultural Goods: Procedures and guidance for exporters of works of art and other cultural goods* https://www.artscouncil.org.uk/sites/default/files/downloadfile/Guidance%20for%20Exporters%20Issue%201%202020.pdf (accessed 26 February 2021).

be cultural heritage under the export-licensing regime would be deemed to be a pre-existing control of use, rather than an expropriation under A1P1.[478] Policies involving the protection of national cultural heritage are deemed to engage the 'public interest' required by A1P1 and public authorities have a wide margin of appreciation in determining what is in the wider general interest.[479] The English system of cultural heritage does not deprive owners of the value of cultural objects, but rather attempts to control their eventual geographic location and would not be viewed as a deprivation or expropriation.

There are various open licences permitting the export of certain specified objects without the need to obtain an individual export licence; different regimes[480] apply to intra-European exports and temporary exports to third countries. Miss Lucky's application for an export licence would have been referred to a non-statutory independent body, the Reviewing Committee on the Export of Works of Art and Objects of Cultural Interest (the Reviewing Committee), which advises the Secretary of State for Culture, Media, and Sport. The Reviewing Committee has eight permanent members with varied cultural expertise and they are normally also assisted by three independent assessors, who are experts in the particular object under discussion.[481]

The Reviewing Committee assesses objects against a variety of criteria ('the Waverley Criteria') in deciding whether or not the object is a 'national treasure' and its departure from the UK would be a misfortune on the grounds that: (a) it is closely connected with the history and national life of the UK; (b) it is of outstanding aesthetic importance; it is of outstanding significance for the study of some particular branch of art, learning or history.[482] Miss Lucky would have an opportunity to submit representations and evidence to the Reviewing Committee explaining why the painting should not be considered as a national treasure. Where the object does not satisfy one or more of the Waverley Criteria, the Reviewing Committee will recommend the grant of an export licence.

However, where an object is found to satisfy one of the Waverley Criteria, as appears to have happened here to Miss Lucky's painting, the Reviewing Committee will recommend that the Secretary of State defer any export licence decision for a specified time, normally four to nine months. This delay then allows cultural institutions to raise funds and to make an offer to purchase the object at or above the fair market price (as assessed by the experts on the Reviewing Committee), so that the object remains in the UK. The Secretary of State takes the Reviewing Committee's advice into account and can decide the fair market price for the item. Miss Lucky is not obliged to accept such an offer, but a refusal is taken into account when deciding on the export licence application and is likely to be refused.[483] It is possible for private offers to be made

[478] *Sporrong and Lönnroth v Sweden* (1983) 5 EHRR 35.

[479] *Beyeler v Italy* (2001) 33 EHRR 52.

[480] See eg Council Regulation (EC) No 116/2009 on the export of cultural goods.

[481] Department for Culture, Media & Sport, *Export Controls on Objects of Cultural Interest: Statutory Guidance* (7 March 2015) [15]. https://www.artscouncil.org.uk/sites/default/files/download-file/Export_criteria_March_2015.pdf (accessed 26 February 2021).

[482] Arts Council, *UK Export Licensing for Cultural Goods: Procedures and guidance for exporters of works of art* 11–13, [39–41] https://www.artscouncil.org.uk/sites/default/files/download-file/Guidance%20for%20Exporters%20Issue%201%202020.pdf (accessed 26 February 2021).

[483] Department for Culture, Media & Sport *Export Controls on Objects of Cultural Interest: Statutory Guidance*, March 2015, 8, [21]..

for objects, but these need to be combined with signed undertakings guaranteeing reasonable public access to the object, satisfactory conservation and a moratorium on sale for a specified period. If there is no offer to buy the object during the deferral period, a licence will normally be granted. In the event that an offer is rejected it is possible to reapply at a later date for an export licence for the same object. However, any such reapplication will still be subject to the same reviewing procedure; if the application is made within ten years of a licence being refused or an owner declining to consider an offer, the application needs to explain what circumstances have changed.

The Reviewing Committee presents an annual report to Parliament outlining their policy discussions and giving detailed information of the cases considered. Miss Lucky will not be deprived of the market value of her painting as a result of if being declared a national treasure since either it will receive a matching market value and remain in the country, or it will not and she will be able to sell it overseas. In the event that she is unhappy with the handling of her licence application she can have any complaint reviewed by the Parliamentary Ombudsman, an independent officer of the House of Commons. It would also be possible to judicially review the exercise of the Secretary of State's discretion in awarding or withholding an export licence, but there do not appear to have been any cases on these grounds.

L. The United States

IS

I am not aware of any federal law that allows the United States government to ban the sale or export of a cultural artifact owned by a private entity, merely because the government declares it to be part of the 'cultural heritage' of the United States (or of a specific city, such as the fictional Gotham). However, the Archaeological Resources Protection Act of 1979 (ARPA) does restrict the export of cultural items found on land owned by the federal government or by Native American tribes.[484] The sale or export, across state lines or international boundaries, of 'archeological resources' illegally removed from privately owned land is also prohibited.[485]

Thus, Miss Lucky can only be barred from exporting the portrait in the unlikely event that she removed it from federal or tribally owned land, or if she illegally removed it from someone else's private property.

M. International investment law

FF

For IIL to apply, the scenario needs tweaking: a painting is not an investment. States' cultural policy can create restrictions harming the investors' businesses.

[484] See 16 USC §§ 470CC, 470EE(a).

[485] 16 USC § 470BB(1) (2015); *United States v Gerber* 999 F2d 1112 (7th Cir 1993) (prosecution of dealer for selling artifacts illegally removed from private land and transferring them across state lines).

In 1978, Egypt declared the area surrounding the Pyramids 'public property (antiquity)', withdrew approval for a development project, and reversed a decree designating the land for tourist utilisation.[486] The tribunal found that, while Egypt could 'cancel a tourist development project situated on its own territory for the purpose of protecting antiquities',[487] cancelling the project constituted expropriation and warranted compensation.[488] As regards compensation, the loss of profits (*lucrum cessans*) could be calculated only until when the area was registered under the UNESCO Convention, as no sale or development could occur afterwards.[489]

In *Glamis Gold v USA*, a mining project would have disrupted areas sacred to the Quechan Indian tribe, whose members 'travel physically and spiritually along the Trail of Dreams ... conduct traditional religious activities ... [and] use the Indian Pass-Running Man ATCC for traditional cultural educational programs'.[490] Upon review, the government rezoned the area, proscribed all mineral activity, and denied the investor's plan, in short succession. The tribunal, without pronouncing on the site's cultural significance, acknowledged that the state had relied on expert advice and that the outcome was not predetermined.[491]

Investors might challenge the designation of their investment as cultural heritage as discriminatory, showing that similar investments were unaffected or that the decision creates a class of one ('targeting'). The tribunal should then ascertain whether the executive action applies (or could apply in the future) to similar investments, or whether the cultural rationale plausibly explains the singling out of the investment.[492] In *Parkerings v Lithuania*, the tribunal dismissed the discrimination claim, noting that the investor's plan to build a parking lot inside a UNESCO heritage site was more intrusive than its competitor's plan; the allegations of more favourable treatment were therefore unfounded.[493] The tribunal held that:

> [t]he refusal by the Municipality of Vilnius to authorize BP's project [extending near the Cathedral] was justified by various concerns, especially in terms of historical and archaeological preservation and environmental protection. These concerns are peculiar to the extension of BP's project in the Old Town and thus could justify different treatment with [the competitor's project].[494]

[486] *SPP v Egypt* ICSID Case No ARB/84/3 Award (20 May 1992) paras 62–65.
[487] ibid para 158.
[488] ibid para 172.
[489] ibid para 190.
[490] *Glamis Gold v USA* (NAFTA, UNCITRAL) Award (8 June 2009) para 110.
[491] ibid para 788.
[492] ibid para 795.
[493] *Parkerings v Lithuania* ICSID Case No ARB/05/8 Award (11 September 2007) paras 392, 395.
[494] ibid para 396.

X. Case 9: Acoustic pollution: exceeding the sound limits

A. Belgium

DR, LC, CD, and KP

An airport has been built near Mrs Owner's home. Since the airport has been operational, Mrs Owner has suffered permanent noise pollution, to the point that it has become impossible to live in his home. The noise impact assessment procedures carried out by the competent authorities prior to the construction of the airport appear to have been carried out incorrectly. Mrs Owner wishes to know whether she could challenge the impact assessment carried out and whether he could claim the right to be expropriated. If not, can he claim for compensation?

Under Belgian law, preparatory acts such as an impact assessments carried out during the process of adopting an administrative act may not be challenged directly with a view to obtaining an annulment.[495] Such acts may, however, be challenged indirectly in the course of an action against the final administrative act—for example, in the case of impact assessment, against the permit issued following the assessment.[496]

To the best of our knowledge, unlike Article 16 of the Constitution, which provides for the right to expropriate in general terms, there is no general provision in Belgian law enshrining a right of expropriation. On the contrary, it is possible, where a specific provision so provides, and in specific situations, for an authority to be obliged to expropriate a private person at their request.[497] For example, in the Brussels Region, a private owner of a classified property may require the region to expropriate it rather than carry out work essential to the preservation of the property himself.[498]

Belgium has several airports. As these airports are located in different regions of the country, the rules applicable to them, particularly on matters of noise and expropriation, are likely to vary. For each airport, it is therefore necessary to check whether the applicable regional law allows a local resident to demand to be expropriated and, if so, under what condition(s).

To cite an example, Walloon law does not envisage such a right. However, people living in the neighbourhood of Walloon airports may negotiate with the competent authority so that the latter can buy back their property.[499] It is interesting to note that the Brussels Court of Appeal has previously considered this procedure insufficient to ensure effective protection of the rights that local residents enjoy under Article 8 of the European Convention on Human Rights in a case relating to Liège airport.[500] This

[495] Council of State case *Commune de Schaerbeek*, No 183.000 of 19 May 2008.

[496] ibid.

[497] Renders, Messaoud, and Ganty, 'Les acteurs de l'expropriation' (n 6) 182.

[498] Brussels Code for Town and Country Planning, art 240, §3.

[499] On the grounds of art 1*bis*, § 4, sub 1(1), of the Act 'On combatting noise' (18 July 1973; publication in the Belgian *Official Gazette* on 14 September 1973), as applicable in the Walloon Region).

[500] Brussels Court of Appeal (2nd chamber) (2 June 2017) RG 2010/AR/2642.

decision of the Brussels Court of Appeal is justified by the fact that, for certain buildings which have become unfit for habitation due to noise pollution, in practice, neighbours have only theoretical freedom of negotiation, as their homes would be difficult to sell to a third party. In reality, they are forced to sell at the price determined by the competent authority.

To the best of our knowledge, neither Brussels nor Flemish law provides for the right of airport neighbours to be expropriated, with or without conditions.

It should also be added that where the owner of a piece of land suffers damage because of a neighbouring plot of land, he or she has the option of claiming compensation from the person responsible for the nuisance on the basis of different legal grounds, depending on the circumstances (extra-contractual civil liability,[501] theory of neighbourhood disturbances,[502] etc). This also applies to people living in the vicinity of airports.

As an example, in the above-mentioned decision concerning Liège airport,[503] the Brussels Court of Appeal found that failure by the authority to comply with certain obligations relating to environmental impact assessment amounts to a fault on the part of the authority, which may result in it being ordered to pay compensation to neighbours if it is established that damage is causally linked to the fault, which must be assessed on a case-by-case basis. By contrast, the Court refused to order the cessation of airport activity.

Lastly, it may be added that the applicable regional legislation may provide for measures to reduce the nuisance suffered by people living near airports. For example, Walloon law provides for subsidies or bonuses for the installation of devices intended to reduce noise or vibrations, absorb them, or remedy their inconvenience.[504]

In the present case, Mrs Owner cannot directly challenge the impact assessment, since it is a preparatory act. If she complies with the procedural conditions for bringing such an action, he will, however, be able to appeal against the assessment in the context of an action brought against the decision authorising the construction of the airport. She may also criticise it in the context of a potential claim for compensation on account of the noise nuisance suffered.

The question as to whether Mrs Owner has the right to be expropriated is, a priori, answered in the negative. Depending on the region in which Mrs Owner's property is located, however, that answer may have to be tempered.

In any event, if he does not have the right to be expropriated, Mrs Owner may seek compensation for the damage she suffers as a result of the nuisance caused by the airport. In this respect, the absence of a proper impact assessment will, more than likely, be regarded as faulty.

501 Civil Code, art 1382.
502 ibid art 544.
503 Brussels Court of Appeal (2nd Chamber), 2 June 2017, RG 2010/AR/2642.
504 Act 'On combating noise', art 1*bis*, § 4, sub 1(2), of the, as applicable in the Walloon Region.

B. France

EG

Mrs Owner is in a delicate situation in that the impact study prior to creating the expressway and airport did not indicate that noise pollution would cause a depreciation of the value of her property. Excessive noise that could affect local residents is regulated by Articles L571-9 and R571-44 to R571-52 of the Environment Code and the decree of 5 May 1995 on road infrastructure noise. The aim is to protect them if a public work is the cause of prejudice.[505] In this sense, Article L571-1 of the Environment Code states that:

> The provisions of this chapter are intended, in areas where it is not provided, to prevent, remove or limit noise pollution, either the emission or propagation of noise or vibration likely to present dangers, to cause an excessive disturbance to people, to harm their health or to harm the environment.

It is therefore necessary to specify the remedies available to the owner to ensure that the value of her property is not reduced due to the construction of this highway and the airport.

In this case, the applicable provisions concern new roads and not those that predate the access to Mrs Owner's property. In French law, the principles were determined by the '*Loi Bruit*' of 1992 to protect local inhabitants who might suffer from noise pollution following the construction of public infrastructures. To ensure this protection, noise indicators are defined by decree. The '*maître d'ouvrage*'[506] must ensure that the increase in noise levels does not exceed 2 dB(A), particularly for private dwellings. He is subject to an obligation of result, so he must ensure that the regulations relating to noise pollution are respected.

In the case of Mrs Owner, the noise was found to be excessive and therefore necessarily above the statutory thresholds. Therefore, she can sue the state, which owns the highway, or the private company that holds the concession, in her rightful place. The Environmental Code does not envisage expropriation to settle such disputes. However, according to the concept of damage caused by public works, the claimant does not have to prove the fault of the state. It is sufficient for her to prove her loss and justify the causal link between constructing the infrastructure and the damage suffered.

In order to receive compensation, three criteria must be met. First, the judge must be able to determine that an abnormal and exceptional prejudice has been caused. This is the case of Mrs Owner, who can prove that the nuisance exceeds the regulatory thresholds. Secondly, the conditions of the claimant's existence will be taken into

[505] The *Conseil d'État* may have to analyse the impact study and judge its validity in terms of noise pollution: CE, Decision of 27 February 2006, Nos 257688, 259624, and 2600504, Association Alcaly, in particular by analysing that the impact study includes a chapter devoted to road noise, in which the impact of this noise along the route of the project, divided into three geographical sectors, is presented in order to reject the plea of the insufficiency of the impact study.

[506] In French law, this term refers to the contracting authority on whose behalf the work is performed.

account, particularly the geographical location of her property: it is understood that a property located in an urban area is more likely to suffer from noise pollution. It is specified that Mrs Owner's property is 'close' to the airport and the highway, so the conditions of existence will be considered to be met. Lastly, the admissibility of the action for compensation is subject to the criterion of anteriority. This means that the claimant must not have known about the construction of the infrastructure before acquiring the property. This is the case with regard to the owner.

All the criteria seem to be fulfilled, so Mrs Owner will be able to bring a motion before the administrative judge regarding the nuisance to which she is being subjected.

Regarding the noise that would emanate from the new airport construction, it should be noted that special legislation governs this area. Residents can benefit from soundproofing work. On the other hand, if it is established that the work would be too costly and ineffective, the residents can be expropriated or rehoused.[507]

C. Germany

FS

Airports may only be constructed if a planning approval procedure is carried out.[508] The planning approval procedure ends with a planning approval decision. If the planning approval decision has an error, for example, because the authority has made an incorrect impact assessment, the person concerned must challenge the planning approval decision before the competent administrative court.[509] The action must be lodged within one month from the date of the announcement of the planning approval decision.[510] This has not been done in the present case. The planning approval decision itself can therefore no longer be challenged. If the planning approval decision has become incontestable, claims to cease airport operations are excluded.[511]

If unforeseeable effects of the project occur after the plan has become incontestable, the person concerned may demand precautions to exclude the adverse effects.[512] The precautions include noise protection measures, which the planning approval authority can impose on the airport operator by order.[513] In the present case, however, the noise protection measures fail, and Mrs Owner's property is no longer habitable. If it is impossible to take noise protection measures, there is a claim for reasonable financial compensation.[514] Mrs Owner has to submit the application for appropriate compensation to the planning approval authority in writing. The period for such an application is three years and runs from the time when Mrs Owner becomes aware of the adverse effects of the project.[515] Mrs Owner can further assert a claim for the

507 Environmental Code, art R 571-85 of the.
508 LuftVG, § 8 sec 1 sentence 1.
509 cf ibid § 10 sec 4 sentence 1.
510 cf VwGO, § 74 sec 1 sentence 2.
511 LuftVG, §§ 8 sec 1 sentence 10; VwVfG, 75 sec 2 sentence 1.
512 LuftVG, §§ 8 sec 1 sentence 10; VwVfG, 75 sec 2 sentence 2.
513 LuftVG, cf §§ 8 sec 1 sentence 10; VwVfG, 75 sec 2 sentence 3.
514 LuftVG, §§ 8 sec 1 sentence 10; VwVfG, 75 sec 2 sentence 4.
515 LuftVG §§ 8 sec 1 sentence 10; VwVfG, 75 sec 3 sentences 1 and 2.

takeover of the land against compensation. This claim presumes, however, that the property has been drastically devalued as a result of the planning approval.[516]

D. Italy
SM

According to the rules provided by the Italian Civil Aviation Authority, territorial planning and management are effective means to ensure that activities in the vicinity of airports are compatible with the traffic flows that occur in these areas.

The main objective is to minimise the population affected by aircraft noise by introducing the so-called 'acoustic zoning' of the area around airports. The authority provides some guidelines for local administrations in order to plan urban development.

The municipal authorities are responsible for containing urban-planning activities in the areas around airports. National urban law regulates the planning and use of the territory around airports, clearly specifying the responsibilities of local administrations. The main planning tool in the areas around airports envisaged by current regulations is the definition of the 'areas of respect'.

Administrative case law has pointed out that an airport represents a single, however complex, source of noise pollution, caused by a plurality of noise-producing components, determined essentially by normal aircraft activity (in the landing and take-off phases), but also by the airport infrastructure as a further source of noise (by way of example, the different composition of the materials making up the covering of a runway or landing strip, which can affect the type and intensity of noise when manoeuvring aircraft). The Council of State therefore stated that the responsibility for the control and supervision of the compliance with limits allowed must be entrusted to a single subject (ie to the airport manager), which actually has the power to monitor the noise of the entire airport infrastructure.[517]

If the local authorities have the competence to reduce the consequences of noise through the territorial planning tool, the technical activity of abating the noise produced by aircraft and airports as a whole must be carried out by the managing body of the airport itself.

Residents and owners of properties located in neighbouring areas are entitled to appeal against the acoustic zoning of an airport. For this reason, administrative case law uses both the criteria of proximity and of the danger of an abstract prejudice to their situation.

By applying these criteria, it can be said that Mrs Owner can challenge the impact assessment by asking the administrative judge to evaluate if the planning tool has been lawfully applied by the local administration in determining the acoustic zoning, and, if so, if there is any responsibility of the airport manager for an incorrect monitoring and lack of an effective activity of noise abatement.

[516] P Wysk, '§ 74' in FO Kopp and U Ramsauer, *Verwaltungsverfahrensgesetz: Kommentar* (21st edn, CH Beck 2020) paras 163a and 163b.

[517] See Cons Stato, Sec VI (7 March 2016) No 907.

Regarding compensation, a distinction must be made between noise that exceeds the limit established by special laws and noise that remains below this limit. In the first case Mrs Owner would be entitled to compensation for damages; in the second case it would be possible to request an opinion from the ordinary judge who assesses whether the values are tangibly intolerable bearing in mind the situation of the place and the characteristics of the applicant's property.

E. The Netherlands

JS and NvT

Under Dutch law there is no right to expropriation. However, assuming that it is an objective fact in this case that the noise exceeds the initial expectations and results in a situation that makes the property unsuitable for habitation, Mrs Owner might be able to enforce expropriation by means of a loophole.

Part of the preparation of the environment plan that formed the basis for the development of the airport would be an environmental impact assessment. Part of that assessment would be a calculation of the expected noise caused by the use of the airport to (among others) adjacent properties. Evidently the outcome of this assessment was that the expected amount of noise was tolerable: the (extra) noise would not result in the house of Mrs Owner becoming unsuitable for (continued) habitation. The (expected) noise limits would be integrated in the environment plan.

The increase of noise on the basis of those limits—and the impact of this noise on the value of the property—would, of course, entitle Mrs Owner to compensation.

If the actual noise proves to be (much) higher than expected, the noise limits in the environment plan will be violated. Violation of those limits is something that Mrs Owner will be able to bring to the attention of the (administrative) court. The public authority might then do one of two things: either force the operator of the airport to reduce the noise or raise the noise limits. The latter course is the more likely, but this would result in a situation where the new noise limits conflict with the house of Mrs Owner being suitable for habitation. The outcome would then be that the public authority purchases or—if necessary—expropriates Mrs Owner in order to solve the noise issue.

F. Poland

IK and ŁK

Mrs Owner's legal and procedural opportunities are largely dependent on whether her property lies within a limited use area (LUA), which can be established around airports or other similar facilities serving public transport. LUAs are set up when it transpires, from an ecological review, an environmental impact assessment required by the Act of 3 October 2008 on making information concerning the environment and its protection available, the participation of society in environmental protection and environmental impact assessments (IEAA)[518] or a post-implementation analysis, that despite using available technical, technological, and organisational measures the relevant environment quality standards outside of the airport area cannot be met. LUAs are established by resolutions of county councils or provincial assemblies, where their boundaries are specified, as well as restrictions on land purpose, technical requirements related to buildings, and the manner in which such land can be used.

Compensation for owners of property lying within LUAs is due, pursuant to Article 129(2) of the 2001 Environmental Protection Act (EPA), if restrictions have been introduced as to the manner in which such property can be used. The legislator does not foresee any compensatory duty for a lower level of property use comfort as a result of legal changes in its environment, theoretically leading to the property's decreased value. Notably, inhabitants of inner city zones where due to tight urban development and car/track vehicle traffic (including buses and trams) noise standards are exceeded (as shown on acoustic maps) may not seek compensation for it, even if the value of their property goes down. The legislator compensates only for direct consequences of its intervention in the form of normative prohibitions or orders. They are introduced in order to protect human health by correctly managing the way land around airports can be developed as well as ordering building facilities following the standards ensuring appropriate acoustic insulation of the buildings.

As noise generated by aircraft can spread, a LUA can be extended. To that end, environmental noise is subject to monitoring. Measurement results serve as the basis for acoustic mapping where average values are presented on an annual basis. Such information is the basis for installing acoustic screens, which Mrs Owner can apply for.[519] Furthermore, if a LUA does not include Mrs Owner's property, the most effective legal remedy she may have access to is an application to the competent county council or provincial assembly for a resolution on the extension of the LUA. In case of its rejection, which also takes the form of a resolution of that body, she has access to all procedural options provided for in the Code of Administrative Procedure.

G. Portugal

RGdF

The construction of an airport and the connecting railway would certainly be subject to environmental impact assessment, and noise levels would actually be one of the items covered by the assessment (Articles 13/1 and 14/3, and annex V of the Decree-Law 151-B/2013, of 31 October (AIA)).[520]

The impact assessment can be challenged in the administrative courts of law (Article 37 of the AIA), but Mrs Owner might be faced by various obstacles. First,

[518] Uniform text: JoL of 2020, item 283.

[519] The relevant guidelines can be found in Annex 16 to the Chicago Convention and in *Doc 9184 Airport Planning Manual, Part II—Land Use and Environmental Control*. The instruction contains guidelines related to the use of various tools in order to minimise, control, or prevent aviation noise impact in the vicinity of airports, as well as describes spatial planning and development practices used by certain EU countries, including Poland.

[520] Lastly amended by Decree-Law 152-B/2017 of 11 December.

she would have to demonstrate that she could not possibly have known the assessment was flawed until the airport and the railway started operating and producing unbearable noise, because the general rule is a deadline of three months after the act for its challenge (Article 58 of the Code of Process in the Administrative Courts of Law (CPTA)). Then, Mrs Owner would have to show that the assessment clearly violated applicable principles and rules (for instance, by not using the correct instruments) or overlooked the facts (because separation of powers forbids the courts allowing technical assessments that only the public administration can make).

Anyway, challenging the impact assessment would not necessarily bring closure to Mrs Owner's pretentions. Even if it were illegal, and its illegality would reflect on the (il)legality of the construction of the airport, the existence of the latter is already a de facto situation that would certainly not be revised. So, Mrs Owner could claim damages: but she could do this anyway.

The authority responsible for works like these has the obligation to provide noise abatement systems, as in Mrs Owner's case.[521] If this is insufficient, because as in Mrs Owner's case the property is no longer fit for habitation, alternatives have to be considered.

Could Mrs Owner ask to be expropriated? Article 96 of the CE accepts the possibility of expropriation at the request of the owner, but only if a special legal rule so provides. That is to say that the CE does not provide such a right by itself, and so this is an exceptional right in Portuguese law. There are some examples: Article 163 of the LPIL gives proprietors the right to claim for an expropriation themselves when that is necessary for setting correct limits of land for the execution of detailed plans;[522] Article 50 of the BPCHPV allows the owner of a classified building or estate to ask for its expropriation. But the exceptionality is understandable: expropriations are justified by general interests, and expropriation at the request of the owner is intended to satisfy the latter's interest. Of course, the background to these situations is always the negative impact on a private property of a public use which is legitimate by law, but that did not justify an expropriation because there were other solutions less grave for the owner and public interest considered together.

The most common situation of expropriation at the request of the owner is for the total expropriation of a piece of land when only a part of it is needed for a particular public use: the owner has such a right if the remaining part of the land does not allow the same uses as the whole property did, or if the remaining part is (objectively) of no economic interest for the owner (Article 3 of the CE). These are classic situations, long supported by law and case law in Portugal. But these situations are justified by the existence of an expropriation: what happens is it would be excessively (disproportionately) damaging for the proprietor to carry the burden of a non-useful part of a land which they cannot use normally. So, it is still a form of compensation for the expropriation.

[521] For a similar situation involving a highway see Decision on appeal of the Supreme Court of Justice 58/01 (1 March 2001).

[522] See above.

Mrs Owner had no such luck, that of being expropriated, that is, she can only be compensated for damages in the general terms of civil responsibility of public authorities,[523] which can be higher than those of the CE.

H. Spain

LAJ and DUFB

Under Spanish law, the environmental impact assessment is shaped as required preparatory opinion for the approval of certain projects, ie as one of the procedural steps of a broader procedure leading to a final decision on the relevant project's approval. Therefore, the party concerned cannot challenge the environmental impact assessment in isolation; rather, it should file the relevant appeals against the final administrative decision authorising the project (Articles 41(4) LEA, 112(1) LPAC and 25(1) LJCA).[524] In specifically provided cases, environmental legislation does allow to modify the conditions set forth in the environmental impact statement, one of these cases being that, 'whilst monitoring compliance with the environmental impact assessment, it be found that the preventive, corrective or compensation measures are insufficient, unnecessary or inefficient (Article 44(1) LEA)'. The modification procedure can only be initiated by the project developer or *ex officio* by the relevant public authorities, although the latter may also initiate the procedure upon receipt of a complaint (Article 44(2) LEA). Thus, Mrs Owner could urge the environmental authority to initiate *ex officio* the modification procedure.

In view of the case at stake, it must be stressed that Article 18 LR provides Mrs Owner with a legal remedy to seek protection against noise pollution on top of the appeal against the project's approval or the modification of the environmental impact assessment. On the one hand, under Article 18(2) LR, public authorities must implement

> any appropriate measures to avoid noise pollution, specifically by applying those technologies with the least noise impact amongst the cutting edge available techniques, ie, the most noise-friendly technologies technically and economically feasible, having regard to the characteristics of the relevant noise polluters.

On the other hand, Article 18(3) LR provides that 'the competent public authorities may examine the substance of the authorizations, approvals, permits and other instruments … without giving rise to compensation, in order to meet the noise emission thresholds'. If Mrs Owner exhausts all legal remedies available, thus being left with a real estate asset unsuitable for residential use, she would not have a right to be expropriated, but she would be entitled to compensation for the damage suffered. In this regard, it must be taken into account that Spanish expropriation law defines the

[523] See Law 67/2007, of 31 December.

[524] STS of 17 November 1998 (Rec 7742/1997), of 11 December 2002 (Rec 3320/2001) and of 13 October 2003 (Rec 4269/1998).

administrative decision to expropriate as a discretionary prerogative.[525] There are partial expropriations, where only a part of the property is taken; these expropriations render the remaining part unprofitable. In these cases, expropriated owners can request public authorities to expropriate the remaining part (Article 23 LEF). However, even under these circumstances, the relevant public body may decide, at its discretion, whether or not to broaden the extent of the expropriation. In the latter case, the relevant public authority will be required to pay compensation for any loss or damage caused to the expropriated owner (Article 46 LEF) subject to the general public law standards on non-contractual liability (Articles 106(2) CE and 32 LRJSP). On an exceptional basis, Article 69 TRLS76 provides that, in certain cases, owners of land plots affected by urban planning may require public authorities to expropriate the affected plots, thereby rendering expropriation mandatory.[526] However, this only applies if the urban plan provides for the expropriation of the plot for subsequent construction works thereon and public authorities fail to order the expropriation within five years from the entry into force of the plan.

It I readily apparent that this provision does not *ratione materiae* to the case at hand. Consequently, Mrs Owner may not claim a right to be expropriated. Nevertheless, she could seek compensation for the loss or damage resulting from the project's approval by the authorities (Articles 106(2) CE and 32 LRJSP). This compensation could not only be based on the harm caused to her right to property (Article 33(1) CE), but also on the violation of her fundamental rights to privacy and to the inviolability of her home (Article 18 CE). Indeed, the Spanish Constitutional Court, in line with established case law of the European Court of Human Rights,[527] has ruled that noise pollution can be considered an undue interference with the said fundamental rights.[528] This is a very significant detail because, although the requirements to award compensation for public authority liability are the same in both cases (Articles 106(2) CE and 32 LRJSP), the interference with the rights to privacy and the inviolability of the home opens Mrs Owner two additional legal remedies that are not available to secure the right to property: (i) the extraordinary expedited proceedings before administrative law courts; and (ii) the appeal for constitutional protection of fundamental rights (*recurso de amparo*) before the Constitutional Court (Article 53(2) CE).

I. Sweden

PJ

Mrs Owner does not have the right to challenge the impact assessment per se (Environmental Code, *Miljöbalken* 1998:808, section 8, Chapter 6).

She should nevertheless have the right to ask for damages as noise is one of the environmental harms that may be compensated for (Chapter 32, Environmental Code).

[525] STS of 24 February 2003 (RJ 1203) and of 2 July 2010 (RJ 3593).

[526] STS of 4 December 2012 (RJ 8328) and of 20 December 2011 (RJ 8509).

[527] ECtHR judgments of 16 November 2004 *Moreno Gómez v Spain* App no 4143/02; of 12 June 2014, *Martínez v Spain* App no 56030/07; and of 16 January 2018, *Cuenca Zarzoso v Spain* App no 23383/12.

[528] STC 150/2011, FJ 5-9. C Alonso García, 'La contaminación acústica' in L Ortega and C Alonso (eds), *Tratado de Derecho ambiental* (Tirant lo Blanch 2015) 695–730.

The condition is nevertheless that 'the disturbance that caused the injury should not be reasonably tolerated given the conditions of the locality or its general occurrence under comparable conditions' (section 1, Chapter 32 of the Environmental Code). Mrs Owner should also have the right to redemption of property according to section 11, Chapter 32 of the Environmental Code, which states that

> If an activity referred to in this chapter entails that a property is wholly or partly useless to the owner or that particular damages arise when the property is used, the property or part of the property shall be redeemed at the owner's request to the business owner.

J. Ukraine

HD

The Law of Ukraine 'On environmental impact assessment' provides the possibility of post-project monitoring. However, this will be conducted if it is provided for in the conclusion of an environmental impact assessment. The order, terms and requirements relating to this monitoring must be specified in the conclusion. On this basis, a business will ensure post-project monitoring in order to detect any divergences in predictable levels of impact. If a business activity's essential negative impact on human life and health or on environment has been confirmed, and if this impact was not evaluated during the environmental impact assessment, the decision regarding the activity would have to be annulled by a court, and the activity would have to cease (Article 13). Anyone has a right to challenge the conclusion regarding the environmental impact assessment in the court (Article 12).[529]

The Code of Administrative Proceedings of Ukraine provides that every person has a right to bring a case before the administrative court if he or she considers that his or her rights, freedoms, or legal interests have been infringed by the decision, action or inaction of the competent authority. Anyone is entitled to claim damages for prejudice arising from the decision, action or inaction of the competent authority (Article 5(1).[530]

Hence, Mrs Owner is entitled to challenge the impact assessment. However, the Law of Ukraine 'On alienation' does not provide the possibility of expropriating property *post factum* and on the owner's initiative.[531] Thus, Mrs Owner could not ask for her land to be expropriated. She could claim compensation or seek another remedy.

The Code of Administrative Proceedings of Ukraine provides that protection against violated rights, freedoms, or interests of a person who brings an action before

[529] Law of Ukraine 'On environmental impact assessment' (23 May 2017) https://zakon.rada.gov.ua/laws/show/2059-19 (accessed 5 May 2021).

[530] Code of Administrative Proceedings of Ukraine (6 July 2005) https://zakon.rada.gov.ua/laws/show/2747-15 (accessed 5 May 2021).

[531] Law of Ukraine 'On alienation of land plots, other real property assets located on them which are private property for the public needs or on the grounds of public necessity' (17 November 2009 https://zakon.rada.gov.ua/laws/show/1559-17 (accessed 5 May 2021).

the court may be ensured in any way compatible with the law and that guarantees effective protection from breaches committed by public authorities (Article 5(2)).[532]

In this situation, cases *Grimkovskaya v Ukraine*[533] and *Hatton and Others v the United Kingdom*[534] could be applied. The case law of the ECtHR is recognised as a source of law in Ukraine.

K. The United Kingdom
EW

An environmental impact assessment (EIA), which would have been carried out as part of the planning process[535] before the airport and railway were constructed,[536] should have considered the likely significant environmental impacts of the scheme, including noise. There are three different ways that EIA decisions can be challenged including: (i) procedures under the EIA Regulations 2017; (ii) under the statutory appeal route offered by section 288 of the TCPA 1990; or (iii) by judicial review. Given that the impact assessment has occurred and the project now exists, the most applicable route for challenge would be an application for judicial review, perhaps on the grounds that adequate reasons for allowing the project had not been given despite the impact of noise on properties, or that there had been a failure to take account of all relevant considerations in deciding what the environmental impact would be on properties. Mrs Owner would have standing on the grounds of having sufficient interest in the matter given that her home is affected, but she would only have six weeks from the date on which the grounds for the claim first arose[537] to make her application for judicial review.[538] In the event that Mrs Owner's claim is successful, the court has a number of remedial options including a declaration, an injunction, or a mandatory order. Given that the airport is functional and operating, any court is unlikely to quash a decision to grant planning permission. Mrs Owner would be more likely to gain a useful remedy by seeking financial compensation available under other legislation. English law allows for compensation to be paid in some circumstances where public works negatively affect neighbouring land and would otherwise be construed as an actionable nuisance. Mrs Owner's land has presumably already had all possible noise

[532] Code of Administrative Proceedings of Ukraine (6 July 2005 https://zakon.rada.gov.ua/laws/show/2747-15 (accessed 5 May 2021).

[533] Judgment: *Grimkovskaya v Ukraine* App No 38182/03 (ECtHR 21 July 2011) https://www.menschenrechte.ac.at/orig/11_4/Grimkovskaya.pdf (accessed 5 May 2021).

[534] Judgment: *Hatton and Others v. the United Kingdom* [2003] ECHR 338 http://hudoc.echr.coe.int/eng-press?i=003-788265-805159 (accessed 5 May 2021).

[535] The EIA Directive 2011 (Directive 2011/92/EU of the European Parliament and of the Council of 13 December 2011) as amended by the EIA Directive 2014 (Directive 2014/52/EU of the European Parliament and of the Council of 16 April 2014) were implemented into English planning law by the Town and Country Planning (Environmental Impact Assessment) Regulations 2017 (SI 2017/571) ('EIA Regulations 2017').

[536] An EIA is required because airports fall within the definition of developments necessitating an EIA under Schedule 1 to the EIA Regulations 2017.

[537] In *R (Burkett) v London Borough of Hammersmith and Fulham (No 1)* [2002] 1 WLR 1593 the House of Lords held that the time limit for applying for judicial review runs from when the planning permission is granted.

[538] Civil Procedure Rules 1998/3132, r 54.5.

mitigation works carried out unsuccessfully, but if not, it is possible for public authorities to insulate buildings against noise caused by the construction or use of public works (including airports).[539] Since Mrs Owner did not have any land taken from her as part of the scheme, she cannot benefit from compensation available for injurious affection and severance under section 7 of the Compulsory Purchase Act 1965.

However, she can make a claim for a loss in the value of her home due to the noise from the airport under Part 1 of the Land Compensation Act 1973 ('Part 1 claim'). There are potential claims for both the harm suffered during the construction of the airport and railway, and for the harm caused by their use. Given that the airport and railway are now operational, Mrs Owner should focus on making a claim for any depreciation in the value of her property due to the use of the airport and railway. Whilst Part 1 Claims can be difficult to make out, it appears that Mrs Owner may be able to claim financial compensation for the depreciation of her land's value. She needs to demonstrate that the depreciation is due to one of seven statutorily defined 'physical factors' caused by the use of the public works. These physical factors include noise,[540] so Mrs Owner would be able to bring a Part 1 Claim since the depreciation in value caused by the noise is associated with the use of the airport and railway, rather than just their mere existence. In addition to the noise, Mrs Owner will qualify for a Part 1 Claim since she is an owner of a 'dwelling'.[541] She needs to serve a notice on the acquiring authority setting out: the land that the claim relates to; her interest in the land and date of acquisition; the public works to which the claim relates; the amount of compensation claimed; and any details of contiguous or adjoining land that she owns.[542] The Part 1 Claim cannot be made until twelve months have passed since the public works were first used,[543] and Mrs Owner has six years from this date to bring her claim.[544] Compensation is calculated on the depreciation caused by the 'physical factors', that is the noise, rather than the nearness of the airport and railway.[545]

It is also open to an acquiring authority to exercise a discretion to purchase land which is not directly required for the scheme, but which is affected to such an extent that compensation under a Part 1 Claim cannot adequately mitigate the hardship caused.[546] The acquiring authority is empowered to purchase the property, but is not obliged to do so. A contract for a purchase on the grounds of nuisance from the new airport must be signed within a year from the date after the development comes into use.

[539] Land Compensation Act 1973, s 20; Civil Aviation Act 1982 section 79 provides for grants to protect against noise and vibration attributable to the use of an aerodrome (airport); The Noise Insulation (Railways and Other Guided Transport Systems) Regulations 1996 applies to the railway noise if they are within 300 metres of the railway.

[540] LCA 1973, s 1.

[541] ibid s 2.

[542] ibid s 3.

[543] B Denyer-Green, Compulsory Purchase and Compensation (11 edn, Routledge 2018) para 23.4.4.

[544] LCA 1973, s 19(2A) and Limitation Act 1980, section 9.

[545] LCA 1973, s 4.

[546] Section 26 of the Land Compensation Act 1973 allows land to be acquired by agreement to mitigate any adverse effect which the existence or use of public works (this includes an airport) has on the surroundings, or where the enjoyment of land is serious affected by the construction, alteration or use of public works.

L. The United States

IS

This is another issue that varies greatly based on the laws of particular local and state governments. Different localities have different laws on noise pollution. However, the US Supreme Court has ruled in *United States v Causby*, that '[f]lights of aircraft over private land which are so low and frequent as to be a direct and immediate interference with the enjoyment and use of the land' qualify as takings that require compensation under the Fifth Amendment.[547]

M. International investment law

FF

The scenario revolves around international investment law (IIL) protection against private nuisance attributable to the authorities, imputable to an erroneous impact assessment.

Nuisance from large infrastructural projects is commonplace in investor–state dispute settlement, but usually investment operations are scrutinised, not state conduct. Noise control is routinely included in the checklist of impact assessments, which investors must present to obtain clearance for mining, drilling or other projects entailing environmental encroachments.[548] Host states name-check domestic nuisance law, trying to justify their acts (limiting noise levels, or sanctioning breaches) as legitimate regulatory decisions warranting no compensation. For instance, the USA explained in *Glamis Gold* that land use limitations could not amount to expropriation, because domestic law already precluded the right to cause irreparable harm to sacred Native American sites:

> [t]he prohibition 'inhere[s] in the title itself, in the restrictions that background principles of the State's law of property and nuisance already place upon land ownership', [therefore] no compensation will ever be due, regardless of the economic impact of the challenged regulations.[549]

Instead, the scenario refers to state actions interfering with the investor's use of property for economic purposes.[550] The classic reference for this predicament is the 1906 *Trail Smelter* case on transboundary pollution,[551] standing for the principle that a business reduction 'caused by a nuisance' does not warrant compensation. However,

[547] 328 US 346 (1946).

[548] By way of example see *Burlington v Ecuador*, ICSID Case No ARB/08/5, Decision Counterclaims (7 February 2017) para 182; *Clayton and Bilcon v Canada* Award (10 January 2019) para 171; *Windstream v Canada* PCA Case No 2013-22 Award (27 September 2016) para 164; *Pac Rim* (n 189) para 7.15.

[549] *Glamis Gold* (n 490), Rejoinder (15 May 2017) 14.

[550] The scenario refers to 'suitability for living', but an adjustment is necessary for the land to achieve the status of investment.

[551] *Trail Smelter* (USA v Canada) 3 RIAA 1906, 1911 (first decision 1938).

IIL might provide the investor with a better cause of action than is available under customary law.

Since the impact on the investment seems unintentional, the state must be informed of it. If the investor obtains no redress, she could bring a claim for expropriation, breach of fair and equitable treatment (FET) or FPS. Mrs Owner could plead indirect expropriation, arguing that the airport's operation 'affects the environment or conditions under which [she planned to carry on] its business'[552] resulting in de facto deprivation 'of the greatest part and the economic heart of [her] investment'.[553] She could also bring a FET or 'non-impairment'[554] claim, based on the measure's arbitrariness (it relied on a mistaken impact assessment) or its discriminatory character (it disproportionately affected her investment for no reason). Evidence of arbitrariness and/or discrimination could strengthen Mrs Owner's claim that the state's conduct frustrated her reasonable expectations about the investment's economic viability, especially if domestic law conditioned the construction of the airport to an (accurate) impact assessment.

Alternatively, Mrs Owner could characterise noise pollution as environmental harm, invoking the authorities' responsibility for breaching the FPS standard, by undermining the integrity of her land. In *Allard v Barbados*,[555] the investor accused the authorities of failing to operate a sluice gate between the ocean and the wetlands, thus causing environmental degradation to the investor's land. Moreover, the state had reclassified the lands adjacent to the investor's, with the alleged effect of reducing the site's 'tranquillity'. The tribunal held that state conduct had caused no degradation, therefore it did not have to determine whether the FPS standard includes 'an obligation of the host State to protect foreign investments against environmental damage'.[556]

A faulty impact assessment, depending on the circumstances, could strengthen, or weaken, the investor's claim. On the one hand, it created a specific assurance by the authorities that Mrs Owner's land would be unaffected by the airport's construction. Accordingly, she could plead a breach of legitimate expectations generated by specific governmental acts and warranties.[557] On the other hand, the state could invoke the impact assessment to prove its due diligence and rebuff an FPS claim. FPS clauses create an obligation of conduct, not of result, thus the subsequent discovery of a mistake might be immaterial if the impact assessment was carried out diligently.

Ultimately, however, Mrs Owner's request for damages would be limited to the property's loss of value caused by the de facto constraints on its original business destination.

552 *Burlington* (n 548), Decision on Liability (14 December 2012) para 397.
553 *UP v Hungary* ICSID Case No ARB/13/35 Award (9 October 2018) para 354.
554 *Tethyan* (n 415) para 1365.
555 *Allard v Barbados* PCA Case No 2012-06 Award (27 June 2016).
556 ibid para 252.
557 However, her investment seemingly predates the assessment, so the decision to make the investment did not rely on the assessment's conclusions.

XI. Case 10: A new urban planning act

A. Belgium

DR, LC, CD, and KP

Based on a decision to enact a new urban planning act, Belleville City decides to expropriate Miss Busy's land in order to build a bus station.

Miss Busy is then expropriated on these grounds, and the works start on the area.

This situation is not rare in Belgian law.

In effect, a local municipality can request authorisation from the competent authority—in principle, the concerned regional government—to order expropriation to ensure the execution of an urban planning act that the municipality has adopted.[558]

The urban planning act should be considered a different and autonomous decision from the decision allowing the expropriation.

As mentioned in the chapter by D Renders, L Ceci, C Delforge, K Polet, 'Procedural Requirements for Administrative Limits to Property Rights in Belgium' in this volume, Belgian law requires the regularity of the decision allowing expropriation to be examined by a court before the transfer of property and thus before the public works begin.

After ascertaining the regularity of the expropriation, the court must also establish the amount of compensation that may be claimed by the expropriated owner under Article 16 of the Belgian Constitution.

In the case at hand, the question is whether the annulment of the urban planning act could imply the unlawfulness of the decision allowing expropriation.

Miss Busy could try to argue that the decision allowing expropriation has become unlawful due to the annulment of the urban planning act.

The argument could be based on this logic: Article 16 of the Belgian Constitution only envisages expropriation in the situations permitted by law. Belleville's decision to enact a new urban planning act is precisely a case of expropriation provided for by urban legislation. If this act no longer exists, Miss Busy could claim that the expropriation is no longer justified and, thus, that the expropriation in question breaches Article 16 of the Constitution.

Miss Busy could use the unlawful situation in various ways.

First of all, Miss Busy could claim repossession of the property, as mentioned in Part I of this volume. This option would, however, probably be inadequate in the case in question as the right to retrocession can normally only be claimed when the public purpose pursued by the public authority has not been achieved.[559] This is not the case, as Belleville City does not seem to have abandoned construction of the bus station.

558 Local municipalities in the Walloon Region are authorised to expropriate properties in order to execute urban planning decisions. This could concern several types of urban planning acts (a '*schéma de développement communal*' or a '*schéma d'orientation local*', for example; see Code of Territorial Development, art D.VI.1, 2, and 3 (20 July 2016; publication in the Belgian *Official Gazette* on 14 November 2016).

559 M Vrancken and M Pâques, 'Le droit de rétrocession, une garantie constitutionnelle pour l'exproprié?' (2015) 3 Administration publique 425.

Secondly, it should be noted that, even without considering the right to retrocession, established case law states that when expropriation is unlawful, the owner concerned may claim the return of his property if the works in question have not yet been executed.[560] However, in the case at hand, such a request would be unlikely to be successful because the works are currently ongoing. It is thus very probable that the court will consider Miss Busy's claim excessive.

Consequently, the only realistic option might be to request compensation based on Articles 1382 and onwards of the Belgian Civil Code. Indeed, when an expropriation is considered unlawful, the legal grounds for requesting compensation change as they do not concern compensation for the loss of a property under Article 16 of the Belgian Constitution, but reparation of the damage caused by a fault of the public authority under Articles 1382 and onwards of the Belgian Civil Code.[561] In principle, modification of the legal basis for compensation has a limited impact because, in general, loss of a property and all its accessories are equally compensated for in both cases.[562]

B. France
EG

Miss Busy had her property expropriated by the Belleville City Council. The declaration of public utility concerned the construction of a bus stop on her land. However, one of the primary documents justifying the declaration of public utility was cancelled after her expropriation.

The question that arises is whether the annulment of this administrative act—the local urbanisation plan—consequently leads to the annulment of the expropriation and de facto to the retrocession of the property or to compensation.

It is only possible to modify local urban planning rules, including the local urban plan, if the project's usefulness is not called into question. Therefore, it is accepted that minor modifications can be made to the town planning rules without altering their content. Thus, the 'general economy of the project' must not be called into question. The new local urban plan may also be useful to modify the previous permit, which contained a procedural irregularity. Thus, it appears that Miss Busy will be able to challenge the expropriation only if the new local urban plan did not comply with the former urban planning one. If it is only a procedural or formal defect, the court will not grant her request.

In any event, Miss Busy cannot claim damages because the five-year period for bringing her claim has not expired. Finally, Miss Busy will only be able to bring an action if the annulment is the result of an internal legal defect and, furthermore, she will not be able to assert her right of retrocession because the work has already begun.

560 Wéry, 'L'expropriation pour cause d'utilité publique' (n 2) 788 and relevant references.
561 ibid.
562 ibid.

C. Germany

FS

According to the Federal Building Code, expropriation is possible in order to use a piece of land in accordance with the provisions of the land-use plan.[563] A precondition is, however, that the land-use plan is legally effective.[564] If the planning act has been quashed due to illegality, the expropriation is generally unlawful. In the present case, the urban planning act was quashed after one year. However, the act of expropriation had become incontestable and final. Miss Busy will therefore not be able to challenge the expropriation in court, but will only be able to apply to the authorities to withdraw the unlawful expropriation act.[565]

The withdrawal can break through the validity of the administrative act in order to preserve the principle of legality. The authority shall not be permanently bound to unlawful administrative acts.[566] The withdrawal is a discretionary decision by the authority. The authority has to balance the principles of legal certainty and individual justice. In this respect, the authority must also take into account that the works on the bus station have begun in the meantime. The withdrawal of the expropriation act is only permissible within one year from the date on which the authority becomes aware of the facts justifying the withdrawal.[567]

Irrespective of the possibility to apply for the withdrawal of the expropriation act, Miss Busy may assert a claim for damages against Belleville City on the basis of public liability.[568] This claim presumes that Belleville City committed a breach of official duty when the urban planning act was issued. This is the case if, for example, Belleville City violated a higher-ranking law.

D. Italy

SM

The expropriation procedure starts with the imposition of the 'pre-established constraint for expropriation'. This is the first formal act of the procedure and it may derive from a general regulatory plan, from a variant or from another act which in any case entails a modification to the regulatory plan. The second step is the declaration of public utility that can be contained in the approval of the definitive project of the public work or in the specific plans such as the detailed plan, the development plan, the recovery plan, the reconstruction plan, the plan of the areas to be used for production sites, or the area plan.

The case in question does not specify if the urban planning is the general regulatory plan of the town or a specific one. But as the expropriation of Miss Busy's land has already begun and the public works to build the bus station are going on, we have to assume that the administrative authority also issued a declaration of public utility.

563 BauGB, § 85 sec 1 No 1.
564 Battis, '§ 85' in Battis, Krautzberger, and Löhr (n 19) para 2.
565 cf VwVfG, § 48 sec 1 sentence 1.
566 J Müller, '§ 48' in Bader and Ronellenfitsch (n 15) before para 1.
567 VwVfG, § 48 sec 4.
568 cf BGB, § 839 in conjunction with GG, art 34.

The quashing of the urban plan involves the invalidity of the expropriation procedure. The declaration of public utility is no longer effective along with the pre-established constraint for the expropriation that was established by the urban plan.

Case law says that in such a situation the whole expropriation procedure is void, and the jurisdictional competence lies with the ordinary judge. The expropriation power exercised by the public authority is lost because of the quashing of the urban plan, and the owner has the right to compensation for damages. The case is called 'encroaching occupation' by the Italian courts, meaning an occupation of private land made by public authority without any formal and lawful administrative decision.

In any case, since the public works have started and are still ongoing, it is not certain that Miss Busy will be able to regain possession of her land. If the public works cause an irreversible transformation of her property, the public administration can decide to acquire it on the basis of Article 42-*bis* of the Expropriation Act (DPR No 327/2001), according to which the authority that uses a property for public interest purposes, modified in the absence of a valid and effective provision for expropriation, may order that it be acquired, not retroactively, and that an indemnity be paid to the owner for the monetary and non-monetary damage. The acquisition order can also be adopted during the pending judgment and even after the quashing of the planning act that contained the constraint for the expropriation. So in this case it would be possible for the competent authorities to acquire Miss Busy's property in order to continue the public works for the bus station.

E. The Netherlands

JS and NvT

Under Dutch law a situation as described above would never occur. In the event of the already mentioned expropriation procedure to develop an environment plan the actual expropriation—ie the transfer of ownership from the expropriated party to the expropriating party—can only take place once the environment plan that underlies that expropriation has become irrevocable. There is—to be clear—no possibility provided for by law for the public authority to already be carrying out works on a property that is not already expropriated.

F. Poland

IK and ŁK

The regulation in Article 6 of the IPMA does not specify criteria or ways of recognising anything as a public purpose. It does contain a list of various activities, facilities or actions considered to be public purposes. Undoubtedly, however, building a public bus station belongs to such purposes found in Article 6(1) of the IPMA, as it is a public transport facility.[569] In the case of Miss Busy, the factual and legal circumstances

[569] More: E Bończak-Kucharczyk, *Ustawa o gospodarce nieruchomościami: Komentarz* (Wolters Kluwer 2020); E Klat-Górska and L Klat-Wertelecka, *Ustawa o gospodarce nieruchomościami: Komentarz* (Wolters Kluwer 2015).

indicate that the expropriation decision meets the conditions of Articles 119 and 112 of the IPMA. The procedure was carried out correctly and Miss Busy received appropriate compensation. In the circumstances, the return of the expropriated property could take place only if it became redundant given the non-attainment of a public purpose.[570] If the purpose were attained on a section of that land, the owner could apply for the remaining part to be returned. As an investment project of bus station construction has begun and continues on Miss Busy's land, the circumstances specified above do not take place. By the same token, circumstances have taken place that preclude such property return. Similarly, it seems impossible that her land could be brought back to its previous condition, which is one of the requirements for its return.

On the day the expropriation decision was issued, the contested area was covered by a local urban planning act, then quashed. The factual circumstances in Miss Busy's case do not indicate why. Assuming that it ceased to apply as a result of the adoption of a new spatial development plan, Article 34(1) of the SPDA will be applicable, under which the entry into force of a local plan results in the invalidity of other spatial development plans or their parts related to the land covered by them. At the same time, however, Article 34(2) provides that the loss of the binding force of a local plan does not result in the expiry of administrative decisions issued on its basis.

One could yet assume here that the commune's resolution concerning the local plan was quashed because of a vital breach of the principles of local plan drafting, a vital breach of the local plan drafting procedure, as well as a breach concerning the competence of the authority in that regard. That could have led to the invalidity of the resolution of the commune council in its entirety or part, declared by both the *voivode* and an administrative court. Last but not least, one could also assume that the ascertainment of the invalidity of the resolution on a local spatial development plan has the same result as if that local plan has never circulated in the system of legal transactions.

Given the above, Miss Busy would need to consider whether to exercise her right to seek the ascertainment of the invalidity of the expropriation decision as well whether such a demand is actually in her legal interest, if only given the mutual settlements related to the already paid and received compensation.

G. Portugal
RGdF

Expropriation of land and buildings is a legal instrument for the execution of urban programmes and planning, as well as for public interventions, infrastructure and public utility facilities (Article 159/1 of the LPIL). These expropriations follow the procedures of the CE, and the general interest situations in the law are mere examples (Article 159/2 and 3 of the CE). It is plausible that Miss Busy could see her land being expropriated for this purpose, and depending on the type of planning in question, the competent authority could be the municipality[571] or the state (Article 14/2 of the CE).

[570] IPMA, art 137.
[571] In the case of plans of urbanisation and detailing plans (see above).

It is always possible that a plan faces issues of legality and ends up being 'quashed'. According to Portuguese law, if otherwise not expressly determined, the declaration of nullity of a certain plan does not affect the effectiveness of the administrative acts issued under the plan (Article 129/3 of the LPIL). This norm is considered to be only for declarations of nullity issued by the administration itself.

But if the plan is judicially quashed, being an administrative regulation, one of two things might happen (Article 76 of the CPTA). First, the court may—for reasons of certainty, equity or exceptional relevant public interest—determine that the effects of the quashing are only for the future (safeguarding previous acts). Secondly, even if the court did not determine the previous limitation, the administrative acts that cannot be challenged any more will stand (and given that a year has passed, in Miss Busy's case, this would probably be the case).

In any case, the quashing of the plan would not necessarily determine the illegality of the expropriation (bear in mind that the 'dup' is an administrative act). The 'dup' would always have to specify the cause of public interest for that particular land. And theoretically this specification could stand even without the plan. Certainly, an expropriation must be in accordance with the specifications of the plans for the area (many rules of the CE count on that). But the non-existence of a plan (regardless of the reasons for that) does not in itself impede expropriation. The situation would be more complicated if the quashing would determine the reinstatement of a previous plan which would clearly not allow the bus station.

Eventually, the 'dup' might need to be renewed, which is a possibility expressly thought of for situations of expiry (Article 13 of the CE). But the point is that the grounds for expropriation are not provided by the plan solely by itself. And anyway, the 'dup' would probably stand after the court's decision.

H. Spain

LAJ and DUFB

In this case, the applicable legal framework depends on how the expropriation occurred. One could expect that Belleville City first enacted an urban plan—which, as discussed in the chapter by L Arroyo Jiménez and D Utrilla Fernández-Bermejo, 'Procedural requirements for administrative limits to property rights in Spain' in this volume, qualifies as administrative rulemaking—wherein Miss Busy's property was declared 'of public utility or social interest', in order to subsequently issue the declaration of the need to expropriate—ie a single-case administrative decision adopted in the implementation of the plan the plan. Had the expropriation been conducted as stated above, the implications of the urban plan's judicial annulment would be as follows.

First, if the plan was invalidated after two months from the issuance of the declaration of the need to expropriate, the latter would be final and unappealable (Article 73 LJCA). Consequently, Miss Busy would not be entitled to challenge the expropriation, although she could claim compensation for any loss or damage resulting from the unlawful expropriation (Articles 106(2) CE and 32 LRJSP).

Secondly, if the plan was invalidated within the said 2-month period following the issuance of the declaration of the need to expropriate, it would not be final and thus could be challenged first before the expropriating authority, and next before the administrative law courts. If this were the case, Miss Busy could seek (i) the annulment or invalidation of declaration of the need to expropriate (Article 31(1) LJCA); (ii) the declaration of her right to regain possession of her property, and (iii) compensation for any loss or damage arising from the unlawful expropriation (Articles 106(2) CE and 32 LRJSP), which could be claimed before the administrative law court (Article 31(2) LJCA).

Having regard to the aforesaid time periods, it would be possible that the works had not yet started or otherwise that they had not yet substantially and irrevocably altered Miss Busy's property, so that restitution would remain an option. However, if the works had already commenced and irreversibly transformed Miss Busy's property—thereby rendering restitution de facto impossible—the only available forms of relief would be the invalidation of the declaration of the need to expropriate (Article 31(1) LJCA) and compensation for any loss or damage (Articles 106(2) CE and 32 LRJSP), which could also be directly claimed before the competent administrative law court (Article 31(2) LJCA). In this case, the relief in the form of compensation applies by default—ie, as secondary protection (*tutela secundaria*) of the right to property—given that granting legal relief in the form of restitution—primary protection (*tutela primaria*)—to Miss Busy had become de facto impossible.[572]

I. Sweden

PJ

The expropriation having taking place Miss Busy has received full compensation for her long-term property. She has no rights left in the property.

It is interesting to note that a possibility to get expropriated property back existed in the past, ie in the Expropriation Act (1917:189), but was not introduced in the current Act enacted in the 1970s. The issue was discussed again thoroughly in the 2010s.[573] Nevertheless, the legislator decided not to introduce a provision regarding the repurchase of previously expropriated properties. The reasons are that 'it is very complicated to create a regulatory framework that fully covers all the conditions that should apply to how such a repurchase right can be actualised and exercised' and that 'it seems unlikely that such a rule would be perceived as fair by all concerned'.[574]

[572] S Díez Sastre, 'La tutela de los competidores en los procedimientos administrativos de adjudicación' in L Arroyo and D Utrilla (eds), *La administración de la escasez* (Marcial Pons 2015) 214–18.

[573] SOU 2010:92 *En effektivare förvaltning av statens fastigheter*, dir 2010:51 (Preparatory work).

[574] SOU 2010:92, 168–69. The committee in charge of investigating the issue end its concluding remarks writing that it would like to point out that an in-depth analysis work could provide further information on possible avenues. It would be of particular interest to investigate whether Government decisions on expropriation should include provisions on repurchase options (SOU 2010:92, 169—Preparatory work).

J. Ukraine

HD

As has already been mentioned in case 5, Ukrainian legislation provides for the possibility of having property returned to the owner after it has been compulsorily alienated (expropriated). The special procedure for this is established by law.

If the need for use of the land plot that was bought out for public needs or was compulsorily alienated on the grounds of public necessity has passed, the authorities that issued the decision on redemption of this object must adopt the decision regarding it. This must be done within one month of the situation becoming known to the authorities, which are obliged to inform the previous owner or his or her heirs that the public need or necessity is over. Land plots that were bought out or compulsory alienated, and other objects located on the land plots can be bought back by the previous owner if he or she files an application for it. The actual price for the time of the redemption will be set, and the application should be filed within six months of the day when the previous owner received notification from the authorities or from the day this information was published in the print media (Article 19 of the Law of Ukraine 'On alienation').

Miss Busy cannot challenge the court decision about the expropriation by claiming that after a year there is no longer a proper basis in the planning act because it is assumed that the forced alienation was carried out lawfully. Rather, the inactivity of the local authorities should have informed Miss Busy about revision of the urban planning act and the possibility of buying her property back could be recognised as unlawful. The burden of proof lies with the local authority (Article 77(2) of the Code of Administrative Proceedings of Ukraine).[575] It should be taken into account that the works have already started and that there is also no legal ground to stop them or to demolish the constructions that have already been built. The court will probably hold that despite the lack of public necessity, there is no possibility of reversing the redemption.

The Code of Administrative Proceedings of Ukraine provides that if a court endorses Miss Busy, it could also apply other ways of protecting her rights that will ensure their effective protection (Article 245(10)).

K. The United Kingdom

EW

The third-party effects of unlawful administrative acts are a complex area in English law. It has been observed by Lord Radcliffe that an order:

> [E]ven if not made in good faith, is still an act capable of legal consequences. It bears no brand of invalidity upon its forehead. Unless the necessary proceedings are taken at law to establish the cause of invalidity and to get it quashed or otherwise upset it will remain as effective for its ostensible purpose as the most impeccable of orders.[576]

[575] Code of Administrative Proceedings of Ukraine (6 July 2005) https://zakon.rada.gov.ua/laws/show/2747-15 (accessed 5 May 2021).

[576] *Smith v East Elloe Rural District Council* [1956] AC 736, 769–70.

Here, the authorising urban planning act has been quashed but the circumstances bring into play Lord Denning's 'domino effect'[577] where the question arises as to the validity of the subsequent actions made in reliance on the (now) quashed urban planning act. The 'second actor' doctrine developed by Forsyth,[578] suggests that where an act appears to be valid and is relied upon by others for subsequent acts, the validity of those subsequent acts depend on the legal powers of that 'second actor' irrespective of the validity of the first (void) act. Debates about the legal effect of void and voidable acts reveal 'terminological and conceptual problems of excruciating complexity'.[579] The courts have taken different approaches to avoiding the domino effect of administrative chaos that could otherwise occur, if acts subsequent to an apparently valid but later void act were also tainted. Applying the domino effect strictly would make the compulsory acquisition also unlawful because it was predicated on a valid planning act. Sometimes the courts have treated unlawful decisions as decisions of fact rather than law; the discretionary nature of judicial review remedies has also allowed the courts to tailor solutions to the particular context of specific cases on the grounds that 'a claimant may be disabled from obtaining the full relief he seeks … [due to] grounds pertaining to the facts of a particular case'.[580]

Despite the quashing order it is worth noting that the English courts retain a wide discretion in deciding what remedies should apply in any successful judicial review challenge. Here, a quashing order was made. It would have been open to the court to consider the third-party effects of the quashing order and to have explicitly countermanded the continuing building works. This does not appear to have happened. On a pragmatic basis, there were several chances for the compulsory purchase order (CPO) to be challenged before the construction works started, for example when the CPO was first advertised, when the property was singled out for expropriation, and so on. Additionally, the project would not have proceeded to this stage without the payment of compensation and the transfer of the affected property. From a practical viewpoint, it is possible to argue that no loss has been suffered since the deprivation of property was fully compensated for under the CPO. The fact that the CPO has been quashed without this extending to undoing the validity of the construction works indicates that any challenge to the construction work may be unlikely to succeed.

L. The United States

IS

It is most likely Miss Busy would lose. While the planning act may now be repealed, it was still in force at the time the condemnation occurred, and therefore was duly authorised. Things would, of course, be different if the legislation repealing the act

577 *Director of Public Prosecutions v Head* [1959] AC 83.

578 CF Forsyth, 'The Metaphysics of Nullity' in W Wade and I Hare (eds), *The Golden Metwand and the Crooked Cord: Administrative Law Essays in Honour of Sir William Wade QC* (OUP 1998) 142.

579 H Woolf and others, *De Smith's Judicial Review* (8th edn, Sweet & Maxwell 2018) [4–058].

580 *McLaughlin v Governor of the Cayman Islands* [2007] 1 WLR 2839, 2847 [16].

indicated that the repeal has retroactive effect, thereby invalidating takings that had already occurred.

M. International investment law

FF

In this scenario, the state expropriated an investment and, thereafter, it transpired that the expropriation had a defective legal basis. Originally, the expropriation might have been lawful (ie carried out for a public purpose, with due process, against compensation) but it might be deemed unlawful if the quashing of the urban planning act results in the lapse of a genuine public purpose (see international investment law (IIL) Case 6 and Case 7) or evinces a serious want of due process.

In these circumstances, the investor might bring a claim of unlawful expropriation. It must be ascertained whether the remedy sought would differ from any amount already obtained by the state under the framework of the original expropriation process.[581]

Since (a) the only remedy available is monetary compensation and (b) there is little difference between compensation granted voluntarily and compensation ordered as a remedy, this scenario is an unlikely fit for investor–state dispute settlement arbitration.

[581] For a thorough discussion see IIL Case 5.

XII. Case 11: Regulatory taking

A. Belgium

DR, LC, CD, and KP

In the context of the case in question, the competent authorities decide to restrict entry to the Belle Coast and the activities authorised in the area.

This decision alters Mr Mad Hatter's situation as he owns fifty acres of land near the Belle Coast and has set up a tourist resort in the area.

Several forms of interference with the right to property must be distinguished in Belgian law.

Interference could take the form of an expropriation based on public purpose—in the strict sense—which implies a transfer of property and the obligation to follow a specific procedure, as described in the chapter by D Renders, L Ceci, C Delforge, K Polet, 'Procedural Requirements for Administrative Limits to Property Rights in Belgium' in this volume. In this case, under Article 16 of the Belgian Constitution, a 'fair compensation paid beforehand' must be paid to the owner who has been deprived of his right to property.

In addition, as also mentioned in Part I of this volume, the case law has sometimes acknowledged that severe forms of interference with the right to property might be seen as an expropriation—qualified as 'expropriation in fact'[582]—and that the conditions required for expropriation in the narrow sense must be respected. Therefore, owners deprived of their right to property must be awarded compensation.

Lastly, there are situations where interference with the right to property is based on a legal provision and does not imply a transfer of property. In this case, the owner can still use his or her property, albeit only in part.

In this case, the interference is described as a public servitude, which does not fall within the scope of Article 16 of the Belgian Constitution.[583] In effect, under Article 544 of the Belgian Civil Code, the legislator can establish limits to the right to property if this is in the public interest. No compensation is granted in this case.[584]

When a public servitude is created with regard to a given property, the concerned owner has, in principle, no right to compensation, unless the text on which the public servitude is based allows it.[585]

However, if, according to Article 1 of Protocol No 1 to the European Convention on Human Rights, the public servitude in question creates a disproportionate interference with the right to property, the European Court of Human Rights has ruled that the owner concerned may be entitled to compensation.[586] Based on this case law, the

[582] See especially M Denys, 'De la quasi-expropriation ou de l'indemnisation des interdictions de bâtir' [1983] Journal des Tribunaux 405; Wéry, 'L'appropriation des biens immeubles par les pouvoirs publics' (n 201) 34–37; D Lagasse, 'L'indemnité et la quasi-expropriation' in Renders (ed), *L'expropriation pour cause d'utilité publique* (n 4) 565–604.

[583] Lagasse (n 286) 599.

[584] ibid 567, 568.

[585] ibid 583.

[586] *Chassagnou and Others v France* (n 215); *Alatulkkila and Others v Finland* (n 215); *Anonymos Touristiki Etairia Kritis v Greece* (n 215); *Hermann v Germany* (n 215); Constitutional Court case No 55/2012 of 19 April 2012; Court of Cassation (24 June 2010) *Pasicrisie*, 2010, 2004.

Belgian court has also already established that public servitudes may imply a right to compensation.[587]

In the case at hand, the authorities have restricted entry to the Belle Coast and the activities authorised in the area.

There is thus no transfer of property, and Mr Mad Hatter can still use his property. It is only a *limitation* of his right to property.

In this respect, the Council of State has previously considered that the protection of a site as cultural heritage—as a semi-natural site in the concerned case—is a form of interference with the right to property but is not, in principle, an expropriation, 'as there is no transfer of property in favour of the authority'.[588]

The court could just as well consider, in the case in question, that the absence of transfer of property between Mr Mad Hatter and the authorities shows that the measure is not an expropriation but a public servitude.

If Mr Mad Hatter challenges the interference with his right to property, the court should first examine whether the measure taken by the authorities is based on a legal provision allowing the restriction of entry to the Belle Coast and the activities authorised in the area.

If there is no legal basis allowing interference with the applicant's right to property, the court should quash the challenged decision or grant refusal to apply it, regardless of whether Mr Mad Hatter decides to bring the case before the Council of State or before an ordinary court. In addition, the court might consider that the authorities are at fault under Articles 1382 ff. of the Belgian Civil Code and could grant the applicant an indemnity if he has suffered damage.

If the measure adopted by the authorities is grounded in a legal provision allowing the limitation of Mr Mad Hatter's right to property, the court should consider that this interference is a public servitude for which no compensation is due, unless the text on which the public servitude is based allows it.

If no compensation is granted, Mr Mad Hatter could attempt to demonstrate disproportionate interference with his right to property. The court should then examine whether there is a balance between the interference and the aim pursued by the measure. In the event of imbalance, the applicant may be entitled to compensation.

In Belgian law, this solution could be applied regardless of whether Mr Mad Hatter is a Belgian citizen or a foreign investor.

B. France

EG

The administration decided to classify the Belle Coast, but Mr Mad Hatter had grand ambitions for the land he occupies near this area. The Environment Code allows local and national authorities to determine new 'registered or classified sites' for reasons of

[587] Constitutional Court case No 55/2012 of 19 April 2012. See also the principles stated by the Court of Cassation regarding the compensation of interferences with the right to property: Court of Cassation 24 June 2010, *Pasicrisie*, 2010, p 2004.

[588] Council of State, *Immo Fond'Roy*, No 161, t717 of 8 August 2006.

general interest as stated in Article L341-1 of the Code: 'In each department, a list of natural monuments and sites whose conservation or preservation is of general interest from an artistic, historical, scientific, legendary, or picturesque point of view is established.' However, following this classification, the administration also restricted public access in order to preserve the Belle Coast. This has resulted in a direct prejudice to Mr Mad Hatter as its activity is tourism and risks damaging the coast. It will therefore be necessary to examine the remedies available to the applicant in order to annul the decision or, failing that, to obtain compensation.

First of all, it should be noted that the classification procedure requires a public inquiry of which the owner is an integral part. Thus, if the owner has been directly notified that a classification procedure has been initiated, and if he has not explicitly expressed his refusal, his silence is equivalent to an agreement, as stipulated in Article R341-5 of the Environmental Code: 'At the end of this period, the silence of the owner is equivalent to a lack of consent. However, when the owner has been personally notified of the decision to put the project under investigation, his silence at the end of the period is equivalent to tacit consent.'

It is therefore important for Mr Mad Hatter to have previously indicated his refusal at the time of the investigation phase in order to be able to contest the classification decision. If this was the case, in the absence of an amicable agreement, the Environmental Code provides a clear answer to settle the dispute in Article 168: 'In the absence of the owner's consent, the classification is pronounced, after the opinion of the higher commission, by decree in the Council of State.' Thus, the only outcome open to the owner is that the higher commission refuses the classification decision. If this is the case, the decision will be annulled. However, if the classification is carried out, the owner may claim compensation as provided for in the article mentioned above: 'The classification can give right to compensation to the benefit of the owner if it entails a modification to the State or the use of the premises determining a direct, material and particular prejudice.'

In this case, it appears that the classification will most certainly have a direct impact on the tourist activity insofar as public access will be limited. Moreover, the decrease in the number of visitors to the establishment will decrease the owner's turnover, which constitutes material damage—more precisely, monetary damage. Finally, the attractiveness of the tourist establishment run by Mr Mad Hatter is based on the presence of the Belle Coast, which suggests that attendance will inevitably and undoubtedly be reduced.

Mr Mad Hatter can challenge the classification of the Belle Coast. If he does not obtain the cancellation of the classification decision following the commission's decision, damages will be awarded to him following the prejudice that his activity has suffered. The Environmental Code does not differentiate between owners based on their nationality, so the remedies available to foreign owners would have been perfectly equivalent.

C. Germany

FS

The authorities have severely restricted access to the Belle Coast and the activities permitted there. These restrictions concern the coast located near Mr Mad Hatter's property, but not directly the property of Mr Mad Hatter. The property right guarantees the owners of land or buildings the possibility of 'external contact'. However, the main focus here is on the access to public roads. Any location advantages beyond this are in principle not protected by the right to property.[589] Mr Mad Hatter is therefore not entitled to unrestricted access to the coast because his property is close to Belle Coast. Compensation is only possible if access to the natural zone was part of the permission or if access was assured to Mr Mad Hatter. If this is not the case, the administrative decision cannot be challenged.

Besides, the property right guarantees the right to use the property itself or to generate income from the contractual transfer of use.[590] Accordingly, Mr Mad Hatter can use his land as a tourist resort that benefits from the access to the coast. However, the fundamental right to property does not protect the most lucrative use of the property.[591]

Even a foreign investor would have no further protection under German law. At most, claims from bilateral investment treaties (BIT) would be considered. The object of protection under these treaties is usually the 'investment' or 'capital investment' in the broader sense.[592] This could include the property of land near the coast if Mr Mad Hatter had acquired it under a bilateral investment treaty.

D. Italy

SM

Assets constituting natural beauties can be the object of distinct forms of environmental protection, also cumulatively, depending on the profile considered, with the consequence that landscape protection is perfectly compatible with urban-planning provisions.

In its general planning activity, the public administration (ie the municipality) has the authority to introduce constraints or preordained provisions for the satisfaction of landscape interests.

The constraints and destinations of areas with an environmental and landscape vocation must be introduced in the general urban planning or in the variants that the competent authority has the discretionary power to adopt at any point.

Administrative case law currently recognises the discretion of the public authority in the exercise of the planning power and specifically in imposing new environmental and natural constraints.[593] The administration has therefore the power to carry out an independent evaluation of the interests involved, comparing the reason of environmental protection with other interests, such as territorial organisation or the residential, commercial or economic needs of the area.

[589] Papier and Shirvani (n 297) paras 220 ff.
[590] BVerfGE 98, 17 <35>; 101, 54 <75>.
[591] ibid 91, 294 <310>; 100, 226 <243>.
[592] Papier and Shirvani (n 297) para 85.
[593] See eg Cons Stato, Sec IV (13 October 2010) No 7478.

In the case under examination such an evaluation has been carried out by the competent authorities in order to impose some constraints on the area of Belle Coast and on the activities allowed there, in order to introduce stronger landscape and nature protection. It is a legitimate assessment that falls within the discretionary power of the public administration. Judicial control on this administrative decision is limited to the consideration of its lawfulness, and particularly on the grounds of illegality and the excess of power in all its meanings, such as irrationality, insufficient motivation or lack of preliminary investigation.[594] These are the only grounds on which Mr Mad Hatter could challenge the administrative decision, seek its annulment and consequently ask for damages.

In the Italian legal system there are no other remedies, there is no allowance provided for the application of naturalistic constraints. The solution would not be different if Mr Mad Hatter were a foreign investor because the discipline on the constraints and destinations of areas with an environmental and landscape vocation would apply in any case.

E. The Netherlands

JS and NvT

The remedies available to Mr Mad Hatter depend on the nature of the decision. Has the administrative authority adopted a new zoning plan/environmental plan or has the land been designated a Natura 2000 site?

Under the former law, a new zoning plan only applied to developments after the zoning plan (with its prohibition) had come into force. Current legitimate use was—based on rules of transitional law—therefore allowed.[595] The current use could continue, but could not be expanded. Mr Mad Hatter did not have to seek the annulment of the contested decision. It is still unclear what the answer to the above question will be under the Environment and Planning Act, under which the aforementioned transitional law will not continue. One of the main reasons is the fact that the environment plan regulates a lot more than the former zoning plan. Therefore, standardised transitory law is not considered appropriate. Briefly, under the Environment and Planning Act the principle of legal certainty will decide whether Mr Mad Hatter can continue with his business.

If he is not allowed to continue his business, he can possibly seek compensation for losses resulting from an administrative act (namely the adoption of an environment plan). However, this will only entitle him to compensation for part of his damage. If the environment plan has been adopted according to the prescribed rules, Mr Mad Hatter will not be able to seek for the annulment of the contested decision.

In case the land that is listed as a Natura 2000 site, the activities that take place on the land are subject to a licensing obligation.[596] Under the Environmental and Planning

[594] See in this regard Cons Stato, Sec VI (2 December 2019) No 8246.
[595] Spatial Planning Decree, art 3.2.2.
[596] Nature Conservation Act, arts 2.7–2.9 The Nature Conservation Act is the successor of the Nature Conservation Act 1998, in which the Habitats Directive was implemented.

Act, it seems to be the case that a former exception comes back into play.[597] If there is so-called existing use—that is, a use that was known or should have been known to the competent authority on 31 March 2010—there is no licensing obligation. Since we assume Mr Mad Hatter started his enterprise after that date, he will not be able to invoke this exception. The authorities are therefore allowed to restrict Mr Mad Hatter's activities. Just as with the environmental plan, he can possibly seek compensation. He will not receive a full compensation. The outcome of such a request will depend—among other things—on the foreseeability of the designation of the land as a Natura 2000 site.

If the authorities really want to make sure Mr Mad Hatter stops operating a tourist resort, they will have to start expropriation proceedings.

The answer to this question does not change if Mr Mad Hatter were a foreign investor, albeit that compensation issues might also be brought forward under an arbitration clause in some applicable investment treaties. However, it is hard to imagine that such proceedings would lead to more compensation than Dutch law provides for.

F. Poland

IK and ŁK

In order to explain Mr Mad Hatter's case, one should begin by indicating that Polish law includes a number of administrative regulations concerning nature protection. The Nature Protection Act of 16 April 2004 (NPA) is not the only legal act that regulates matters related to the broadly understood environment. Apart from it, the EPA of 27 April 200 (JoL of 2016, item 672, as amended), the Water Law Act of 20 July 2017 (JoL of 2017, item 1566, as amended) and many others legal acts are in force. Equally broad is the objective scope of act-of-law legislation. Pursuant to Article 76 of the Environmental Protection Act (EPA), local spatial development plans and building and zoning decisions take into account limitations stemming from the establishment, under the NPA, of: a national park, a nature reserve, a landscape park, a landscape protection area, a Natura 2000 site, a nature and landscape complex, an ecological site, a documentary site, monuments of nature, as well as their adjacent areas[598]. Also considered is the establishment of LUAs or industrial zones as well as the delineation of quiet zones within urban agglomerations and elsewhere. Further, considered are decisions made under the WLA related to the conditions of using waters from a water region and a catchment area as well as setting up of protective water intake zones and protective water reservoir areas. The establishment or an extension of a national park or a nature reserve is a public purpose in the meaning of the IPMA. When such establishment covers areas that are immovable property not of the state treasury, it takes place with the owner's consent, and in the absence thereof—by means of expropriation.

[597] This exception was found in art 19d of the Nature Conservation Act 1998 and originally in Nature Conservation Act, art 2.9. Due to the Emergency Act to Combat Nitrogen, this exception was revoked.

[598] If amendments of Acts of law necessitate amendments of a study or a local plan, such amendments of a local development plan shall be carried out in a scope needed for them to be effected (art 33 of the SPDA).

The introduction of specific forms of nature protection can result in restricting the right of property use. The introduction of such forms of nature protection as, for instance, national parks or nature reserves may entail serious restrictions on the right of ownership and other rights in rem. That is why Articles 129 and 130 of the EPA regulate solutions that make it possible to seek purchase of property, in its entirety or part, the use of which has been restricted, or payment of compensation. Article 130(2) of the EPA does not exclude the possibility of restrictions on the use of property due to planning solutions aimed at protecting natural resources. At the same time, in such cases Article 129(5) of the EPA excludes the possibility to make compensatory claims under Article 36 of the SPDA.[599] In case of the property use restriction referred to in Article 130(1), that is making areas or facilities subject to protection pursuant to the provisions of the NPA, the competent starost—upon the request of the injured party—sets, by means of a decision, the compensation amount. The decision may not be contested at that instance. The party not satisfied with the compensation granted may appeal against the decision in a common court within thirty days after having been served the said decision. The court may also be seized if the competent authority fails to issue the decision within three months after the request was made by the injured party. Launching a court case does not suspend the execution of the contested decision.[600]

The purchase demand in cases of restrictions on the use of property referred to in Article 130(1) of the EPA is regulated accordingly by the principles and procedure laid down in the IPMA.

Given the above, Mr Mad Hatter could seek compensation because of the possible consequences of the restrictions introduced near the Belle Coast. Also, it should be noted that under some conditions he could also make claims under civil law. He also has a legal interest in contesting the planning activities of local government bodies, if the restrictions have been applied as a result of their resolutions. If that is the case, he could request that such resolutions be declared invalid. Similarly, in line with general principles, he could complain before higher-instance bodies and competent administrative courts against the governmental administrative bodies that issued the contested decisions.[601] However, the list of actions the petitioner can think of taking is somewhat determined by the fact that certain restrictions stem directly from the provisions of Acts of law or Regulations. Consequently, in many cases lifting them would require a ruling on the incompatibility of the said provisions with the Polish Constitution or relevant Acts of law. Only such a ruling would result in opening the road towards seeking the invalidity of administrative decisions issued in individual cases.

[599] The claims formulated on the basis of art 129(1) and art 129(2) of the EPA are also subject to serious restrictions. Pursuant to art 129(4) of the EPA, they shall be made within three years since the entry into force of a regulation or a bye-law that enforces a restriction on the way immovable property is used. This means that, once that period lapses, the claims expire and the relevant obliged entity may meet them by making a natural commitment, yet no legal enforcement shall be made against it.

[600] See further W Radecki (ed), *Teoretyczne podstawy odnowy przyrody* (Wolters Kluwer 2006).

[601] Yet it should be remembered that if a spatial management plan resolution or a voivode's administrative decision is found invalid, the compensation received may need to be returned.

G. Portugal

RGdF

Mr Mad Hatter was affected by what were formerly in Portugal 'coastal planning instruments' and are now called 'coastal planning programmes', after the LPPSPU. These were special plans, and now, as programmes, they must be integrated in municipal planning.

In accordance with the LPPSPU, Article 171 of the LPIL determines that restrictions imposed on landowners by planning give them the right to claim damages if there is no other compensation possible (like urban-planning compensation, with the transfer of building rights to another parcel of land). The situation has some similarities with Mrs Sheraton's (see above). Mr Mad Hatter has pre-existing and solid legal rights, which need to be compensated, since the entry into force of the new planning rules determine the end of his licences/permits.

The compensation would be paid to Mr Mad Hatter according to the criteria of the CE, but other expenses that he incurred in order to adapt his land to the use laid down in the plan would also be covered as damages. But Mr Mad Hatter would have to be diligent: after the entry into force of the new plan, he only has three years to claim damages; after that, his right expires.

The result is the same even if Mr Mad Hatter is a foreign investor: the protection of his property rights is the same regardless of his nationality (Articles 15 and 62 of the Constitution). It is possible that one of the multiple bilateral investment treaties would place him in a better position than the general one granted by the Constitution and the laws, but never in a less protected situation.

H. Spain

LAJ and DUFB

Yet again, this case involves a limitation of the contents or substance of the right to property based on the underlying social function of the relevant category of assets (Article 33(2) CE, and see the chapter by L Arroyo Jiménez and D Utrilla Fernández-Bermejo, 'Procedural Requirements for Administrative Limits to Property Rights in Spain' in this volume). It resembles Spain—Case 8 regarding the artwork being declared an asset of cultural interest. A priori, Mr Mad Hatter could bring annulment and compensation claims. His chance to bring an annulment claim depends on how the measure was actually enacted.

From a procedural or formal standpoint, the new rules restricting the use of the area may have been provided either (i) in the declaration of Belle Coast as a natural protected area, thus subject to the relevant legal framework, which can be national (LPN and LPNB) or regional—stemming from any of the 17 regional governments—; or (ii) in an amendment to the local urban plan, which can also lay down a protection regime covering part of the municipal land on environmental grounds (Article 13(1) TRLSRU). In both cases we could assume the instrument for approval to be an administrative rule. Accordingly, Mr Mad Hatter could file an appeal with the administrative law courts seeking annulment (Article 25(1) LJCA). In the first case, it is nonetheless possible that the declaration as a natural protected area be made through a statutory provision passed by the national or a regional legislature. As already mentioned, Parliamentary statutes are not subject to appeal by citizens, neither before administrative law courts nor before the Constitutional Court. Thus, Mr Mad Hatter would have to challenge an act implementing the relevant statutory provision before an administrative law court in order for this judicial body to refer an exception of unconstitutionality (*cuestión de inconstitucionalidad*) to the Constitutional Court (Article 163 CE).[602]

From the perspective of substantive law, the measure will be valid if it fulfills a set of specific requirements, laid down in environmental and urban planning legislation, along with several general conditions: (i) there must be a well-reasoned public purpose, such as protecting natural heritage and biodiversity (Articles 45 CE and 4 LPNB); (ii) the relevant measure must pass the proportionality test, ie it must be suitable, necessary, and strictly proportional to achieve the aims pursued, although in recent rulings the Constitutional Court seems to have lowered this standard, solely applying a suitability test—rational basis review;[603] (iii) it must preserve the right's essence—to that end: Mr Mad Hatter should retain some sort of individual economic advantage and (iv) the demarcation of the protected site must abide by the principle of equality, ie, it must be based on objective and reasonable criteria.[604]

In the judicial appeal against the administrative provision restricting his right to use his property, Mr Mad Hatter cannot only seek annulment. He can also claim compensation for any loss or damage resulting from such restriction during the time period between the enactment of the measure and its judicial annulment. However, the right to compensation can be recognised even in the absence of judicial invalidation of the measure. Including land in a national park is a form of limiting the right to property based on its 'social function' (see the chapter by L Arroyo Jiménez and D Utrilla Fernández-Bermejo, 'Procedural Requirements for Administrative Limits to Property Rights in Spain' in this volume) which, on its own, does not give rise to compensation.[605] Nevertheless, the measure might be lawful—it might meet the aforesaid substantive requirements—and yet entail an 'extraordinary loss' or a 'distinct sacrifice' to be borne by Mr Mad Hatter; this 'sacrifice' can be of such intensity so as to breach the equality principle regarding equal contribution to public expenses and burdens. In that case, the provision—whether Parliamentary or administrative—would still be valid, but the enactment thereof gives rise to Mr Mad Hatter's right to compensation for any loss or damage. If the competent public authority declared the area a natural park under Article 7(5) LPN, the said right to compensation will fall within the scope of expropriation (Article 33(3) CE).

[602] JM Rodríguez de Santiago, 'Artículo 33' in ME Casas and M Rodríguez Piñero (eds), *Comentarios a la Constitución Española* (Wolters Kluwer/BOE 2018) 1170–72.

[603] STC 16/2018 and 32/2018.

[604] Rodríguez de Santiago (n 9) 1160–63.

[605] STC 170/1989, 28/197, and 248/2000.

Otherwise, it falls within the scope of public law non-contractual liability (Articles 106(2) CE and 48 TRLSRU). Mr Mad Hatter could thus receive compensation on the grounds that he is unable to recover his investment in Belle Coast. In this case, public authority liability is not triggered by unlawful or wrongful acts, but rather by the breach of Mr Mad Hatter's legitimate expectations. However, under this last ground, compensation will only amount to the actual loss suffered by the injured party (*interés negativo*).[606] Accordingly, the amount of compensation would hardly cover loss of profit resulting from Mr Mad Hatter's being precluded to run his resort under the initially provided terms.

If Mr Mad Hatter were a foreign investor covered by an investment treaty and he brought arbitration proceedings against the Kingdom of Spain, the Spanish constitutional and legal framework could be set aside. The substantive law applicable in this case will obviously depend on the applicable treaty, since expropriation standards might be very diverse.[607] Nonetheless, investment protection standards within international investment law tend to be more investor-friendly than Articles 33 and 106(2) CE. Although in Spain public authorities may be held liable for indirect expropriations, property's underlying 'social function' justifies greater restrictions when it comes to define the content of the right to private property than the ones usually admissible under most investment treaties. In any event, this statement would have to be verified having regard to the specific treaty under which Mr Mad Hatter files his claim.

I. Sweden

PJ

Mr Matter would have the possibility to ask for damages according to section 4, Chapter 31 of the Environmental Code (the chapter is entitled 'Compensation and Redemption Due to Certain Regulations, Injunctions and Prohibitions').

The kind of decision addressed to Mr Hatter—on measures and restrictions relating to nature and cultural reserves—entitles him to compensation.[608]

Mr Hatter would also have the right to the redemption of his property according to section 8, Chapter 31 of the Environmental Code, which states: 'if special inconveniences arise in the ongoing use of the property, the property owner has the right to have the property redeemed instead of receiving compensation'. The same rules apply to national and foreign investors.

[606] L Medina Alcoz, 'Confianza legítima y responsabilidad patrimonial' (2006) *130* Revista Española de Derecho Administrativo 275.

[607] SA Spears, 'Public Interest in International Investment Agreements' in C Brown and K Miles (eds), *Investment Treaty Law and Arbitration* (CUP 2011) 276–279; M Beltrán de Felipe, '¿Puede haber responsabilidad patrimonial de las Administraciones públicas al margen de la LRJAPyPAC? El arbitraje internacional de inversiones (y el estándar universal de trato justo y equitativo) como inesperado sustitutivo de la legislación interna' (2007) *16* Revista General de Derecho Administrativo 1.

[608] Indeed, according to this provision, the property owner is entitled to compensation due to a decision which means that land is utilised or that ongoing land use within the affected part of a property is considerably hampered.

J. Ukraine
HD

The Code of Administrative Proceedings of Ukraine provides that every person has a right to file a suit against the administrative court if he or she considers it within his or her rights and freedoms, or their legal interests have been infringed by the decision, action, or inaction of the competent authority. A person is entitled to claim for damage arising from the decision, action, or inaction of the competent authority (Article 5(1)).

Reimbursement of damages caused by the creation of a nature reserve is regulated by the Land Code of Ukraine[609] as well as the Law of Ukraine 'On the nature reserve fund of Ukraine'.[610] Damages (including loss of profit) have to be reimbursed if the right to use a plot of land is limited.[611]

Thus, if Mr Mad Hatter supposes that the decision is illegal, he could seek its annulment and sue for damages. If the decision was adopted in accordance with the law, Mr Mad Hatter could ask for damages, citing the limitation of his rights.

The Law of Ukraine 'On the regime of foreign investment' establishes a nationwide regime on this matter (Article 7). It sets out guarantees for investors if an investment is terminated. A foreign investor is entitled to have his or her investments returned.[612] So, if Matt Hatter were a foreign investor he could also ask for damages. Moreover, if he decides to terminate his investment activity he could have his investments returned.

K. The United Kingdom
EW

Natural England is responsible for identifying and protecting sites of special scientific interest (SSSIs) in England under the Wildlife and Countryside Act 1981 (WCA 1981). Under section 28 WCA 1981, Natural England has a duty to notify the local planning authority, or owners and occupiers of the land, and public bodies that the land is of special interest by reason of its flora, fauna, or geological or physiographical features.[613] The regime is set out in sections 28 to 33 of the WCA 1981.[614] Any notification under section 28(1) WCA 1981 must specify the time (not less than three months from the date of the notification) within which and the manner in which representations or objections to the order. Under sections 28F to 28L, owners and occupiers of and anyone with an interest in SSSIs can appeal against a decision by Natural England

[609] Land Code of Ukraine (25 October 2001 https://zakon.rada.gov.ua/laws/show/2768-14 (accessed 5 May 2021).

[610] Law of Ukraine 'On nature reserve fund of Ukraine' (16 June 1992) https://zakon.rada.gov.ua/laws/show/2456-12 (accessed 5 May 2021).

[611] Procedure for Determining and Reimbursement of Damages to Landowners and Land Users (19 April 1993) https://zakon.rada.gov.ua/laws/show/284-93-%D0%BF (accessed 5 May 2021).

[612] Law of Ukraine 'On Regime of Foreign Investment' (19 March 1996) https://zakon.rada.gov.ua/laws/show/93/96-%D0%B2%D1%80 (accessed 5 May 2021).

[613] https://jncc.gov.uk/our-work/guidelines-for-selection-of-sssis/ (accessed 26 February 2021).

[614] WCA 1981 as amended by the Countryside and Rights of Way Act 2000 and Natural Environment and Rural Communities Act 2006.

in relation to a refusal of consent to carry out an operation on the SSSI, the conditions imposed (including time limits), or a revocation or modification of an existing consent. Natural England can help owners to manage SSSIs and inform them of funding that is available.

A similar situation to the scenario occurred in *R (on the application of Trailer and Marina (Leven) Ltd v Secretary of State for the Environment, Food and Rural Affairs*.[615] Here, the Court of Appeal confirmed a High Court decision that statutory provisions relating to SSSIs *were* compatible with Article 1 of Protocol No 1 of the European Convention on Human Rights (A1P1) and that a fair balance had been struck between public interest and individual rights. The claimant bought the Leven canal, which was then designated as a SSSI and annual compensation was paid to the claimant in return for agreeing not to carry out commercial activities. Later legislative changes restricted the uses of such SSSIs, without requiring the payment of compensation for these further limitations. The claimant argued that the restrictions made the land virtually valueless and that the lack of compensation was a breach of A1P1. The Court of Appeal held that, whilst A1P1 normally required compensation when a deprivation occurred, there was no requirement for compensation in a control of use situation. In this case, which controlled the use of property in the public interest, a fair balance had to be struck between the general public interest and the individual rights. The government could properly take the view that the benefit to the community outweighed the detriment to the individual. The legislative provisions had been discussed in a consultation paper where the government noted that it was inappropriate to compensate landowners for agreeing not to carry out damaging operations because resources should be devoted to the encouragement of conservation. The SSSI scheme was not inherently incompatible with A1P1 and its provisions for the control of use of property did not amount to a disguised appropriation since the legislation was not so manifestly disproportionate that it offended against A1P1.

It would appear that the current scenario would be decided in a similar way. The imposition of further restrictions, as well as the absence of compensation, would not be automatically problematic from an A1P1 perspective in the English context. It would be open to the claimant to argue that the lack of compensation makes the restrictions disproportionately unjust. The line between expropriation and control is fraught and difficult to predict. The Supreme Court held in the *Mott* case that the 'distinction between expropriation and control is neither clear-cut, nor crucial to the analysis' since in that case the loss of 'at least 95% of the benefit… was clearly relevant to the fair balance'.[616]

If therefore all meaningful use of the land has been affected, it might be possible to categorise the actions as an unjust deprivation requiring compensation. However, given the wide margin of discretion afforded to public authorities imposing control of use restrictions, especially in an environmental capacity,[617] a challenge seems unlikely to succeed.

615 *R (on the application of Trailer and Marina (Leven) Ltd v Secretary of State for the Environment, Food and Rural Affairs* [2005] 1 WLR 1267.
616 *R (Mott) v Environment Agency* [2018] 1 WLR 1022, 1033.
617 *R (Mott) v Environment Agency* [2018] 1 WLR 1022, 1034.

L. The United States

IS

Mr Hatter could file a claim for a regulatory taking under the Fifth Amendment. Unless the regulation in question destroyed all the economic value of his property, the claim would be governed by the US Supreme Court's decision in *Penn Central Transportation Co v City of New York* (1978), which sets out three factors that must be weighed in determining whether a regulatory action that doesn't involve a physical invasion of property is a taking: 'The economic impact of the regulation on the claimant', the 'extent to which the regulation has interfered with distinct investment-backed expectations', and the 'character of the government action'.[618] Whether the restrictions on Mr Hatter's use of his property would qualify as a taking under the *Penn Central* test would require a complicated analysis of facts not included in the question, such as how much of an economic loss Mr Hatter would suffer as a result of the regulation. But, in general, application of the *Penn Central* test tends to favour the government.

If Mr Hatter were to win the case, he would get financial compensation for the 'fair market value' of the rights lost as a result of the regulation.[619]

It makes no difference whether Mr Hatter is a US citizen or a foreign investor. The takings clause protects the rights of all persons, not just US citizens, so long as the property in question is located in the United States.[620] There is an exception for situations where the government seizes the property of 'enemy aliens'—citizens of a nation with which the United States is at war.[621]

M. International investment law

FF

Rezoning decisions can lead investors to claim that the state has (a) committed regulatory expropriation or (b) frustrated their legitimate expectations and thus breached the fair and equitable treatment (FET) clause.

Changes to local laws or governmental decisions premised on public purposes can interfere with the right to use or profit from investments.

For example:

- the government repurposes the area of a port, frustrating the investor's plan to thereon operate a facility for off-loading tankers;[622]

[618] *Penn Central Transportation Co v City of New York* 438 US 104, 123 (1978).

[619] See discussion of the fair market value requirement earlier in this chapter.

[620] See eg *Russian Volunteer Fleet v United States* 282 US 481,489, 491–92(1931); *Ashkir v United States* 46 Fed Cl 438 (2000).

[621] See eg *Cummings v Deutsche Bank* 300 US 115, 120 (1937).

[622] *Mamidoil v Albania* ICSID Case No ARB/11/24 Award (30 March 2015). See Dissenting Opinion of Steven A Hammond, para 3.

- the minister passes a zoning order that freezes the designation for the land's use; the investor's pending request for a quarrying permit is therefore dead on arrival;[623]
- the state creates a national park, frustrating a mining company's plan to start extraction after exploration and construction;[624]
- the state develops a park for the protection of leatherback sea turtles, with expropriatory consequences on the investors' plots of land;[625]
- the state designates an area of archaeological interest, frustrating the investor's plan to build tourist and residential resorts.[626]

Two overarching principles emerged. First, the societal purpose alone cannot spare state measures from scrutiny.[627] Regulatory changes attributable to the state must respect international investment law (IIL), irrespective of their professed rationale. Secondly, investors cannot count on local laws staying immutable: host states can 'decide [their] urban policies and legislation'.[628] Compliance with laws at a given time cannot insure against future changes. Conversely, when state authorities make representations raising legitimate expectations of stability to the investors,[629] their FET and expropriation claims are viable when laws change without notice and damage their business.

Foreign investors often invoke the wrongfulness of zoning and rezoning measures.[630] The two principles introduced above influence the assessment. Assuming a damage to the investor, it must be determined whether compensation follows automatically ('sole effects' doctrine) or depends on the measure's design and purpose. Merely invoking environmental protection will not be a sufficient defence for the state.[631] Merely proving an unexpected loss will not vindicate the investor's claim (a point that is increasingly made explicit in treaties[632]). The outcome typically flows from the tribunal's discretionary assessment of the state measure with respect to both elements (impact and purpose[633]), rendered through nuanced arguments (using proportionality) or heuristic classification (referring to police powers). Until recently, express mentions to proportionality and police powers have been absent in IIL treaties.

[623] *St Mary's v Government of Canada* (NAFTA/UNCITRAL) Consent Award (29 March 2013).

[624] *Cosigo v Colombia* UNCITRAL Statement of Claim (19 February 2016) para 15.

[625] *Berkowitz v Costa Rica* ICSID Case No UNCT/13/2 Interim Award (30 May 2017) para 2. See also *Unglaube* (n 332); *Santa Elena* (n 329) (the *Santa Elena* and *Unglaube* cases concern an instance of direct expropriation).

[626] See IIL Case 8 above.

[627] *Tecmed* (n 53) para 121.

[628] *MTD v Chile* ICSID Case No ARB/01/7 Award (25 May 2004) para 98.

[629] *Mamidoil* (n 622) para 705.

[630] F Ortino, *The Origin and Evolution of Investment Treaty Standards: Stability, Value, and Reasonableness* (OUP 2019) 57 notes an early commentator wondering 'where indirect deprivation of property ends and, for instance, planning legislation, or property law reform begins'. See G Schwarzenberger, 'The Abs-Shawcross Draft Convention on Investment Abroad: A Critical Commentary' (1960) 9 JPL 147, 157.

[631] *Vivendi v Argentina* ICSID Case No ARB/97/3 Award (20 August 2007) para 7.5.21.

[632] See eg EU–Vietnam Investment Protection Agreement (2019, not in force), Understanding on Expropriation (Annex 4), art 2.a; EU–Singapore Investment Protection Agreement 2018, art 2.2.

[633] *Glamis Gold* (n 490) para 356; *Total v Argentina* ICSID Case No ARB/04/01 Decision on Liability (27 December 2010) fn 232.

However, recourse to these notions has been inevitable in arbitration, not so much as unwritten sources of law but rather as argumentative devices:

> [n]otwithstanding that [the BIT provision on expropriation] does not provide for proportionality as a core guarantee towards the investment, the undersigned has no doubt that a literal interpretation contrary to the spirit of the rule would be untenable, since proportionality is an element underlying various of the difficulties that would ensue and the damages claimed.[634]

Ultimately, both proportionality and police powers point to a basic principle, which underpins the FET standard as well: state action cannot unduly restrict individual rights:

> [a] finding of a violation of the FET standard necessarily entails a determination that the State exceeded its reasonable right to regulate, and to interfere with investors' rights. There is no need for a separate, 'duplicative' assessment of the State's right to regulate under the police powers doctrine.[635]

1. Breach of legitimate expectations and other FET standards

Regulatory autonomy must be exercised within the limits set by international obligations. The badge of 'police powers' does not spare state actions from scrutiny; rather, it is pinned on acts that are proportionate and respectful of due process.[636] Immunity by labelling is not a viable option: IIL compliance is not inherent in regulatory action but rather gained by diligent exercise.[637]

State measures damaging the investor's industrial plans, while lawful in principle, might breach IIL if they renege on specific representations upon which the investor relied to make the investment (breach of legitimate expectations). The notion of legitimate expectations considers both the investor's need for stability and the state's right to adapt its law: 'Both aspects have to be balanced when establishing the right point in time during a long and complex process from when a State is restricted in the use of its sovereign power and the investor is protected.'[638] For instance, states approving an investment, create an expectation that it complies with applicable urban regulations.[639] A licence can generate a valid expectation that the investment will not be subsequently threatened by its revocation or withdrawal, even if domestic law would permit them.[640]

[634] *South American Silver* (n 68) Separate Opinion of Orrego Vicuña (30 August 2018) para 4. See also *MTD* (n 628) para 109; *Armas* (n 279) para 342.

[635] *United Utilities v Estonia* ICSID Case No ARB/14/24 Award (21 June 2019) para 767.

[636] *Tza Yap Shum v Peru* ICSID Case No ARB/07/6 Award (7 July 2011) para 174.

[637] *Serafín Armas* (n 24) paras 291, 342.

[638] *Mamidoil* (n 16) para 703.

[639] *MTD* (n 628) para 166. Conversely, the investor must bear the consequences of negligence if it ignored applicable urban legislation: see ibid para 178; *Tulip v Turkey* ICSID Case No ARB/11/28 Award (10 March 2014) paras 403–405.

[640] *Mamidoil* (n 16) para 726, citing also *Tecmed*(n 53) paras 120–21; *Eureko v Poland*, Ad hoc, Partial Award (19 August 2005) paras 231–34; *MTD* (n 628) paras 165–66.

In the absence of specific undertakings (through licences, representations or promises), investors must accept that land is subject to expropriation for environmental protection: 'lawful expropriation for urban planning (with compensation) is a business risk to be accepted by a foreign investor ... just as it must be for a domestic' one.[641]

Even without asserting frustration of expectations, investors could challenge state measures—including the designation of the territory as environmentally protected—under other FET standards (eg reasonableness, due process, transparency, non-discrimination).[642]

For instance, an investor attacked the creation of a national park that stifled its operations, alleging arbitrariness and discrimination: '[n]o geographic and environmental features to be purportedly protected by the National Park can be found in the Claimants' property. By contrast, other properties that would affect the Baiguate Waterfall and its river were expressly excluded from the National Park'.[643]

2. Expropriation

Formal expropriation's public purpose does not spare states from compensation duties. In fact, public purpose and compensation are equally necessary for the expropration's lawfulness.

When investors challenge the effects of regulatory changes, instead, the adequacy of compensation is never at stake, because there was none by definition. States passing regulations do not frame them as expropriatory; compensation is not on the cards. Rather, the damaged subject raises the equation between regulation and expropriation, for tribunals to validate or reject. Accepting the equation simply based on the act's effects ('sole effects') renders the regulatory purpose irrelevant expand indefinitely the range of state acts amounting to partial or total expropriation. Commenting on *Metalclad*, the Supreme Court of British Columbia noted that: '[t]he Tribunal gave an extremely broad definition of expropriation [including] covert or incidental interference with the use of property ... This definition is sufficiently broad *to include a legitimate rezoning of property by a municipality or other zoning authority*'.[644] The 'sole effects' test, therefore, is normally reserved for properly expropriatory acts (whether openly or covertly so).[645] Regulatory measures are commonly assessed differently, through tests that accept that lawful measures can produce negative externalities on economic activities: 'As a matter of principle, general regulations, even if having negative effect on an investor's property, are not to be considered as expropriatory'.[646]

First, an accepted *de minimis* threshold applies to expropriation. There is no expropriation when investors suffer less than permanent,[647] 'substantial deprivation'[648] of the

[641] *Beheer v Poland* PCA Case No 2013-01 Partial Award (29 April 2014) para 352.

[642] *Ballantine* (n 426), Award (3 September 2019) para 341.

[643] ibid para 372.

[644] *Mexico v Metalclad* 2001 BCSC 664, 89 BCLR (3d) 359, para 99 (emphasis added).

[645] *Yukos* (n 190) paras 1579–80; *Middle East Cement v Egypt*, Award (12 April 2002) para 107; *Santa Elena* (n 329).

[646] *Oxus v Uzbekistan* UNCITRAL Final Award (17 December 2015) para 740.

[647] *Burlington* (n 548) paras 471–73.

[648] *Pope & Talbot v Canada* (NAFTA, UNCITRAL) Interim Award (26 June 2000) para 102.

value or the economic benefit[649] of their investments.[650] Slicing investments down to their components to argue deprivation of each separately is normally to no avail.[651] Claims under other IIL standards, especially FET, remain possible.[652] Conversely, substantial and permanent losses caused by administrative measures can amount to expropriation:

> in the absence of the concessions, which were NMM's raison d'être, the Claimants' investment in NMM was virtually worthless ... this deprivation was permanent and was not justified by the police powers doctrine ... the revocation of the concessions indirectly expropriated Quiborax of the value of its investments.[653]

Secondly, more general state measures are less likely to constitute expropriation.[654] This rule of thumb builds on the intuition that harming investors is not the aim, but at most the collateral damage of genuine regulations pursuing public goals. These measures thus fall within the state's exercise of police powers.[655] Conversely, a similar specificity test applies to the investor's expectations: if they are distinct and reasonable[656] the finding of expropriation is more likely.[657] In other words, expropriation is more probable if the measure targets one investment (specificity of harm) or a general measure frustrates a tailored promise (specificity of expectation). Recent IIL instruments list these specificity cues when defining indirect expropriation:

> [a determination of indirect expropriation requires consideration of] the extent to which the measure or series of measures interferes with *distinct* and reasonable expectations arising out of investments ...
>
> Except in rare circumstances, such as when a measure or a series of measures of a Contracting Party is extremely severe or disproportionate in light of its purpose, *non-discriminatory measures* of a Contracting Party that are designed and applied to protect legitimate public welfare objectives, such as public health, safety and the environment do not constitute indirect expropriation.[658]

Thirdly, if a measure's positive effects exceed its harmful impact, tribunals are more likely to consider it a legitimate exercise of police powers. General legislation applied

[649] *Occidental v Ecuador* LCIA Case No UN3467 Award (1 July 2004) para 89.
[650] *Gami v Mexico* (NAFTA, UNCITRAL) Final Award (15 November 2003) para 126; *Glamis Gold* (n 490) para 536.
[651] *Electrabel v Hungary* ICSID Case No ARB/07/19 Award (25 November 2015) para 6.57; *Dreyfus v India* PCA Case No 2014-26 Award (11 September 2018) para 419.
[652] See eg *9REN v Spain* ICSID Case No ARB/15/15 Award (31 May 2019) para 370.
[653] *Quiborax* (n 69) para 239.
[654] The taxonomy in this section is inspired by Y Zhu, 'Do Clarified Indirect Expropriation Clauses in International Investment Treaties Preserve Environmental Regulatory Space?' (2019) *60* Harv Intl LJ 377.
[655] *Saluka* (n 282) para 255.
[656] On expectations' reasonableness/legitimacy, the FET practice can serve as guidance. States occasionally regulate future contingencies in more detail. The Annex on Expropriation of the Uzbekistan–South Korea BIT (2019, not in force) reads: '[f]or example, an investor's expectations that regulations will not change are less likely to be reasonable in a heavily regulated sector than in a less heavily regulated sector.'
[657] *Bear Creek* (n 53) paras 375, 451.
[658] Japan–Morocco BIT, Annex to art 9, art 3(b), 4 (emphasis added); Canada–Peru FTA, Annex 812.1, (b)(ii), (c).

consistently and evincing a plausible purpose—like environmental protection—typically passes this test. Accordingly, no compensation is due, irrespective of the damage caused to specific investors. Bona fide regulatory changes can cause disproportionate suffering to investors. A NAFTA tribunal, commenting on a public ban on a harmful chemical, concluded that:

> the [regulatory agency] took measures within its mandate, in a non-discriminatory manner, motivated by the increasing awareness of the dangers presented by lindane for human health and the environment. A measure adopted under such circumstances is a valid exercise of the State's police powers and, as a result, does not constitute an expropriation.[659]

Zoning authorities denying or withdrawing building permits might apply general rules, but state measures are aimed at specific investments. It is difficult, therefore, to distinguish indirect expropriation (based on the 'sole effects' doctrine) from legitimate regulatory action. The 'specificity' test yields mixed results: a specific measure flows from general law. In *Invesmart*, the tribunal found that revoking a bank's licence occurred under a generally applicable law that was 'a bona fide non-discriminatory regulation aimed at the general welfare'.[660]

Regulatory expropriation, ultimately, is rarely found in connection with general legislation pursuing genuine public interests.

[659] *Chemtura v Canada* (NAFTA, UNCITRAL) Award (2 August 2010) para 266; *Methanex v USA* (NAFTA, UNCITRAL) Award (3 August 2005) para 15.

[660] *Invesmart v Czech Republic* (UNCITRAL, Ad hoc) Award (26 June 2009) para 269.

PART IV
COMPARATIVE ANALYSIS

16

Comparative Perspectives on Expropriation and Other Takings

England, France, Germany, and the United States

*Vincent Martenet**

I. Introduction

In many countries, administrative limits to property rights are subject to procedural requirements. These limits may be anchored in constitutions or statutes. State interference regarding property rights is usually subject to procedural or substantive boundaries framed by human and fundamental rights. These boundaries or limits may also result from case law, so a comparative study of countries with different legal traditions is interesting in this context. However, constitutional or legal provisions are normally drafted in rather broad terms and leave a certain margin of appreciation to administrative authorities. Consequently, case law in many countries, including the four compared in this chapter, provides useful insight as to the actual meaning and scope of these requirements.

There are many administrative limits to property rights, and the most salient issue in this regard relates to land expropriation. Procedural requirements not only differ among jurisdictions but within a given jurisdiction; such requirements also differ depending on the administrative limits imposed. This 'double diversity' makes both intra-jurisdictional and inter-jurisdictional comparisons particularly interesting. That procedural requirements are imposed in several countries for a certain type of administrative limit to property rights may signal the need for reforms in another country where similar limits are lacking. This invites reflection on property rights from a comparative and procedural perspective, considering the historical, constitutional, legal, and judicial context prevailing in each country, as each country's history and legal order shape the protection and regulation of property and vice versa. Accordingly, a comparative study of countries with a strong normative history, notably regarding property, sparks a high level of interest. In England, France, Germany, and the United States, many issues relating to expropriation in the broad sense have been addressed by legislatures and courts over decades or even centuries—notably from a procedural perspective.

The four countries selected for this comparative analysis share many commonalities and some distinctive features regarding procedural requirements for administrative limits to property rights. Although similarities may be noted, the four countries differ in terms of their constitutional and statutory framework (section II) and how their courts

* The author would like to thank Emma Guernaoui, Foroud Shirvani, Ilya Somin, and Emma JL Waring for their extremely helpful comments.

Vincent Martenet, *Comparative Perspectives on Expropriation and Other Takings* In: *Procedural Requirements for Administrative Limits to Property Rights*. Edited by: Martina Conticelli And Thomas Perroud, Oxford University Press. © Vincent Martenet 2022.
DOI: 10.1093/oso/9780198867586.003.0016

and authorities deal with administrative limits to property rights (section III). Some cross-cutting issues highlight various commonalities and differences and may even challenge the general view of procedural requirements for certain administrative limits to property rights (section IV). Lastly, on the basis of this comparison, some fundamental remarks can be made regarding property and its limits from a procedural point of view (section V).

II. The constitutional and statutory framework

In terms of their constitutional and statutory framework, England, France, Germany, and the US differ to varying degrees. A comparative study is therefore difficult and must be conducted very carefully. One interesting approach, which this chapter adopts, consists in examining the nature of the key procedural requirements for administrative limits to property rights. Written laws, especially statutes, seem almost inevitable, considering the fundamental issues raised by expropriation, its political dimension, and the need for some transparency and predictability for property owners.

In England, land expropriation is known as compulsory purchase and is not based on a constitutional provision, as England has no written constitution. Historically, compulsory purchase was derived from a combination of legislative powers, prerogative powers, and judicial decisions. Nowadays, it is governed almost exclusively by a number of statutes. The highly fragmented legal landscape relating to compulsory purchase is noteworthy, with many general statutes coming into play. This characteristic of English law highlights the need for consolidated legislation on this issue to avoid legislation spreading among an array of statutes. Moreover, specific compulsory purchase laws apply in Scotland and Northern Ireland, while in Wales the rules are basically the same as in England. Lastly, it is worth mentioning that the incorporation of the European Convention on Human Rights (especially Article 1 of Protocol No 1) through the Human Rights Act 1998 (HRA 1998) applies to compulsory purchase law in England. Thus English courts will, when considering whether or not there is 'a compelling case in the public interest' for the specific compulsory purchase scheme, consider the impact that it will have on the human rights of those affected by the proposed acquisition.[1]

In France, Article 17 of the Declaration of the Rights of Man and of the Citizen guarantees the right of property in these terms: 'Property being an inviolable and sacred right, no one can be deprived of private usage, if it is not when the public necessity, legally noted, evidently requires it, and under the condition of a just and prior indemnity.' A Code of Expropriation for Causes of Public Utility unites the legislative and regulatory provisions relating to expropriation. This Code contains many strict rules applicable to expropriation decisions in France. French regions, departments, or communes may not enact laws relating to expropriation. In other words, expropriation legislation is solely national in France.

In Germany, Article 14 section 3 of the German Basic Law contains a provision on expropriation for reasons of the public good:

[1] See Department for Levelling Up, Housing & Communities' *Guidance on Compulsory purchase process and The Crichel Down Rules* (2019), p 12.

> Expropriation shall only be permissible for the public good. It may only be ordered by or pursuant to a law that determines the nature and extent of compensation. Such compensation shall be determined by establishing an equitable balance between the public interest and the interests of those affected. In case of dispute concerning the amount of compensation, recourse may be had to the ordinary courts.

According to case law, the constitutional term 'expropriation' is narrowly interpreted and does not cover, for instance, prohibitions or restrictions of use provided for in laws concerning building or nature conservation. Such restrictions are qualified as determinations of the content and limits of property (Article 14 section 1, sentence 2, of the German Basic Law). The German *Bundesländer* have enacted expropriation laws that implement the requirements of Article 14 section 3 of the German Basic Law. They regulate the expropriation procedure, while other provisions relating to expropriation are found in various laws at Federation or *Bundesländer* level.

In the United States, the Takings Clause of the Fifth Amendment of the Federal Constitution and similar provisions in the state constitutions preclude taking private property without just compensation. The Fifth Amendment also limits the use of eminent domain to property for public use. The US Supreme Court interprets this notion broadly.[2] In reaction, states have amended their constitutions or adopted new statutory laws that notably ban many types of takings transferring property to private parties; since the *Kelo* decision of the Supreme Court in 2005, there are vast differences between states in this regard. In essence, the individual states' statutes play a decisive role in expropriation as they define the conditions under which an expropriation is lawful. In addition to the Takings Clause, the Fifth and Fourteenth Amendments also preclude federal and state governments from depriving individuals of property without due process of law.

III. Commonalities and differences among the countries under comparison

A. Commonalities

In all four countries compared, expropriation or a similar institution must be authorised by a specific statutory provision.[3] In other words, the acquiring authority must possess the statutory power to expropriate land. This may be considered a fundamental requirement resulting from the rule of law or, in the continental European context, from the *Rechtsstaat* or the *État de droit*.

Expropriation is usually limited to cases of public use or that are in the public interest, though these notions may be broadly or narrowly interpreted by courts. With some exceptions, notice of expropriation is normally required, and basic procedural guarantees of due process must be respected. Expropriation decisions must be reasoned, and challenges may normally be brought by way of judicial review. Owners must be able to contest the legality of any expropriation, and when applicable conditions are

[2] *Berman v Parker* 348 US 26 (1954); *Kelo v City of New London* 545 US 469 (2005).
[3] Regarding the United States see eg *Delaware L & W R Co v Town of Morristown* 276 US 182 (1928).

met, just compensation—usually based on fair or open market value—is due.[4] If an expropriation or another taking is found to be illegal due to lack of public use or interest, then the expropriation decision is annulled by the seized court. Violation of procedural requirements may also lead to an annulment or to the repetition of procedural steps in compliance with the applicable laws.

The nationality of the condemned expropriated owners is, in principle, irrelevant in all four countries. Nationals and foreigners are both protected, for instance, by due process or similar requirements in expropriation proceedings. Bilateral investment treaties may however apply in specific cases and may contain special rules benefiting foreign investors. In such a case, the investment itself is usually protected rather than the property as such.

B. Differences

Many important or minor differences exist among the four countries compared. As described above,[5] the constitutional and legal framework differs considerably from one country to another. Moreover, depending on the country, the power to expropriate land can be either centralised or decentralised. This power usually belongs to government and other public bodies, but may even be granted to private entities under certain specific circumstances. This issue is extremely important, as granting this power is one—if not the most—essential feature of the expropriation regimes in any of the countries in question.

In England, two statutory stages must be distinguished: (i) legislation empowering authorised entities to acquire land compulsorily for a specified purpose; and (ii) legislation setting out the relevant acquisition procedures, such as making and confirming a Compulsory Purchase Order (CPO) under the Acquisition of Land Act 1981 as amended (ALA 1981). Various Acts of Parliament enable public bodies to acquire land by compulsory purchase, and it is possible for an Act of Parliament to give such powers to a private entity.[6] However, the power to make a compulsory purchase of land is normally given to a public body, for example a local authority. Private entities are then normally involved at the second stage, ie in exercising the power. For instance, section 226(4) of the Town and Country Planning Act 1990 (TCPA 1990) grants a local authority power to acquire land but 'it is immaterial by whom the local authority propose that any activity or purpose … [relating to the project] should be undertaken or achieved'. This allows a local authority to use its powers of compulsory purchase to then involve private entities in exercising and

[4] Regarding the United States (fair market value) see eg *Kirby Forest Industries Inc v United States* 467 US 1, 10 (1984). In England (open market value), the Land Compensation Act 1961 uses the notion of 'open market value', which is based on the principle of equivalence, ie that the owner should not be worse or better off after the acquisition. In assessing the open market value, the evaluation is supposed to ignore any increase or decrease in the land's value attributable to the development scheme that underlies the compulsory purchase order. Other payments can, however, be made in addition to land value, eg disturbance payments, severance where some land is retained, fees for surveyors, etc.

[5] See section II above.

[6] See eg the various statutes relating to the Channel Tunnel or the Crossrail Act 2009.

implementing the scheme.[7] English law seems open regarding the involvement of private entities in expropriation matters.

In France, the state is entitled to expropriate. Local and regional authorities also have this right, but need the agreement of the state's services. Private entities providing a public service and private organisations pursuing a public purpose also may expropriate where an expropriation is necessary for the accomplishment of their mission. Nevertheless, most expropriation decisions are made by the state or require its agreement in some form.[8] Not surprisingly, in terms of expropriation rules, France has the most centralised system of the countries compared in this study.

In Germany, most of the expropriation decisions are made at the local level of the *Bundesländer*. Expropriation is primarily regulated by laws of the *Bundesländer* which also designate the competent expropriation authority. In principle, legal actions against expropriation measures may be taken in local administrative courts at first instance. The Federation *(Bund)* may expropriate for certain major projects, as envisaged by some federal statutes. Private entities may not initiate an expropriation procedure but can be the beneficiaries if they implement a project in the interest of the public good.

In the United States, governments at all levels can expropriate property to build public infrastructure, public buildings or public utilities. However, most decisions to expropriate are taken at the local or state level. An expropriation can be decided, at least in certain states, for developing a private project for public use. Private entities do sometimes have the delegated power to use eminent domain in the United States. This may be allowed, nowadays, for pipeline owners, and—historically—has been allowed for railway companies, among other businesses.[9]

Lastly, an expropriation procedure may coexist with a nationalisation procedure in certain countries, but not in others. The very notion of nationalisation may not even exist in some countries such as the United States or England, where nationalisation schemes have not been used. When it exists, a nationalisation procedure cannot, as a rule, be launched in order to avoid procedural or substantive requirements relating to expropriation. Moreover, nationalisation—in France, for instance—concerns private companies and regards shares in the latter, not any land they may own.

IV. Some cross-cutting issues

A. Due process in various contexts

1. Urban planning

The adoption or revision of urban plans may have a significant impact on property and its possible use. Participatory or specific procedural requirements may exist in many

[7] See Supreme Court, *R (Sainsbury's Supermarkets Ltd) v Wolverhampton City Council* [2011] 1 AC 437. On this case see EJL Waring, 'Private-to-private Takings and the Stability of Property' (2013) 24(2) King's LJ 237.

[8] See C-S Marchiani, *Le monopole de l'Etat sur l'expropriation* (LGDJ/Thèses 2008).

[9] See I Somin, 'Eminent Domain in the United States' in I Kim, H Lee, and I Somin (eds), *Eminent Domain: A Comparative Perspective* (CUP 2017) 38–66.

countries. These are, however, not equivalent to guarantees of procedural due process. In several countries, such as the United States, urban planning is not assimilated to proceedings where procedural guarantees of due process apply as such. In England, neighbourhood development orders can only be challenged at specific stages in the urban planning procedure. However, the involvement of citizens in urban planning procedures is increasingly allowed or even favoured in many countries, including the four compared in this study. Community participation especially concerns the local level of government.

In England, the 2011 Localism Act strengthened neighbourhood planning at a more local level, allowing communities to influence the development of local areas and encourage community participation. It is, for instance, possible to challenge compulsory purchase orders, and there are public local inquiries that can be held to deal with objections, or where written representations may be made. A property owner whose land has been included in a list of assets of community value may apply for this inclusion to be reviewed under section 92 of the Localism Act, for example. Normal administrative law protections (eg judicial review) have not been ousted by the Act, so it is possible for a community group (or a property owner) to challenge a decision by requesting judicial review on grounds of bias or irrelevant consideration, for example.

In France, participatory procedure in urban planning exists at local level. When a given planning includes some land expropriation, participation is carried out through mandatory 'public inquiries' prior to a declaration of public utility. The project must be publicised, and all documents in the file must be made available to the public. This allows for interaction between citizens and those responsible for urban projects. Property owners whose land may be expropriated are treated the same way as in other expropriation procedures. When a given urban planning does not imply any expropriation, a participatory procedure is optional, and property owners directly affected by an urban planning project may invoke some rights in the planning proceedings and challenge the plan, but these rights are much less protective than the ones in usual administrative proceedings leading to individual decisions.

In Germany, the public must be involved when a land-use plan is adopted or amended.[10] The public must, as early as possible, receive information about general aims and purposes of planning, different planning solutions, and expected effects of the planning. The public must have the opportunity to comment on and discuss the plan.[11] Affected property owners may invoke some specific rights in urban planning proceedings, and the building planning authority must take these rights into account.

In the United States, some state and local governments have created opportunities for citizens to comment and participate in urban planning proceedings. Procedural guarantees of due process are not applicable as such, and property owners cannot invoke them in these proceedings, even if they are directly affected by the planning at stake, except when their land is expropriated, of course.

Considering the implications of urban planning on property owners, the involvement of the owners and other stakeholders seems to be justified. A purely top-down approach creates tensions and problems that can hinder sound urban planning. From this perspective, some bottom-up features seem recommendable, if not required by

[10] *Baugesetzbuch* (BauGB, Federal Building Code), §§ 1 sec 8 and 3.

[11] ibid § 3 sec 1 sentence 1.

applicable constitutional or statutory provisions. This, however, is not to say that due process requirements should—fully—apply to urban planning. Some *sui generis* procedural requirements may be appropriate in order to find the right balance between, inter alia, the protection of property value and the legitimate need to plan for land use.

2. Urgent situations

In urgent situations, the occupation or even destruction of private property by law enforcement is usually not treated as expropriation but is regarded as the exercise of police power. It is regulated by rules other than those applicable to land expropriation. Compensation may or may not be required, depending on the applicable laws and the concrete circumstances of each case.

In England, under the Civil Contingencies Act 2004 (CCA), emergency regulations can include 'providing for or enabling the requisition or confiscation of property, with or without compensation'.[12] Courts are likely to accept a restriction on due process requirements when Parliament has approved emergency regulations. The CCA cannot, however, amend or abridge the 1998 HRA, which incorporates the European Convention on Human Rights into domestic law. Courts could, therefore, declare any emergency regulations adopted by the Government to be legally invalid where these contradict protections secured by the HRA.[13] With respect to an Act of Parliament, however, courts are only allowed to make a declaration of incompatibility under Section 4 HRA. In practice, the Covid-19 pandemic has demonstrated the potential weakness of these protections. The government did not trigger the CCA but instead brought in new legislation under Coronavirus Act 2020, which was based on a public health mandate but has fewer checks than the CCA. For example, most of the emergency measures in Coronavirus Act 2020 are limited to two years (compared to the normal thirty-day period during which such regulations last under the CCA).

In France, a requisition ordered by local or national authorities in an emergency situation is coercive. The affected person must comply with the order but is protected by various guarantees. The order must be reasoned and written—although it may provisionally be verbal, and there may be exceptions.[14] It is notified to its addressee. If an administrative court concludes that the requisition order was not justified by the emergency and contrary to the principle of proportionality, the state may be held liable, and damages may be claimed. However, when litigation arises, judges tend to rule in favour of the administration. By way of example, the expropriated party may attack the declaration of public utility by means of a summary suspension (emergency referral to the administrative judge). Few requests are successful since only a 'sufficiently serious and immediate' infringement of the applicant's rights allows for the suspension of the administrative act permitting the expropriation.[15]

In Germany, temporary occupation of a piece of land by the police can constitute a seizure under police and security laws. Such a seizure may be carried out to avert a current danger. It must not unreasonably and excessively burden the affected owner.[16]

[12] CCA 2004, s 22(3)(b).
[13] ibid s 30(2).
[14] Council of State decision *Chavat* (2015) Rec 62.
[15] Council of State decision *Confédération nationale des radios libres* (2001) Rec P 29.
[16] See BVerfGE 122, 374, 391–92 (2009).

In other words, a proportionality test is required. If the interference with property, such as a police seizure, is unlawful, the owner must file a complaint with the administrative court. If the court considers the seizure to be unlawful, the owner is entitled in principle to claim compensation under state liability law.

In the United States, the occupation or even destruction of private property by law enforcement as part of an operation to prevent crime or maintain public order does not require compensation.[17] In other urgent situations, government occupation and destruction of property may qualify as a compensable taking, especially if the property was not itself the source of the threat to the public.

In specific situations, the distinction between the exercise of police power and taking may prove to be blurred in many countries, including the four compared here. A case-by-case approach would be preferable in order to determine whether or not the concrete circumstances of a given case justify proper compensation. The discussion should not be framed in rigid legal categories, and the exercise of police actions, where any compensation is categorically excluded at the outset, should be significantly limited.

B. Public utility and private facilities

One of the most sensitive issues with respect to the expropriation of land relates to the creation or expansion of *private* facilities. Intuitively, one may think that expropriation typically benefits public infrastructures or facilities. However, the public nature of the use or of the interest—rather than the public nature of the facilities at stake—is usually at the core of expropriation laws. Accordingly, the reality is more complex and nuanced, as one would expect.

In England, an acquiring authority can use its powers of compulsory acquisition to benefit a private company. Section 226(1) TCPA 1990 provides local authorities with broad powers to make a compulsory acquisition of land where the authority is satisfied that the expropriation will, for instance, contribute to the promotion or improvement of the economic, social, or environmental well-being of the local area. Section 226(4) TCPA 1990 also allows for schemes to be carried out by private companies or entities, such as private hospitals, so there is no need, in such a case, for the public body to carry out the scheme itself, remembering that the compulsory purchase of land will normally be decided by a local authority.[18]

In France, as mentioned above,[19] private entities providing a public service, and private organisations pursuing a public purpose, may also expropriate when necessary for the accomplishment of their mission. Constructing a private hospital contributes, in principle, to improving the health system. According to the case law of the Council of State, the fact that the project only concerns private health care facilities does not cause it to lose its character of general interest.[20] It is widely accepted that

[17] See eg *Lech v Jackson* 719 Fed Appx 711 (10th Cir 2019).
[18] See section III.B above.
[19] ibid.
[20] Council of State decision *Société du Tertre Rouge* (2005) Rec T 922; Juris Data N 069125.

private actors can work in the same way as public law bodies when the circumstances justify it, particularly in matters of health or road infrastructure.

In Germany, an expropriation decision may transfer a plot of land from a private party to another one. Private projects can serve the public good; indeed, constructing a public or private hospital usually constitutes a public interest. The measure could nevertheless prove disproportionate if health care is already sufficiently available in the area, or if another plot of land is manifestly more suitable, due—for instance—to better accessibility.

In the United States, some states also allow for the expropriation of private property for transfer to private parties, simply to promote 'economic development'.[21] In many states, private facilities offering public benefits such as healthcare may qualify as 'public uses' under the state constitution and statutory laws.[22] Other states are more restrictive and do not allow expropriation of private property in favour of private parties.

With regard to public utility and private facilities, a nuanced approach is probably appropriate. On the one hand, private actors often provide essential services to the public, such as private hospitals and transport infrastructures. In these cases, expropriation of neighbouring properties should not categorically be excluded. On the other hand, the sole promotion of economic development—a fortiori by private parties—may not be deemed sufficient to justify expropriation, even with just compensation.

C. Regulatory taking

Regulatory taking is a very difficult issue in many jurisdictions. Identifying general rules in this matter seems challenging, as the relevant circumstances of each case play an important role in the legal analysis. Compensation is, in principle, not excluded upfront, but rather limited to specific situations where all or most of the meaningful use of property is suppressed. As we describe, it seems that, in all four countries compared here, administrative practice and case law are very restrictive in this respect. One may wonder whether property is *de facto* and *in concreto* sufficiently protected.

In England, the line between expropriation and control of use, where there is typically no requirement for compensation, is blurred. In the *Mott* case, the Supreme Court held that the 'distinction between expropriation and control is neither clear-cut, nor crucial to the analysis' since in that case the loss of 'at least 95% of the benefit ... was clearly relevant to the fair balance'.[23] In other words, the suppression of almost all meaningful use of land may qualify as an unjust deprivation requiring compensation. However, the chance of success of a challenge seems remote due to the wide margin of discretion afforded to public authorities imposing control of use restrictions, especially in an environmental capacity.[24] The other area in which this issue has been raised tangentially is in relation to adverse possession of land. The Grand Chamber of the European Court of Human Rights decided in 2007 that the

[21] See I Somin, *The Grasping Hand:* Kelo v City of New London *and the Limits of Eminent Domain* (rev edn, University of Chicago Press 2016) ch 7.

[22] ibid ch 5.

[23] *R (Mott) v Environment Agency* [2018] 1 WLR 1022, 1033.

[24] ibid 1034.

laws relating to adverse possession were a justified limitation and control of use rather than compensable deprivation.[25]

In France, deprivation of the right to property, in particular due to expropriation, must be distinguished from the infringement or limitation of this right. In the latter case, compensation can only be claimed if the limitation is 'so serious that the resulting infringement of the right to property distorts the meaning and scope of this right guaranteed by Article 17 of the Declaration of the Rights of Man and of the Citizen'.[26] There may be special rules in some statutes. The classification of a site under the Environmental Code, for instance, 'can give right to compensation to the benefit of the owner if it entails a modification to the state or the use of the premises determining a direct, material and certain prejudice'.[27]

In Germany, the constitutional right to property guarantees the right to use the land itself or to generate income from it.[28] However, this right does not protect the most lucrative use of the property.[29] Moreover, the suppression of almost all meaningful use of a piece of land, due to legislation or regulation, is not treated as an expropriation. Such a 'factual expropriation' does not fall within the scope of Article 14 section 3 of the German Basic Law. Indeed, Article 14 section 3 of the German Basic Law contains a provision on expropriation for reasons of the public good. Expropriation is the sovereign access to private property, which results in the complete or partial deprivation of specific property rights and involves the acquisition of goods for the benefit of the public authorities or, in specific circumstances, private parties. Access to property must lead to a complete or partial deprivation of the property. Otherwise, the measure is not an expropriation, but a determination of the content and limits of property (Article 14 section 1, sentence 2, of the German Basic Law). Where, as an exception, the application of the law leads to an unreasonable burden on the owner, compensation regulations can be considered to maintain the proportionality of the measure at stake (within the scope of Article 14 section 1, sentence 2, of the German Basic Law). The legislature must regulate the compensation.

In the United States, three factors must be weighed in determining whether a regulatory action without a physical invasion of property is a taking: 'the economic impact of the regulation on the claimant,' the 'extent to which the regulation has interfered with distinct investment-backed expectations,' and the 'character of the government action'.[30]

The authority and, in case of judicial review, the court must examine these three criteria and make a comprehensive assessment. Any compensation may be due only in situations where a regulatory action is treated as a taking. Additionally, without having to review it under the aforementioned three-factor test, a government action qualifies as a 'per se' (automatic) taking if it is a permanent physical occupation of the owner's property according to a long-standing Supreme Court precedent,[31] or if the government's regulations destroy 100% of the economic value of the property in question (eg—if the government bans all development and the property has virtually no value in its undeveloped state).[32] In a recent case involving a challenge to a California

[25] *JA Pye (Oxford) Ltd v UK* App no 44302/02 (ECtHR, 30 August 2007).
[26] Constitutional Council decision 96–373 (1996).
[27] Environmental Code, art 168.
[28] BVerfGE 98, 17, 35 (1998); BVerfGE 101, 54, 75 (1999).
[29] BVerfGE 91, 294, 310 (1994); BVerfGE 100, 226, 243 (1999).
[30] *Penn Central Transportation Co v City of New York* 438 US 104, 123 (1978).
[31] See *Loretto v Teleprompter Manhattan CATV Corp* 458 US 419 (1982).
[32] See *Lucas v South Carolina Coastal Council* 505 US 1003 (1992).

law requiring agricultural growers to grant union organisers access to their property for three hours per day, 120 days per year, the Supreme Court held, as a general rule with several exceptions listed in the opinion of the Court, that "a physical appropriation is a taking whether it is permanent or temporary".[33] Such a decision makes it easier to obtain protection under the Takings Clause of the Fifth Amendment and reinforces constitutional property rights. In many takings cases, the outcome actually depends on whether the property owner can demonstrate that the government's actions qualify as a "*per se*" taking. If it does not demonstrate this, the owner is likely to lose and, accordingly, the government usually prevails. Finally, some state Supreme Courts have provided broader protection for property owners under their state constitutions, and a few states have also done so by constitutional amendment or by statutory law.

As this comparative study demonstrates, regulatory taking remains a very sensitive issue. A case-by-case approach, based on general statutory provisions and limits resulting from case law, seems almost unavoidable. Any endeavour to regulate regulatory taking in many detailed statutory provisions would require a strong commitment from the legislature for arduous, precise, technical, and generally thankless work.

V. Conclusion

There are several different administrative limits to property rights. Expropriation and other similar takings belong to the most severe category, although a strict categorisation is difficult, considering the many situations in which property is limited by state action. The occupation and destruction of private property by law enforcement or a regulatory action, for instance, may not qualify as expropriation or similar taking, but, considering all the relevant circumstances in a given case, compensation may be fully appropriate. From this perspective, a nuanced approach may be preferred. Statutes may create categories of administrative limits to property rights allowing compensation, but these limits should have some degree of flexibility for the government, an administrative body or a court to extend the right to compensation to situations where the specific circumstances of a case call for such a right.

The same can be said of procedural requirements. A binary approach, where some limits would be subject to the full set of due process guarantees and other limits to almost no guarantee, may prove inadequate. Here again, a nuanced and more refined approach should be favoured. Both the legislature and, subsequently, courts should determine, in various groups of cases, the extent of protection needed to ensure the overall legitimacy and the individual acceptability of limitations to property.

Finally, concrete facts and specific situations matter—or should matter—when property rights are subject to administrative limits. True, the framework is usually set by legislatures in rather general terms, and the importance of statutes should not be underestimated in this area. Nevertheless, the role of governmental or administrative bodies and of reviewing courts, in case of litigation, is of great importance. Their activity must be based on, and limited by, law. At the same time, they should enjoy some discretion in order to take into account all the relevant facts in a given situation.

[33] See *Cedar Point Nursery v Hassid* 594 US ___ (2021); 141 S. Ct. 2063, 2074 (2021).

17

Public and Private Sovereign Powers in Liberal Models of Property Protection

Belgium, Sweden, and the Netherlands

Yseult Marique

I. Introduction

In his Pulitzer award winning book, *The Power Broker*,[1] Robert Caro documents the thirst for power animating Robert Moses, the mastermind behind the transport network and urban planning in New York between the 1920s and 1960s. In particular, Moses used extensively and creatively intricate statutory authorisations granting expropriation powers to his private corporations (we would call them 'special purpose vehicles' in today's parlance), shielded from public scrutiny. In this way, Moses socially reshaped whole parts of New York and struck compromises with major property owners around the city. Major differences awaited minorities living in socially close-knit—albeit somewhat deprived—sections of New York and establishment members living on large estates. Caro's minute investigations highlighted the interplay between law, social positions, and political preferences. This story calls to mind the intricate political and legal links between the protection of private property as the stronghold of individual freedom and security, and the rule of law as the bastion against executive arbitrariness on the other side of the Atlantic.[2]

International investment law pays close attention to the protection of property rights and the rule of law, especially to legal certainty: it focuses on the existence of a general principle of 'fair and equitable treatment'.[3] While international investment law draws on comparative public law,[4] identifying European core principles of expropriation has been largely the task of private law.[5] Focusing on comparing liberal systems (Belgium, Sweden, and the Netherlands) as such highlights how deeply expropriation lies at the crossroads between different areas of public law (eg constitutional law, fundamental rights and freedoms, and general administrative law), private law (eg property as a right), and mixed fields (eg environment and planning law). Despite an overall system protecting property rights against administrative arbitrariness at a rather similar level

[1] R Caro, *The Power Broker: Robert Moses and the Fall of New York* (Knof 1974).

[2] J Sluysmans, S Verbist, and E Waring, 'Expropriation in Europe' in J Sluysmans, S Verbist, and E Waring (eds), *Expropriation Law in Europe* (Kluwer 2015) 1–26, 9.

[3] OECD, 'Fair and Equitable Treatment Standard in International Investment Law' Working Papers on International Investment No 2004/3 (September 2004).

[4] S Schill (ed), *International Investment Law and Comparative Public Law* (OUP 2010).

[5] J Sluysmans, S Verbist, and E Waring (eds), *Expropriation Law in Europe* (Kluwer 2015).

Yseult Marique, *Public and Private Sovereign Powers in Liberal Models of Property Protection* In: *Procedural Requirements for Administrative Limits to Property Rights*. Edited by: Martina Conticelli And Thomas Perroud, Oxford University Press.
 DOI: 10.1093/oso/9780198867586.003.0017

in Belgium, Sweden and the Netherlands, many technical compromises and concrete solutions are reached via different routes, highlighting variations in preferences in liberal systems to curtail administrative powers: Belgium provides fragmented answers as it relies heavily on judge-made law in addition to its federalised system, whereas the Netherlands sequences the administrative process, compartmentalising it in fairly watertight stages where environmental plans and expropriation are kept separate, and Sweden addresses issues pertaining to expropriation topic by topic.

II. Shared background and its limits

Belgium, the Netherlands, and Sweden are all representatives of the French model of expropriation, ie a model strongly influenced by the Napoleonic idea of sacred property, as proclaimed in the French Civil Code of 1804 (Article 544), with 'sovereign' property owners enjoying full control over their property: the first part of Article 544 provides that '[p]roperty is the right to enjoy and dispose of things in the most absolute manner'. In this liberal approach, property is deemed inalienable (see Article 17 of the 1789 French Declaration of the Rights of Man and the Citizen[6]). Article 545 of the French Civil Code confirms this by providing that '[n]o one may be compelled to surrender his property, except in the public interest and in return for fair and prior compensation'. Thus, in contrast to a more social model, property is not understood as having a social function as the core of its very essence (as it would be in the German model of property rights). However, Article 544 of the French Civil Code opens the door for limits to the absolute sovereign power of the property owner when it states that '[p]roperty is the right to enjoy and dispose of things in the most absolute manner, *provided that they are not used in a manner prohibited by laws or regulations*',[7] which together with Article 545, allows for regulating property rights and expropriation in the name of the general interest. A specific act of 1810 was adopted to regulate expropriation in France, which then travelled across Europe, including Belgium, the Netherlands, and Sweden.

As a response to industrialisation and the need to develop railways,[8] key legislation regarding expropriation, strongly modelled on the French approach, was adopted in all three countries in the 19th century (in 1835 in Belgium, and it is still in force although more recent legislation applies in very urgent circumstances; in 1845 in Sweden—it was in force until 1917, and was reformed again in 1972; in 1851 in the Netherlands—it will be in force until a reform adopted in 2016 enters into force; at the time of writing, the official date is not known). The Dutch and Belgian constitutions also included the specific protection of property (Article 164 of the Dutch Constitution of 1815,[9] included in Article 14 of the Dutch Constitution of

[6] 'Since the right to property is inviolable and sacred, no one may be deprived thereof, unless public necessity, legally ascertained, obviously requires it, and just and prior indemnity has been paid.'

[7] Emphasis added.

[8] For Sweden see T Kalbro and J Paulsson, 'Development of Swedish Legislation Regulating Compensation for Compulsory Acquisition: A Law and Economics Perspective' (2014) 3(3) European Property LJ 215, 222.

[9] The protection of property can be officially traced back to 1798 (https://www.denederlandsegrondwet.nl/id/vkugbqvdtzxh/artikel_14_onteigening (last accessed 28 June 2021).

1983; Article 11 of the Belgian Constitution of 1831, formally coordinated under Article 16 in 1994 with no substantive change), while Sweden included no bill of rights in its first Constitution of 1809 but supplemented that of 1974 with a specific chapter on fundamental rights in 1980 (and the protection of property in Article 15 of the Instrument of Government).

This shared liberal approach to property across the three countries is especially noteworthy as it is not as straightforward as it might seem. Indeed, in many other respects, France, Belgium, the Netherlands, and Sweden have different traditions when it comes to civil law and state organisation. Space allows us to mention only some of these differences here, such as the reception of Roman law in France, Belgium, and the Netherlands but its absence in Sweden.[10] However, Grotius left his mark all over Europe, including Belgium, the Netherlands, and Sweden.[11] In terms of executive power evolving into absolutism, the three countries did not have a long-lasting and shaping experience of deep-seated absolutism such as the one that peaked in France from the 17th century onwards. The 1809 Swedish Constitution marked the transition from some form of absolutism to a constitutional monarchy,[12] confirmed by the Act of Succession of 1810, which regulated the right of French Prince Bernadotte to accede to the Swedish Throne. The Low countries (the Netherlands and Belgium) had long been part of the Habsburg Empire until the French Revolution. They then had close ties with Napoleonic France, as Belgium had been annexed in 1795, and from 1806 to 1810 the Dutch King was Napoleon's brother, leaving traces of a Napoleonic approach to administration in the Dutch system up until the famous *Benthem* arrest.[13] Overall, in reaction, Belgium developed a pragmatic stance against all things authoritarian once it gained independence in 1831.[14]

After the Second World War, Belgium, the Netherlands, and Sweden also became party to the same international instruments, such as the European Convention on Human Rights, and in particular the First Protocol to the European Convention on Human Rights, whose Article 1 protects property. More recently, there have been reforms or additional pieces of legislation regulating expropriation in all three countries. In Belgium, the legislation most often used now dates back to 1835 and 1962 (in the case of very urgent circumstances);[15] in the Netherlands, a major expropriation reform is due to enter into force in 2022; in Sweden, major socio-economic reforms have been adapting the landscape since the 1970s.

[10] T Lundmark, *Charting the Divide between Common and Civil Law* (OUP 2012) 418.

[11] Sluysmans, Verbist, and Waring (n 2) 4.

[12] Lundmark (n 10) 425, according to whom the Swedish kings never enjoyed the power of absolutist monarchs in the same way as they did in France: they shared power with a more or less independent parliament and with a judiciary that often sided with parliament in confrontations with the king.

[13] *Benthem v Netherlands* App no 8848/80 (1986) 8 EHRR 1 (ECtHR, 23 October 1985).

[14] Y Marique, 'Belgian Constitution (1831)' *Max Planck Encyclopaedia of Comparative Constitutional Law* available at https://oxcon.ouplaw.com/view/10.1093/law-mpeccol/law-mpeccol-e640 (last accessed 3 May 2022).

[15] Until 2007, the 1962 Act had provided the default procedure, but judges then started to intensify their scrutiny of 'very urgent circumstances', hence limiting the use of the 1962 Act, which resulted in a revival of the 1835 Act.

Despite these changes, the core features of the expropriation procedure and the protection of property against expropriation remain faithful to the liberal approach. Overall, expropriation is seen as an ultimate solution when no other option has proved successful.[16] All three legal systems lay strong emphasis on achieving an amicable transfer of property to the public authority based on negotiations with the property owner. Secondly, a legal ground is needed for expropriation. Thirdly, the expropriation has to pursue a public purpose. This condition is framed differently in the three systems. In Belgium, the public purpose is interpreted very widely and may include private interests (but not speculation: eg the provision of a hospital by a private entity is accepted). Judges have only limited power to scrutinise this public purpose. In the Netherlands, the expropriation needs to be in the interest of the development, use, or management of the physical environment. In Sweden, an exhaustive list of ten public purposes is set out. These ten purposes range widely from urban development to '*the need for space for a building ... of significant importance to the state or to a certain population group*'. In addition, a condition of emergency exists for one of the main expropriation procedures used in Belgium, while necessity and urgency are required in the Netherlands. A balance between the general and individual inconvenience and the benefit resulting from the expropriation needs to be made in Sweden. Furthermore, the possibility of 'self-realisation' is open in the Netherlands and Belgium, allowing property owners to carry out a public project if they have the capacity to do so. The importance of property as such (and not only as an economic value that can be swapped for money) can be identified to various degrees across the three legal systems. Indeed, in Belgium and the Netherlands there is a right to repurchase the property when the public purpose has not been achieved within a certain period of time or when the property has turned out not to be needed for the public project to be realised. Much discussed in Sweden, this option has been dismissed as resulting in too many intricated issues with no clear and fair outcomes. A last point pertains to the fact that while there is no general right in Belgium[17] or in the Netherlands for a property owner to request a public authority to purchase a property, Sweden does recognise a right of redemption in some circumstances (see the discussion of the cases pertaining to excessive noise and taking).

III. Structural differences

Despite these commonalities, four major features need to be discussed to understand how Belgium, the Netherlands, and Sweden organise expropriation in administrative terms: their state organisation, the outlook of their constitutional and administrative law, the content of property rights, and their legislative strategies.

[16] It has been noted that Belgium historically opted for this solution because it was mindful of the limited resources of the newly created State rather than for reasons linked to the political ideals enshrined in the constitution (S Verbist, 'Expropriation Law in Belgium (Flanders)' in J Sluysmans, S Verbist, and E Waring (eds), *Expropriation Law in Europe* (Kluwer 2015) 27–59, 27). This is one illustration of Belgian pragmatism.

[17] Specialised legislation such as the one applicable to Walloon airports is a rare exception to this.

A first major difference between the three administrative systems is the degree of centralisation. Indeed, Sweden and the Netherlands are centralised states, while Belgium is a federal system,[18] with a distinctive legal framework regarding a range of matters relating to expropriation, such as the regulation of airports, urban planning, and cultural heritage. However, this does not seem to be determinative of the entities that are allowed to proceed with expropriation. In Belgium, local, regional, and federal government enjoy this right. In the Netherlands, municipal, provincial, and state government also enjoy expropriation rights despite stronger centralisation there. In Sweden, by contrast, only the central government enjoys this right, but delegation to the country administrative board or to another public authority is provided for in limited circumstances. In addition, local self-government is recognised in different ways in the three countries. For instance, due to the Dutch spatial configuration, water authorities are a distinctive form of local government in the Netherlands, enjoying expropriation powers on a par with 'ordinary' local government. Although Belgium also had sophisticated legislation regulating water authorities, they do not enjoy expropriation powers: another public authority will in principle carry out the expropriation required to manage the water system.[19]

A second major difference between the three administrative systems relates to structural features of administrative law and constitutional review. Indeed, Belgium, the Netherlands, and Sweden share a similar view on parliamentary sovereignty when it comes to the allocation of roles between Parliament and the Executive, although the Swedish administration is more independent from the Executive than it is in principle in Belgium and the Netherlands.[20] However, the role of courts varies deeply when it comes to their contribution to guaranteeing that the constitution and the legislation are complied with. When it comes to the system of constitutional review, only Belgium has a centralised system with a constitutional court and an extensive constitutional review with detailed case law on the protection of fundamental rights and freedoms, including the protection of property rights.[21] In Sweden, courts play only a limited role in deciding on fundamental rights, yet public authorities are expected to review whether a decision complies with norms of a higher rank.[22] Constitutional review is prohibited in the Dutch Constitution.[23] By contrast, the three legal systems are placed

[18] This means that a Flemish Decree (*Vlaams Onteigeningsdecreet* 24 February 2017) and a Walloon Decree (Decree 22 November 2018 *relatif à la procédure d'expropriation)* coexist with the federal legislation of 1962 (L 26 July 1962 *relative à la procédure d'extrême urgence en matière d'expropriation pour cause d'utilité publique*).

[19] No right to expropriate in *Loi* 5 July 1956 *relative aux wateringues*. In Wallonia, the Government may expropriate (eg *Décret relatif au Livre II du Code de l'Environnement constituant le Code de l'Eau*, art 171 §2 second sentence); in Flanders, regional, provincial, or local government may expropriate as a matter of principle (Decree 15 Juni 2018 *coordinatie van Decreet van* 18 July 2003 *betreffende het integraal waterbeleid*, Art 1.3.3.1.1).

[20] J Rechel, 'The Pan-European General Principle of Good Administration in Sweden: Undeniable but Partial Vehicles of Changes' in U Stelkens and A Andrijauskaite (eds), *Good Administration and the Council of Europe: Law, Principles, and Effectiveness* (OUP 2020) 256–74, 258.

[21] For one illustration see Constitutional Court No 69/2005 (20 April 2005). In addition, the Constitutional Court links art 16 of the Constitution with art 1 of Protocol No 1 see G Rossoux, *Vers une dématérialisation des droits fondamentaux* (Bruylant 2015) 873–94.

[22] H Wenander, 'Administrative Constitutional Review in Sweden: Between Subordination and Independence' (2020) 26(4) European Public Law 987.

[23] Dutch Constitution, art 120.

in a mirroring position when it comes to the formalisation of administrative procedures, another technique used to limit and channel administrative power. Indeed, there is a formal procedural act codifying administrative procedures in Sweden (since 1971) and the Netherlands (adopted in stages since 1994),[24] while Belgium did not adopt such a codification of the administrative procedures: it relies on general principles of good administration developed by courts to supplement a very fragmented legal and constitutional framework organising the duties of the administration.

A third major difference between the three legal systems is that property rights are actually *not* conceived in the same way in the civil law. Belgium stayed close to the French civil code until 2020,[25] while the Netherlands has evolved away from it to a larger extent as the civil code was deeply reformed in 1992 and Sweden was influenced by legal realism from the early 20th century onwards.[26] These differences need to be noted as they point towards a key distinction between the ways property is protected as such against arbitrary encroachment by public powers under constitutional and administrative law on the one hand, and how property is regulated and understood in private relationships under private law, on the other.

A fourth major difference between the three legal systems relates to general legislative strategies. Indeed, Sweden provides many highly specific solutions in specialised legislation (such as the Civil Protection Act or the Heritage Act). The Netherlands also has specialised legislation, but the most noteworthy feature is that many legal issues related to the expropriation procedures in other legal systems have been hived off outside the expropriation framework, in a different legislative framework, namely that of the adoption of the environment plan. This means that certain legal issues are supposed to have been addressed elsewhere prior to the expropriation. By contrast, Belgium has a system that relies more extensively on solutions developed through case law. There is specific legislation providing partial answers to questions pertaining to some aspects of expropriation, but this legislation, by and large, does not exhaustively or systematically cover the legal issues arising in expropriation, and judges fall back on two default provisions, either Article 1 of the First Protocol to the European Convention on Human Rights or Article 1382 of the Civil Code on general (administrative) liability with a view to awarding compensation.

IV. Direct expropriation: process and substance

In Belgium, the Netherlands, and Sweden, a classic expropriation procedure when the property owner sees a piece of real estate being compulsorily taken away from her is a two-stage process, with an administrative stage, a judicial stage, and a possible outcome: full compensation.

[24] JB Auby (ed), *Codification of Administrative Procedure* (Bruylant 2014).

[25] There has been a reform of property rights in Belgium (*Loi* 4 February 2020—*Nouveau Code Civil, Livre 3 'Les biens', Official Journal* (17 March 2020) entry in force for the most part on 1 September 2021). Belgian property rights will become less absolute in the future. See *Le droit des biens réformé* (Bruylant 2020).

[26] For the development in relation not to real estate but to movables see K Rakneberg Haug, 'The Historical Development of the Scandinavian Functional Approach to Transfer of Ownership: A Tale of Change and Continuity' (2017) 6(2) EJPL 236, 237.

A. Judicial stage

As a matter of principle, courts play a crucial role in ensuring that property rights are respected and that the administrative process is regular in the three legal systems. In Belgium, expropriation is, by its very nature, a judicial decision rather than an administrative one: the administrative authorities have to submit a request to a court, which will examine the legality of the expropriation and decide on prior compensation. In the Netherlands, expropriation can only come into force after an administrative court has acknowledged it: the authorities have to initiate the judicial proceeding themselves. In Sweden, expropriation is an administrative decision, but ordinary courts decide on the compensation, and the Supreme Administrative Court may review the lawfulness of the decision on expropriation.

B. Fair administrative process

Belgian, Dutch, and Swedish judges broadly address substantive and formal defects in the administrative process concurring with expropriation and have a tendency to quash a decision if it has adversely and substantively affected the rights of the property owners. However, beyond this basic core similarity, differences appear that are not per se connected with the protection of property rights but with the ways in which administrative decisions are understood to be lawful in each system.

A first difference regards the information organised around the expropriation, the ways notice is given, and the consequences of defects at this stage. In Belgium, a case such as the one of Mr Burns would be unlikely. The expropriation decision needs to be notified to the addressees, including the property owners, and it is likely that specialised procedures will set out how the public needs to participate in greater detail, and the property owner will ordinarily be notified of the expropriation as a part of the judicial proceedings. In the Netherlands, the authorities have the duty to notify the (draft) expropriation decision. However, the court might not conclude that failing to notify will lead to quashing the decision as the property owner may not have been adversely affected by this lack of notification, and even if this were the case, it may still be possible to repair the defect during judicial proceedings. In Sweden, property owners have a right to be heard during the expropriation procedure. However, if they are not, a court may accept that such a hearing was not 'obviously necessary', as the relevant legislation recognises this to be a ground for leaving a decision to stand despite procedural defects.

A second difference in the administrative process appears in relation to the right to participate in the revision of an urban plan, which may affect a property subject to expropriation. In Belgium, revisions of urban plans usually require such public participation. According to the case law of the administrative judge, the lack of such public participation can be considered to be an essential formality whose violation leads to quashing the resulting administrative decision. In the Netherlands, property owners have no individual right to be notified of the revision of the plan, but notification is widely organised, and the owner can object to the revision. If participation requirements are not complied with, this procedural defect does not lead to automatic quashing of the plan, as the court will have to deem it to be a substantial defect to reach such a result. In Sweden, property owners have the right to be consulted, and notification takes place by means of publicity on the municipal noticeboard and in a local newspaper. If these requirements are not complied with, the property owner can appeal to the Land and Environmental Court. Through application of the relevant legislation, failure to comply with participatory requirements leads to quashing the revision to the plan, and the decision is remanded to the decision-making authority. In short, as a matter of principle, each system organises a form of participation but with different modalities. Methods of ascertaining that the participation requirements have not been adequate differ: it should lead to automatic quashing of the defective decision in Sweden and, according to the case law, will probably lead to quashing in Belgium, while it will depend on the facts of the case in the Netherlands.

A third difference concerns the duty to give reasons. In Belgium there is a formal obligation to give reasons in individual administrative decisions, such as expropriation: the legal and factual grounds of the decisions need to be communicated to the property owner. This allows for a discussion about the reasons the expropriation was necessary and how other possible options were assessed. From the substantive standpoint however, once the formal duty to give reasons has been complied with, the judge only exercises marginal control over the decision taken by the administration. There is no such duty to explicitly provide reasons in Sweden. In the Netherlands, the duty to give reasons is more limited as discussions about which property needs to be expropriated to carry out a public project should be held prior to the expropriation, when the environment plan is adopted.

C. Outcome: full compensation

In all three legal systems, compensation needs to be paid prior to expropriation and is deemed to be 'full'. There may however be questions about how the economic value of the property is assessed. Experts are normally involved in this assessment in some way.[27] Beyond compensation being paid in relation to the economic value of the expropriated property, the right to compensation can vary. Indeed it can be deemed 'full' in different ways and to varying extents. In the Netherlands, moral damages are excluded; in Belgium, compensation includes the economic value of the property as well as a range of expenses that the property owner had to reasonably cover ensuing the expropriation. In addition, compensation may be obtained if the property owner can prove moral damage; in Sweden, compensation is calculated at 125 per cent of the economic value of the property to cover both the loss and moral damages.

[27] Sluysmans, Verbist, and Waring (n 2) 1–26.

In addition, compensation can be claimed in court when a property owner has suffered some harm following a procedural error or when the interference with personal property rights is disproportionate.

V. Property related rights and indirect expropriation

International investment law draws attention to interferences in property rights other than the classic case of expropriation of real estate, namely the so-called 'indirect expropriations'.[28] Nationalisation is, of course, the most extensive case, at one end of the spectrum of these other interferences, and there are a range of lesser interferences with property rights that can be material in nature or limit or reduce the use and enjoyment of property rights to varying extents, at the other.

Belgium, the Netherlands, and Sweden have no specific legislative framework for nationalisation, but there is little doubt that the same principles as those governing expropriation would apply. When it comes to 'lesser' interferences, the similarities and differences are more difficult to map. Indeed, one first important step in the reasoning process consists in correctly labelling the interference and its legal consequences. In this case there is no clear pattern. For instance, a licence (to exploit a public estate) does not have the same administrative features in the three legal systems. It is a contract in Sweden, while it is considered a unilateral administrative decision in Belgium. The legal consequences are then consistent with the label attributed in each legal order. Other examples are discussed further, based on two cases analysed in the national chapters of this edited collection.

A. Cultural heritage

Limitations to property rights such as the sale of artefacts belonging to the national cultural heritage would not be understood as an expropriation *sensu stricto* in Belgium, the Netherlands, and Sweden: first it may relate to movables only, and secondly, there may be no compulsory purchase by public authorities, but limits are set on the right to sell the artefact. Dedicated legislation applies in Belgium, the Netherlands, and Sweden. The details and technicalities of each piece of legislation differ deeply. In the Netherlands, a negotiation between the property owner and the public authorities will ensue regarding the price and conditions of the sale, while in Sweden, the procedure only regards obtaining permission to transfer an artefact outside the country with no possibility of compelling the public authority to purchase or compensate for a refusal to export the artefact. There is no compensation in Belgium either, except if the interference with property rights is deemed to be disproportionate and therefore non-compliant with Article 1 of the First Protocol to the European Convention on Human Rights.

[28] OECD, *International Investment Law: A Changing Landscape: A Companion Volume to International Investment Perspectives* (2005) ch 2.

B. Urban planning

One of the widest, if not the widest, differences across the three countries relates to the interplay between expropriation and urban planning. Indeed, in Belgium problems frequently arise due to the unlawfulness of an urban planning act and its ripple effect on expropriation decided on the basis of a planning act later found to be unlawful. In the Netherlands, this situation is only impossible because technically an expropriation can only happen if there is no possibility to challenge the environment plan at the basis of the expropriation. In Sweden, there would be no problem either but for another technical reason: once the expropriation has happened, the former owner no longer has any right over the property. After long discussions, the legislator consciously decided there would be no right to re-purchase the property as the situation would become too complicated.

Behind this difference in outcome, one may pinpoint diverging views regarding the interconnections between the autonomy of the various administrative procedures and rights over a specific piece of real estate. Sweden and the Netherlands adopt a 'compartmentalising' view, where rights and administrative processes are kept separate, located in different 'boxes' deemed to become as watertight as possible so as to prevent the weakening of new rights created over the real estate. The specific technique for this compartmentalisation seems to differ, however. On the one hand, Sweden adopts a problem-oriented approach[29] (providing solutions to identified problems),[30] while, on the other, the Netherlands adopts a process-oriented approach, where each phase of the overall process represents a slice, and one can proceed to the next stage only if a stage is completed (ie there is no longer any way to challenge it). Contrasting with these compartmentalising strategies, Belgium adopts a far more 'overlapping' view, where multiple rights (such as public servitudes or the theory of neighbourhood disturbances in the case of excessive noise for instance, where personal rights conflict with rights *in rem*) are accepted as coexisting with each other over time. This statement is striking because Sweden is a country where property is usually understood to be seen as more segmented, so it is approached through its different functions.[31] Providing an explanation for the existing solution in Belgium is not easy. One possible explanation may lie with the liberal approach favoured there when it comes to the protection of subjective rights. This has two expressions: on the one hand there is a strong tendency to protect property, even if it becomes fragmented, in the hope that, over time, partial rights will either be bought back or will elapse, allowing for full property rights to be reunited to the property owner (this is also in this sense that the property owner is 'sovereign'); on the other hand, the liberal protection of subjective rights also means that the exception of illegality is understood in a broad sense with no time limit

[29] S van Erp, 'Comparative Property Law and Politics' (2015) 4(2) EPLJ 81, 83.

[30] In addition to the acts mentioned in the Swedish chapter in this collection, a list of the specific acts applicable to expropriation can be found in T Kalbro and J Paulsson, 'Development of Swedish Legislation Regulating Compensation for Compulsory Acquisition: A Law and Economics Perspective' (2014) 3(3) EPLJ 215, 224, table 1.

[31] Rakneberg Haug (n 26) 236.

in principle (Article 159 of the Constitution),[32] hence allowing the unlawfulness of an administrative decision (eg an urban plan) to be open to dispute down the line, such as an expropriation.

VI. Liberal protection and its administrative variations

This comparison between Belgium, the Netherlands, and Sweden highlights the enduring French legacy outside France. In a 2019 world ranking of countries with expropriation risks, Belgium was ranked number 132, the Netherlands 157, and Sweden 168.[33] All three belong to the category with the lowest risk of expropriation. Rankings and quantitative indicators are often difficult to interpret in a more qualitative way. However, a public authority wanting to expropriate a property in Belgium, the Netherlands, or Sweden can reach its objective even if the negotiations with the owner fail. The procedure may be varyingly cumbersome, lengthy, and expensive, but there is little doubt that in the majority of cases, the expropriation will succeed. But liberal protection lies elsewhere. Despite the reforms, the Belgian, Dutch, and Swedish systems remain deeply liberal in the sense that individual owners do not primarily have duties to use property for a social purpose: the public authorities will take care of this, directly or indirectly.

Against this background, the deepest difference between these legal systems relates to the overarching structure of the solutions to issues relating to expropriation. Belgium relies heavily on case law and its pragmatism, while the solutions are differentiated across the sub-national entities and supplemented by general provisions by default (Article 1382 of the Civil Code and Article 1 of Protocol No 1 to the European Convention on Human Rights); the Netherlands tends to limit litigation and problems in removing possible objections to a public project and hives them off in a different procedure with its own logic. Sweden, however, tends to favour legal certainty by cutting all links between the property owner and the property after expropriation, and for the rest has many detailed specific solutions across specialised pieces of legislation. In short, the differences between the administrative cultures are not primarily about the level of individual protection but about the means of achieving it, especially how balances of interests are struck and how the court grounds its decisions on the interplay between special solutions and general legal provisions.

[32] J Theunis, S Van Garsse, and E Vleugels, 'Balancing Legality and Legal Certainty: The Plea of Illegality in Belgian Public Law and the Role of the Council of State and Other Judicial Bodies' in M Eliantonio and D Dragos (eds), *The Plea of Illegality in Europe* (Routledge 2020).

[33] See https://www.theglobaleconomy.com/rankings/expropriation_risk/ (last accessed on 28 June 2021).

18

Procedural Safeguards of Property Rights in Southern Europe

Italy, Spain, and Portugal

*Nuria Magaldi**

I. Introduction

The three legal systems selected for this analysis have many points in common but also some distinctive features. On the whole, comparative study allows us to state that they all rely on the same legal tradition.

II. Constitutional framework

A. Expropriation as an instrument to restrict property rights

The three legal systems selected for this case-based analysis on expropriation and limits to property rights all spring from very similar constitutional foundations. The origins of the constitutional expropriation system in all of them very likely date back to their first, liberal, fundamental texts, drafted and passed in the first half of the nineteenth century, in which private property was considered an absolute right.[1]

In that regard, it can be stated that there are no big differences among Spain, Italy and Portugal when it comes to the traditional constitutional concept of expropriation and property limitations. All three Constitutions recognise the right to property as a fundamental right, even though its location within the constitutional texts varies from one to another. Once recognised, however, the right of property is immediately subject to the possibility of being limited (specially through expropriation). Three main conditions must be fulfilled, however: deprivation of property must have its foundation in law, it has to be based on reasons of general interest, and it can only take place if the citizen is compensated for it.[2]

* Associate Professor of Administrative Law (*Profesora Titular*) at the University of Córdoba (Spain). Her research activities fall within the framework of the Research Project 'Seguridad pública, actividad administrativa de limitación y derecho sancionador' PGC2018-093760-B-00 (MCIU/AEI/FEDER, UE).

[1] This principle was first found in art 17 of the Declaration of Human and Civil Rights of 26 August 1789, which established that 'Since the right to Property is inviolable and sacred, no one may be deprived thereof, unless public necessity, legally ascertained, obviously requires it, and just and prior indemnity has been paid'.

[2] See Italian Constitution, art 42, Spanish Constitution, art 33, and Portuguese Constitution, art 62/2.

Nuria Magaldi, *Procedural Safeguards of Property Rights in Southern Europe* In: *Procedural Requirements for Administrative Limits to Property Rights.* Edited by: Martina Conticelli And Thomas Perroud, Oxford University Press. © Nuria Magaldi 2022.
DOI: 10.1093/oso/9780198867586.003.0018

It is important to emphasise that in all three systems the institution of expropriation has a dual nature. Admittedly, it is an exceptionally strong instrument of public power (generally, of public administration) geared to achieving a general interest. Thus, and provided that the above-mentioned conditions are fulfilled, public power can deprive a citizen of his or her property rights. On the other hand, the institution of expropriation must be seen also as a very essential guarantee for citizens: the safeguard vis-à-vis their property rights may not to be taken away unless a law provides for it, there is a general reason of public interest, and fair compensation is established and paid.

Given its above-mentioned dual nature, the institution of expropriation is established and regulated mainly by formal law adopted by Parliament. In this regard, all three Constitutions under analysis, after establishing the core regulation, defer to ordinary law to define expropriation cases, compensation rules, and procedural requirements.[3] Additionally, and since Spain and Italy are both politically and administratively decentralised states, it is also necessary to note the distribution of legislative competences on expropriation between the state and regional parliaments. Analysis of the Italian and Spanish system leads to the conclusion that legislative competence on expropriation in both countries appertains mainly (but not exclusively) to the state. Thus, they try to reach a single type of expropriation procedure, in which procedural guarantees and compensation rules do not vary from one territory to another. Otherwise, the equality principle may be jeopardised.

B. The social function of property

The transition from liberal state to welfare state seem to have produced similar legal transformations regarding property and expropriation in all three countries. This evolution led to the inclusion of the so-called 'social function of property' at a constitutional level. This social function of property is twofold. On the one hand, it means that there are more reasons of general interest able to justify the deprivation of property rights: expropriation may be used to obtain land in order to build, for example, hospitals or highways (traditional approach) but also to launch an economic hub in a region or to challenge big landowners (broad approach). On the other hand, the social function of property allows law to regulate different sets of rights and duties for owners of goods and assets of a different nature. Therefore, legal restrictions are imposed on these categories of owners without even giving rise to any right to compensation.

Both aspects of the social function of property are to be found in the three constitutional systems under analysis, albeit with some differences. The most visible one is that there is no clear and explicit mention of the social function of property in the Portuguese Constitution. On the contrary, the reference in both the Italian and the Spanish Constitutions is explicit.[4] However, despite the lack of any express mention

[3] These are *Testo Unico delle disposizioni legislative e regolamentari in materia di espropiazione di pubblica utilità* (*Decreto del Presidente della Reppublica* no 327) (8th June 2001); *Ley de Expropriación Forzosa* (16 December 1954); *Código das Expropriaçaos, Lei* 168/99 (18 September 1999).

[4] See the wording of both provisions: 'the content of these rights [property, inheritance] shall be determined by the social function which they fulfil, in accordance with the law' (Spanish Constitution, art 33.2); 'private property is recognised and guaranteed by the law, which prescribes the ways it is acquired, enjoyed

in the Portuguese system, it seems clear that the idea of social function must be considered as implicitly included in the Portuguese Constitution too. This follows on from the fact that it has been consistently used in that country to justify limits to property based on health or the environment.

Two of the most paradigmatic fields in which the social function of property has clearly emerged in past decades are the protection of cultural, artistic and historical heritage, and protection of the environment and landscape. In fact, two of the cases proposed refer to these, posing the question whether an intervention on goods or assets due to the need for artistic or environmental protection is to be considered a limit of property rights that must be compensated or not.

From a procedural point of view, the general rule in all three systems is that the declaration as part of the cultural heritage of a good (for instance, a valuable portrait) or the declaration of a piece of land as a natural protected area triggers a set of duties and obligations for the owner. Among others we can mention the following: to preserve goods, assets or lands in fair condition and to use them in a way that is compatible with their artistic, historical or environmental character; in the case of movable goods, the duty to communicate and be previously authorised to export them; the right (for public authorities) of first refusal in the event of an auction; a restriction of the activities that can be conducted in the land; restriction to public entry and access to the protected zone, etc. Failure to fulfil these obligations may lead to sanctions and, in some cases, even to compulsory expropriation of the economic good concerned, as in Spain.

The said declaration usually takes place through an administrative procedure in which the owners or holders of goods or assets of (artistic, historical, or environmental) value must have the right to participate (for instance, in order to submit observations). Moreover, the administrative decision declaring the cultural interest or the environmental protection of a good or asset can always be challenged before the courts. We have to bear in mind, however, that administrative authorities in all three systems enjoy a wide margin of technical appreciation here, which consequently leads to partial judicial review. The courts will thus generally verify the factual basis and possible lack of preliminary investigation, the procedural requirements, and sufficient motive (including well-reasoned public purpose), as well as any excessive use of powers. They will also ascertain that general limits such as rationality or proportionality have not been infringed, but they will not go beyond that.

In Spain, however, a declaration that assets or goods are of cultural interest or represent naturally protected areas can also take place through statutory provisions passed by Parliament. Admittedly, this is not typical, but when it happens, the judicial remedies that a citizen has at hand are considerably fewer. This is because the Spanish system does not allow an individual to challenge a law before an ordinary court and to ask for constitutional review. Therefore, the only option at his/her disposal would be to challenge an (administrative) act implementing the declaration and ask the court to raise a question as to constitutionality before the Constitutional Court. The fundamental right to an effective judicial remedy seems to be put into question under these circumstances.

and its limitations so as to ensure its social function and make it accessible to all' (Italian Constitution, art 42).

From a substantive perspective, the starting point is that there is no compensation in either Spain or Italy when duties and obligations are imposed on a category of owners or holders of these types of goods or assets. In this regard, it seems that those obligations and duties are not considered expropriation in the true sense but as a general regulation of the right of property regarding certain types of categories of goods or assets. This may sometimes occur through urban planning. For instance, in both countries the right to export a valuable portrait is not considered to be a part of the set of rights that the ownership of cultural goods entails. Likewise, the existence of building constraints on natural areas does not mean that property rights are being 'limited' but regulated according to their social function. Thus, the legal recognition of a good or asset as part of the cultural or natural heritage does not imply that its owner is entitled to compensation in either Italy or Spain.

However, this statement must be reviewed in those circumstances in which a general regulation might have material expropriative effects. This would occur, for instance, when a new regulation or an urban planning change entails an 'extraordinary loss' for the owner or holder of property rights. Let us imagine, for instance, a case in which a change in the public authorities' assessment of the natural value of a piece of land where a tourist resort is located leads to severe restriction of the activities that can be carried out there. This could be also the case of a building declared of cultural interest; as a consequence, its owner must preserve it and use it appropriately, without being granted any compensation. But what happens if, according to previous urban planning, the owner had the right to demolish the building to build a new (more profitable) one, and this is no longer possible?

Under those exceptional circumstances, at least in the Spanish system, compensation for loss might be possible. Changes like those described above may be formal general regulations, but they have material expropriation effects. They entail extraordinary sacrifice on the part of the affected persons, giving rise to compensation. This kind of reasoning, although complex, has been frequently used in the Spanish legal literature and constitutional case law.

On the contrary, Portugal seems to follow quite a different approach, and the threshold for granting compensation may be lower. For instance, the fact that an owner cannot freely decide to sell the good to anyone (even to a buyer living abroad) very likely entitles him to seek damages, unlike in Italy or Spain. Also, as a rule, restrictions on landowners stemming from changes to urban planning give rise to a right to compensation, as they are considered pre-existing and legal consolidated rights the deprivation of which should be compensated. It seems, therefore, that the Portuguese system strikes a different balance among interests in comparison with the Italian and the Spanish frameworks.

III. Safeguarding property rights through administrative procedure

One of the most significant points in common that emerge from comparative analysis is the crucial role that the administrative expropriation procedure plays when a public authority decides to deprive a party of his or her property rights. As has already been pointed out, expropriation implies enormous public power but, at the same time, an essential safeguard for citizens.

Among the guarantees available to citizens who have been affected by expropriation, one of the most important is the expropriation procedure itself. This means that a deprivation of property rights can only take place following legally established procedural steps. Generally speaking, this fundamental idea is enshrined in all three legal systems in question. Thus, the lack of essential procedural acts in a case of expropriation may lead to its invalidity in all three, as we will see in greater detail under A and C. However, the controversial Italian institution of 'constructive expropriation' (*occupazione acquisitiva*) will raise doubts about whether and how individuals are protected when the Italian authorities expropriate unlawfully (without respecting procedural safeguards).

A. A declaration of the general interest that justifies the expropriation is required in all three systems, with severe consequences in the event of failure to comply with this requirement

There is no question that every expropriation in these three systems has to be based upon a public interest that must be indicated in a formal act, which is usually called 'declaration of public utility'. Sometimes this declaration is not truly a part of the expropriation procedure. This is the case of Spain, where the *declaración de utilidad pública o interés social* is a precondition to be fulfilled in order to trigger administrative proceedings. In other cases, however, the declaration is one of the steps that make up the whole expropriation procedure. This happens in Portugal, where the declaration (*declaraçao de utilidade publica*) constitutes one of the formal steps in the expropriation procedure. It must clearly identify the reasons of general interest that justify taking away property rights. Very similarly, in the Italian declaration of public utility (*dichiarazione di pubblica utilità*) the authorities have to indicate the public interest in relation to the realisation of a public work or interference in private property rights.

In any case, this declaration must always exist in order for an expropriation to be lawful; otherwise, it would be declared invalid if challenged. One conclusion can be drawn from this: in all three systems, all lawful expropriations need to be justified by the existence of a sufficiently important public reason benefiting the community.

In this regard, however, analysis of the Italian system shows a peculiarity that deserves some attention. As a matter of principle, and according to Italian law, if expropriation has taken place without respecting procedural guarantees (for instance, in the absence of a declaration of public utility), the expropriation will be invalid. The affected person could thus request the restitution of the goods or assets. Nevertheless, if the land or economic good has already been seized and transformed, the authorities have the option to keep the acquisition after compensating the private owner for damages (including a percentage in terms of non-pecuniary loss for the unlawful expropriation). This controversial doctrine, usually known as 'constructive expropriation', has been repeatedly questioned by the European Court of Human Rights, since it places lawful and unlawful expropriation on the same level.

B. The requirement of a statement of the reasons for expropriation acts is to be found in all three systems, although the intensity of this requirement varies from one to another

The duty to state reasons regarding the choice of the specific goods or assets to be expropriated is clearly recognised in both Spain and Portugal.

In Portugal, the duty to state reasons is considered a fundamental right by itself and it stems directly from constitutional provisions. Thus, courts require the reasons justifying the subtraction of property rights to be clearly identified; however, there is no need to justify why other lands or goods were passed over. In any case, there is an obligation to explain to the affected owners why a specific decision was taken, which implicitly includes, among other things, an explanation regarding the property to be seized. Consequently, a breach of this duty to state reasons could lead to a court declaring the expropriation invalid, if challenged.

In Spain, according to the general rules of administrative procedure, these administrative acts, which are discretionary or restrict individual rights or interests, must be motivated. There is, thus, a general duty to state reasons regarding the identification of the rights or assets to be expropriated. This aspect is stressed in the Spanish Law on Expropriation, which lays down that deprivation may only include goods or assets 'strictly necessary to fulfil the purposes of the expropriation'. Accordingly, the reasoning should seek to justify the choice of the goods expropriated. The extension and depth of the reasoning may of course vary, depending on the complexity of the situation. In any case, expropriation without any reasoning pertaining to why a specific piece of land was taken rather than a neighbouring property (or, in general, without any or sufficient reasons why this property was suitable for expropriation) constitutes a breach of the duty to state reasons. Consequently, the expropriation could be declared invalid if challenged before a court.

Things look different when analysed from the Italian perspective. In Italy, the decision concerning which goods or property are to be expropriated falls wholly within the technical discretion of the public authorities. Judicial review is therefore ruled out, except when there are factual errors, breaches of procedure, or examples of administrative irrationality or arbitrariness. On this basis, Italian case law deems that a very general motive (just indicating general criteria) regarding the chosen properties is sufficient and there is thus no need to provide reasons for the seizure of a specific area or good rather than another.

In conclusion, it may be stated that the requirement for reasoning does exist in all three legal systems under analysis. However, the thoroughness of the motive that must be provided by each public administrative authority varies considerably depending on the legal system under scrutiny. As far as Italy is concerned, the threshold seems to be lower since it would be difficult for a court to declare an expropriation invalid on the sole basis of a lack of reasons stated regarding the choice of property involved. On the contrary, Spanish and Portuguese courts seem to be more demanding. Accordingly, an absence of reasoning may lead to the expropriation being declared invalid in both countries if an affected citizen can prove the impossibility of defending his or her property rights effectively for that reason.

C. The requirement to formally notify the essential expropriation acts is also to be found in all three systems and has similar consequences in the event of failure to notify

The three legal systems under analysis impose an individual, formal notification of the most relevant acts of the expropriation procedure. In all three cases, the aim is to guarantee the participation and defence rights of the owners and persons affected by the expropriation (to submit observations, for instance).

The consequences of a lack of notification are severe, usually following the general rules regarding administrative acts and administrative proceedings. In Portugal, for instance, what has to be individually notified is the declaration of public utility, which is a condition for its effectiveness. As this is an administrative act, should the declaration produce no effects (because it was not notified), any further expropriation acts will be declared unlawful if challenged before a court.

As regards the Italian case, the formal act that must be notified is the one that triggers the expropriation procedure. The absence of formal notification of the said act, if challenged before the courts, would also lead to the invalidity of further expropriation acts (significantly, that of the expropriation decree). However, once again, 'constructive expropriation' could be applied in those cases, preventing the affected person from having his or her property returned and allowing the authorities to 'remedy' an unlawful expropriation.

As for Spain, the administrative act to be individually notified is the 'declaration of the need to expropriate' (*declaración de necesidad de ocupación*), whose objective is to select the property and assets to be expropriated. A failure to individually notify this declaration leads to the invalidity of further expropriation acts. In fact, according to Spanish Law this would be tantamount to expropriation with no procedure at all, which would be null and void.

D. Procedural protection may be lawfully set aside only under very exceptional circumstances

Up to now, we have stressed the importance of the procedural guarantee in the event of deprivation of property rights exercised by a public power. As a general rule, serious flaws in the expropriation procedure may have legal consequences, probably leading to an invalid expropriation, as shown above.

However, it is conceivable that, under some very exceptional circumstances, the procedural safeguard (or, at least, most of it) could be ruled out. In this regard, all three systems include the institution of 'requisition', defining it in a similar way. According to this notion, a requisition implies that, for very exceptional underlying reasons of public interest, public authorities are entitled to deprive a person of his or her property rights or assets—for which compensation is generally available—but without respecting basic procedural requirements. Since procedural requirements are part of the constitutional protection of property rights, this safeguard can only be lawfully set aside in extraordinary circumstances.

As may be expected, all three systems tend to link this extraordinary power to situations where public order, public security or public health are put at risk.[5] Only exceptional reasons related to serious dangers concerning public order, public security or public health may justify procedural requirements yielding to the urgent need to deprive someone of property rights. In such cases, the expropriation procedure is shortened or speeded up, which inevitably means a weakening of the owner's procedural safeguards. One of the procedural guarantees that is usually set aside is the participatory one, meaning that the participatory rights of the affected persons are reduced or simply removed. This is clearly the case of Italy, where the decision to impose requisition is adopted in an emergency procedure without formal notice, and the participatory rights of the owner are excluded. Very similarly, the Spanish authorities can deprive a person of his or her property rights through requisition by skipping the essential steps (and consequently, his or her participatory rights) in the expropriation procedure.[6] On the contrary, and quite surprisingly, participatory rights cannot be set aside in Portugal: those affected always have the right to be heard before the decision on the requisition is formally taken by the competent body (the government).[7]

In any case, the proportionality principle emerges as the crucial one to be considered in determining the lawfulness of any requisition in all three systems. This means that judicial control of a requisition decision will be based on an analysis of proportionality according to the following model: (a) this extraordinary measure is apt for achieving the aim pursued; (b) the said measure is necessary, meaning that the aim pursued cannot be achieved in another less intrusive way (for instance, through ordinary expropriation and an ordinary expropriation procedure); (c) the measure is strictly proportionate (after weighing the interests and rights at stake). Regarding the last step, it must be highlighted that, as already mentioned, Portuguese law strikes a different balance insofar as participatory rights cannot be sacrificed even with regard to the extraordinary measure of requisition.

A requisition decision can be challenged before the courts in all three systems. If the decision is quashed, damages (and/or an eventual restoration of the prior situation) may be awarded to the owner or affected person under certain circumstances. However, it is important to outline that deprivation of participatory rights would not be a ground for review either in Italy nor in Spain. On the other hand, in Portugal the adoption of a requisition decision without giving the affected persons the right to be heard leads, if challenged, to the courts annulling the said requisition.

[5] Paradigmatic in this regard is the wording of the relevant Spanish Law: 'serious grounds of public order or public security, or in the face of epidemics, floods, or other emergencies'.

[6] In fact, requisition can take place in Spain without serving on the affected person the so-called 'declaration of the need to expropriate', an essential step in an ordinary expropriation procedure.

[7] Admittedly, the Portuguese Government could approve a dispensation to set aside participatory rights in exceptionally urgent cases; however, in order to do so the degree of justification required is very demanding.

IV. Safeguarding expropriated property rights beyond the expropriation procedure: the right of reversion

As already noticed, all three systems selected for this analysis clearly establish that a lawful deprivation of property must be based on reasons of general interest. The regulations on the expropriation procedure in Italy, Spain, and Portugal try to guarantee that the general interest underlying all expropriations really exists; if this is not the case, no seizure of goods or assets and subsequent transfer of property can take place. In this regard, it has already been shown (under section IIIA) that a declaration of general interest is a crucial requirement for lawful expropriation. However, nothing has yet been said about what happens afterwards. Are there any consequences if, once a public authority has, for instance, seized the good, no public works ever started, or, if they did, they were interrupted later?

Expropriation is not an end in itself but a means to achieve a public purpose, a general interest. Accordingly, there must always be a public purpose behind every lawful expropriation. In this light, it is clear that if the reason of general interest behind an expropriation no longer subsists, this may have consequences in all three systems under scrutiny. However, as we will discuss below, Italy shows some peculiarities that deserve attention.

If, for whatever reason, the general interest no longer subsists after an expropriation procedure has been lawfully completed, the original owner may have the right to claim, under certain circumstances, the restitution of the goods or assets expropriated. In this regard, all three systems have means of reversing the expropriation on the grounds of a failure to fulfil its intended purpose. Nevertheless, it is worth mentioning that this right of reversion does not seem to be a constitutional safeguard stemming directly from constitutional provisions but simply a statutory right deriving from the general regulation of expropriation. This has been expressly stated by the Spanish Constitutional Court, and similar conclusions can be drawn from an analysis of the Italian and Portuguese frameworks.

The general rule is that (through statutory provisions) public authorities are given a deadline for at least starting the public works necessary to achieve the aim pursued by the deprivation of goods. The right of reversion can emerge after expiry of the said deadline without fulfilling the intended purpose, leading to the eventual restitution of the expropriated goods or assets. In Spain, the right of reversion can be triggered if public works are suspended for more than two years or do not start within the five years following the seizure of the property. As for Portugal, the reason of general interest—expressed in the declaration of public utility—no longer exists if the works are suspended or interrupted for more than three years. In this case, the declaration of public utility would remain without effect, and so would the other steps in the expropriation procedure. In both systems, the right of reversion means that the previous owner can request the restitution of the expropriated goods or assets. In return, he or she will have to pay back the compensation received.

Of course, both in Spain and Portugal additional rules are applied when the expropriated goods or assets have suffered the effects of depreciation or have been transformed in such a way as to add value to the original ones (in such cases, the compensation to be paid back may be adjusted). A fairly common situation is, however, when restitution becomes impossible due to a definitive physical or legal transformation of the status of the expropriated good or asset; in that case, it would appear possible to seek compensation.

Even though the right of reversal exists in the Italian system of expropriation (*retrocessione del bene espropriato*), so-called 'constructive expropriation' may, once again, prevent the past owner from exercising it. As already illustrated (see section IIIA), this Italian institution allows the public authorities to 'remedy' an unlawful expropriation (the consequences of which would be its annulment and the restitution of the property) by ordering the acquisition of the land unlawfully seized and physically or legally modified. Consequently, the previous owner cannot ask for restitution, but has to accept compensation (which includes a percentage of non-pecuniary damages). The interesting thing here is that failure to comply with the works scheduled can be considered a well-founded reason for seeking annulment of the seizure. Consequently, 'constructive expropriation' can be triggered by the authorities. Quite surprisingly, Italian law does not establish any deadline for doing so, and this controversial institution may even be applied years after the land has been occupied.

V. Conclusions

This comparative analysis has shown that the three legal systems have many points in common, even though some differences among them have also arisen. A general remark that could be highlighted in this concluding section is the important role played by procedural guarantees. As expropriation is an important limit to, or even a deprivation of, property rights, safeguards throughout the expropriation proceedings (and even afterwards) are of great significance for the affected persons. All three systems therefore give utmost importance to the expropriation procedure. Precisely for this reason, the procedural requirements vis-à-vis administrative limits to property rights offer several interesting insights for the 'Common Core of European Administrative Law' research, as shown throughout this chapter.

19

The Value of Property in Central and Eastern Europe

Comparative Expropriation in Poland, Ukraine, and Hungary

*Balázs Szabolcs Gerencsér**

I. Introduction and historical background

This study aims to compare relevant legal regulations in Poland and Ukraine, as well as relevant provisions in Hungarian law. The recent history of these three countries has led to a special emphasis on the right to property. All three lacked free (private) property during the time of their communist dictatorships, as their extreme collectivist ideology rejected the importance of private property and proclaimed only the primacy of state property.

In the democracies re-emerging after 1989, private property once again became the primary foundation of civil society. The Constitutional order is based on the recognition of private property and its fullest possible respect and primacy. The right to property is fundamental, and is important both in the relationship between citizens and in the relationship between citizens and state power. The recognition of private property therefore limits the intervention of state power in the civil sphere, and it puts an end to the direct relationship between economic and political power. Private property thereby restricts the power of the state.

Changes of regime were also accompanied by Constitutional amendments in each of the countries examined. The earlier communist constitutions did not (or only seemed to) regulate the right to property and other fundamental rights. One of the most important manifestations of the change in the political regime is, therefore, the redefinition of fundamental rights and, during this process, the rediscovery of the idea that these human rights and fundamental freedoms are based on private property. If an individual's right to property is restricted, his/her political rights also become limited.

One of the means of building a Soviet-style dictatorship was the nationalisation of private property. This, in fact, was a historically unique, arbitrary confiscation. The dictatorships deprived citizens and various legal entities (such as local governments, churches, social organisations, insurance institutions, cooperatives, and commercial companies) of almost all of their productive assets. With this, all asset-based sources

* PhD, Habil, Director of Ereky Public Law Research Center (ereky.jak.ppke.hu), associate professor at Pázmány Péter Catholic University, Faculty of Law, Budapest.

Balázs Szabolcs Gerencsér, *The Value of Property in Central and Eastern Europe* In: *Procedural Requirements for Administrative Limits to Property Rights*. Edited by: Martina Conticelli And Thomas Perroud, Oxford University Press. © Balázs Szabolcs Gerencsér 2022. DOI: 10.1093/oso/9780198867586.003.0019

of income and the entire material basis of society were taken away. All this entailed a significant loss and destruction of property. Total state ownership, coupled with political power, resulted in unlimited dictatorship. The entire society was deprived of property, and its citizens lost their independence and became economically vulnerable.[1]

Given all this, it is understandable that the social and economic reorganisation of the former socialist countries relied on the restoration of private property. Controlled restrictions on property rights had to be created, the most important element of which was the codification of legal guarantees for expropriation. Controlled restrictions on property rights had to be created, the most important element of which was the codification of guarantees for expropriation. Property rights and their restrictions are well-regulated at the constitutional level in these three countries; however, detailed provisions can be found at statutory levels: in addition to civil codes, separate laws were enacted in all three countries to regulate the compulsory transfer of property.

II. Comparison of constitutional provisions

Article 21 of Poland's Constitution contains provisions on the right to property. Provisions concerning the right to property are contained in Chapter I (The Republic) of the Constitution. This precedes Chapter II, which summarises fundamental rights and freedoms (The Freedoms, Rights and Obligations of Persons and Citizens).

The fact that the right to property appears as a peculiar human right and is also given emphasis in the text of the Constitution is not unique in CEE constitutions. As far as the countries analysed are concerned, the Hungarian Constitution in force between 1989 and 2012 (Act XX of 1949 on the Constitution of the Republic of Hungary, amended in 1989) enshrined the right to property in the introductory chapter in its Article 13, like in Poland's Constitution.[2] This highlights the special role of the right to property in each of the countries freed from the pressures of Socialism; the restoration of the value of the right to property was a milestone in the establishment of a modern democratic political regime and a market economy.

According to the text of Article 21 paragraph 1 of Poland's Constitution 'The Republic of Poland shall protect ownership' as a fundamental right. In addition, paragraph 2 defines two pivotal elements of expropriation: 'Expropriation may be allowed solely for public purposes and for just compensation.'

The Polish Constitution, however, also declares the right to property among the fundamental rights, thus striking a balance between the political significance of

[1] A Horváth (ed), *Magyar Állam- és Jogtörténet (History of State and Law in Hungary)* (Nemzeti Közszolgálati Egyetem 2014) 280–81.

[2] This text is already the result of the advent of democracy in 1989. The text of the Hungarian Constitution in force in 1949 clearly avoided declaring the protection of private property. The one drafted during the communist era, based on Soviet, Stalinist principles, initially provided for state property: 'The bulk of the means of production in the Hungarian People's Republic, being the property of society, is in the ownership of the State, the community or the co-operatives. The means of production may also be in private ownership' (art 4(1)). In addition, art 8 also stipulated that '[t]he Constitution recognises and protects property acquired by work.' This restrictive provision was further limited in the Constitution by stating, 'Private property and individual initiative may not infringe public interests.' 'Protecting the property of the people' and 'strengthening social property' were also declared to be fundamental duties of the citizens of the Hungarian People's Republic (art 59).

property and its place among fundamental rights. Article 64 of the Constitution provides for the protection of 'ownership, [and] other property rights', and it stipulates that 'Everyone, on an equal basis, shall receive legal protection regarding ownership, other property rights and the right of succession.' (paragraph 2). All these rights may only be restricted in a manner regulated by law, without restricting the essential content of the fundamental right ('the substance of such right').

Constitutions adopted after the regime changes not only differentiated private property but also public property. The Constitutions analysed declare the right of local governments to property, which was also a revived legal instrument of public law in these countries (Poland's Constitution Article 165, Hungarian Fundamental Law Article 32, Ukrainian Constitution Article 14).

The Ukrainian Constitution provides for the right to property in its Chapter II on Human and Citizens' Rights, Freedoms and Duties. Article 41 guarantees the right to property and the right to disposal of things. The first sentence of Article 41 provides almost a civil law definition of the content of the right to property. Among the restrictions, the requirement of legality is mentioned in the text first; in other words, the right to property may only be restricted by law (see sentences 2 and 4: 'The right of private property is acquired by the procedure determined by law.' 'No one shall be unlawfully deprived of the right of property. The right of private property is inviolable').

Expropriation is provided for in paragraph (5) of Article 41. The Ukrainian Constitution emphasises that private property may be withdrawn only in exceptional cases and for reasons of social necessity. The text makes no reference to the object of ownership (movable or immovable property). Expropriation may only be applied by the procedure established by law and on condition of advance and complete compensation of a property's value. In this context, the Constitution also stipulates that the legal grounds for expropriation may be determined from two sources: martial law or a state of emergency. Regarding the state of emergency, this provision is unique as far as the three countries are concerned. In the event of an extraordinary legal order, the right to property can be temporarily restricted but cannot be withdrawn in Poland and in Hungary (Article 228 of Poland's Constitution; Articles 49, 50 and Article I of the Fundamental Law of Hungary).

Article 41 paragraph (6) of the Ukrainian Constitution also mentions another form of restriction: confiscation. Three conditions are set forth here: (i) a court decision is needed for its application, (ii) it may only be decided on a case-by-case basis, and (iii) it may only be decided and applied to the extent and according to the procedure established by law.

The Fundamental Law of Hungary has several parts providing for the right to property, but the text does not contain legal regulations; rather, it makes a political declaration. In its first Chapter, entitled 'Foundation', Article U (1) d) and g) makes reference to communist responsibility. These reasons derive from the same source that was mentioned at the beginning of the chapter.[3] It is also the first Chapter which

[3] According to the Hungarian Fundamental Law, art U paras (d) and (g) states that The Hungarian Socialist Workers' Party and its legal predecessors and the other political organisations established to serve them in the spirit of communist ideology were criminal organisations, and their leaders shall have responsibility without statute of limitations for ... putting an end to the economy based on the freedom of property, and indebting the country; depriving citizens and certain groups of citizens of their fundamental human

provides for the acquisition of the ownership of arable land (Article P).[4] In the second Chapter, on Freedom and Responsibility, Article XIII contains the right to property. Like Poland's Constitution, the provisions regarding expropriation are laid down in parallel to the declaration of the fundamental right (Article 21 para 2).

The property of local governments is provided for in a different part of the Fundamental Law of Hungary, namely in Article 32, which contains provisions for local governments. Article 38 regulates the property of the state and local governments in detail.

III. The object of expropriation

Expropriation always concerns the transfer of property, and the object over which the right to property can be exercised may be *movable or immovable*. The special and exceptional deprivation of property can therefore apply, in theory, to both types of property.

The three regulations analysed show significant differences in the possible legal grounds for deprivation of ownership. Constitutional Provisions remain silent about the types of things in all three countries, so one needs to look at lower-level provisions and legal practice to learn more about the exact content.

In accordance with the detailed Polish country report, the Constitutional Court of Poland interprets the definition of property broadly, and in its view not only immovable property but also movable property may be expropriated. In theory, this also applies to cases where the right in rem attaches to the immovable property (eg the right of usufruct).

Ukrainian legislation is also silent on the types of things. The country report finds that there are no separate or special provisions for land expropriation in the text. Article 350 of the Civil Code, on the other hand, is more specific when applying the rule of forced alienation to immovable property.

In Hungary, Act CXXIII of 2007 on Expropriation contains detailed provisions. Section 1 stipulates that according to Hungarian law, only immovable property may be expropriated. *In rem* rights attached to immovable property, such as the right of usufruct mentioned above, may also be expropriated, however. The amount of compensation also has to be specifically determined in the course of the procedure (section 17). The Hungarian law defines the arable land as a special object of limitation of property rights.

Case 8 raises both the issue of movable property and the restriction of property rights due to cultural heritage. The latter is a legal institution recognised in all the examined countries, ie, cultural protection (mainly related to immovable property) as defined by law may mean a restriction of property (eg alienation). Polish legislation

rights or seriously restricting such rights, in particular for … restricting their rights to property; totally depriving citizens of their liberties.

[4] Hungarian Fundamental Law, art P para (2)states that [t]he limits and conditions for acquisition of ownership and for use of arable land and forests that are necessary for achieving the objectives referred to in paragraph (1), as well as the rules concerning the organisation of integrated agricultural production and concerning family farms and other agricultural holdings, shall be laid down in a cardinal Act.

emphasises that only at the request of the owner can an asset be entered in the register of cultural heritage property. In none of the countries studied can an *ex officio* decision be made to place a private property under cultural heritage protection.

IV. Subjects of expropriation

The subject of the right to property is the *owner*. If any change in ownership (alienation) or dispute arises, the legal relationship becomes multipolar. In civil law terms, the former owner and the new owner, the seller and the buyer, will be the main subjects of the legal relationship. In addition to civil law, a very significant branch of administrative law also plays a role in expropriation. There will in any case be two inevitable subjects of a public administrative procedure (the client and the authority) who will not be the same as the civil subjects (at least on the buyer's side). As a result of expropriation, the property passes to the state (or local government), ie private property becomes public property. However, in expropriation procedures, more actors would typically have to be reckoned with.

If we look at the expropriation procedure in general, the *administrative body* (authority) channels in a forced sale between the seller and the buyer. The *seller* is the client, and the *buyer* is the person requesting the expropriation (for whom the law makes it necessary or mandatory for the task that requires the expropriation of a property). This means there are at least three subjects. In addition, however, there may be further actors such as the Land Registering Authority, which can prove the legal status of the property, or the expert who helps to determine the purchase price.

The expropriation procedure is normally carried out by a (usually regional) body of the centralised state administration in the three countries examined. In Poland it is the *stratost*, while in Hungary it is the county government office (*megyei kormányhivatal*). Both bodies are administrative units at NUTS-3 level. In Ukraine, according to the country report, the range of actors involved is wider: government bodies, decentralised state authorities, and decentralised municipalities can also conduct expropriation proceedings.

The person requesting the expropriation will normally be an actor appointed or authorised by law. This most extreme restriction on ownership is usually justified for the expansion of infrastructures, the energy sector, mining, or similar reasons, as we will see in the next subsection. A similar feature among them is that most of them are market activities; therefore it is not to be excluded that a business may also request the expropriation of a property in favour of the state to achieve a public purpose specified in the law.

Now we come to perhaps the most hidden and, at the same time, problematic part regarding the subjects. The owner is on the other side of the subject circle. His/her identity and the existence of property must be credibly proven in the proceedings. To this end, the authority has recourse to credible sources such as *state registers*. It may not even appear at first, but one of the keys to an effective and lawful expropriation is the public credibility of the state register and the security of data management. There is, unfortunately, usually little talk about this, but if we were to remove it from the procedure, complete expropriation would not be possible at all.

V. The content and framework of expropriation

A. The question of the legal bases

Expropriation is the most complete restriction on property rights. It is an extreme case of forced alienation in which the seller is forced into this position even against his/her will. Therefore, in the context of expropriation, it is worth examining the legal bases that may justify expropriation.

We have already seen that expropriation must be the ultimate means, where this forced transfer of ownership must be preceded by a hearing and a normal sale and purchase process. However, it is interesting to see what grounds appear in the legislation of the countries in question upon which a legal expropriation can be based.

Poland's Constitution identifies public purposes as a reason encompassing the common features of legal bases (Article 21). Article 31 of Poland's Constitution lists, among the general rules for the restriction of fundamental rights factors, those that may serve as a legal basis for the restriction of property rights: protection of security or public order, the natural environment, health or public morals, or the freedoms and rights of other persons. The Hungarian Fundamental Law also designates public interest and the criterion of exceptionality (Article XIII). The Ukrainian Constitution mentions another—broader—concept: reasons of social necessity (Article 41).

In order to find detailed legal bases in the Hungarian legislation we must, therefore, see the sources of law below constitutional level. Section 2 of the Hungarian Expropriation Act CXXIII of 2007 lists twenty grounds (points a–t) that may establish public interest: from energy and the development of transport infrastructure to environmental protection and communications. The list is exhaustive; however the amendment falls within the simple majority of Parliament's decision-making power, so it is up to the respective parliament to decide what falls within this scope.

Article 8 of the Ukrainian Law on Alienation also provides a detailed list of the reasons for expropriation: national security and defence, communication, utility, transport, energy and other facilities, mining, and objects of national importance.

The rules examined show that infrastructures (of all kinds) and critical infrastructures clearly have an advantage, as they are the service engines of society and the economy. In the same way, the law stipulates the condition of public interest necessary for expropriation for the operation of environmental, as well as other, protection and security objects.

Similarly, in terms of content, how does the law speak about *compensation*? The Polish Constitution emphasises the criterion of *just* compensation (Article 21). The Constitution of Ukraine, however, mentions *advance* and *complete* compensation of a property's value (Article 41). According to the Hungarian Fundamental Law, expropriation can only take place with *full*, *unconditional*, and *immediate* compensation (Article XIII).

Among the restrictions on ownership, the most severe (and restrictive) is expropriation, meaning the actual withdrawal of ownership. However, it is also worth mentioning *other restrictions on property ownership*, which have a milder effect, usually limiting only certain entitlements to property. This occurs when the state authority or municipality modifies building requirements within the framework of spatial or urban planning, thereby restricting the freedom of ownership. The limitation of building or alienation may also be due to some pre-defined public interest, such as the protection of cultural heritage, monument protection, landscaping, security regulations, environmental protection, and so on. These are restrictions that exist in all three countries examined and are regulated by law. A peculiarity of these restrictions is that the expropriation procedure appears as a kind of reference point.

Case 10 raises the question of the consequences of a quashed law that served as a legal ground for expropriation. Each of the countries examined assumes that the first condition for the legality of expropriation is a correct legal basis. If the authority orders expropriation on the basis of a valid and effective law (and thus the bus station works begin), the expropriation is lawful even if the legal basis is later repealed or quashed. Public purpose is a compulsory condition for expropriation in all the countries examined and can only be defined by law. In the case of all three countries, it can be stated that the law in force at the time of the administrative decision will be the keystone of the basis of legality.

The subsequent repeal of the legislation does not imply an obligation to restore the expropriation—especially if 'in integrum restitutio' is not even possible due to the work in progress and the fact that the owner has already received full and legal compensation. Ukrainian law allows the former owner to apply for repurchase within a period of 6 months.

Case 4 further details the issue of the legal basis. Solutions to this case show the need for special rules for both critical infrastructure (such is a hydropower plant) and the state of emergency. The protection of a critical infrastructure is necessary both for society and the economy, irrespective of whether it is privately or publicly owned, even at the cost of restricting property rights. Blocking the power plant in the example may also create a life-threatening situation if, for example, the power plant also supplies a hospital with electricity. Thus, several fundamental rights may conflict in this situation: in particular the right to life, human dignity, and the right to property.

If a state of emergency arises, then the law (constitution) must regulate in detail what can trigger the state of emergency. However, decisions made in such circumstances (even restrictions on ownership) can only be temporary.

B. Administrative Procedures

The procedure whereby expropriation is carried out is also part of the framework of protection. The Ukrainian and Hungarian constitutions explicitly state that expropriation may only take place within the framework of a procedure specified by law. The Polish legal environment has a similar prescription.

With regard to the procedures of the countries examined, the following key points may be highlighted. The first step is to request expropriation and/or to decide to order expropriation. Secondly, in order for the authority to be able to make a bid on the basis of relevant information, an expert decision on the price is required. In my own experience, most of the legal disputes are the most common at this point. This is followed, thirdly, by notification to the owner, and then a hearing. Finally, if the negotiation is unsuccessful, ie the purchase contract cannot be concluded, an expropriation decision must be made. This last step shows that expropriation must indeed be the tool of last resort in the hands of the state.

In case 2, the expropriation was carried out without notice and in violation of procedural rights. In all three countries examined, the right to a fair trial requires that all clients, in this case the owner, be informed of the initiation of the administrative procedure, and that they be able to express their views in person before the authority. A decision breaching this fundamental right will certainly be annulled by the courts of all three countries.

C. Legal Remedies

Administrative decisions on expropriation can be reviewed by a court in all three countries. The Polish country report specifically states that the court primarily has cassation powers (similar to Hungary), ie the court has little or no powers of reparation.

VI. Conclusions

We should note that the three countries studied—Poland, Ukraine and Hungary—are former Socialist countries for which private property is of outstanding value. This is stated primarily by the Constitutional rules of each, as well as by the decisions of the Constitutional Courts.

Among the rules of constitutional protection, we can highlight first of all the fact of declaration, ie the Constitutions in each examined country contain rules on the guarantee of property rights and the limits of expropriation. Secondly, all three constitutions emphasise that the right to property is fundamental and can only be restricted in the manner prescribed by law. This means the representative body—parliament—refers to the competence to regulate the restriction of fundamental rights.

Although all three countries have different definitions of expropriation in some ways, a common element is that the competent authority, the procedure, and the guarantees must be defined and designated in law; secondly, expropriation may be carried out only for reasons of public interest; and thirdly, expropriation can be ordered only on condition of paying full compensation. This also means that nationalisation, ie property withdrawal without compensation, is not a legal tool in the countries studied above and is therefore not an option.

20

Property Rights, Administrative Limits and Procedural Requirements in the EU, the ECHR, and the IIL

Martina Conticelli

I. Preface and background remarks

This comparative chapter addresses the approach to property rights of the European Union (EU), the European Convention on Human Rights (ECHR), and the legal regime for the protection of foreign investors (which we will refer to in general as international investment law or IIL).

The work's purpose is not only to compare legal systems from a merely abstract point of view and a theoretical perspective but also to highlight the major issues raised in the questionnaire through an analysis of the chosen hypotheticals.

The detailed story of the jurisdictions selected cannot be told in this chapter: we apologise in advance should some parts of this work appear axiomatic.

As a matter of fact, from an overall perspective, the regimes in question share many background commonalities and some distinctive features.

First and foremost, all of them are located beyond the state, with distinctions, however. While the EU can be classified as a supranational legal system,[1] the ECHR is part of the system of public international law, and the various bilateral regimes for the protection of foreign investments may be considered to operate both in a transnational dimension[2] and a global one.[3]

Not surprisingly, in terms of both quantitative and qualitative assessment, the list of overarching divergences proves quite significant. Legal experiences interplay with domestic contexts in various ways, but the same systems differ from each other from the point of view of their reach and the parties involved.

Last but not least, the purposes each legal regime stands for, their respective institutional setting, their legal machinery, and their effectiveness, may vary profoundly.

1 Case 26–62 *NV Algemene Transport- en Expeditie Onderneming van Gend & Loos v Netherlands Inland Revenue Administration* ECLI:EU:C:1963:1 (Judgment of the Court, 5 February 1963).

2 G Shaffer, *Transnational Legal Ordering and State Change* (CUP 2013); G Shaffer and C Coye, 'From International Law to Jessup's Transnational Law; From Transnational Law to Transnational Legal Orders' in P Zumbansen (ed), *The Many Lives of Transnational Law: Critical Engagements with Jessup's Bold Proposal* (CUP 2020) 126; G Shaffer and TC Halliday, 'With, Within, and Beyond the State: The Promise and Limits of Transnational Legal Ordering' in P Zumbansen (ed), *Oxford Handbook of Transnational Law* (OUP 2021).

3 On this issue but from different perspectives see G Van Harten and M Loughlin, 'Investment Treaty Arbitration as a Species of Global Administrative Law' (2006) 17 Eur J Intl L 121 ff; SW Schill, 'Multilateralizing Investment Treaties through Most-Favored-Nation Clauses' (2009) 27(2) BJIL 496.

Martina Conticelli, *Property Rights, Administrative Limits and Procedural Requirements in the EU, the ECHR, and the IIL*
In: *Procedural Requirements for Administrative Limits to Property Rights*. Edited by: Martina Conticelli And Thomas Perroud, Oxford University Press. © Martina Conticelli 2022. DOI: 10.1093/oso/9780198867586.003.0020

II. Foundations

It might appear trivial to state that discussion of the 'constitutional framework' concerning property rights and their deprivation in the EU, the ECHR, and the IIL must take into due account the uniqueness of each regime, but this is a necessary starting point.

First and foremost, as they are beyond state level, neither the ECHR nor the IIL take an active part in rule-making/executive rule-making/adjudication: their jurisdiction is limited to assessing compliance with given standards of action by public entities. The same issue could be addressed with regard to the EU. In addition, the EU enjoys a wide range of competencies in many policy areas, both in legislative and executive terms. Because of this, the same EU action might occasionally be questioned from the standpoint of its likely conflict with property issues.

Essentially, the three regimes primarily provide standards with which third parties must comply if they are to interfere with private property lawfully, while, at the same time, the EU also qualifies as a recipient of standards, as well as acting as a standard setter.

Secondly, from the viewpoint of formal constitutional provisions (as distinct from the substantive provisions existing also in countries without a formal Constitution in that sense) the question regarding constitutional property clauses should be answered in the negative for the jurisdictions selected. In contrast, our answer may change once we refer to the place assigned to property rights in acts considered to be primary sources by each legal system.

In general terms, the right to property is enshrined in Article 17 of the Charter of Nice, Article 1 of Protocol No 1 to the ECHR, and *ad hoc* provisions in most of the treaties protecting investors from a contracting state in the territory of another contracting state.

As far as the EU is concerned, a suitable starting point may be the absence of a formal provision concerning the 'right to property' in the Treaties, given that Article 345 TFEU provides that: 'The Treaties shall in no way prejudice the rules in Member States governing the system of property ownership' (replacing former Article 222 of the Treaty of Rome).[4]

The above-mentioned provision enshrines the principle of neutrality of the Treaties regarding the systems of property ownership in the EU Member States. Its scope may appear controversial: initially referring to public or private ownership of companies, the provision was intended to signify an abstention from formal expropriation, which still remains within the prerogative of the legal systems, both in terms of discipline and administrative implementation.

[4] Further, minor, references to property are included in the limits on implementing measures for the free movement of goods in the form of industrial and commercial properties and among the guarantees of implementation of the freedom of establishment from the beginning: see Treaty of Rome, arts 13, 36, 54.

Nevertheless, the picture changes once the Charter of Nice is approved, and thanks to the reference included in Article 6 TEU by the Treaty of Lisbon, given that Article 17 of the Charter of Rights provides that:

> 1. Everyone has the right to own, use, dispose of and bequeath his or her lawfully acquired possessions. No one may be deprived of their possessions, except in the public interest and the cases and under the conditions provided for by law, subject to fair compensation being paid in good time for their loss. The use of property may be regulated by law in so far as is necessary for the general interest. 2. Intellectual property shall be protected.

It would be mistaken, however, to think that the EU approach to property and other fundamental rights was actually neutral before 2000.

On the contrary, in striving to look for the real status of property within the EU, analysis of its jurisprudence provides quite a different picture. Primary references can be found in the supranational courts' rulings delivered in the nineteen-seventies. By that time, the approach to the protection of fundamental rights, broadly speaking,[5] and property rights, more specifically,[6] was mostly linked to the constitutional traditions of the Member States and the ECHR.[7]

At the same time, the Court used to refer to non-discrimination on the grounds of nationality and fundamental freedoms.

Initially, therefore, concern for property rights was conceived potentially as an additional tool of the common market. Until the turn of the twenty-first century, in fact, judicial review served to check the lawfulness of actions in terms of their potential implications for intra-community discrimination.

We may consider though, that the affirmation of a catalogue of rights itself did not immediately lead to the attribution of an autonomous space for protection of the right of property, due to the massive space occupied by the overarching freedoms of the Single Market, and particularly, the right to establishment and the freedom to provide services.

Thus, the restrictions covered by Article 17 of the Nice Charter are still frequently read in conjunction with the freedoms referred to in Articles 15 and 16 whenever their subject matter may be likely to overlap.[8] Article 52, paragraph 1 of the same Charter states that:

> Any limitation on the exercise of the rights and freedoms recognised by this Charter must be provided for by law and respect the essence of those rights and freedoms. Subject to the principle of proportionality, limitations may be made only if they are

[5] Judgment of the Court of 17 December 1970, *Internationale Handelsgesellschaft mbH v Einfuhr- und Vorratsstelle für Getreide und Futtermittel*, Case 11–70 [1970] ECLI:EU:C:1970:114.

[6] Case 4–73 *J Nold, Kohlen-und Baustoffgroßhandlung v Commission of the European Communities* [1974] ECR 491 (Judgment of the Court, 14 May 1974); Case 44/79 *Liselotte Hauer v Land Rheinland-Pfalz* [1979] ECR 3727 (Judgment of the Court, 13 December 1979).

[7] P Craig, *EU Administrative Law* (OUP 2006) 484 ff.

[8] See Judgment of the Court (Third Chamber) 30 April 2014, case C-390/12, Pflaeger [2014] ECLI:EU:C:2014:281.

> necessary and genuinely meet objectives of general interest recognised by the Union or the need to protect the rights and freedoms of others.

Furthermore, and needless to say, the reach of the Charter of Rights is still limited to activity involving states and national administrations in the implementation of European Union Law. At the same time, reference to the European Convention on Human Rights has inevitably become considerable after Lisbon.[9]

Again, Article 52 chapter 3 provides that:

> In so far as this Charter contains rights which correspond to rights guaranteed by the Convention for the Protection of Human Rights and Fundamental Freedoms, the meaning and scope of those rights shall be the same as those laid down by the said Convention. This provision shall not prevent Union law providing more extensive protection.

This naturally leads to a discussion of the ECHR. Without a doubt, the framework for protecting human rights provided for by the European Convention deserves a special mention within the context of our investigation. This legal system does not enjoy regulatory functions since it is entrusted with guaranteeing compliance with a series of rights, in so far as its objectives do not include purposes of a finalistic nature.

The significance of the ECHR when dealing with property issues is unprecedented, however. Concerning property deprivations, Article 1, Protocol 1, added lately to the main body of the Convention, states that:

> 1. Every natural or legal person is entitled to the peaceful enjoyment of his possessions. No one shall be deprived of his possessions except in the public interest and subject to the conditions provided for by law and by the general principles of international law. 2. The preceding provisions shall not, however, in any way impair the right of a State to enforce such laws as it deems necessary to control the use of property in accordance with the general interest or to secure the payment of taxes or other contributions or penalties.

It is precisely in the case law of the Court of Strasbourg that significant attention is given to the protection of proprietary rights and the regulation of their deprivation, albeit within the general limits customarily ascribed to the Convention.

The details were first specified in a seminal ruling by the same Court, carefully interpreting the framing of Article 1, Protocol 1, which held what might be understood to refer to three distinct rules:

> The first rule, which is of a general nature, enounces the principle of peaceful enjoyment of property; it is set out in the first sentence of the first paragraph. The second rule covers deprivation of possessions and subjects it to certain conditions; it appears in the second sentence of the same paragraph. The third rule recognises that the

[9] See TEU, art 6 and, before that, Maastricht Treaty, art F para 2.

> States are entitled, amongst other things, to control the use of property in accordance with the general interest, by enforcing such laws as they deem necessary for the purpose; it is contained in the second paragraph.[10]

Further arguments for the respect of property rights pass through the scrutiny of the various investments' protection regimes. Thus, we refer to the environment that seeks to protect foreign investors' rights, some of whose legal bases are to be found in bilateral treaties, and others in multilateral ones.

The thousands of Treaties shaping foreign investment protection complement customary law and the concept of international expropriation in this field.[11] These arrangements have been brought under 'a system' through an exegetical analysis of the texts adopted by arbitral tribunals with jurisdiction over the enforcement of investors' rights.

Property is one of the main focuses of bilateral or multilateral investment treaties. The recognition of investors' expectations represents the need to provide adequate protection for the remuneration of the capital employed in countries other than that of origin.

As far as property and its deprivation is concerned, all the texts convey a 'standard' notion of deprivation of property. There is little room to mention here the multiple provisions on the matter, not to mention model bilateral treaties. For example, one may refer to the Canadian bilateral investment treaty (one of the latest to be re-issued),[12] whose Article 9, first paragraph states:

> 1. No Party shall expropriate a covered investment either directly or indirectly, except (a) for a public purpose; (b) in accordance with due process of law; (c) in a non-discriminatory manner; and (d) on payment of compensation in accordance with paragraph 5.
> 2. A direct expropriation under paragraph 1 occurs only when a covered investment is taken by a Party through formal transfer of title or outright seizure.
> 3. An indirect expropriation under paragraph 1 may occur when a measure or a series of measures of a Party has an effect equivalent to direct expropriation without formal transfer of title or outright seizure. A non-discriminatory measure of a Party that is adopted and maintained in good faith to protect legitimate public welfare objectives, such as health, safety and the environment, does not constitute indirect expropriation, even if it has an effect equivalent to direct expropriation.

Analysis of property clauses reveals that crucial concepts are similar in principle, but there is some degree of divergence.

Basic requirements governing lawful expropriation as set out by the 'constitutional provisions', like in the case of the Charter of Nice and the ECHR, are met when the

[10] See ECtHR, *Sporrong and Lönnroth* (1979) Series A no 52, para 63.

[11] They should amount to 2,290, according to the Unctad Investment Policy Hub: see https://investmentpolicy.unctad.org/international-investment-agreements (accessed 21 July 2021).

[12] See the whole model agreement at the following url: https://investmentpolicy.unctad.org/international-investment-agreements/treaty-files/6341/download (accessed 4 July 2021).

decision is rooted in the public interest, conditions are provided for by law, and fair compensation is promptly afforded (reference is also made to the respect of general principles of international law in the ECHR).

In addition and beyond emphasising the need for a public purpose and the plea for compensation, investment treaties within the IIL commonly claim that expropriation can only occur according to due process of law and concerning non-discriminatory conditions.

Other divergences concern the way the above-mentioned texts consider what property the property in question actually is: while the Charter of Nice and the protocol to the ECHR refer to property rights and possessions, most of the bilateral treaties within what we have qualified as the IIL regime deal with investments.

We argue that divergence is more apparent than real as far as this point is concerned, as the concepts of assets and possessions, in the definition provided by most investment treaties, overlap and almost coincide.

III. Theory and practice

Clearly, the picture provided thus far does not answer all the problems concerning the protection of property rights and deprivation, specifically regarding grounds, procedure, and enforcement. Significant guidance is provided by the courts as far as the EU and the ECHR are concerned and by arbitral tribunals with regard to the IIL. Rulings and 'case law' from the courts mentioned above are of paramount importance in addressing this issue.

Questions and problems are frequently raised concerning the lawfulness of deprivation from the points of view of legality, substantive and procedural requirements, and guarantees. The solutions are eclectic given the nature of the legal systems selected, their interplay with national systems and their possible reciprocal relationships.

As mentioned in the previous pages, it cannot be said that the selected jurisdictions enjoy land expropriation powers in the traditional sense.

However, as their jurisdictions increase and, given the development of functions with specific regard to the EU, actions by supranational institutions or national administrations in the execution of EU law currently interfere with property rights in many ways. EU activities themselves may therefore be assessed as potentially representing deprivation of property.

While the EU, the ECHR, and the IIL are all concerned with expropriation, they regularly scrutinise acts attributable to competent agencies. In this regard, the way powers of expropriation are distributed among different levels of government is usually irrelevant (ie in regional, federal or confederal states).

Their scrutiny acts as a supplement to domestic (and EU) legislation to ensure the rule of law in cases of deprivation attributable to public administrations in the broad sense. Essentially, they double check domestic (and supranational) decisions both in adjudicatory proceedings and rule-making activity or executive rule-making procedures.

If the extinction of owners' legal rights may constitute the essence of a deprivation of property, not only are formal expropriation and transfer of ownership taken into consideration but also *de facto* expropriations and other regulatory decisions that may interfere with property rights in terms of their effects, which are rated as tantamount to expropriation.

Consequently, a proper procedure is not formally ruled out as in the case of traditional expropriation within national legal systems due to the lack of power to expropriate. The EU provides some exceptions in this regard, so when regulatory policies might interfere with property rights, not only a legal basis but a codified procedure for limiting private assets is needed. An excellent example in this regard is represented by the rules for resolving credit institutions in EU countries participating in the Banking Union.[13]

Conversely, standards defining fair procedure are not codified *ex ante*, although they are clearly affirmed mainly in case law, which refers them both to direct deprivations and indirect interference in the enjoyment of property rights.

The consequences of a court finding an act unlawfully depriving property rights vary, depending on the jurisdiction taken into consideration and the specific case in point.

While the Court of Justice may declare an act null and void within the limits on annulment, the ECHR and arbitral tribunals do not have jurisdiction to annul a specific act, nor can they review domestic ones. *Restitutio in integrum* is also excluded; instead, parties seeking monetary damages may be awarded compensation if they are victims unlawful conduct.

IV. Convergence and divergences in practice

Regarding the hypotheticals, it is interesting to reflect on procedural requirements, indirect expropriations, and regulatory takings. A focus on the questionnaire reveals that these topics look particularly meaningful when addressing the main issues regarding property and its deprivation in the jurisdictions of interest here. On the subject of assessing convergence and divergence from the perspective of discussing a common core, we may anticipate that they all contribute to defining the scope of application of shared principles, albeit in different ways.

The duty to give notice and, conversely, the right to be heard are preconditions for the lawfulness of deprivation in all three legal systems.

This is considered a general principle of Community Law.[14] The right to be heard in some EU Court judgments relating to property rights has proved particularly important, as have some pieces of sectoral legislation, even in the absence of any rules governing the procedure in question, or before the appearance of rules prescribing precisely the opposite, since this is part of the system of protection of fundamental rights at the heart of EU law.

[13] See Regulation (EU) No 806/2014 of the European Parliament and of the Council of 15 July 2014 establishing uniform rules and procedure for the resolution of credit institutions and certain investment firms in the framework of a Single Resolution Mechanism and a Single Resolution Fund, amending Regulation (EU) No 1093/2010.

[14] See Joined Cases C-402/05 P and C-415/05 P *Kadi and Al Barakaat International Foundation v Council and Commission* [2008] ECR I-6351.

As for the ECHR, the Court of Strasbourg held that even if Article 1 of Protocol No 1 to the ECHR does not refer to any procedural requirement, the Court must nevertheless consider whether applicable procedures enable reasonable consideration of the views of the interested parties and, in order to ascertain whether those conditions were satisfied, 'a comprehensive view must be taken of the applicable procedures'.[15]

A prominent role is assigned to due process rights, such as the right to be heard or the right to judicial review, also within the IIL regime, with specific reference to formal deprivation of the right of property. On the contrary, sole infringement of the right to be heard cannot be sufficient for conduct to be deemed wrongful if measures are tantamount to expropriation before any regulatory activity.

The consequences of breaches differ across the legal systems selected: neither the European Court of Human rights nor the tribunals seized with IIL cases may void any administrative measure on this basis, unlike the EU courts, but they can award damages or compensation.

A particular interest in indirect expropriations emerges from a factual analysis of the questionnaire.

The case in point arises from the occupation of private lands ordered by the city of Metropolis—including a part of Miss Busy's property—to carry out urgent public works for the renovation and maintenance of a highway. After a long period of land occupation, the issue arises when the works are not carried out and the land is not used.

Paradoxically the unlimited and never-ending occupation of lands deprives the owner of her prerogatives without any expropriation having occurred. In fact, notwithstanding formal ownership of her land, public deficiency in completing the formal expropriation procedure prevents Miss Busy from enjoying the prerogatives associated with ownership or counting on the guarantees and conditions in place for formal ownership expropriations, such as compensation for her loss. Such a condition is condemned in each of the legal systems selected for our comparison.

As for the ECHR, the Court of Strasbourg began to address this issue in 1993[16] and delivered one of its best known rulings on the matter, stating the need to look behind the appearances, holding that 'the Convention is intended to guarantee rights that are "practical and effective"'.[17]

Furthermore, from the IIL perspective, Miss Busy's properties are considered to be the object of indirect expropriation (or *de facto* expropriation),[18] whose unlawfulness rests on several deviations from the formal expropriation model. This may therefore legitimise the investor claimant to seek compensation.

The case regarding regulatory takings is particularly relevant in all legal systems.

As far as the case included in the questionnaire is concerned, the damage suffered by Mr Mad Hatter results from a change in local laws or government decisions that affects the future use of his properties in Belle Coast. The issue at stake highlights the

[15] See Court (Chamber) *Agosi v United Kingdom* (1987) 9 EHRR 1, App no 9118/80, para 55.

[16] ECtHR, *Papamichalopoulos v Greece* (1993) Series A no 260-B.

[17] *Sporrong and Lönnroth* (n 10).

[18] *Compañia del Desarrollo de Santa Elena SA v Republic of Costa Rica* ICSID Case No ARB/96/1 Award (17 February 2000); *PL Holdings Sàrl v Republic of Poland* SCC Case No 2014/163 (2017).

conflict between proprietary rights (which are not absolute in modern democracies) and the power to regulate (which cannot be spared scrutiny).

Protection stands at a crossroads between what constitutes deprivation and what may be considered a form of control over the use of property.[19]

According to settled case law, the right to property is not absolute but must be viewed in relation to its function in society. Consequently, exercise of the right to property may be restricted,

> provided that these restrictions, in fact, correspond to objectives of public interest pursued by the Community and do not constitute, in relation to the aim pursued, a disproportionate and intolerable interference, impairing the very substance of the right so guaranteed.[20]

The Mad Hatter controversy, however, opens the path to a review that might well take into account various issues. These could include the frustration of the owners' legitimate expectations regarding his prerogatives, the basis of police powers,[21] and the role of the principle of proportionality, while, with specific regard to the IIL, we might also mention the potential breach of the fair and equitable treatment (FET) standard.

While, on the one hand, the power to regulate does not escape scrutiny, on the other, the object and purpose of regulation in terms of relevance for public needs and interests must be taken into consideration. If this is the case, policy delivery may be as significant as policy purposes.

Comparison of thee hypotheticals highlights many convergences and some divergences in these legal systems' approaches to property issues, some of which have already been pointed out in the previous pages. Further points of common relevance concern the broad concept of property rights both in terms of objects and deprivations.

As far as the former are concerned, both goods capable of value and vested rights are taken into due account. In practice, abstract definitions of property referring to possessions in the ECHR regime and investments in the IIL system are interpreted broadly in jurisprudence. From vineyards[22] to intellectual rights to social security benefits[23] and licences,[24] a vast range of categories, such as movables, immovables, intangibles, claims, and entitlement rights are represented in the case law of the EU courts, as well as in the rulings settled by the Court of Strasbourg and arbitration proceedings.

[19] As for the ECtHR, reference may be made to art 1. See *Banèr v Sweden* App no 11763/85 (Commission Decision, 9 March 1989).

[20] Lastly see Judgment of the Court (Grand Chamber) of 3 September 2008: Joined Cases C-402/05 P and C-415/05 P *Yassin Abdullah Kadi and Al Barakaat International Foundation v Council of the European Union and Commission of the European Communities* [2008] ECR I-06351.

[21] *Técnicas Medioambientale Tecmed SA v United Mexican States* ICSID Case No ARB AF/00/2 Award (29 May 2003).

[22] Case 44/79 *Liselotte Hauer v Land Rheinland-Pfalz* (n 6).

[23] See Case C-258/14 *Eugenia Florescu and Others v Casa Județeană de Pensii Sibiu and Others* ECLI:EU:C:2017:448 (Judgment of the Court (Grand Chamber), 13 June 2017); *Stec and Others v United Kingdom* App nos 65731/01 and 65900/01 [2005] ECHR 924 (ECtHR (Grand Chamber), 6 July 2005).

[24] See Case C 190/16 *Werner Fries v Lufthansa CityLine GmbH* [2017] ECLI:EU:C:2017:513 (Judgment of the Court (First Chamber), 5 July 2017); *Capital Bank AD v Bulgaria* App no 49429/99 (ECtHR, 24 November 2005); *Case of Centro Europa 7 Srl and Di Stefano v Italy* App no 38433/09 (ECtHR, 7 June 2012).

Moreover, not only do the objects of property rights evade the classical approach anchored in a view of property that mainly refers to immovables, but a wide range of different prerogatives associated with property are taken into serious consideration with clear implications for the concept of what might be considered as 'taking' or as a measure of interference.

As for the latter therefore, in addition to compulsory acquisitions and deprivation, also different forms of restrictions, such as transfer to public ownership/requisitions, and extinguishment/modification of rights regarding rights to possessions, takings, and regulatory takings, are relevant.

In other words, direct expropriation is of concern for the jurisdictions selected but also for indirect expropriation when this is the consequence of regulatory policies capable of affecting private property rights.

Such an approach to property rights and deprivations differs profoundly from domestic approaches, with consequent implications for concrete and adequate protection.

Regarding the focus of this volume, as already mentioned, procedural terms are not generally codified with specific regard to cases involving property. Thus, procedural requirements and guarantees are mainly specified in the case law of all three legal systems.

As a legal basis, fair compensation and public interest are requisites, while reasonableness and proportionality are also commonly recognised as general criteria for valid restrictions in a regular stream of cases in each of the legal regimes in question.

While speaking specifically about procedural requirements and more broadly about rights in the course of procedure, the case law of the three jurisdictions provides a very broad picture. Within the given catalogue, the right to be heard, to be informed, to obtain a reasoned decision, the protection of legitimate expectations, good administration, impartial treatment, respect for procedural steps, and the need for a codified procedure are duly safeguarded.

Particular relevance is given to forms of review as well as to rectification procedures. General attention is paid to the way different values come into the procedure, to the rights of third parties, the position of those directly aggrieved, and the effects on the handling of procedural irregularities, to procedural criteria for the use of discretionary powers, procedural arbitrariness, conditions possibly affecting procedures, and those leading to changes (eg a procedure that is normally unreasonable may be considered reasonable in times of emergency).

V. Property rights, revisited?

Notwithstanding the strong connection between property rights and the sovereign choices expressed by national constitutions, jurisdictions beyond the state are of greater importance to the subject matter of this book.

The main findings of our comparative survey strengthen the belief that the contemporary paradigm of property rights rejects the formal and rigid modules of domestic jurisdictions but at the same time the benefits from the input from legal orders other than the state increase.[25] This is particularly evident if one considers that failure to

[25] D Caruso, 'Private Law and Public Stakes in European Integration: the Case of Property' (2004) 10(6) Eur LJ 751 ff; A Lehavi, 'Unbundling Harmonization: Public versus Private Law: Strategies to Globalize Property' (2015) 15(2) Chic J Intl L 452 ff.

comply with ultra-national standards may translate into unlawful conduct in the view of regional supranational courts, international conventions, or in the course of transnational arbitration proceedings even when the action has been taken in conformity with domestic legality in the broader sense.

If we look at the debate thus far, most of the studies on this subject have focused on property and its state-wide limits, while less attention has been paid to the exercise of authoritative power, particularly with regard to the forms and limits of public interference, at least till the latest decades of the last century. That was the initial outcome of the enormous stream of cases delivered by the former European Communities' courts and the Court of Strasbourg.

Conversely, the lines of the more recent literature show a generalised dissatisfaction with the traditional anchoring of property to domestic regimes in favour of the role of other regimes where attention is devoted mainly to procedural and substantive fairness, as well as on their implication on the overall regime of property and its deprivations.[26]

Looking to the future, the development of international trade and the spread of transnational regimes protecting direct investments may imply first of all a re-reading of some traditional legal categories such as property and deprivation—the object of this volume—but also of the standards of administrative action and decision-making rules relating primarily to deprivation in classic cases of expropriation (whether translational or otherwise), also referring more broadly to regulatory forms of deprivation. The growing importance of standards of fairness in administrative action and their increasing relevance by virtue of multiple relationships across markets, as well as the interplay between legal systems (also in the field of property) are expected to foster not only the development of common principles but also, and even more importantly, their enforcement.

[26] In this sense see U Mattei, *La proprietà, in Trattato di diritto civile: I diritti reali*, vol II (Utet 2015) 429.

21
Concluding Remarks on the Unity of the Liberal World as Regards State Regulation of Property

*Thomas Perroud**

I. What's in a name? The notion of takings

The notion of 'takings' as a legal institution relates to state-imposed limits on private property, that is, administrative limits to property rights. Property rights are recognised as one of the fundamental pillars of the rule of law. It is traditionally connected to the concept of freedom, having been raised to a fundamental right by the liberal constitutionalism of the Enlightenment era.

The right to property was enshrined in the revolutionary declarations and perceived as an inherent right of the human condition itself, coming to be considered an absolute right and 'the universal soul of all legislation'.[1] Although it represents a guarantee of freedom, it is important to note that it is limited and attenuated by certain principles and fundamental rights resulting from historical and social processes.

Both property rights and the notion of takings in each of the selected legal systems refer to principles built up from apparently common ground, interpreted as liberal and individualistic ideas. However, these rights and takings are set in specific social contexts and legal traditions, being also subject to legal frameworks that may be more or less robust.

In fact, the right to property requires a set of legal rules to be effective; these may be found in most of the selected countries' constitutions, either in the fundamental rights chapter or under the headings regarding economic, social, and cultural rights (such as Italy, Spain, and Portugal). In England and Wales, recognition comes from the existence of a specific tort (trespass) and the regulations on takings.

These same legal rules also allow the state to impose restrictions on such property rights. However, in each legal system reviewed, the notions of property and takings have specific contours: some use generic formulas whereas others employ more detailed regulation over scenarios where takings are permitted, including specific enforcement criteria.

* I wish to thank Carolina Mota Mourão for help in drafting this conclusion.

[1] See J Gordley, 'Myths of the French Civil Code' (1994) 42(3) AJCL 459 (quoting Halperin who, in turn, uses this quotation from Portalis—Présentation au Corps Législatif) 463.

Thomas Perroud, *Concluding Remarks on the Unity of the Liberal World as Regards State Regulation of Property* In: *Procedural Requirements for Administrative Limits to Property Rights.* Edited by: Martina Conticelli And Thomas Perroud, Oxford University Press. © Thomas Perroud 2022. DOI: 10.1093/oso/9780198867586.003.0021

On the other hand, although the concept of takings may be subject to distinct approaches depending on the 'legal families' involved,[2] it is connected—directly or indirectly—to certain aspects that may be viewed as a common core, mostly relating to the link between takings and individual freedom. In this sense, even though the notion of takings has different names and legal forms, it is important to seek out its essence and understand its identity-forming attributes ('a rose by any other name would smell as sweet'). In other words, names are arbitrary labels.

Considering the similarities and differences inherent to the concept of takings in each European jurisdiction, the comparative analysis presented here provides a systematic overview of the subject to aid understanding of the common traditions and principles governing the concept of takings. The analysis covers a range of liberal democracies, which, albeit with many variations and particularities, look to the establishment of common standards regarding the moderation of state power, the lawfulness of administrative action, and procedural guarantees.[3]

A. Shared criteria

A comparative analysis of each jurisdiction brings out the principle similarities regarding takings. Each system guarantees the right to property and determines that any restrictions will only apply if they are in accordance with the specific criteria established in the relevant statutes or follow parameters defined by the judiciary.

The different features of takings in each specific legal system are permeated by great issues and are intended to fulfil functions that reveal the existence of a shared substrate[4]. It is essential to understand these common elements.

In the legal systems reviewed in this book, the concept of takings refers to a compulsory transfer of property. Although the notion of expropriation was initially closely related to the transfer of property from an individual to the state, the underlying general principle is the government's power to take private property, even if there is no effective transfer to the state but to other recipients. Thus, property may be transferred to a private entity, as long as there is a public purpose.[5] Furthermore, the boundaries between public and private structures have become increasingly fluid in view of the growing approximation between public administration and the private sector in particularly diverse projects.[6]

This kind of mandatory transfer of ownership relies on two fundamental pillars: public interest and financial compensation for the individual right sacrificed in the name of the common good. The public interest requirement for carrying out

[2] See the comments made by S Cassese on the traditional legal comparison based on the definition of legal types and families in S Cassese, *La Construction du Droit Administratif: France et Royaume-Uni* (Montchrestien 2000) 18–20.

[3] On the specificities and convergences of legal systems see M Fromont, *Droit Administratif des États Européens* (PUF 2006) 353. See also G della Cananea, 'Administrative Law in Europe: a Historical and Comparative Perspective' (2009) 2 IJPL 181.

[4] See della Cananea (n 4) 209.

[5] The cases of Belgium and Germany illustrate this alternative.

[6] See the analysis by Y Marique, 'Public and Private Sovereign Powers in Liberal Models of Property Protection: Belgium, Sweden, and the Netherlands' in this volume.

expropriation draws attention to the need for political or moral justification. In turn, compensation brings the economic dimension of rights at stake in expropriation into play insofar as it constitutes a form of allocation of rights and resources in society.

Regarding the public interest requirement for expropriation, different expressions are adopted by the legal systems analysed; for instance: 'public purpose', 'public interest', 'general interest', 'the public good', 'public use', and 'public utility'.[7] In some cases, the use of qualifiers such as 'pressing' to characterise 'public interests' may indicate a non-standard situation.

There are undoubtedly some significant variations. However, the adoption of different expressions does not necessarily imply totally different perceptions of what the 'common good' is. As Magaldi shows in her analysis of Italy, Portugal, and Spain, the fact that there are fluctuations does not mean we are facing a conceptual crisis.[8]

In reality, this plurality of expressions emphasises that, in the countries analysed, expropriation generates a common obligation to present reasons of a public nature that (i) benefit the community to some extent, and (ii) are sufficient in the face of the sacrifice suffered by an individual on behalf of the entire community. In this way, the 'common good'—and the respective theoretical and practical work involved in its construction—has the function of meeting the need for appropriate public justification. To some extent, it establishes a balance between the public purpose and the interest and rights of those involved.[9]

There are other important aspects that permeate, from a theoretical point of view, the need for a justification of expropriations since they present specificities in comparison to other kinds of intervention regarding property. As Elazar explains, this occurs for two main reasons. The first is because the expropriation of assets over which the individual has a legitimate right is made asymmetrically by the state. This means the restriction on ownership does not arise from broader economic regulations applicable to groups or segments of society but from a specific decision that leads to a very specific sacrifice for an individual or group. The second reason is because it affects a good whose nature is not entirely fungible. In other words, even pecuniary compensation may not repair the damage resulting from expropriation due to the different interests and expectations of the owner in relation to his/her property.[10]

In this sense, the need to justify emerges as a truly 'universal principle' underlying the legal institute of takings. Any limitation over property rights must entail some level of justification based on some consideration of the relationship between the public and the private, even if it is vague and unclear. Thus, the justification of a public reason is usually one of the first elements legally required in carrying out the expropriation process.

[7] These expressions were taken from the reports presented by the countries analysed in this book.

[8] See N Magaldi, 'Procedural Safeguards of Property Rights in Southern Europe: Italy, Spain, and Portugal' in this volume.

[9] This demand for equitable balance between the public interest and the interests of those affected is expressly stated in the German report.

[10] M Elazar, '"Public Use" and the Justification of Takings' (2004) 7 U Pa J Const L 249 https://scholarship.law.upenn.edu/jcl/vol7/iss1/5 (accessed 15 July 2021).

Another common general principle is compensation. At least since 1789 and the French Declaration, financial compensation has been the remedy for any restrictions imposed on private property. Found in all the legal systems analysed, it remains untouched in the context of liberal democracies.

Nonetheless, such compensation may be subject to specific modulations. This is the case in jurisdictions where we identify qualifiers as 'just' or 'fair', or jurisdictions that provide for 'full' compensation (such as Sweden). Therefore, there is a general rule of compensation that must comply with certain requirements that, in practical terms, may substantially change the effects of takings.

The concept of compensation raises several relevant questions about the proper instruments to determine the fair value due to property limitations and the authorities empowered to make such a decision on fair valuation in each case. The calculation of the value of a property goes beyond the merely financial dimension, also involving issues concerning political, moral and economic rationality: how to quantify adequate and fair compensation? What criteria should be adopted? How much is society willing to pay for expropriated property? What rights and interests should prevail? What is really at stake from the point of view of compensation? Compensation often expresses the tensions underlying social relations and raises a discussion about distribution, equality, and social purposes of state power over property.

In every expropriation there is, implicitly, a reaffirmation (or criticism) of the 'social pact'? Theoretically, there is indeed a recognition that expropriation is part of the rules for living in society and the 'common good'. In short, revisiting Rousseau, 'each one of us puts into the community his person and all his power under the supreme direction of the general will; and as a body, we incorporate every member as an indivisible part of the whole'.[11]

Thus, in expropriation, especially in democratic regimes, there is an evident intertwining of justification and compensation (*Romeo and Juliet*). In both, there is a social construction around public interest and how much it effectively justifies the restriction of fundamental rights. However, for the construction of this public reason to be plural and democratic, it is essential to have an administrative law enabling state action based on legality, due process, transparency, and the participation of society. The cases analysed—which address these aspects—are a rich source of research to further examine this theme.

In line with these general principles emerging from different national realities, Protocol n. 01 to the Convention for the Protection of Human Rights (Article 01), protecting property, recognises public interest and compensation as central elements of expropriation while establishing standards for the interpretation and application of these general principles as a way of approaching the members of the European Union[12]—something that can be understood as a 'Europeanisation of administrative law', according to Fromont[13] and Schwarze.[14]

[11] See JJ Rousseau, *The Social Contract* (GDH Cole tr, 1762) Bk 1, ch 6, 11 https://socialpolicy.ucc.ie/Rousseau_contrat-social.pdf (accessed 15 July 2021).

[12] See della Cananea (n 4) 209.

[13] Fromont (n 4) 354.

[14] J Schwarze, *European Administrative Law* (Sweet & Maxwell 2006).

B. The variations

If, on the one hand, there are common principles, on the other, there are variations that can change the meaning of these more general rules to a greater or lesser extent. The comparative study in this volume allowed the identification of cross-cutting issues that clearly show some differences between countries with regard to administrative limits to property rights.

As seen above (*primo atto*), an important convergence lies in the requirement for the competent authority to give reasons for expropriation. However, despite the general principle of justification, the reasons for takings presented by the state or the person with delegated powers may be robust to varying degrees, depending on each legal tradition or even the cultural context in which they are produced.[15]

Indeed, even given the parameters established by Protocol No 1 of the Convention for the Protection of Human Rights, countries have a margin of appreciation over what can be considered public purpose and whether the expropriation is justified in any specific case. In this sense, countries apply different meanings to 'public good', as well as different competences to define it.

In a narrower view, takings carried out in the name of the 'common good' require the transfer of private property to be made to a state entity that has been assigned the task of implementing a project in the public interest. However, there is also a broader understanding whereby private projects can be considered of public interest with no restrictions on the transfer of ownership to a private company. This is the case in most countries, such as Germany, the UK, and others, but not without some controversy.

In practice, not all public purpose hypotheses for takings are equivalent: each country seems to address the issue in its own way. In some countries, takings must be based on public interest purposes duly listed in law.[16]

In turn, in many countries it is understood that the use of this instrument is only possible *if there is no other less burdensome way* to achieve the public good.[17] In Italy, Portugal, and Spain, there must be a *public reason important enough* to benefit the community.[18] Thus, an analysis of proportionality regarding the 'costs' of expropriation is required—with the caveat that these costs can be evaluated both from a strictly economic point of view and from a perspective that takes into account social variables. Generally speaking, the competence to take this decision rests with the administrative authorities, with variations dependent on the administrative organisation in each country.

Lastly, there are countries where it is sufficient to have *some public benefit* justifying expropriation, regardless of the degree of deprivation of the violated rights by the state action. In such countries there is a considerably broad conception of the meaning of public purpose. The North American scenario fits into this broader conception,

[15] The duty of justification is inserted in cultures that can be more or less argumentative. In this sense see A Sen, *The Argumentative Indian: Writings on Indian History, Culture and Identity* (Picador 2005).

[16] See Sweden report.

[17] See Germany report.

[18] See Magaldi (n 9).

considering that, according to the US Supreme Court, 'for purposes of the Fifth Amendment's Takings Clause, promoting economic development is a traditional and long accepted function of government'.[19]

Thus, there are legal systems in which the indication of potential benefit to the community as a valid reason is sufficient (*weaker rationality of justification*), whereas in others there must be a more consistent demonstration of the relationship between cost and benefit of the decision taken by the state, as well as an analysis of the variables involved in takings with a view to a more equitable distribution of the sacrifices involved (*stronger rationality of justification*).[20]

The same goes for the definition of compensation. Compensation for takings is a common element among all the countries analysed, but they adopt different interpretations as to what is considered adequate compensation. Adequate compensation can be one that fully reflects the loss felt by the owner compared to market value. But it can also be an 'equitable' or 'fair' compensation, in which case it would be admissible to either pay above market value, if there are extraordinary losses, or only partial payment when necessary for social justice.[21] In summary, there are multiple ways to reach the compensation amount.

In addition to justification and compensation, other cross-cutting issues addressed in the reports also bring out differences in procedures relating to the imposition of administrative limits on property rights, namely: cultural heritage, urban planning, and noise.

In the European countries analysed, cultural heritage is protected by a multiplicity of rules, both at national and supranational level. The international regulation of cultural heritage protection is quite robust, as it is in national contexts: the protection of cultural heritage has a strong 'local' connotation, as it involves a relationship between goods (tangible or intangible), culture, and territory. We may find in each country's report the definition of what is considered cultural heritage, what are the procedures and competent authorities for its declaration as a property subject to specific protection, the administrative burdens that fall on them and whether or not there is a right to compensation against property restrictions, with significant variations in substance, and to a greater extent in form, with regard to the protection of historical heritage.

This protection imposes several restrictions on the owner's right to property, such as the establishment of standards for its conservation, rules for public access, restrictions, even prohibitions on circulation, and negotiation and sale, especially when this implies the property leaving national territory. The manifestation of this state regulation is found in administrative law; thus, the tensions between cultural and property rights emerge more concretely.

As evidenced in the reports, the restrictions imposed on this type of property are not considered effective expropriations despite the burden that falls on the property. There is no compulsory transfer of ownership, as it continues to belong to its original

[19] See the case of *Kelo v City of New London* 545 US 469 (2005), quoted in the USA report.

[20] Elazar (n 11). In addition to these models of 'weak rationality justification' and 'cost-benefit justification', Elazar also proposes the model of 'deontological justification', in which it is considered that the importance of certain fundamental values 'makes them not to be annulled by any public benefit' (252–53).

[21] See the Polish report.

owner, which is why, as a general rule, these restrictions do not give rise to the right to compensation (see, in this regard, Belgium, Germany, Ukraine, Italy, Sweden, and the UK).

However, one cannot speak of the existence of a pattern among European countries, since the approach by national laws varies considerably. This regulation follows the specific political and cultural interests of the states, and it is possible to observe distinctions, especially (i) in the (exceptional) cases of compensation for measures to protect cultural heritage resulting in excessive restrictions on property rights, (ii) in the degree of state interference in the commercialisation of goods and, finally, (iii) in the greater or lesser participation of the owner and other interested parties in the process of declaration and protection of the property of cultural value. Nonetheless, common principles also emerge, such as proportionality.

Other than cultural heritage protection, it is worth mentioning the restrictions on property rights stemming from the government's role in urban planning and territorial ordering, and infrastructure projects.

In activities related to urban management and planning, the state can call upon 'police power' to control and establish restrictions on the use and occupation of urban land in cities, as well as urban planning instruments specifically aimed at policies for land use, building, land tenure and regularisation, among others. Expropriation can be understood as an instrument favouring urban development with a focus on broader expropriation resulting from state planning, as it reaches larger areas for the purposes of urbanisation and the requalification of certain sectors of cities.[22] However, there is no uniform understanding among the countries quoted here about a more specific relationship between urban planning and expropriation. The main divergence concerns the level of connection between the urban development plan and the expropriation intended by the government for urban purposes.

Similar issues arise when the property right is attained by infrastructure projects implemented for the benefit of the community but with negative impacts—such as noise pollution—and they limit or even prevent the full use of the property by its owner. In this case, the adverse effects resulting from noise do not confer on the owner an automatic right to expropriation or purchase of the land by public authorities (Belgium, the Netherlands). Nevertheless, excessive noise pollution allows the interested party to claim before the administrative authorities that his/her property should be expropriated in specific situations (Belgium, United Kingdom), such as, for example, in cases of excessive devaluation of the property after approval of an impact assessment (Germany).

II. A man's property is his castle! Protections

The classic phrase of English jurist Sir Edward Coke uttered in the early seventeenth century—considered the starting point of the common law principle known as *knock-and-announce*—is quite emblematic as it symbolically portrays the relationship

[22] See the narrative and analysis of Y Marique on the connection between urban planning and expropriation in the 1920s to 1960s in New York.

between modern man and property. In other words, ownership does not just mean ownership of 'things' and 'pieces of land'. It is also part of the very essence of the individual, granting a set of powers and serving as an instrument of social distinction.[23]

It is no wonder that property protection mechanisms have been consolidated over the centuries: if property were previously protected by walls and fences, it has gradually become the object of legal guarantees preventing government or third-party violation or limitation. In this sense, the requirement of formal law, dating back to the Magna Carta of 1215, became the main protection mechanism against possible restrictions and deprivations of private property.

Other mechanisms were added to the list of protections concerning property rights, such as guaranteed due process for the imposition of restrictions on this fundamental right and the judicial control of public administration by the courts, the ultimate guardians of property.

A. The sources of protections: ownership democracy

In liberal democracies, constitutional texts broadly affirm the 'right to property', protecting the owner from interventions by state powers. However, the concept of ownership has not always been the same. Although it may be perceived as stable and immune to historical circumstances, property is an institution in constant transformation.

During the nineteenth and twentieth centuries, the concept of property was broadened beyond the definition of traditional property to include entire individual net worth, not just real estate. This enlargement is not innocuous. The growing list of things likely to become private property—'that multiply to infinity', according to Carbonnier—shows that property is permeated by not always apparent interests and disputes and often crystallises relations of inequality through legal structures.[24]

However, as evidenced in this comparative study, ownership is not absolute. On the contrary, property is also intrinsically connected with social purposes. In this sense, recognition of the 'social function of property' led to an alteration of its original conception whereby the idea of property protection remains, but not to the same extent that individualism had already recognised in it. Thus, the administrative restrictions imposed by the government also came to be considered as an instrument to respond to the demand for social equality and, more specifically, for the distribution of wealth within society.[25]

Considering this historical-social transformation process, several countries began to expressly foresee the 'social function' as a limit to the right to property. This is the case, for example, in Spain, Italy, and Germany. However, the meaning and scope of the social function of property is not uniform across the countries examined here.

Despite the different paths countries may have taken in shaping property rights and defining their functions, there is an underlying premise that gives identity to liberal

[23] P Bourdieu, *La Distinction: la critique social du jugement* (Les éditions de minuit 1979).

[24] J Carbonnier, *Flexible Droit: Pour une Sociologie du Droit Sans Rigueur: Titre III: La Propriété. Chapitre premier: Le droit de propriété dans la vision révolutionnaire* (10th edn, LGDJ 2007) 353.

[25] See della Cananea (n 4) 173.

democracies: the requirement that there be a law to limit administrative action and whose purpose is the restriction of property rights. In the countries analysed, there is a shared vision that the law is the principal mechanism for containing administrative discretion and protecting fundamental rights. This is what we can observe from the empirical research described in this book.

Thus, there is a preference for a model of democracy based on individual property in which property is under parliamentary protection. This model is not necessarily translated into 'egalitarian' democratic regimes of proprietary citizens[26] and it is clearly reflected in the case of takings. In this sense, as a general principle, it is up to the legislator to define the hypotheses and conditions under which the government is authorised to impose the compulsory transfer of private property for purposes of public interest.

Even when confronted with legislative authorisation to impose restrictions on property rights, administrative authorities remain with considerable margin of discretion to carry out the command of the law. Furthermore, there are situations in which expropriation is feasible even in the absence of a specific law. However, the theme is quite controversial, as can be seen even in historical cases such as 'The Steel Seizure Case' in the US in 1952, in which the then President arranged for the seizure of most of the steel industry in the country with no basis in legal authorisation, being eventually limited by the Supreme Court in a case that called into question the limits of the rule of law.[27]

B. Procedure: is there a global due process for takings?

The growing demand not only to limit the power of public authorities, but also to establish more predictable, transparent, and democratic standards of state action, has given rise to a general principle of respecting procedural guarantees to protect individual rights vis-à-vis administrative authorities.[28]

Even though expropriation is traditionally understood as a unilateral administrative act, in all the countries examined here, without exception, there are specific procedures for decisions imposing restrictions on private property. Even though legal authorisation for takings is required, administrative procedure plays a fundamental role as a mechanism for protecting citizens from the discretion of authorities to determine the compulsory transfer of property.[29]

[26] The idea of property-owning democracy is adopted by some political philosophers (in this sense see J Rawls, *Justice as Fairness: A Restatement* (Belknap Press 2001) 135–40) as a way to ensure the equitable distribution of economic freedom and security in society.

[27] D Gray Adler, 'The Steel Seizure Case and Inherent Presidential Power' (2002) 19(155) Constitutional Commentary 1 https://scholarship.law.umn.edu/concomm/251/ (accessed 15 July 2021).

[28] According to della Cananea, the procedural dimension of administrative law is central not only in the US, but also in Europe. Although few address the issue at the constitutional level, countries have increasingly regulated the issue with a view to strengthening democracy. It is also for this reason that 'a new wave of laws regulating administrative procedures followed the fall of the Berlin Wall in 1989' in della Cananea (n 4) 185–88.

[29] See Magaldi (n 9).

There are several common elements in takings procedures in the different countries analysed, including: (i) decision-making by a competent authority through pre-established stages[30]; (ii) declaration of public utility; (iii) formal notification to the owner; (iv) definition and payment of any compensation; (v) transfer of ownership.

These legal systems attach great importance to the duty to give the reasons for the administrative decision and to formally notify the owner that his/her property will be expropriated (Spain, Portugal, Belgium, Ukraine, Sweden, France). It is for no other reason that the absence of these two elements can lead, to a greater or lesser extent, to the invalidation of an administrative decision to proceed with taking.

Nevertheless, there are variations that imply a different understanding of the role of due process in moderating the power of authorities and protecting individual rights. In some countries the reason for the decision and even the declaration of public utility can be of a more fluid nature, allowing a generic justification, as well as an implicit declaration of public utility as the result of another administrative act.[31]

Another important variation that deserves a closer look is the scale of participation in the takings proceeding. This is a fundamental dimension for an administrative law that intends to support democratic regimes. Generally speaking, the proceedings provide some kind of opportunity for the owner to have a voice. However, the degree of owner participation and that of interested third parties is quite variable.

In some countries, participation through oral hearing is a mandatory stage of the proceeding (Germany, Poland). The hearing can take place before (Portugal), or after (Spain), the declaration of public utility. Furthermore, it can involve different governmental instances and be more or less open to the participation of interested third parties.

Other than differences in participation, the configuration per se of the administrative procedure of takings varies from country to country due to the political organisation of the state and the executive, legislative, and judicial branches. In addition to the participation of parliament, responsible—in a broader sense—for enacting laws authorising expropriation, administrative or judicial courts may be required to guarantee due process.

On the one hand, empirical studies reveal the existence of models grounded in decision-making exclusively by the administrative authority based on its discretionary power. In these cases, administrative or judicial courts are only responsible for reviewing the decision in the event of the violation of rules of procedure or unlawful takings. On the other hand, models exist in which courts, whether administrative or judicial, have powers to effectively participate in decision-making. Examples include defining the amount of compensation or when expropriation occurs non-consensually (as in the case of Belgium, Ukraine, or France). For this reason, courts can often be decisive in determining the real protection of fundamental rights, whether because of their technical specialisation that limits administrative discretion or even because of their institutional autonomy. Even though there are not always equivalent institutional structures in the different systems, it may be said that, in many contexts, there

[30] Countries adopt different configurations regarding the subject of the administrative process. See della Cananea (n 4) 185–88.

[31] See the Italian report and the comparative report by Magaldi (n 9).

are 'functional equivalences', to use Sabino Cassese's expression in his comparative analysis of the French administrative justice and the English system.[32]

Despite the numerous variations in the legal and institutional design of takings procedures and the challenge to systematise them, there seems to be growing convergence towards procedures that ensure, at least, the organs of the public administration's duty to provide justification and guarantee some degree of participation and proportionality in its decisions. Nevertheless, this analysis cannot fail to consider the role of the international dimension, such as the ECHR, in establishing minimum procedural standards to contain the excessive centralisation of power, given that the configurations of due process can be quite different in terms of the protection of the right to property.

C. Remedies: courts as ultimate guardians of property

We turn now to the ultimate guardians of property: the courts. Alongside the legislative, courts play a fundamental role in protecting the individual from a public authority's discretion in making decisions regarding expropriation. Indeed, the effectiveness of a system protecting property rights—considered one of the main axes of liberal democratic regimes—requires some level of judicial review, provided the affected individual can have access to the review, as well as the guarantee that unlawful takings will be reversed and any damages indemnified.

Review of decisions by administrative authorities is a prerequisite of the rule of law. However, their institutional design is strongly marked by political choices relating to the organisation of the state and the authorities in each country, including the adoption of monism or jurisdictional dualism. Thus, some systems are constituted on the basis of a strict separation of powers in which the judiciary exercises control over the legality of administrative action through ordinary courts, while other systems are based on courts with specific jurisdictions—that can even be part of the administration itself—in which the model of specialisation around disputes involving public law prevails.[33] We must remember that the systems of control for administrative action are the result of practices built up from historical and cultural processes and arise from a greater or lesser degree of trust in specific state institutions.

This plurality of institutional arrangements is quite visible in the control of administrative decisions relating to takings. There are variations in both the adopted institutional model (administrative courts that supplement the administration: Italy and Netherlands, or judicial courts separated from the administrative structure: Belgium) and the scope of judicial review: in some cases, review of the decision is limited to assessment of the legality of the act (Italy, Belgium), while in other cases the merits will be examined (the Netherlands). In Sweden, expropriation is an administrative decision, but it is up to a specialised court to assess the amount of compensation due in a specific procedure.[34]

[32] Cassese (n 3) 136. See also G della Cananea and M Andenas, *Administrative Procedure and Judicial Review: A Common Core Research* (OUP 2021) 5.

[33] See della Cananea and Andenas (n 33) 8.

[34] Marique (n 7).

The treatment courts reserve to possible errors or violations of the takings procedure also involves different solutions: in some countries they lead to the annulment of the proceeding as a whole due to the violation of a fundamental right (Portugal); in other systems, annulment depends on manifest unlawfulness, albeit with a margin of tolerance (Spain).

This plurality of alternatives shows an aspect crucial not only to the protection of property rights but to the very essence of the rule of law: there is no legal-institutional arrangement that can be considered better or more adequate or that should be adopted uniformly by countries declaring themselves liberal-democratic regimes.

III. Conclusions

The similarities and differences between legal systems in relation to the imposition of administrative restrictions on property rights, notably takings, provide concrete evidence for the existence of an intrinsic content of administrative law constituted by a set of common principles, as Cassese claims.[35]

Thus, in our view, the experiences highlighted here demonstrate that, despite the historical and cultural differences among the countries examined in this book, there is a common moral political substrate on the theme of takings that affects administrative law in each country.

There is a common underlying notion around the idea of property—private property in liberal democracies—as a fundamental pillar of the rule of law. For this reason, its limitation by the state in the name of the common good requires the proof that there will be a benefit to the community and that this is sufficient to justify the sacrifice of an individual on behalf of society as a whole. In this sense, in the regimes under discussion, any restriction on ownership includes some degree of justification, however vague it may be. Furthermore, the different terms to name the 'common good' do not necessarily imply irreconcilable perceptions on the subject.

Within this liberal conception of property, every expropriation requires compensation to be paid to those who have been deprived of their right to property, even though it may include modulations. This is a crucial issue to understand identities and differences between the systems and how they conceive and implement the 'social contract?' since compensation expresses a way of allocating rights and resources within society, bringing a discussion about the distribution, equality, and social purposes of property ownership.

Likewise, there is a common set of protections for the right to property, such as the legal requirement authorising its limitation and the guarantee of due process and judicial review: it gives courts (administrative or judicial) their role as ultimate guardians of property. There is a shared vision, in the liberal world, that these protections are the mechanisms *par excellence* for containing administrative discretion and protecting fundamental rights.

[35] Cassese (n 3) 142.

Nevertheless, it is important to highlight that empirical research also reveals variations in the institutional configuration and in the more specific legal treatment to takings process. These distinctions in structures often result from fundamental political choices related to the organisation of the state and powers in each country. These variations confer the unique nature of each legal system, even though it may be found within a similar legal tradition.

In this framework, the exact understanding of the meaning and scope of these variations requires an analysis of the different legal arrangements in the light of their functions. Indeed, legal variations may have little impact on the more general meaning of takings; even subtle variations can reveal a greater or lesser commitment to moderating the power of administrative authorities and promoting democratic values. These variations gain effectiveness in the field of administrative law and can be decisive for the success or, on the contrary, the deterioration—often imperceptible—of the protection of fundamental rights and guarantees, creating the conditions for the rise of the so-called illiberal democracies where there is a lack of civil liberties. After all, the boundaries between democratic regimes and modern autocracies are blurred. Literature and history are replete with examples in this regard.

Selected Bibliography

Ackerman B, *Private Property and the Constitution* (Yale University Press 1977)

Alegre Ávila JM, *Evolución y régimen jurídico del patrimonio histórico* (Ministerio de Cultura 1994)

Allen T, *The Right to Property in Commonwealth Constitutions* (CUP 2009)

Alonso García C, 'La contaminación acústica' in L Ortega and C Alonso (eds), *Tratado de Derecho Ambiental* (Tirant lo Blanch 2015) 695

Alves Correia F, *Manual de Direito do Urbanismo, II* (Almedina 2010)

Auby JB (ed), *Codification of Administrative Procedure* (Bruylant 2014)

Bader J and Ronellenfitsch M (eds), *BeckOK VwVfG* (50th edn, CH Beck 2021)

Baño León JM, 'Artículo 149.1.18º' in ME Casas and M Rodríguez-Piñero (eds), *Constitución Española: LV Aniversario* (Wolters Kluwer/BOE 2018) 1376

Battis U, Krautzberger M, and Löhr R-P, *Baugesetzbuch: Kommentar* (14th edn, CH Beck 2019)

Bell A and Parchomovsky G, 'Givings' (2001) 111 Yale LJ 547

Beltrán de Felipe M, '¿Puede haber responsabilidad patrimonial de las Administraciones públicas al margen de la LRJAPyPAC? El arbitraje internacional de inversiones (y el estándar universal de trato justo y equitativo) como inesperado sustitutivo de la legislación interna' (2007) 16 Revista General de Derecho Administrativo 42

Bengtsson B, *Speciell fastighetsrätt: Miljöbalken* (Iustus 2018)

Bengtsson B, 'Skadestånd vid överträdelse av Europakonventionen: den nya lagstiftningen' (2018) 2 SvJT 93

Bobrika V, Spasibo-Fateeva I, and Banasko O (eds), *Civil Code of Ukraine: Scientific and Practical Commentary*, vol 5 (Strajd 2011) (in Ukrainian)

Bończak-Kucharczyk E, *Ustawa o gospodarce nieruchomościami: Komentarz* (Wolters Kluwer 2020)

Bouvier P, Born R, Cuvelier B, and Piret F, *Éléments de droit administratif* (2nd edn, Larcier 2013)

Bussani M and Mattei U, 'The Common Core Approach to European Private Law' (1997–1998) 3 Colum J Eur L 339

Carlson L, *The Fundamentals of Swedish Law* (Studentlitteratur 2012)

Caruso D, 'Private Law and Public Stakes in European Integration: the Case of Property' (2004) 10(6) Eur Law J 751

Conticelli M, 'L'espropriazione' in S Cassese, *Trattato di diritto amministrativo, Parte speciale* (Giuffrè 2003) 1929

Couzinet JF, 'From Public Necessity to Public Utility: Changes in the Justifying Factor for Expropriation' ('De la nécessité publique à l'utilité publique: les évolutions du fait justificatif de l'expropriation') in G Koubi (ed), *Property Right and Revolution (Propriété et Révolution)* (CNRS and Toulouse University 1991) 197

Craig P, *EU Administrative Law* (OUP 2006)

Cribbett JE, 'Concepts in Transition: The Search for a New Definition of Property' (1986) 1 Univ Ill Law Rev 1

Dahlsjö A, Hermansson M, and Sjödin E, *Expropriationslagen: En kommentar* (Norstedts Juridik 2010)

Darpö J, 'Tradition och förnyelse på vattenrättens område: Om mötet mellan gamla tillståndsregimer och moderna miljökrav' (2014) 2 Nordisk Miljörättslig Tidskrift 101

della Cananea G, 'Equivalent Standards under Domestic Administrative Law: A Comparative Perspective' in F Ortino and others (eds), *Investment Treaty Law: Current Issues*, vol 2 (BIICL 2007) 149

della Cananea G, *Due Process of Law Beyond the State. Requirements of Administrative Procedure* (OUP 2016)

della Cananea G and Bussani M, 'The Common Core of European Administrative Laws: A Framework for Analysis' (2019) 26 Maastricht J Eur & Comp L 217

della Cananea G and Andenas M, 'Administrative Procedure and Judicial Review: A 'Common Core' Research' in G della Cananea and M Andenas (eds), *Judicial Review of Administration in Europe* (OUP 2021) 3

della Cananea G, 'Commonality and Diversity in Administrative Justice: Fin de Siècle' in G della Cananea and S Mannoni (eds), *Administrative Justice Fin de Siècle: Early Judicial Standards of Administrative Conduct in Europe (1890-1910)* (OUP 2021) 3

Díez Sastre S, 'La tutela de los competidores en los procedimientos administrativos de adjudicación' in L Arroyo and D Utrilla (eds), *La administración de la escasez* (Marcial Pons 2015) 205–242

Dreier H (ed), *Grundgesetz: Kommentar*, vol 1 (3rd edn, Mohr Siebeck 2013)

Ely JW, *The Guardian of Every Other Right: A Constitutional History of Property Rights* (3rd edn, OUP 2007)

Epping V and Hillgruber C (eds), *BeckOK Grundgesetz* (45th edn, CH Beck 15 November 2020)

Epstein RA, *Takings: Private Property and the Power of Eminent Domain* (Harvard University Press 1985)

Ernst W, Zinkahn W, Bielenberg W, and Krautzberger M, *Baugesetzbuch: Kommentar* (CH Beck August 2020)

Favoreu L, 'Le principe de constitutionnalité: essai de définition d'après la jurisprudence du Conseil constitutionnel' in L Favoreu (ed), *Mélanges Eisenmann* (Cujas 1975) 33

Favoreu L, 'La jurisprudence du Conseil constitutionnel et le droit de propriété proclamé par la Déclaration de 1789', Conseil constitutionnel (ed), *La Déclaration des droits de l'homme et du citoyen et la jurisprudence: Colloque des 25 et 26 mai 1989 au Conseil constitutionnel* (PUF 1989) 138

Fernández Torres JR, *Estudio integral de las expropiaciones urbanísticas* (Thomson-Aranzadi 2007)

Fischer H, *Entschädigungsanspruch aus Enteignung und enteignungsgleichem Eingriff* (4th edn, Beck 2017)

Fromont M, *Droit administratif des Etats membres de l'Union européenne* (PUF 2006)

Gambaro A, *Property, Propriété, Eigentum* (Cedam 1992)

García de Enterría E, 'Las expropiaciones legislativas desde la perspectiva constitucional. En particular, el caso de la Ley de Costas' (1996) 141 Revista de Administración Pública 131

García de Enterría E, *Los principios de la nueva ley de expropiación forzosa* (Thomson-Civitas 2006)

García de Enterría E, and Fernández T-R, *Curso de Derecho Administrativo*, vol I (Thomson-Civitas 2017)

García Luengo J, *Las infracciones formales como causa de invalidez del acto administrativo* (Iustel 2016)

Garlicki L and Zubik M (eds), *Konstytucja Rzeczypospolitej Polskiej: Komentarz* (2nd edn, Wydawnictwo Sejmowe 2016)

Graziadei M and Smith L, *Comparative Property Law, Global Perspectives* (Edward Elgar Publishing 2017)

Guerra da Fonseca R, *Comentário à Constituição Portuguesa, II, coord P Otero* (Almedina 2008)
Guerra da Fonseca R, and Assis Raimundo M (eds), *Direito Administrativo do Mar* (Almedina/ICJP—CIDP 2016)
Hansmann H and Mattei U, 'The Functions of Trust Law: A Comparative Legal and Economic Analysis' (1998) 73(2) NYU L Rev 434
Henckels C, 'Scope Limitation or Affirmative Defence? The Purpose and Role of Investment Treaty Exception Clauses' in L Bartels and F Paddeu (eds), *Exceptions in International Law* (OUP 2020)
Hepburn J, *Domestic Law in International Investment Arbitration* (OUP 2017)
Honoré M, 'Ownership' in AG Guest (ed), *Oxford Essays in Jurisprudence* (Clarendon Press 1961) 161
Horváth A (ed), *Magyar Állam: és Jogtörténet (History of State and Law in Hungary)* (Nemzeti Közszolgálati Egyetem 2014)
Ilnytskyi OV and Ilkiv NV, 'Peculiarities of the Judicial Trial of Cases on Forced Alienation of Land Plots, Other Objects of Real Property Assets Located on them on the Grounds of Public Necessity' (2013) 3(15) Bulletin of High Council of Justice 18 http://irbis-nbuv.gov.ua/cgi-bin/irbis_nbuv/cgiirbis_64.exe?C21COM=2&I21DBN=UJRN&P21DBN=UJRN&IMAGE_FILE_DOWNLOAD=1&Image_file_name=PDF/vvru_2013_3_4.pdf. (accessed 24 May 2022) (in Ukrainian)
Isensee J and Kirchhof P (eds), *Handbuch des Staatsrechts der Bundesrepublik Deutschland*, vol 8 (3rd edn, CF Müller 2010)
Jarass HD and Pieroth B, *Grundgesetz: Kommentar* (16th edn, CH Beck 2020)
Kalbro T and Paulsson J, 'Development of Swedish Legislation Regulating Compensation for Compulsory Acquisition: A Law and Economics Perspective' (2014) 3(3) EPLJ 215
Kim I, Lee H, and Somin I, *Eminent Domain: A Comparative Perspective* (CUP 2017)
Kopp FO and Ramsauer U, *Verwaltungsverfahrensgesetz: Kommentar* (21st edn, CH Beck 2020)
Kossak VM, 'Expropriation' (Експропріація) in VA Smoliy (eds), *Encyclopaedia of the History of Ukraine (Енциклопедія історії України), part 3* (Institute of History of Ukraine 2005) 24 http://www.history.org.ua/?termin=Ekspropriaciya (accessed 5 May 2021)
Langbein J, 'The Contractarian Basis of Trust Law' (1995) 105(3) Yale LJ 625
Lehavi A, 'Unbundling Harmonization: Public versus Private Law Strategies to Globalize Property' (2015) 15(2) Chic J Intl L 452
López Menudo F, 'Títulos habilitantes para la utilización de los bienes y derechos demaniales: Tipología y régimen' in C Horgué (ed), *Régimen patrimonial de las Administraciones públicas* (Iustel 2007) 193
Lundmark T, *Charting the Divide between Common and Civil Law* (OUP 2012)
Macey JR, 'Property Rights in Sweden: A Law and Economics Perspective' SNS Occasional Paper, No 85 (January 2001)
Mangoldt H, Klein F, and Starck C, *Grundgesetz: Kommentar*, vol 1 (7th edn, CH Beck 2018)
Marchiani C-S, *Le monopole de l'Etat sur l'expropriation* (LGDJ/Thèses 2008)
Marique Y, 'Belgian Constitution (1831)' *Max Planck Encyclopaedia of Comparative Constitutional Law* (Oxford University Press 2021)
Martínez López Muñiz JL, 'La publicatio de recursos y servicios' in L Cosculluela (ed), *Estudios de Derecho Público Económico: Libro Homenaje al Profesor Dr. S. Martín-Retortillo* (Civitas 2003) 687
Mattei U, *Basic Principles of Property Law: A Comparative Legal and Economic Introduction* (Greenwood Press 2000)
Mattei U, 'The History, Present Day Applications, and Future of Property Law: Basic Principles of Property Law: A Comparative Legal and Economic Introduction' (2002) 12(2) Int J Bus Manag 126
Mattei U, *La proprietà*, in *Trattato di diritto civile: I diritti reali*, vol 2 (Utet 2015)
Maunz T and Dürig G, *Grundgesetz: Kommentar* (CH Beck 2020)

Medina Alcoz L, 'Confianza legítima y responsabilidad patrimonial' (2016) 130 Revista Española de Derecho Administrativo 275
Mengoli G, *Manuale di diritto urbanistico* (Giuffrè 2014).
Merten D and Papier H-J (eds), *Handbuch der Grundrechte in Deutschland und Europa*, vol 5 (CF Müller 2013)
Mestre Delgado JF, 'La extinción de las autorizaciones y concesiones demaniales' in C Chinchilla (ed), *Comentarios a la Ley 33/2003, del Patrimonio de las Administraciones Públicas* (Civitas 2004) 491
Mirate S, 'Occupazione nel diritto amministrativo' in *Digesto delle discipline pubblicistiche, Aggiornamento* (UTET 2008) 520
Moringiello JM, 'Towards a System of Estates in Virtual Property' (2008) 1 IJPL 3
Möstl M and Schwabenbauer T (eds), *BeckOK Polizei: und Sicherheitsrecht Bayern* (15th edn, CH Beck 2020)
Oliveira FP, *Regime Jurídico dos Instrumentos de Gestão Territorial* (Almedina 2012)
Ortega Álvarez L and Arroyo Jiménez L, 'Artículo 128' in ME Casas and M Rodríguez-Piñero (eds), *Constitución Española: LV Aniversaio* (Wolters Kluwer/BOE 2018) 833
Ortino F, *The Origin and Evolution of Investment Treaty Standards: Stability, Value, and Reasonableness* (OUP 2019)
Ossenbühl F and Cornils M, *Staatshaftungsrecht* (6th edn, CH Beck 2013)
Nicolas C and Faure Y, 'News from the Public Utility Judge, Commenting CE Decision of July 9, 2018, Commune de Villiers-le-Bâcle et autres' [2018] AJDA 1661
Pâques M, Donnay L, and Vercheval C, 'La cause d'utilité publique' in D Renders (ed), *L'expropriation pour cause d'utilité publique* (Bruylant 2013) 209
Parejo Alfonso L, 'El régimen de la utilización de los bienes y derechos de dominio público. Autorizaciones y concesiones demaniales' in C Chinchilla (ed), *Comentarios a la Ley 33/2003, del Patrimonio de las Administraciones Públicas* (Civitas 2004) 433
Parejo Alfonso L, 'La actuación administrativa, a caballo entre normación y simple ejecución y el caso e la planificación y el plan' (2020) 1 Revista de Derecho Público: Teoría y Método 7
Petit J, 'Intangibility and Unfinished Public Work' (*Ouvrage public inachevé et intangibilité*) (2013) 1 RDP 79
Philbrick FS, 'Changing Conceptions of Property in Law' (1938) 86(7) U Pa L Rev 691
Pritchett W E, 'The "Public Menace" of Blight: Urban Renewal and the Private Uses of Eminent Domain' (2003) 21 Yale Law & Policy Rev 1
Radajewski M, 'Normatywna treść konstytucyjnych przesłanek dopuszczalności wywłaszczenia' (2018) 1(103) Przegląd Legislacyjny 23
Rakneberg Haug K, 'The Historical Development of the Scandinavian Functional Approach to Transfer of Ownership: A Tale of Change and Continuity' (2017) 6(2) EJPL 236
Rechel J, 'The Pan-European General Principle of Good Administration in Sweden: Undeniable but Partial Vehicles of Changes' in U Stelkens and A Andrijauskaite (eds), *Good Administration and the Council of Europe: Law, Principles, and Effectiveness* (OUP 2020) 256
Reich C, 'The New Property' (1964) 73 Yale LJ 733
Reinisch A and Schreuer C, *International Protection of Investments: The Substantive Standards* (CUP 2020)
Reis Novais J, 'Ainda sobre o ius aedificandi (… mas agora como problema de direitos fundamentais)' in *Estudos Jurídicos e Económicos em Homenagem ao Prof. Doutor António de Sousa Franco* (Coimbra Ed 2006) 493
Renders D, *Droit administratif général* (3rd edn, Larcier 2019)
Renders D, Ben Messaoud D, and Ganty D, 'Les acteurs de l'expropriation' in D Renders (ed), *L'expropriation pour cause d'utilité publique* (Bruylant 2013) 65

Rivero J, 'Le droit positif de la grève dans les services publics d'après la jurisprudence du Conseil d'État') (1951) 14 DS 595
Rodríguez de Santiago JM, 'Artículo 33' in ME Casas and M Rodríguez Piñero (eds), *Comentarios a la Constitución Española* (Wolters Kluwer 2018) 1147
Rossoux G, *Vers une dématérialisation des droits fondamentaux* (Bruylant 2015)
Sacco R, 'Legal Formants: A Dynamic Approach to Comparative Law I' (1991) 39 AJCL 1
Sachs M (ed), *Grundgesetz: Kommentar* (8th edn, CH Beck 2018)
Saitta F, 'Verso un "giusto" procedimento espropriativo (2013) 4 Dir amm 627
Schill SW, 'Multilateralizing Investment Treaties through Most-Favored-Nation Clauses' (2009) 27(2) BJIL 496
Schill SW (ed), *International Investment Law and Comparative Public Law* (OUP 2010)
Scoca FG, Stella Richter P, and Urbani P, *Trattato di diritto del territorio*, vol 1 (Giappichelli 2018)
Shaffer G, *Transnational Legal Ordering and State Change* (CUP 2013)
Shaffer G and Coye C, 'From International Law to Jessup's Transnational Law; From Transnational Law to Transnational Legal Orders' in P Zumbansen (ed), *The Many Lives of Transnational Law: Critical Engagements with Jessup's Bold Proposal* (CUP 2020) 126
Shaffer G and Halliday TC, 'With, Within, and Beyond the State: The Promise and Limits of Transnational Legal Ordering' in P Zumbansen (ed), *Oxford Handbook of Transnational Law* (OUP 2021) 987
Sjödin E, Ekbäck P, Kalbro T, and Norell L, *Markåtkomst och ersättning: För bebyggelse och infrastruktur* (Wolters Kluwer 2016)
Sluysmans JAMA, 'The principle of Full Compensation under Dutch Expropriation Law' (2019) 8(2) EPLJ 161
Sluysmans JAMA, Verbist S, and Waring E, *Expropriation Law in Europe* (Wolters Kluwer 2015)
Sluysmans JAMA, Verbist S, and Waring E, 'Expropriation in Europe' in JAMA Sluysmans, S Verbist , and E Waring (eds), *Expropriation Law in Europe* (Kluwer 2015) 1
Sluysmans JAMA, and de Graaff RL, 'Expropriation Law in The Netherlands' in JAMA Sluysmans, S Verbist , and E Waring (eds), *Expropriation Law in Europe* (Wolters Kluwer 2015) 337
Sluysmans JAMA and N van Triet, 'Reclaiming Property, Changes of Purpose or Non-Realization of Public Purpose after Expropriation' in B Hoops and others (eds), *Rethinking Expropriation Law I: Public Interest in Expropriation* (Boom Eleven 2015) 185
Sluysmans JAMA and Waring EJL, 'Core Principles of European Expropriation Law' (2016) 5(3) EPLJ 142
Sluysmans JAMA and Nielen MG, 'The Principle of Good Governance in Expropriation Law' in B Hoops and others (eds), *Rethinking Expropriation Law II: Context, Criteria, and Consequences of Expropriation* (Boom Eleven 2016) 299
Smits JM, 'Convergence of Private Law in Europe: Towards a New Ius Commune?' in E Örücü and D Nelken (eds), *Comparative Law: A Handbook* (Hart Publishing 2007) 219
Snijders-Storm EJ and Procee JS, 'Terugvordering op Grond van Artikel 61 Onteigeningswet; Stand van Zaken' in EWJ de Groot and RD Harteman (eds), *Bijzonder Geschikt voor het Werk* (IBR 2012) 127
Somin I, *The Grasping Hand:* Kelo v City of New London *and the Limits of Eminent Domain* (rev edn, University of Chicago Press 2016)
Somin I, 'Eminent Domain in the United States' in I Kim, H Lee, and I Somin (eds), *Eminent Domain: A Comparative Perspective* (CUP 2017) 38
Spannowsky W and Uechtritz M (eds), *BeckOK BauGB* (51st edn, CH Beck 1 November 2020)
Spears SA, 'Public Interest in International Investment Agreements' in C Brown and K Miles (eds), *Investment Treaty Law and Arbitration* (CUP 2011) 276

Snijders-Storm EJ and Procee JS, 'Terugvordering op Grond van Artikel 61 Onteigeningswet; Stand van Zaken' in EWJ de Groot and RD Harteman (eds), *Bijzonder Geschikt voor het Werk* (IBR 2012) 127

Theunis J, Van Garsse S, and Vleugels E, 'Balancing Legality and Legal Certainty: The Plea of Illegality in Belgian Public Law and the Role of the Council of State and Other Judicial Bodies' in M Eliantonio and D Dragos (eds), *The Plea of Illegality in Europe* (Routledge forthcoming)

Tolivar Alas L, 'Artículo Administración expropiante y beneficiario' in F Sosa Wagner (ed), *Comentarios a la Ley de Expropiación Forzosa* (Thomson-Aranzadi 2003)

Tuleja P (ed), *Konstytucja Rzeczypospolitej Polskiej: Komentarz* (Wolters Kluwer Polska 2019)

Utrilla Fernández-Bermejo D, *Expropiación forzosa y beneficiario privado* (Marcial Pons 2015)

van der Feltz GCW and others, *Schadeloosstelling voor Onteigening: Telders, Nieuw voor Oud* (Kluwer 2006)

Van der Walt A, *Constitutional Property Clauses: A Comparative Analysis* (Kluwer Law International 1999)

van Erp S, *European and National Property Law: Osmosis or growing antagonism?* (European Law Publishing 2006)

van Erp S, 'Comparative Property Law and Politics' (2015) 4(2) EPLJ 81

Van Harten G and Loughlin M, 'Investment Treaty Arbitration as a Species of Global Administrative Law' (2006) 17 Eur J Intl L 121

Vandevelde KJ, 'The New Property of the Nineteenth Century: The Development of the Modern Concept of Property' (1980) 29 Buff L Rev 325

Verbist S, 'Expropriation Law in Belgium (Flanders)' in J Sluysmans, S Verbist, and E Waring (eds), *Expropriation Law in Europe* (Kluwer 2015) 27

Victorin A, 'Real Property' in M Bogdan (ed), *Swedish Law in the New Millennium* (Norstedts Juridik 2008) 428

von Münch I and Kunig P, *Grundgesetz: Kommentar*, vol 1 (7th edn, CH Beck 2021)

Waring EJL, 'Private-to-private Takings and the Stability of Property' (2013) 24(2) King's LJ 237

Wenander H, 'Administrative Constitutional Review in Sweden: Between Subordination and Independence' (2020) 26(4) Eur Pub L987

Wéry O, 'L'expropriation pour cause d'utilité publique: chronique de jurisprudence (2000-2014). Première partie' [2014] Journal des Tribunaux 773

Woś T, *Wywłaszczanie nieruchomości i ich zwrot* (LexisNexis 2011)

Zenkov AV, 'The Notion of Expropriation in the Legislation and Doctrine of the Soviet Period' (2013) 3 J Intl L & Int'l Rel (журнал международного права и международных отношений) 22 http://evolutio.info/ru/journal-menu/2013-3/2013-3-zenkov (accessed 5 May 2021) (in Russian)

Index

For the benefit of digital users, indexed terms that span two pages (e.g., 52–53) may, on occasion, appear on only one of those pages.